THE TWELVE HOUSES

To Scorp,

Happy Astrology

love Goat xx

Available in this series

CHINESE ASTROLOGY Derek Walters
MUNDANE ASTROLOGY
Michael Baigent, Nicholas Campion & Charles Harvey

THE TWELVE HOUSES

Understanding the Importance of the Houses in your Astrological Birthchart

HOWARD SASPORTAS
D F ASTROL S

FOREWORD BY
LIZ GREENE

Illustrated by Jaqueline Clare

Thorsons
An Imprint of HarperCollins*Publishers*

Thorsons
An Imprint of HarperCollins*Publishers*
77–85 Fulham Palace Road,
Hammersmith, London W6 8JB

Published by The Aquarian Press 1985
Thorsons edition 1998

20 21 22

A catalogue record for this book
is available from the British Library

ISBN 0 85030 385 0

Printed and bound in Great Britain by
Creative Print and Design (Wales), Ebbw Vale

To my parents, with love

CONTENTS

Part 3: A Guide to Life's Possibilities

ILLUSTRATIONS

ACKNOWLEDGEMENTS

Many people have helped, supported and tolerated me through the agony and ecstasy of writing this book and my sincere appreciation extends to all of them.

In particular, an especially heartfelt thanks goes to Max Hafler for all we shared and for pushing me in the beginning; and to Robert Walker for pushing me through the middle and end, for his excellent advice, criticism and suggestions, his patient support through my more difficult periods, and just for being there when I needed help.

My appreciation also goes to Mary Ann Ephgrave for her adept transcription of the 'Houses Seminar'; to Christine Murdock for her expert and much needed help, guidance and encouragement; to Lesley Cottrill for her professional advice; and to Sheila Sasportas for her warm support.

I am naturally indebted to all those people who have shared their knowledge with me over the years. Special acknowledgements go to Maharishi Mahesh Yogi for his invaluable teaching and for the experience of meditation and what it opened up for me; to Darby Costello for titillating me with her Geminian insights and for introducing me to astrology way back when; to my first astrology teachers, Betty Caulfield and Isabel Hickey; to Ean Begg for helping me to begin to understand myself a little better; to Ian Gordon-Brown, Barbara Somers and Diana Whitmore for the enormous amount I learned from them; to Judy Hall for her generous and constant support, wisdom, healing and help; and a very warm thanks to Liz Greene whose insight and grace as a good friend, teacher and astrological colleague have left a deep mark on all my work.

Two more people deserve special mention. Words can't express my feelings of appreciation to a certain Dona Margarita, Our Lady of Gomera, for sharing with me the power of her Leonine love and spirit and for providing me with an idyllic atmosphere (in all senses) to begin writing. And last, but certainly not least, I am especially grateful to Jaqueline Clare for being a true friend through all of this and for the impeccable diagrams she so caringly produced.

PREFACE

The houses of the horoscope form one of the basic building-blocks with which every student of astrology must learn to work at the outset of any serious study of the subject. Because the houses are basic, it is often assumed that therefore they are simple — perhaps the most simple and accessible of the trinity of planet-sign-house which comprises the foundation of horoscope analysis. And because the houses are often considered so simple and accessible, they are also believed to be the least worthy of any in-depth perusal in the body of astrological literature.

I have found in my own experience, however, that the houses are no simpler than the planets and signs, and perhaps even more subtle. How could they not be so, when after all everyone born on a given day will have the same planets in the same signs, while planetary placements in the houses are dependent upon that most individual of factors, the moment of birth? Because they are so very individual, they portray a map of a very individual destiny, and are worthy of much more extensive interpretation and analysis than is usually offered in astrological textbooks. There is a large and unfortunate gap in this area of the study, and certainly no past author has done full justice to this apparently so simple yet difficult issue of the 'spheres of life'.

I am therefore delighted to be able to write a preface to a book which I feel not only fills this gap in current astrological literature, but also extends the understanding of astrology itself. Howard Sasportas has managed to do this without either violating those aspects of astrological tradition which have proven to be valid, or ignoring — as so many authors do — the current urgent need to bring psychological understanding into a study which has for far too long been purely prognosticative and behavioural in its interpretations. This book seems to me to be unique also in that, although it is 'psychological astrology' at its best, it does not hide behind psychological jargon, and its language speaks both to the beginner and the experienced practitioner equally clearly.

The issue of 'psychological astrology' appears to be a rather thorny one in some respects, because many astrologers who have studied in older traditions feel that their language, which has stood the test of many centuries, is being encroached upon by the language of psychology, and that astrology, in these hands, is no longer 'pure' but is becoming an extension of the helping professions. But psychological astrology in the way it is applied in Howard's book is not an erosion of the beauty and completeness of the astrological model. It embodies, rather, one apparently very simple concept: the reality of the psyche. That an individual's life is characteristic of the individual ought to be obvious, but it is exceedingly difficult to fully grasp unless one's own psyche is a reality to oneself. The interpretation of the houses that Howard offers in such depth in this book is 'psychological' in the most profound sense, because implicit in every chapter is the observation that an individual has certain kinds of experiences in a particular sphere of life because that is how the psyche of the individual perceives, reacts to, and interprets that sphere of life. The author phrases this very eloquently in the first chapter:

> The philosophical premise upon which psychological astrology is based is that a person's reality springs outward from his or her inner landscape of thoughts, feelings, expectations and beliefs.

This is certainly astrology, and not an extension of anything else; but it is an astrology which preserves the essential dignity and value of the individual psyche, and in which the houses, no less than the signs and planets, are inside as well as outside, and become full of meaning for the individual rather than remaining static 'places' or 'events' in life which have no connection to the soul.

The personal experience of astrology which is evident throughout the book is extensive and impressive. I have had many occasions to learn from and have my own astrological insights enhanced by Howard's work, as we have jointly founded and co-direct the Centre for Psychological Astrology in London which is focussed on precisely this approach to astrology. I can therefore recommend Howard's book not only for the clarity and depth of its content, but also because I am well aware that the interpretations which he offers are built upon many years of direct experience, and not merely upon clever intellectual theorizing. Also implicit in the book is a personal commitment to the astrologer's own development and inner confrontation, which I have always felt to be the chief criterion for any person wanting to take up the responsibility of counselling others in any way. The psyche is obviously a reality to the author, and therefore he is able to communicate its reality and its subtleties to the reader through the astrological model. Genuine authority of this kind cannot be faked, although numerous astrological writers appear to offer excellent theories which have never been put to the test in life. No one observing the effects of a particular planet in a particular house can really understand the complex issue of how an individual unconsciously creates, brick by brick, the apparently 'outer' reality which he or she encounters unless there is some relationship with the unconscious. Otherwise the interpretations are descriptions of behaviour, which leaves us back where we started. When this happens, the creative, teleological dimension of astrology — its capacity to open doors to a person and allow that person to see how an attitude might be shaping outer life and therefore how some consciousness of that attitude might shape a different quality of life — cannot be present. Astrology then ceases to be creative, and becomes quite pointless except as a method of justifying issues for which the individual does not wish to take responsibility.

As a learning textbook, Howard's book is invaluable, because it begins at the beginning with basic principles and takes the reader further and further into the complexities of interpreting the houses while retaining throughout an essential clarity of writing and a disciplined structure. I have no doubt that it will become an essential textbook for any serious student of astrology wishing to develop his or her understanding. As a statement of what psychological astrology is really about, it is also invaluable, because it could not put the point more clearly. Psychological astrology is not about abandoning astrology to psychotherapy, but about a way of understanding and reading the symbols of the horoscope which encompasses both inner and outer levels of experience, and points the way to the essential archetypal patterns which underlie both. Usually the houses are confusing because of the apparent diversity of themes which often occur under one umbrella. For example, the profundities and mysteries of death are conjoined with life insurance policies in the eighth, and the complexities of the relationship between body and spirit are mixed up with 'small animals' in the sixth. Howard's book provides the essential meaning which underlies all these apparently disparate themes connected with one house, which thereby allows the reader to understand why all these 'outer' circumstances are part of one core. This kind of insight is rare and cannot be overestimated in its value.

It is therefore with great pleasure that I can introduce a book which I am certain will provide an important and unique contribution to the body of astrological literature.

LIZ GREENE

INTRODUCTION

> Man is asked to make of himself what he is supposed to become, to fulfil his destiny.
>
> Paul Tillich

All around us in nature, life unfolds according to certain inner designs. A rosebud opens into a rose, an acorn grows into an oak, and a caterpillar emerges as a butterfly from its cocoon. Is it unreasonable to assume that human beings share this quality with the rest of creation — that we, too, unfold according to an inner plan?

The concept that each of us has a unique set of potentialities yearning to be realized is an ancient one. St Augustine wrote that 'there is one within me who is more myself than my self.'[1] Aristotle used the word *entelechy* to refer to the evolution and full blossoming of something originally in a state of potential. Along with *entelechy*, Aristotle also spoke of *essence* as those qualities which one could not lose without ceasing to be oneself. In like manner, Eastern philosopy applies the term *dharma* to denote the intrinsic identity and latent life-pattern present from birth in all of us. It is the *dharma* of a fly to buzz, a lion to roar, and an artistic person to create. Each of these patterns has its own kind of truth and dignity.

Modern psychology attaches many different names to the perennial quest 'to be that self which one truly is'[2] — the individuation process, self-realization, self-actualization, self-development, etc. By whatever label it is called, the underlying meaning is clear: all of us possess certain intrinsic potentials and capabilities. What's more, somewhere deep within us there is a primordial knowledge or preconscious perception of our true nature, our destiny, our abilities, and our 'calling' in life. Not only do we have a particular path to follow, but on some instinctive level, we know what that is.

Our fulfilment, happiness and well-being hinge on discovering this pattern and co-operating with its realization. The Danish philosopher Kierkegaard observed that the most common form of despair is that of not being who we really are, adding that an even deeper form of despair stems from choosing to be someone other than oneself.[3] The psychologist Rollo May wrote, 'When the person denies his potentialities, fails to fulfil them, his condition is guilt.'[4] Theologians have interpreted the fourth cardinal sin, sloth or *accidie,* as 'the sin of failing to do with one's life all that one knows one could do'.[5] But how can we connect to that part of ourselves which knows what we could be? How can we find the path again, once we have lost the way? Is there any map that exists which can guide us back to ourselves?

The astrological birthchart is such a map. A picture of the heavens as it appeared at one's place and time of birth, the chart symbolically portrays our own unique reality, innate pattern and inner design. A knowledge of the chart enables us to perceive those things which we would naturally be doing, if we had not been frustrated by family, society and, perhaps most crucially, *by the ambivalences of our own nature.*

Our being is not only given to us but demanded of us, and it is up to us to make of ourselves what we are meant to become. In the end, we alone are responsible for what we do with our lives, for the degree to which we accept or reject our true nature, purpose and identity. The birthchart is the best guide we have to lead us back to ourselves. Each placement in the chart reveals the most natural and appropriate way to unfold who and what we are. Why not listen to the clues the chart has to offer?

HOWARD SASPORTAS

PART I: THE LANDSCAPE OF LIFE

1. BASIC PREMISES

> One may indeed say that it is not the event which happens to the person, but the person which happens to the event.
>
> Dane Rudhyar

There are three basic ingredients which combine to make up an astrological chart — *planets, signs* and *houses.* Planets represent particular psychological drives, urges and motivations. Like verbs, they depict a certain action which is going on — for example, Mars *asserts,* Venus *harmonizes,* Jupiter *expands,* Saturn *restricts,* etc. The signs represent twelve qualities of being or attitudes towards life. The drive of a planet is expressed through the sign in which the planet is placed. Mars can assert in an Arien way or Taurean way; Venus can harmonize in a Geminian or Cancerian fashion, and so on. *Houses,* however, show the specific areas of everyday life or fields of experience in which all this is occurring. Mars in Taurus will assert itself in a slow and steady manner, but its placement by house determines the exact area of life in which this slow and steady action can most obviously be observed — whether it is in the person's career that he or she acts that way, or in his or her relationships, or at school, etc. Put very simply, the planets show *what* is happening, the signs *how* it is happening, and the houses *where* it is happening.

Serving as the lens to focus and personalize the planetary blueprint onto the landscape of actual life, the houses bring the chart down to earth. And yet the meanings and functions of the twelve houses are usually the least understood of all the basic astrological factors. It is the purpose of this book to examine how a proper appreciation of the signs and planets in each of the twelve houses can guide us to our true identity, illuminating the path of self-discovery and the unfoldment of our life-plan.

There are a few reasons why the full significance of the houses has been so often overlooked. Most astrological textbooks dwell on the traditional 'outer' meaning of each house and neglect its more subtle or basic underlying principle. Unless the core meaning of a house is grasped, the true essence of that house is lost. For instance, the 11th house is normally known as the 'House of Friends, Groups, Hopes and Wishes'. At first this may seem strange — what do friends and groups have to do with hopes and wishes? Why are these things all lumped together under the same house? However, when the deeper, most basic principle of the house is explained, then the connection becomes clear. The kernel of the 11th house is 'the urge to become something greater than we already are'. We do this by connecting to something greater than our separate selves — by aligning ourselves with friends and social circles, by joining groups, by identifying with causes which lift us out of ourselves and encompass us in a vaster scheme of things. But the desire to become something greater than we already are must also be accompanied by the capacity to envision new and different possibilities. In other words, hoping and wishing for something moves us beyond existing images and models of ourselves. We must have a dream before we can have a dream come true. Understood in the context of the desire to extend our already existing sphere of experience, the 11th house labels of 'friends, groups, hopes and wishes' begin to make sense in relationship to one another.

The conventional way in which the influence of planets and signs in the houses has been interpreted is another obstacle to fully appreciating the significance of each house. Perceiving events as purely external circumstances which befall us, traditional astrology interprets placements in the chart in a deterministic and fatalistic light, and fails to comprehend the part we play in shaping and constituting what happens to us. An 'event-orientated' astrologer, for instance, might say to a man with Saturn in the 11th house something like 'Your friends will restrict and disappoint you.' This may be true, but what good does such an interpretation do for anyone?

The philosophical premise upon which psychological astrology is based is that a person's reality springs outward from his or her inner landscape of thoughts, feelings, expectations and beliefs. For the man with Saturn in the 11th, trouble with friends is only the tip of the iceberg — the outer manifestation of something which he, himself, is responsible for creating. His difficulty relating with companions is the surface manifestation of something much deeper: his fear of expanding his boundaries to include something other than himself. He wants to become greater than he already is — to identify with something beyond his existing sense of self — and yet he is afraid of endangering the identity he already has. The 11th house urges him to encompass a greater reality but Saturn says 'hold on, preserve what you are already familiar with.' Understood in this way, it is not friendship which restricts him, but *his own restrictions* which limit his friendships. The astrologer who points out this dilemma ushers the man into the vestibule of change. Confronting these apprehensions, examining their origins, and looking at the possible ways of dealing with his fears, are the keys which open the door to further growth and development. When appreciated in the context of unfolding his potential and realizing his life-plan, this man's difficulties with friends becomes a necessary and productive phase of experience. Grappling with Saturn in the 11th, rather than avoiding it or blaming it on others, is one way he 'makes of himself what he is supposed to become'. How infinitely more beneficial this interpretation of an 11th house Saturn is than 'Sorry, old chap, your friends are no good.'

In his book *The Astrology of Personality,* Dane Rudhyar, a pioneer of person-centred astrology, proposes that reading the chart is to read the *dharma* of the person.[1] In a later work, *The Astrological Houses,* he elaborates more fully on this, emphasizing that the planets and signs in each house offer 'celestial instructions' on how a person can most naturally unfold his or her life-plan in that area of existence.[2] As far as possible, this book interprets the planets and signs through the houses in this perspective. However, besides just indicating the most authentic way to fulfil our intrinsic potentialities, the house placements also show our *innate predisposition* to perceive the experiences associated with each house in the context of the signs and planets found there. For example, a woman with Pluto in the 7th house is predisposed from birth to expect Pluto in connection with the affairs of that house. What's more, because Pluto is what she is expecting there, Pluto is precisely what she will find.

What we see in life is coloured by what we expect to see. Twenty-eight students were asked to describe what they saw when a deck of playing cards was flashed one-by-one onto a screen. Their basic expectation (or orienting paradigm) was the preconception that a pack of cards consists of four suits: two black (spades and clubs) and two red suits (hearts and diamonds). However, when the experimenters slipped a *red* six of spades into the deck, many of the students simply refused the evidence of their own eyes and 'converted' the red spade to black in their descriptions. In other words, when the red six of spades was flashed onto the screen, they didn't even notice the card's incongruity to their expectations of what a six of spades should look like. They saw only what they expected to see, not what was *actually* there.[3]

Similarly, our archetypal expectations, as seen through the signs and planets in the houses, precondition us to certain ways of experiencing life. The woman born with Pluto in the 7th, then, will filter issues relating to partnership through the lens of that planet. In this sense, she is 'stuck' with Pluto in that dimension of life, just as an acorn is stuck with becoming an oak. Nothing she can do will change that planet being there. But once she becomes *consciously aware* that Pluto is the context in which she views the 7th house, a few alternatives open to her which didn't exist previously.

To begin with, she can ask herself what purpose the 7th house Pluto serves in the overall unfoldment of her life-plan. In this way, she accepts and begins to co-operate with her inborn nature. Secondly, instead of blaming life or other people for the state of affairs in that house, she can try to understand the role she has played in creating the circumstances there. By doing this, she imbues the experiences in her life with greater meaning and significance — they are not just random events which 'happen' to her. Finally, if she can 'use' Pluto in its most constructive connotations, she is less likely to have to suffer its gruelling side any longer than necessary. On one level, Pluto implies the tearing down of forms and the collapse of existing structures. But on another level, Pluto represents transformation and rebirth into a whole new way of being. Through altering the perspective in which she views what is happening, she can understand Pluto's upheavals as necessary opportunities for growth and change. By facing and coming to terms with the kinds of traumas associated with this planet, she 'shifts' levels and finds that Pluto has a whole other dimension of experience to offer. She learns what Paracelcus observed so long ago, that 'the deity which brings the illness also brings the cure.'

Awareness brings change. Through examining the house placements in our charts, we not only are given clues as to the best way to meet life in that area, but we also gain insight into the underlying archetypal expectations operating within us. Once we become aware that we have an inborn bias to see things in a certain context, we can begin to work constructively within that framework, gradually expanding its borders to allow for other alternatives. Bearing this in mind, the reader can use this book both as a tool for personal development and as a guide for chart interpretation. The suggested meaning of each planet and sign through the houses is intended to serve as a broad and general outline, hopefully inspiring further thought and reflection on the nature of each placement.

My suggestions should not be taken as gospel or applied too rigidly, and I apologize for the inherent limitations of the 'cookbook' format. My firm belief is that every factor in the chart can only be fully appreciated in the light of the whole chart. Furthermore, the expression of any placement in the horoscope is contingent on the X-factor of the level of consciousness of the entity for whom it is drawn. A woman might be born at the same time, place and date as her pet frog, and the two charts would look exactly the same. But the frog expresses the birth map according to its level of awareness, and the woman according to hers. Because our level of consciousness plays such a crucial role in determining the 'outcome' and meaning of placements in the chart, no rigid interpretation of any one factor can be fixed. Each of us is more than the sum of the parts of the chart. Each of us has the potential for greater awareness, freedom and fulfilment.

2.
SPACE, TIME AND BOUNDARIES

> A human being is part of the whole, called by us 'Universe';
> a part limited in time and space.
>
> Albert Einstein

According to the Bible, God began His great work by creating the universe and then dividing it into different parts. He made the heavens separate from the earth, light separate from darkness, and day separate from night. In an attempt to manage, understand and make sense of existence, human beings exhibit this same tendency to divide the wholeness of life into various component parts and phases. Similarly, the birthchart, the map of an individual's existence, reflects this slicing of life into different sections — the sum total of which make a whole.

The Division of Space

No matter how haphazard the universe might seem at times, it is, nonetheless, fairly orderly. Cyclic and predictable, the celestial bodies manage to keep on their paths and adhere to their proper motion. Perhaps in an attempt to ascribe meaning and order to their lives, our early human ancestors observed a relationship between celestial events (the movements of the Sun, Moon and planets) and life on earth. But they needed to have a frame of reference or backdrop by which to plot and pinpoint the positions of these moving lights in the sky. In order to do this, space was divided into different sections and labelled.

Modern astrologers are faced with the same problem — how to divide space to create a frame of reference by which to identify the positions of the celestial bodies. It so happens, from a geocentric point of view, that the Sun, Moon and planets all appear to move in a broad circular path around the earth. This path extends

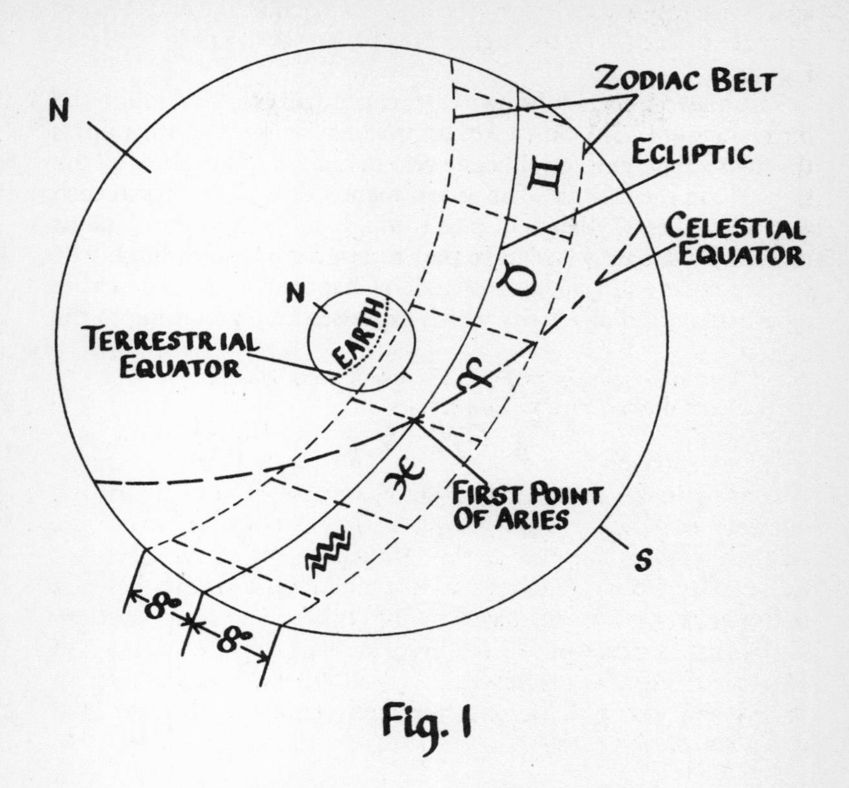

Fig. 1

THE DIVISION OF SPACE

approximately 8 or 9 degrees on either side of what is known as the *ecliptic* — the apparent path of the Sun around the Earth — and is called the *Zodiac Belt.* The ecliptic is then divided into twelve signs of thirty degrees each, starting with 0 degrees of Aries, the point where the Sun's path intersects the celestial equator (the Earth's equator projected into space) at the Spring Equinox. In this sense, the signs of the Zodiac (Aries, Taurus, Gemini, etc.)* are subdivisions of the ecliptic, the apparent yearly movement of the Sun around the Earth (see Figure 1). The positions of the planets are mapped

* The signs bear the same names as the constellations, but due to a phenomenon known as the *Precession of the Equinoxes,* the signs and constellations no longer coincide.

against these divisions of the ecliptic, showing what sign each planet happens to be passing through on any particular day of the year (see Figure 2).

The planets, each at its own rate, continually move through the different signs. The Sun takes approximately one month to pass through a sign, and roughly one year to make a full circle of all the signs along the ecliptic. The Moon spends about 2½ days in each sign and takes 27⅓ days to pass through all twelve signs. Uranus takes approximately 7 years to pass through a sign and roughly 84 years to make a full circle. As stated in Chapter 1, a planet describes a particular kind of activity which expresses itself according to the

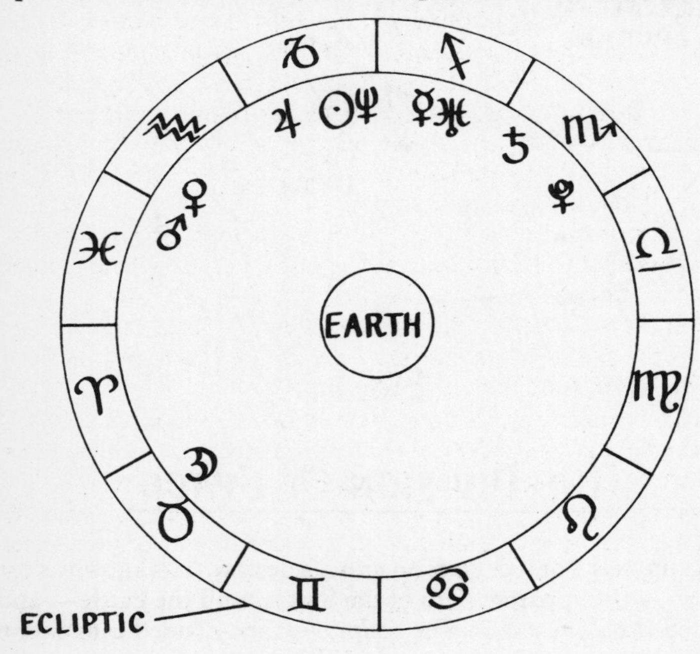

Fig. 2

PLANETS MAPPED AGAINST THE ECLIPTIC FOR JANUARY 1st, 1985

nature of the sign in which it is placed.

The Division of Time

The word *horoscope* comes from the Greek word 'horoscopus', meaning 'consideration of the hour' or 'consideration of the ascending degree'. In other words, the horoscope is literally a 'time-map'. By dividing the space in the heavens into signs, the early astrologers were able to plot the position of the planets in the sky. But they soon realized that something more was needed — a frame of reference to link the planetary pattern to a particular person born at a certain time and place.

Besides the movement caused by the apparent revolution of the Sun, Moon and the planets around the Earth, there is another type of movement which the horoscope must take into consideration: *the daily rotation of the Earth on its own axis.* The early astrologers had to find some way to correlate the celestial phenomena of planets moving through the signs to the terrestrial phenomenon of the daily rotation of the Earth on its own axis.

The most obvious way of doing this was to divide the twenty-four-hour rotation of the Earth into sections based on how long it took the Sun to move from its position at dawn to its position at noon, and from its noon point to its sunset point, etc. Because at certain times of the year the Sun would spend longer above the horizon, these divisions would not always be equal.

Martin Freeman, in his book *How to Interpret a Birth Chart*[1], helps the beginning student of astrology conceptualize the kind of movement caused by the rotation of the Earth. He suggests that we imagine a day in early spring. From the point of view of the Earth, the Sun in early spring is situated in that part of the Zodiacal Belt which is known as Aries. At sunrise on the day in question, the Sun and the sign of Aries will be seen appearing over the eastern horizon of the observer on Earth. By noon of that day, however, the Sun and Aries are no longer due east — they have moved to a position more or less overhead of the observer, and a different sign, probably Cancer, is on the eastern horizon. By sunset, the Sun and Aries will be seen to be setting over the western horizon, and the opposite sign of Libra (180 degrees away from Aries) will be rising over the eastern horizon. At sunrise the next day, the Sun and Aries will again be seen in the east, but the Sun would have moved approximately one degree further along in the sign of Aries. Thus, due to the daily rotation of the Earth on its own axis, the position of the signs (and any planets which happen to be in them) changes in relation to the horizon.

The Division of the Chart into Angles

To understand houses it is essential to remember that we are dealing with two kinds of movement — that of the Earth and the other planets around the Sun, but also the movement of the Earth on its axis. The division of the mundane sphere into what eventually became known as the houses arose out of a need to relate the axial rotation of the Earth with the movement of the planets in the sky. While signs are subdivisions of the apparent revolution of the Sun, Moon and planets around the Earth, houses are subdivisions of the Earth's diurnal (daily) rotation on its own axis.

In *The Astrological Houses,* Dane Rudhyar expands Cyril Fagan's view that what we now refer to as houses were originally periods of time called 'watches'. Watches were based on the movement of the Sun as it rose in the east, passed overhead of the observer, and set in the west. Each watch covered approximately six hours of time, marking the points of sunrise, noon, sunset and midnight. By the advent of the Renaissance, astrologers had devised several methods

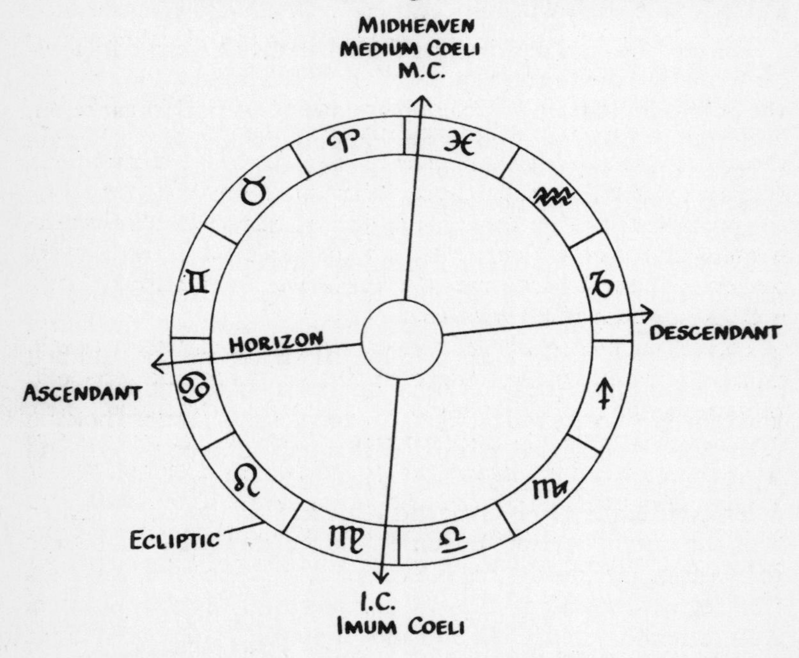

Fig. 3 THE FOUR ANGLES

of dividing these watches into the twelve houses of the horoscope. Furthermore, they had developed a correspondence between various types of human activity and the different watches or houses. In this way, the houses became the frame of reference through which the potentialities of a planet and sign combination could be related to the actual events and concerns of life. Without the structure of the houses, astrologers cannot bring the significance of celestial events down to earth.

It is an easy step from the four watches to the four points in the chart known as *the Angles* (see Figure 3). From the point of view of an observer's position on earth, at any time of day, a certain sign will be seen to be rising in the east while its opposite sign (180 degrees away) will be seen to be setting in the west. The degree of the sign occupying the easternmost point in the sky is called the *Ascending Degree* and the sign it is in is called the *Ascendant* or *Rising Sign*. Astronomically, the Ascendant marks the intersection of the ecliptic with the observer's horizon — in other words, the meeting of heaven and earth. The opposite point to the Ascendant is the *Descendant*, the sign setting in the west. The line connecting the Ascendant and Descendant is called the *axis of the horizon*.

Likewise, at any time of the day for an observer on earth, a particular degree of a certain sign will be 'culminating' at the upper meridian, the point due south of the place in question. This is called the *Midheaven* or *MC*, an abbreviation for the Latin term *Medium Coeli*, the 'middle of the heavens'. The opposite point to the Midheaven is called the *Imum Coeli* or *IC*, an abbreviation for 'the lowest heavens'. The line connecting the Midheaven to the Imum Coeli is called the *axis of the meridian*.

These four points are determined astronomically. Collectively called *the Angles*, the signs found on these points reveal a great deal about an individual's orientation to basic experiences in life. Their significance is more fully discussed in later chapters. The intersection of the axis of the horizon and the axis of the meridian give rise to the four *Quadrants* of the chart. Owing to the tilt of the Earth, the size of the quadrants arising from this fourfold division are seldom equal, and will vary according to the latitude and time of year of the birth.

The Division of the Four Angles into the Twelve Houses

While determining the angles does not raise too many problems, the manner in which the four angles should (or should not) be trisected to form the twelve houses is a major controversy in astrology.

On the whole, there seems to be general agreement that the line of the horizon — the Ascendant-Descendant axis — is the basis upon which the division of the chart into houses should rest. In other words, most astrologers agree that the Ascendant should mark the *cusp* or beginning point (or leading edge) of the 1st house and the Descendant should mark the cusp or beginning point of the 7th house. After that, astrologers disperse in all directions. Those who support the Equal House System of house-division provide the least complicated solution. Calling the Ascendant the cusp of the 1st house, they simply divide the ecliptic into twelve equal-sized houses of thirty degrees each. So, if the Ascendant were 13 degrees of Cancer, then the 2nd house would be 13 degrees of Leo, the 3rd house 13 degrees of Virgo, etc. In the case of Equal House charts, the Midheaven does not necessarily coincide with any house cusp.

However, in Quadrant systems of house-division, the four points of the angles all correspond to house cusps: the Ascendant becomes the 1st house cusp, the IC becomes the 4th house cusp, the Descendant becomes the 7th house cusp, and the Midheaven becomes the 10th house cusp. But how the intermediate house cusps (that is, the cusps of the 2nd, 3rd, 5th, 6th, 8th, 9th, 11th and 12th houses) should be calculated raises many questions. In some of these systems, *space* is divided to determine these cusps; in other systems *time* is the factor upon which the division is made. A fuller discussion of the question of house-division is included in Appendix 2. Personally, and for reasons explained in the Appendix, I favour Quadrant systems over the Equal House System and for the purposes of this book, will generally relate the cusp of the 10th house to the Midheaven, and the cusp of the 4th house to the *Imum Coeli*.

One way or another, we want to end up with twelve houses. Why twelve? The most obvious reason for this is that astrologers believed that the division of the mundane sphere into houses should mirror the division of the ecliptic into twelve signs. Rudhyar offers a more philosophical answer. He argues that each quarter of the chart (as defined by the Ascendant, IC, Descendant and Midheaven) should be divided into three houses because 'each operation of life is basically threefold, including action, reaction, and the result of both.'[2] In his opinion, then, the 2nd and 3rd houses carry out the significance of the Ascendant and 1st house; the 5th and 6th houses fulfil what is begun by the IC and 4th house; the 8th and 9th houses continue what is started by the Descendant and 7th house; and the 11th and 12th houses complete what was initiated by the Midheaven and 10th house. Besides justifying the need for twelve houses, Rudhyar's reasoning helps us to appreciate the fact that the meaning and relevance of each house follows on logically from the previous one. More will be said on the cyclic process of the houses later.

The houses are traditionally counted anti-clockwise from the Ascendant. The 1st and 7th houses are always opposite one another — this means that the sign on the 7th house cusp will be the opposite sign to the one on the 1st house cusp, although the actual degree on the cusp will stay the same. This same rule applies to the other pairs of opposite houses: the 2nd and 8th, the 3rd and 9th, the 4th and 10th, the 5th and 11th and the 6th and 12th.

Martin Freeman makes the relationship between the signs of the zodiac and the twelvefold division of the houses clearer by picturing the zodiac as a 'great wheel surrounding the earth along whose rim the planets move'. This wheel is fixed against the background of the heavens, and the signs are marked along the edge. The twelve houses are like the 'spokes of a moving wheel superimposed on the greater wheel'. The spokes of the houses rotate a full circle every twenty-four hours in line with the daily rotation of the Earth. The particular way the wheel of the houses is related to the wheel of the zodiac at the time and place of birth is what makes the chart unique for each individual.[3]

Since the Earth rotates once every twenty-four hours, the twelve signs and ten planets pass through the twelve houses in that period. The birthchart is a frozen moment in time which shows the particular alignment of planets, signs and houses for the time and place of birth. Two people may be born on the same day and have the same sign positions of the planets, but because they are born in a different place or at a different time, the planetary pattern will be seen in a different area of the heaven, i.e. in different houses.

So far we have divided space into signs, divided time into four quadrants, and divided four quadrants into twelve houses. That's enough dividing for now. It's time to assign meaning to the houses, and consider their relationship to one another, and to our lives.

The Natural Zodiac

Since the houses are determined by the line of the horizon (where heaven and earth meet), they relate the activities and energies symbolized by the planets in the signs (celestial events) to actual life on earth (terrestrial events). In other words, the houses show specific areas of everyday experience through which the operations of the signs and planets manifest. Each of the twelve houses represents a different department of life — a particular phase of what Rudhyar calls 'the spectrum of experience'.[4]

But we still have the problem of assigning meaning to the different houses. Generally, the meaning of each house mirrors the meaning of the twelve signs of the zodiac: Aries is considered similar to the 1st house, Taurus is considered similar to the 2nd house, and so on right through to the connection of Pisces with the 12th house. In what is called the *Natural Zodiac* (see Figure 4), the first degree of Aries is placed on the Ascendant, the first degree of Taurus is placed on the cusp of the 2nd house, the first degree of Gemini is placed on the cusp of the 3rd house, etc. The Natural Zodiac is symbolic, and its main purpose is to help the student gain a deeper understanding of what the houses signify. *In actual practice, the*

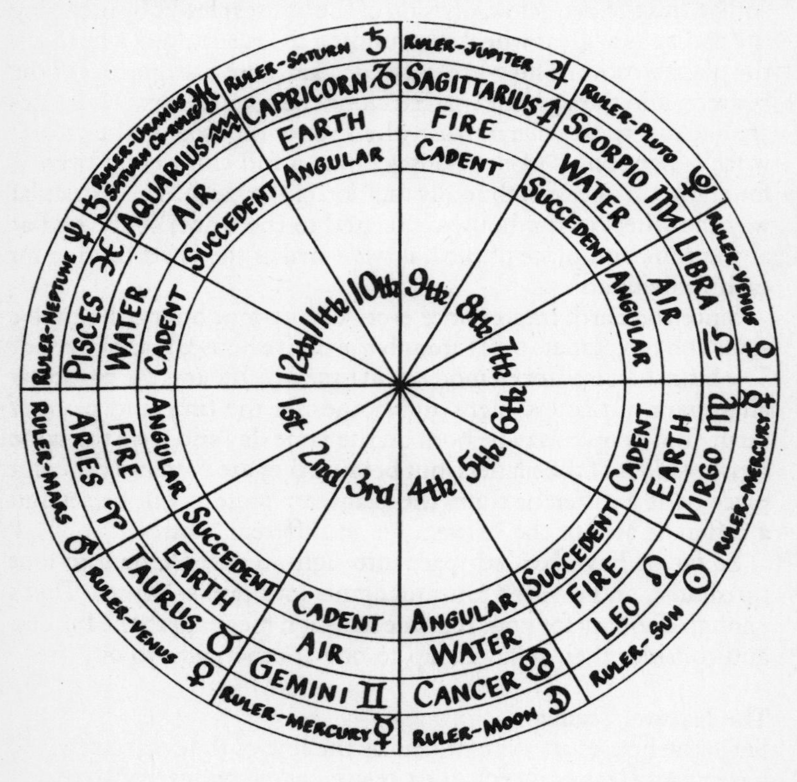

Fig. 4

THE NATURAL ZODIAC

houses in a person's chart will almost never align themselves in such an exact correspondence with the signs as in the Natural Zodiac.

The coupling of 0 degrees of Aries with the Ascendant does make sense, however, because both Aries and the Ascendant (cusp of the 1st house) are beginning points in their respective cycles. The yearly cycle of the Sun's apparent movement around the Earth begins with 0 degrees of Aries — the point where the celestial equator intersects the ecliptic at the Spring Equinox. The daily cycle of the Sun through the houses symbolically begins with the Ascendant — the point where the horizon of the observer on earth intersects the ecliptic. Since Aries and the Ascendant both connote beginnings, it is understandable that they should share a similar meaning. Aries is a sign which implies 'initiation', fresh starts, and the first impulse to act. The Ascendant and 1st house are associated with birth and the way in which we meet life. The ruler of Aries, Mars, also denotes initiatory energy, the will-to-be, and the urge to make an impact on the environment.

Zipporah Dobyns, in *The Astrologer's Casebook,*[5] describes astrology as a symbolic language in which the signs, planets and houses form the alphabet. She feels that astrology depicts twelve ways of being in the world, or twelve sides of life. These twelve aspects of the totality of life can be written in different ways, just as in the English alphabet we have upper case, lower case and italic letters. Signs symbolize one form of the letters of the alphabet, planets another, and houses another still. Signs, planets and houses, in other words, represent different ways in which the same twelve basic principles can be expressed. More specifically, Aries, Mars and the 1st house represent one letter; Taurus, Venus and the 2nd house another; Gemini, Mercury and the 3rd house represent a third letter, etc. It must be remembered, however, that any planet or any sign can be located in any house depending on the exact time, place and date of birth. Therefore, the factors symbolized by a sign, planet or house will be found to be mixed.

The Houses as Fields of Experience

In many textbooks, each house is generally allotted a field of experience, describing a particular set of circumstances in a person's life. For instance, one traditional meaning of the 4th house is 'the home', of the 9th house is 'long journeys', and one of the areas covered by the 12th house is 'institutions'. Texts tell us that if we want to know what a person's home is like, we should examine that person's 4th house. If we want to know what will happen to a person on long journeys, we should analyse the 9th house; and if we want to find out how someone will fare in hospitals or prisons we should consider the placements in the 12th. While sometimes quite accurate, this way of interpreting houses is flat, boring and not very helpful. In Chapter 1, I emphasized that the core meaning of the house must be grasped — that essential inner meaning from which spring all the endless associations and possibilities connected to that house. The 4th house is referred to as the house of 'the home' for a reason, and that reason should be understood. The 9th house is associated with 'long journeys' because travel is just one way that a more general process associated with the 9th house can be lived out. 'Hospitals and prisons' hardly scratch the surface of the 12th house. In Part 2 of this book, we crack the shell of each house in an attempt to cut through all its layers and 'get at' the meaty, archetypal kernel.

Planets and signs in a house reveal much more than just what might be waiting 'out there' for us. Placements in a house describe the inner landscape — the inborn images we carry within which are then 'projected' onto that sphere. We filter what is happening outside through the subjective lens of the sign(s) or planet(s) in a house. If Pluto is in the 4th house, even something 'nice' someone does for us in our home might be perceived as dangerous, underhand and threatening. But, most importantly, the signs and planets in a house suggest the best and most natural manner in which we 'should' meet that area of life in order to unfold and realize our inherent potentialities. As Dane Rudhyar writes, 'each house of the chart symbolizes a specialised aspect of [our] *dharma*.'[6]

The Houses as Process

In a lecture entitled 'Creating a Sacred Psychology',[7] the psychologist Jean Houston related an anecdote about the life of Margaret Mead. As a child, Margaret asked her mother to teach her how to make cheese. Her mother replied, 'Yes, dear, but you are going to have to watch the calf being born.' From the calf being born to making cheese — Margaret Mead was taught as a child to do entire processes, from beginning, to middle, to end.

Dr Houston laments that we are the victims of an 'age of interrupted process'. We turn on a switch and the world is set in motion. We know a little about the beginning of things; we know a little about the end of things; but we have no idea about the middle. We have lost the sense of the natural rhythms of life.

Our current culture is insufferably imbalanced. Before the sixteenth century the dominant world view was organic. People lived close to nature in small social groups, and perceived their own needs as subordinate to those of the community. Natural science had its basis in reason *and* faith, and the material and spiritual were inextricably linked. By the seventeenth century, this world view had changed dramatically. The sense of an organic, spiritual universe was replaced by a different notion: the world as a machine, which functioned on the basis of mechanical laws, and which could be explained in terms of the movement and arrangement of its various parts. The earth was no longer the Great Mother, sentient and alive, but a mechanism, reducible to bits and pieces like a clock. Descartes' famous statement, *'Cogito, ergo sum'* — I think, therefore I am — heralded a major split between mind and matter. People moved into their heads and left the rest of their bodies behind. Fragmentation became the rule of the day, and continues to reign even though twentieth-century physics has shown that *relationship is everything* — that *nothing* can be understood isolated from its context.

Ironically, astrology, the study of nature's cycles and movements, also lost its sense of process and its feeling for the organic wholeness of life. The mechanistic world view led to a belief that nature could and should be controlled, dominated and exploited. Similarly, astrology came to emphasize prediction and outcome at the expense of an understanding of the deeper significance of things. Houses were described by keywords and meanings which made them seem as if they were unrelated to one another, or only loosely connected. Why is the 2nd house of 'money, resources and possessions' followed by the 3rd house of 'the mind, immediate environment, and brothers and sisters'? Why is the 6th house of 'work, health and small animals' spawned by the 5th house of 'creative self-expression, hobbies and spare-time activities'? Surely, just as summer follows spring and day turns into night, there must be some fundamental reason why one house leads on to the next.

Houses are not separate, isolated, dangling segments of life. Conceived in their totality, they unfold a process of supreme significance — the story of the emergence and development of a human being. Starting at birth from the Ascendant, we are not even aware of ourselves as distinct from anything else. Gradually, house by house, through a series of steps, phases, dances and changes we build an identity which can ultimately expand to include all of creation. We emerge out of an amorphous sea, take shape, and then merge back again. Unless appreciated as a process of unfoldment, both life and the houses forfeit their essential meaning. Process is embedded in the very root of human experience. Division is only one part of the entire cycle, and yet we imprison ourselves in it. But wholeness is everything.

PART 2: MAPPING THE JOURNEY

3. THE ASCENDANT AND THE FIRST HOUSE

> What we are looking for is what is looking.
>
> St Francis

Take a few seconds to imagine how existence in the womb might feel. Floating rhythmically in the waters of life — there is no sense of an individual or separate identity, no awareness of body, feelings or mind as distinct from anything else. Dreamily immersed in a primal paradise, there is only unity or oneness with the rest of creation. The universe is the self, and the self is the universe.[1]

Birth rather dramatically jolts us out of this realm of oceanic totality. Being born means 'taking on' a body, and heralds the self as a unique and distinct individual. On the basis of this moment, the birthchart is drawn and our journey through the houses begins.

Marking the cusp of the 1st house, the Ascendant shows the exact degree of the zodiacal sign which is rising over the eastern horizon at the time of birth. Coincident with the first independent breath we take, the Ascendant and 1st house proclaim the beginning of a cycle, the initial step or stage in the process of Becoming.

Whatever is born at a moment in time reflects the qualities of that moment. The Ascending sign comes into light and distinguishes itself from darkness at the same time that we emerge from the dark, hidden, and undifferentiated environment of the mother's womb. In other words, the Ascendant appears as we appear, and its qualities reflect both who we are *and* how we meet life.

The sign of the Ascendant symbolizes a particular facet of the

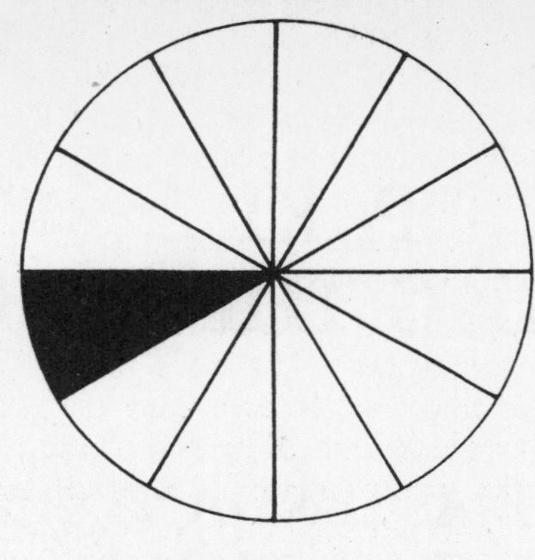

1st

totality of life which literally seeks 'em-bodiment' through what is being born at that moment. Because the Ascendant corresponds with the initial 'flash' or 'hit' of our individual existence, it also impresses itself deeply into the psyche as 'that which life is all about'. We attribute to life the qualities of the sign on the Ascendant or any planets nearby. It is the lens through which we perceive existence, the focus we bring into life, the way we 'bracket' the world. And since we see the world in this way, we invariably act and behave in accordance with our vision. What's more, life obliges our expectations and reflects our own point of view back to us.

Let us pause and consider this concept for a moment. How we perceive the world (our lens) will influence both the way we relate to it as well as what is fed back to us. By consciously or unconsciously 'choosing' certain possible interpretations of situations or people's action and behaviour (while disregarding other ways of assessing the same circumstances), we organize our experience of life according to what we have elected to see. The Ascendant, which is the first notion of life we form at birth, describes something about this sorting out and selection process. Reflecting the inborn image we have of life, the sign on the Ascendant colours our view of existence. If we have on red glasses, the world looks red and we will act accordingly. We may act very differently if we see a blue world through our lenses.

For example, if Sagittarius is rising, we will perceive a world of many exciting options and possibilities which invite us to explore and grow. If Capricorn is rising, however, we will view the world through a narrower lens of fear, doubt and hesitation. The same opportunities for expansion which stimulate and excite the Sagittarius rising into action may provoke the Capricorn rising into a state of dread and apprehension. When presented with a new possibility the Sagittarius Ascendant will exclaim, 'Great, when do I start?' When presented with the same possibility, the Capricorn Ascendant will shudder and drone, 'Must I do it? I know I really should. Am I good enough? Oh, what a big responsibility!'*

We 'dream the world up' according to the sign on the Ascendant, and then we enact the dream. It is both the maze we create, and, at the same time, the way out of the maze. For instance, those with Aries rising interpret the world as a place in which action and decisiveness are prerequisites, and then they proceed to act decisively. Those with Gemini rising create a world in which acquiring knowledge and understanding is necessary and then they endeavour to try to figure life out. In this sense, the sign on the Ascendant is both what we are looking for *and* what is doing the looking. A more detailed description of each Ascendant is found in Chapter 17.

The sign on the Ascendant or any planet near the cusp of the 1st house often describes the individual's experience of his or her birth. For example, Saturn on the Ascendant or Capricorn rising may signify delayed, extended or difficult births. Mars or Aries there seems to plunge into life head-first as if it is eager to 'get out there and get on with things'. Many births with Pluto rising or Scorpio ascending involve a close life-and-death struggle, with the mother or the infant in great danger during the delivery. Regression and rebirthing therapists who also work with astrology confirm the correlation between the sign or planet on the Ascendant and the birth experience.

More broadly, the Ascendant and 1st house denote our relationship to the archetype of Initiation itself. The rising sign not only describes something about the actual birth, but also the inborn expectations and images we have whenever we have to 'get something started'. The Ascendant suggests the fashion or manner by which we will enter into different phases or aspects of life. Anytime we experience something akin to a birth, each time we embrace a new area, facet or level of experience, the qualities of the Ascendant and 1st house are evoked. Each new beginning resonates with the qualities of earlier new beginnings, reawakening similar issues and associations. Capricorn or Saturn rising, for example, hesitates and holds back

* Any planet or sign in a house always suggests the most natural way to unfold the life-plan in the area of life the house represents. To avoid endless repetition of this concept, I do not always state this explicitly in the examples used in this part of the book.

not just with the actual birth but with any transition into a new phase of life.

The style in which we meet life in general is shown by the Ascendant and 1st house. The image which comes to mind is that of a bird pecking itself out of an egg. We can 'hatch' into things in different ways. A Cancer rising bird knows it has to hatch, cracks the shell, and then decides it's safer in the egg it knows. The Taurus rising bird will be slow to hatch but, once the process is begun, will carry it through in a determined and steady fashion. The Leo rising bird will wait until the conditions are suitable to make a dramatic, noble or dignified entrance, exhibiting itself proudly to the world. As an exercise, the reader might try imagining how the other rising signs 'hatch' into life or approach different phases of experience.

The Ascendant may be the way we hatch but what we grow into is the Sun sign. In other words, the Ascendant is the path leading to the Sun. For instance, a woman with the Sun in Aries and Virgo rising might discover her ability to initiate, lead and inspire (Aries) through developing Virgo qualities — such as the measuring of her energy in a focused and precise manner. A man with the Sun in Pisces and Libra rising may discover his way of healing and serving others (Pisces) through an important one-to-one relationship or artistic endeavour (Libra). The Ascendant flowers into the Sun. Or, as Liz Greene expresses it, the Sun is the kind of hero we are, but the Ascendant is the quest on which we must embark. The Sun is why we are here; the Ascendant is how we get there.

The signs and planets in the 1st house indicate the kinds of functions which will be most valuable in the process of realizing our own unique identity. These are the tasks that we need to fulfil in order to more wholly unravel who we are. We cannot be complete until we have recognized, explored and developed these qualities. In this respect, it is useful to bear in mind that the signs and planets (in any house) can be compared to a lift in a department store. The lift can let us off at the first floor for women's shoes, the second floor for men's clothes, or go directly to the restaurant at the top. Similarly, Mars or Aries, for instance, can, on one level, signify impulsiveness and rashness, while on another, courage and bravery. As we expand our awareness, it is possible to shift and change levels, to move from one form of expression of the sign or planet to another. Such shifting of levels may need to be experienced with all the placements in the chart, but it is especially fruitful to experiment in this way with the energies in the 1st house — the area of the chart so crucial to self-discovery.

Along with the 3rd, 4th and 10th houses, the 1st house denotes something about the atmosphere in the early environment. We normally encounter the placements in the 1st house in the highly formative early years of life. For instance, if Jupiter is there, the person may change countries shortly after birth. With Saturn, there may be a sense of hardship or restriction during infancy. Because 1st house energies are met and awakened so early in life, we form a close identification with the archetypes which the planets and signs there represent. Make a small scratch in the bark of a sapling, and once grown, the tree has an enormous cut in it.

Conversely, 1st house energies could describe the effect our 'arrival on the scene' produces on others. With Uranus or Aquarius there, for example, our arrival may signify disruption and change. With Pluto or Scorpio there, our birth may coincide with a major crisis of reorientation for those around us. We bring any sign or planet in the 1st house along with us wherever we go. This is not surprising since this house is naturally associated with the cardinal and fiery sign of Aries and the planet Mars. Cardinal fire represents a principle which radiates out into life. In general, the attributes of any sign or planet in the 1st house are somehow amplified by being in that position, as if the volume of their 'tone' has been raised. If 1st house energies are not obvious in the person, then something else in the chart is probably hampering their expression, and this blockage should be examined.

Since the sign on the Ascendant has such a great influence on the manner in which we meet life, the qualities of this sign will be reflected and embodied to some degree in our overall physical appearance and countenance. Many astrologers claim the ability to rectify an uncertain birth-time by assessing which Ascending sign correlates to the person's shape and looks. However, it is an over-simplification to assign bodily appearance to the Ascendant alone. The whole chart is lived and expressed through the body, and therefore many different factors in the birth map are concretized in the physiognomy.

Geoffrey Dean's *Recent Advances in Natal Astrology* recounts some of the studies which have been conducted on the relationship between placements in the chart and physical appearance. The American astrologer Zipporah Dobyns believes that the position of the ruler of the Ascendant (the planet which rules the sign on the 1st house cusp) is more important in this respect than the sign in which the Ascendant is placed. The German astrologer, Edith Wangemann, reports a correlation between the Ascendant sign and ruler with the shape of the head, forehead, and bones around the eyebrows.[2]

March and McEvers, authors of *The Only Way to Learn Astrology*, Vol. 3, include an interesting chapter on 'Looking for Physical Appearance'. They feel the crucial factors are the sign on the Ascendant, planets in the 1st and 12th houses within 8 or 9 degrees of the Ascendant, the placement of the ruler of the Ascendant, the Sun sign, and planets near the MC.[3]

Obviously, correlating physical appearance with the chart is quite complex. Nonetheless, some of the possible physical manifestations of the Ascending signs are given in Chapter 17.

In general, when assessing any of the workings of the Ascendant, a number of factors need to be considered: the sign on the Ascendant; the ruling planet — its sign, house and aspects; planets near the Ascendant; and aspects to the Ascendant itself. An explanation of these factors is found on pages 158-160.

At the moment of birth, a physical embodiment of one of the myriad possibilities of life rises out of the unbounded matrix of being. As beautiful as this may sound, we are in fact not born with the comprehension of ourselves as separate and individual entities; nor do we arrive with an awareness of ourselves as some manifestation of universal spirit, or as an expression of one of the many faces of what some term God. However, it is through developing the sign on the Ascendant and planets in the 1st house that we will become not only more aware of who we are as unique individuals, but also more conscious of our relation to the greater whole of which we are a part. The next eleven houses describe further stages in that journey.

4.
THE SECOND HOUSE

> Mama may have, Papa may have
> but God bless the child
> that got his own
>
> Billie Holiday

With the 1st house, the initial spark of individual identity has manifested and our general approach to life has been defined. Now the task at hand is the further elaboration of who we are, the forging of a more solid sense of 'I' or the personal ego.* We need more definition, more substance, a greater sense of our own worth and abilities. We need some idea of what it is that we possess which we can call our own. We also should have some notion of what we value, of what we would like to accrue or gain so that we can structure our life accordingly. The 2nd house, associated with the earthy sign of Taurus and the planet Venus, and usually described under the umbrella of 'Values, Possessions, Money and Resources', covers this phase of the journey.

The traditional labelling of the 2nd house makes it sound as if it covers only that which is concrete and tangible and of interest to the tax inspector. Don't be fooled — there is much more under this umbrella than meets the eye.

Although birth is the beginning of our development as a separate individual, it usually takes up to six months before we *recognize* we

* Ego can be defined as 'the centre of the field of consciousness' (Jung's definition). We are born into an ego-less state, because we are unconscious of existing as a separate entity. In the 2nd house, we become aware of our own distinct body; therefore it could be said that we have a body-ego. In the 3rd house, the mind differentiates from the body, and we develop a mental-ego. Once established, the boundaries of the ego can keep expanding.

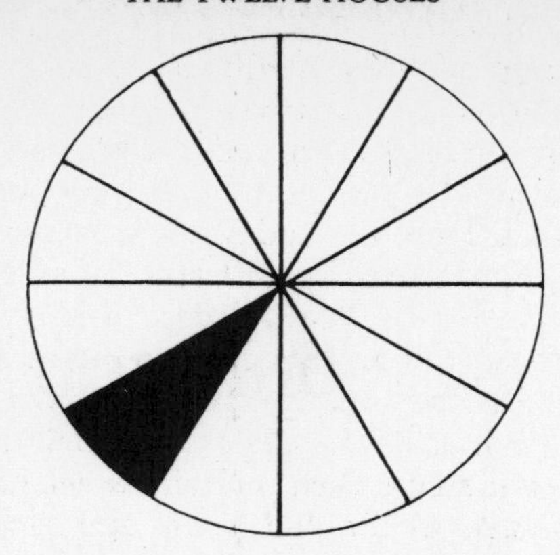

2nd

have a body, and even longer to fully differentiate self from not-self. A big step forward towards establishing ourselves as an entity distinct from everything else is taken when we realize that Mother (who is the whole world to us) is actually *not us*. Before then, she has been seen purely as an extension of who we are. Gradually we develop a sense of inhabiting a physical form which is not hers nor anybody else's: 'These are *my* toes, not Mother's toes; these are *my* hands, not Mother's hands — they belong to me, they define me, they are what *I am* and what *I* possess.' But the discovery of our body as separate also awakens a sense of our vulnerability and finiteness which has not been present before. With this fearful realization comes the need to defend the separate self against death and destruction. We yearn to make ourselves more stable, permanent, solid and enduring.

The body is the first thing by which we define ourselves, but the way is now paved for further self-definition as we attach more and more things to ourselves through which we derive and give substance to our ego-identity. As time goes by we will develop a sense of other things we possess besides the body — a good mind, a clever tongue, a sympathetic nature, a practical ability, an artistic flair, etc. The 2nd house describes what we possess or hope to possess as well as those resources or attributes which, when developed, will give us the sense of substance, value, worth, safety and security previously provided by our identification with Mother. For most people this is money, although its mindless pursuit leads not to self-definition but to despair: witness the number of men queuing to jump off the tenth-floor window-ledge after the crash of 1929. More positively, the desire for money may serve as a spur to develop certain qualities and faculties which otherwise might remain latent. Although the 2nd house is traditionally associated with money, it should be noted that other things can fulfil the need for safety, security and a more substantial sense of identity besides enlarging our bank balance.

On a more basic level, the 2nd house is an indication of what constitutes our personal security. Different things represent security to different people. For instance, if Gemini or Mercury is in the 2nd house then possessing knowledge may be what makes the person feel safe. Those with Pisces or Neptune in the 2nd could derive their security from a 'spiritual' philosophy or religion. If something makes us feel more safe and secure, then naturally we will want to acquire it.

Signs and planets in the 2nd house also serve as guidelines indicating the kinds of inherent faculties and capabilities which we can develop and concretize, and through which we gain a greater sense of self-worth. The 2nd house depicts our innate wealth which can be tapped — our substance or soil which can be tilled productively. For instance, if Mars or Aries should fall there, then potential valuable qualities which the person might actualize would be along the lines of what Mars and Aries represent: courage, directness and the ability to know what one wants and how to get it. Venus and Libra might bestow natural good taste, artistic talent, diplomatic savoir-faire, or physical attractiveness as assets. Any placement in any house gives clues to our most natural path of unfoldment in that area of life. Why not listen to these clues?

In addition to providing a stocklist of potential capacities, the 2nd house also designates our relationship to the sphere of money and possessions: that is, our attitudes towards the material world and the conditions we encounter in this realm. Whether we worship Mammon as a god or consider the world of form as all *maya* or illusion would be shown by placements here. Also indicated is the manner, style or rhythm with which we approach earning money and the development of skills and resources — be it keen, lethargic or fitful. Do we hold on tight or do we allow things to slip through our fingers? Do we have to exert tremendous effort in this area of life or are we blessed with a Midas touch? Do we still want what we have once we have managed to obtain it?

For example, Mars or Aries in the 2nd could indicate an eagerness to amass money as well as the propensity to spend it rashly. There may be a tendency to associate how 'macho' one is with the capacity to earn wealth and acquire possessions. Money could be earned through professions associated with Mars — anything from working for the military establishment to ironmongery. Venus' style in this house is very different — she may lure money to her rather than clamour after it and perceive wealth and riches as a way of augmenting her seductiveness and appeal. Money could be earned through professions associated with Venus — anything from the fine arts to working in the cosmetics department at Harrod's. Liberace, the popular pianist who outrageously parades his wealth and extremes of taste, is born with Uranus in Pisces in the 2nd. Machiavelli, who believed that the end justified any means, was born with Mars in this house. Karl Marx, whose political and economic theories have changed history, was born with both the Sun and Moon in Taurus in the 2nd.

More broadly, 2nd house placements designate what we value and hope to gain in life. This is extremely crucial, because we base our whole existence on such criteria. When our values change, our whole life-focus can alter dramatically. In the 1960s, scores of executives abandoned their secure jobs and offices on Madison Avenue, stripped off their Brooks Brothers' suits and donned their bell-bottoms in search of a new life in California — all because of a shift in values.

The 2nd house shows what we desire. Desire-energy is a mysterious and powerful force: in fact, what we desire, value or appreciate largely determines what we attract into our lives. There is an allegory pertaining to this principle. The people of a small town had such an enormous appreciation for a certain world-famous and acclaimed artist that they wrote to his agent to ask if this illustrious man would deign to visit their town. The agent replied in no uncertain terms that the famous artist had no time to spare to travel to such an insignificant municipality as theirs. Undismayed, the people there established study societies to explore more deeply the work, life and philosophy of their beloved artist, and they even commissioned a statue of him to be erected in the town centre. Eventually the artist heard of the overwhelming enthusiasm and love which these people felt for his work. Naturally, he grew curious enough to journey to this little town where all this fuss was being made over him. In the end, not only did he visit the town but he felt so welcomed there that he decided to make it his new home. Against all odds, the depth and quality of these people's desire and appreciation for the artist had literally drawn him to them. Understood in this way, through valuing and appreciating the qualities associated with a planet which falls in the 2nd house, we are likely to create situations which draw this principle to us, or bring it to the fore. Transits and progressions to the 2nd house indicate those times of shifts and alterations to the desire-nature.

We all tend to form our sense of identity and security primarily from what we own, possess or attach to ourselves — be it the body, the home, the bank balance, the spouse, our children or a religious philosophy. However, deriving an identity from anything external or relative is ultimately precarious and conditional. Any of these could at any time be removed from us or suddenly lose their relevance. Even our body, which is the first thing we have labelled as our own and through which we gained our initial sense of 'I', must eventually be 'let go of' and sacrificed. Perhaps our only real security comes from an identification with that part of us which remains when everything else we thought we were is stripped away. To paraphrase Jung: we only discover what supports us when everything else we thought supported us doesn't support us anymore.[1] It is worth reflecting on the wisdom of certain American Indian tribes which required that at the end of each year, the richest man in the village — the one who had successfully appropriated the most wealth to himself — gave away everything he had accrued.

5.
THE THIRD HOUSE

We read the world wrong, and say that it deceives us.

Tagore

In the womb and for some months after birth, nothing is perceived as separate from ourselves — everything is seen as an extension of who we are. Eventually we become aware of our own distinct body. We discover its biological needs and wants and the kind of equipment we have been given to operate in the world to fulfil these. A sense of physical separateness from the mother develops and thereafter the sense of separateness from the rest of the environment. It is only when we have distinguished ourselves from the totality of life that we can actually begin to see and understand what there is around us, and enter into a relationship with what we find. Having established some awareness of our own boundary and shape, we can now explore the boundaries and shapes of other things. By the time we reach the 3rd house — the area of the chart associated with Mercury and Gemini — we are sufficiently evolved to examine the environment more closely, to interact with it, and to form ideas and opinions about what we meet.

Developmentally, the 3rd house corresponds to the stage in life when we begin to crawl and learn to walk. Provided that we feel reasonably secure (the feeling that 'Mother is at home') and with the stipulation that the environment is not too repressive, we naturally relish our greater independence and autonomy. We *want* to grow and explore. Akin to this is the development of language and the ability to communicate and name things. All this sounds like fun, and yet ironically our growing autonomy and our increasing facility to operate in the world confront us head on with a frustrating sense of our own inadequacy and smallness. There are things out there which are bigger than we are, which are scary and threatening; there

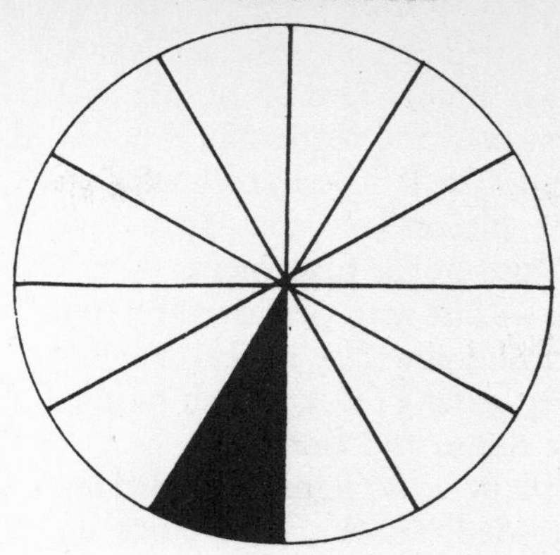

3rd

are certain laws and limits — some things we are allowed to do or say, and are even praised for, while other things we do or say are reprehended with a scowl or firm slap. Welcome to the world of relativity! What a jigsaw puzzle! It is enough of a task to find all the pieces, let alone figure out how to put them together.

Most psychologists affirm that a true sense of individuality does not develop until language is learned: the typical noun-verb structure of most languages helps the growing child to distinguish subject from object, and in this way, the actor becomes separate from the action. (Little Johnny is not the ball, but he can throw the ball.) Accordingly, the child becomes more conscious of the self as a distinct entity — as a 'doer' or the one who is done to. Everything is no longer the same amorphous blob.[1]

Through language, the child also enters the world of symbols, ideas and concepts, and, for the first time, is able to imagine sequences of events beyond what is immediately available to the senses or the body. Attention can now be focused not just on what is present, but also on hypothetical and abstract qualities of existence. In short, with the advent of language, the mind (or mental self) frees and differentiates itself from the body.[2]

Traditionally, astrologers have associated the 3rd house with what is known as 'the concrete mind' and the 9th house (opposite the 3rd) with 'the abstract mind'. Recent scientific investigation confirms what astrologers have always known — that the mind can be divided into two parts. Studies begun in the 1960s have demonstrated that the left and right sides of the brain correspond to different kinds of mental activity.[3] The 'concrete mind' of the 3rd house (in league with the Mercury-ruled 6th house) is analogous to the activities of the left side of the brain. This is the part of the brain which is concerned with rational and sequential thought, the fact-gathering aspect of the mind. The left brain controls that part of us that can talk about, analyse, pigeon-hole, compartmentalize and classify what we experience. Third house placements describe our mental style — how we think — but with particular reference to the left brain functions. Is our mind slow, fast, logical or woolly? Are our thoughts original or do they usually reflect the thinking of those around us? Examine the 3rd house and find out.

Furthermore, planets and signs in the 3rd reveal our relationship or attitude to knowledge itself. For instance, a person with Mars in the 3rd may believe that knowledge *is* power; but those with the Moon in this house may seek knowledge for the security it brings them, for the sense of safety and well-being they gain through mastering how something works.

As children, what we think about is mostly related to what we find in our immediate environment. Signs and planets in the 3rd house indicate what is 'out there' for us. However, as in the case of the Ascendant and 1st house, placements in the 3rd reveal our predisposition to perceive certain aspects of the environment and neglect or miss others. For example, those with Venus in the 3rd 'drink' Venus from the environment. They naturally imbibe the more harmonious and pleasing aspects of what is around them — those things which invite them to be congenial and harmonious in return. But those with Saturn there tend to perceive the more restrictive and colder aspects of the environment, and therefore, in their eyes, it is not a safe enough place in which to freely romp about. In this sense, placements in the 3rd describe both what we attribute to the immediate environment, as well as what we take away from it. '*What you see is what you get.*' Both the chicken and the egg are alive and well and roosting in the 3rd house.

Some of the first things we might bump up against in the immediate environment are brothers and sisters. The 3rd house denotes our relationship with them as well as with uncles, aunts, neighbours, cousins and the like. (Obviously, mother and father are usually present as well, but they are so important that they each warrant other houses of their own.) Signs and planets in the 3rd signify the nature of the bond between us and a sibling, or these placements may be an apt description of the sibling — or at least those qualities we project onto him or her. For example, Saturn in the 3rd could mean that we experience difficulty and conflict in relating with a brother, or we see him as cold and unloving, or that we experience *that part of us* which is cold and unloving as coming from him. It is a common psychological precept that, one way or another, we manage to coerce others to 'act out' or 'take on' those aspects of our own psyche from which we are cut off. The impulse of life is towards wholeness, and if we are not living our wholeness then the outside will bring the missing elements to us. Energies in the 3rd house which we have not acknowledged as our own don't just disappear — instead, they find someone or something else in the immediate environment through which to manifest.

Consultant astrologers will find it useful to question clients about early sibling relationships in the light of placements in the 3rd house. Where were they in terms of ordinal position — eldest, middle or youngest? Was there the feeling that a younger sibling usurped their central position in the family? Did an older sibling take out his or her frustration at being dethroned onto them? How competitive were siblings? Were boy children treated differently from girl children? Finally, issues relating to the death of siblings, either prior to or after one's own birth, are extremely pertinent and more often than not are revealed in the chart. Patterns established with brothers and sisters early in life may repeat themselves with husbands, wives, co-workers, bosses and friends at a later stage of development.

The 3rd house also indicates something about the early schooling experience. School gives us a chance to see what we are like with other people besides our own family, and the opportunity to compare what our parents have told us with what others have to say. We also learn as much from our peers as we do from our teachers. Throughout childhood and early adolescence (the period of time traditionally associated with this house), we assimilate more and more information, which ultimately forms a code of practical rules and 'truths' by which we give order and meaning to life. How we fare during these tricky, formative years is shown by the 3rd house.

In mythology, Mercury (the natural ruler of the 3rd) was in charge of distributing information to and from the various gods. Likewise, all forms of communication — writing, speaking, the media, etc. — come under this house. The 3rd house mind draws connections between one field of study or branch of knowledge and another, and takes pleasure exploring all the myriad forms of life. Bits of information are gathered here and there, and usually some effort is made to perceive how the various parts fit into a larger whole.

The tone and colour of our experiences on short journeys (normally taken to mean within the country of residence) are ascribed to this house. In general, a planet in a house predisposes us to meet the principle it symbolizes on any of the different levels represented by the house: Saturn in the 3rd, for instance, could give problems with studies and/or with siblings and/or with short journeys. Whatever the outer manifestation, it is ultimately 'symptomatic' of a deeper, underlying issue — the desire to explore, discover, and relate to life (3rd house) is beset with fears and apprehensions (Saturn) which are calling out to be examined and understood.

There is sometimes a correlation between having many planets in the 3rd and experiencing frequent changes of environment in the growing-up years. The effect of these moves on a person will vary according to the rest of the chart. Some will develop an exceptional flexibility and ease at fitting into different situations, while others might defend themselves against the pain of being wrenched away from established contacts by avoiding relating too deeply with anyone else. The latter attitude, unless faced and dealt with, could remain with them throughout their lives. Others might compensate for a disruptive childhood by later seeking a stable home at any cost.

Placements in the 3rd often correlate with professions such as teaching, writing, journalism, printing, media work, lecturing, selling, transport work, secretarial jobs and the like. Johnny Carson, reportedly one of the highest-paid American television chat show hosts was born with the friendly conjunction of Moon and Jupiter in the 3rd. Hans Christian Andersen, the Danish writer whose fairy tales continue to enthrall children of all ages, was born with the imaginative Venus in Pisces in the 3rd, along with the Sun and Mercury. Lenny Bruce, the satirical comedian who upset many people by joking about what others considered taboo, was born with shocking Uranus in this house.

In conclusion, the 3rd house describes the context in which we view the immediate environment. It is advisable to remember that *content is a function of context:* the way in which we perceive something determines how we will relate to it.

An Indian story makes this point nicely. A group of people are walking through a town just after sunset when they come upon what appears to be a snake on the ground in front of them. In terror, the alarm is raised, ambulances are summoned, and hospitals are put on alert in case of any mishap. Everyone else scurries back to the safety of their own houses to hide. The sun rises as usual the next morning, and as the light dawns, they discover that what they thought was a snake was in actual fact only a long piece of string someone had discarded on the pavement. All that hubbub because of a piece of string.

Because we so often forget the part we play in constituting the world, it is useful to examine the 3rd house and assess the general context through which we are prone to interpret the immediate environment. Do we tend to see a snake or a piece of string? Becoming conscious of the preconceptions and attitudes that are suggested by the placements in this house ultimately makes it possible for us to work more creatively within their framework.

6.
THE IMUM COELI AND THE FOURTH HOUSE

Who looks outside dreams; who looks inside wakes.

Jung

In the 1st house we are virtually unaware of ourselves in any objective sense. We just *are*. In the 2nd, we discover that we have our own shape and boundary which distinguishes us from everything else. In the 3rd, we turn our attention to what surrounds us, interacting with the other shapes and boundaries in our immediate environment to see what these are all about. By comparing what we are with what we come up against, we formulate even more opinions about ourselves. In the process, we lose the sense that we are *everything*, but gain in return the feeling that we are *a someone* — someone who inhabits a particular body, who thinks in a particular way, and who comes from a particular family background. As we approach the nadir of the chart — the IC and the 4th house — it's time to pause and assimilate what we have learned. The task at hand is to gather our bits and pieces and integrate these around a central point, or 'I', which from now on will form the basis of our identity. Some people carry on gathering new bits of information all their lives and never pause to take root or consolidate at all (too much 3rd house and not enough 4th house). Others settle down and root too soon, before enough of life has been explored (too much 4th house and not enough 3rd).

It is not uncommon for people preoccupied with career and outer achievements in the world to be so active and busy with appointments and meetings that they hardly spend any time at home. Similarly, we all have a tendency to become so 'caught up' and identified with activity and external happenings that we neglect and lose touch with the 'I' that is there underneath it all. We are so engaged in *what* we are seeing, *what* we are feeling, or *what* we are doing, that we

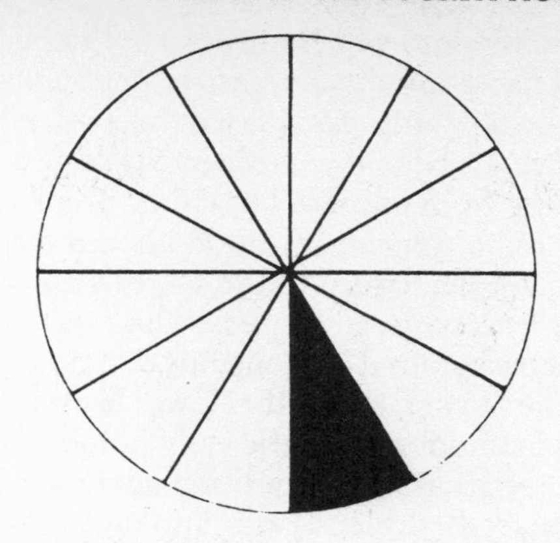

4th

forget about the 'I' that is doing the seeing, having the feelings or performing the actions. What we encounter when we withdraw our awareness from the transitory objects of experience and reconnect with the underlying 'I' which is the subject of all experience, is designated by the sign on the IC (cusp of the 4th house in Quadrant systems) and the planets in the 4th.

The sense of a 'me-in-here' provided by the IC and 4th house lends an inner unity to all thoughts, feelings, perceptions and actions. In the same way that we are biologically self-maintaining and self-regulating, the IC and 4th house serve to maintain the individual characteristics of the self in a stable form.

The 4th house represents where we go when we settle back into ourselves — the inner centre where our 'I' returns to rest before launching into activity again. It is the base of operations from which we meet life. For this reason, the 4th house has been traditionally associated with the home, the soul and the roots of the being. The American Indians believed that you opened your soul to someone when you invited that person into your home. As opposed to our public face, the 4th house describes what we are like deep down inside. The Jungian analyst James Hillman describes soul as 'that unknown component which makes meaning possible'. The soul deepens events into experiences and mediates between the doer and the deed. 'Between us and events . . . there is a reflective moment — and soul-making means differentiating this middle ground.'[1] The subtle way a person turns events into experiences is shown by the IC and 4th house.

The IC and 4th house signify the influence on us of our 'family of origin', the family into which we were born. Planets and signs in the 4th reveal the atmosphere we felt in that home, and the kind of conditioning or 'scripting' we received there — the psychological family inheritance. Delving even deeper, the 4th denotes qualities we carry stemming from our racial or ethnic origins: those aspects of the accumulated history and evolution of our race which reside within us. For example, Saturn in the 4th or Capricorn on the IC sometimes describes a home atmosphere which was felt as cold, strict or unloving, or a background of a long line of staunch conservatives; while Venus in the 4th or Libra on the IC will likely be more attuned to the love and harmony within the early home, and may feel an affinity and appreciation for the tradition out of which it has come. The Moon or Cancer there blend easily into the home environment, whereas Uranus or Aquarius in this position often feels like a stranger in a strange land, curiously wondering how it 'ended up' in that particular family. Marcel Proust, who in *The Rememberance of Things Past* explored in unsurpassed detail his early life and innermost feelings, and the workings of memory itself, was born with the Sun, Mercury, Jupiter and Uranus all in Cancer in the 4th.

The influence parental figures have on us is normally attributed to the 4th-10th house axis. Traditionally it has always made sense to associate the 4th house (naturally ruled by the Moon and Cancer) with the Mother, and the 10th house (naturally ruled by Saturn and Capricorn) with the Father. Most astrologers were content with this classification, but the work of Liz Greene has shed some ambiguity in this area. She has found from her considerable experience and expertise as an astrological consultant that her clients' description of the relationship to their mothers seemed to correlate more closely with the 10th house, while the image of father worked better with the 4th.[2]

There are solid cases for and against both schools of thought. Since the 4th house is linked to Cancer and the Moon, then it would seem reasonable to assign it to the mother. Her womb was our original home, and in infancy we are more responsive to the mother's moods and feelings than to the father's. The father is then connected to the 10th house, Saturn and Capricorn: after all, he is normally the breadwinner and the one out before the public, and it used to be the practice that the son followed the father's profession. However, the opposing arguments are equally convincing. The Moon is not just mother; it is also our 'origins' and we inherit our name from the father. In this way, he can be associated with the 4th house. The 10th house is much more obvious than the 4th, and the mother is much more obvious to the child than the father. The maternity of the child is a clear fact — up front and publicly recognizable like the 10th house. Paternity is more speculative, sometimes hidden and perhaps even a mystery and therefore maybe better correlated to the more hidden and mysterious IC point and the 4th house. Also, in Western society at least, the mother is usually the child's prime socializing influence. She is the great 'nay-sayer' of childhood, the one with whom we spend the most time and whose role it is to watch over us and teach us the difference between what is good and acceptable and what is bad and not allowed. It is normally the mother who toilet-trains the child — the first major adjustment we have to make in order to conform to societal standards (Saturn, Capricorn and the 10th house).

I don't believe that it is possible to fix a view that the 4th is always father and the 10th is always mother or vice versa. It is safer and perhaps more accurate to say that the 'shaping parent' — the one with whom the child spends the most time and who has the most influence on adapting the child to society — should be associated with the 10th house; and the more 'hidden parent', the one who is less visible and who is not so much of a known quantity, should be connected to the 4th house. In practice, after talking with a client the astrologer can formulate an educated guess as to which parent belongs to which house. For instance, if I ascertain that the client's father is a Gemini with an Aquarius Moon and I find Gemini on the client's IC and Uranus in the 4th house, it would seem likely that the 4th house, in this case, is an apt description of the father. Not all charts make it this easy, however.

It is important to remember that placements in the 4th (be it mother or father) may not describe the way the parent actually was as a person, but rather the way in which the child experienced the parent — what is known as the *parent-imago,* the child's *a priori* inborn image of the parent. Traditional psychology normally upholds the view that if something goes wrong between the parent and the child, it is the parent's fault; by contrast, psychological astrology places at least half of the responsibility on the child for experiencing the parent in a particular way. For example (assuming the 4th house to be the father), a little girl with Saturn in the 4th will be most responsive to the Saturnine side of her father's nature. He will probably exhibit many qualities other than those associated with that archetypal principle, but the child in question will *selectively perceive* mainly the Saturn traits. The father may be warm and kind seventy-five per cent of the time, but the twenty-five per cent for which he is cold and critical will be what the daughter registers.

More often that not there is a collusion between the parental image in the child's chart and key placements in the chart of the parent. For instance, the chart of the girl's father with Saturn in the 4th may show the Sun in Capricorn, Capricorn ascending, or a Sun-Saturn conjunction. However, even if her father's chart is not that close a description of the placements in her 4th house, the predilection to see a parent in a particular way often has the effect of turning the person into what is being projected onto him. If she keeps reacting to her father as if he is an unkind person even when he is displaying love and generosity, eventually he might become so frustrated that he turns sour towards her or gives up and avoids her altogether. And then the little girl says to herself, 'The cad — I knew he was like that all along.' But was he?

We are born with the bare bones of certain innate predispositions and expectations, but the experiences we have as children add layers upon layers of flesh to these. We interpret the environment in a certain way and then form concrete attitudes about ourselves and life 'out there' in general based on these perceptions. The little girl we have been discussing with Saturn in the 4th already has a few existential life-statements coming to the fore: 'Father doesn't love me' and 'Father is a cad', to name but two. She will carry these inside her even after she has departed from the parental home where they will blossom into more full-blown attitudes such as, 'Men find me unworthy and unlovable' and 'All men are cads'. Becoming conscious of the origins of these attitudes allows for the possibility of changing them, or finding other ways of organizing experience. Delving into the 4th house, which shows the archetypes activated in the early home life between ourselves and the parent in question, can greatly aid this process.

The 4th house, in addition to describing our inherited origins and that which resides deep within us, is associated with the home base in general. What kind of atmosphere do we create in the home? What do we attract to ourselves there? What qualities in the home environment do we most naturally resonate with? These questions can be answered by examining the planets and signs in the 4th.

T. S. Eliot writes that 'in my beginning is my end.' The 4th house depicts our origins but it is also associated with how we end things. The manner in which we ultimately resolve an issue or 'enact a closure' will be related to placements in the 4th. Venus there ends things neatly and fairly, all tied up in a pretty bundle. Saturn may prolong or begrudge an ending. The Moon and Neptune often slip away quietly and peacefully, while Mars and Uranus 'go out with a bang'.

The 4th also suggests the conditions surrounding the second half of life. What is most deep within us comes out at the end. Many of us, after the age of forty, and perhaps moved by the death of a parent, will become increasingly aware of our mortality and conscious that there is less time to waste. On this basis, we may willingly make more space in our lives to express and vent our innermost needs and feelings. Furthermore, sheer experience of life is a prerequisite for self-discovery, so it is not surprising that our deepest and most intimate motivations may not emerge until the later years. One extreme illustration of this is the death-bed confession, in which people dramatically disclose truths about themselves which they have kept guarded for decades.

Psychotherapy, self-reflection, various forms of meditation — anything which takes us into ourselves — bring 4th house energies to the surface and can make these more *consciously* available to ourselves earlier in life. Rather than neglecting what's down there, it is advisable to deal with difficult placements in this house sooner rather than later. The 4th house, like our past, always catches up with us.

7.
THE FIFTH HOUSE

> Truly, I say to you, unless you turn and become like children, you will never enter the kingdom of heaven.
>
> Matthew 18:3

In the 4th, we discover our own discrete identity, but in the 5th we revel in it. The fire of the 1st house burns without even knowing it is burning; the fire of the 5th rages consciously and is joyfully fanned by the self. The nature of life is to grow, and this house (naturally associated with Leo and the Sun) reflects our urge to expand, to become more and more, and to radiate out into life like the Sun. By the time we reach the 5th house, we now know that we are not everything; but we are not content just to be 'a someone' — we must be *a special someone.* We are not all there is, but we can try to be the most important thing there is.

The function of the Sun in our solar system is twofold: it shines, giving warmth, heat and life to the earth, but it also serves as the central organizing principle around which the planets orbit. In this sense, the Sun is like the personal ego or the 'I', the centre of consciousness around which the different aspects of the self revolve. Individuals with strong placements in the 5th partake of the qualities of the Sun. They need to shine and create from inside themselves; they need to feel influential; and they need to feel that others are revolving around them. To some this means literally always being the centre of attention — a craving to be worshipped like the Sun. One woman I knew with the Sun and Mars in the 5th couldn't tolerate being in the same room with the television on, because it meant that others in the room might focus on it rather than her. We must remember that the Sun, although vitally central and important, is not the only Sun in the galaxy — it is just one of many. The words of a popular song remind us that 'everybody is a star'.

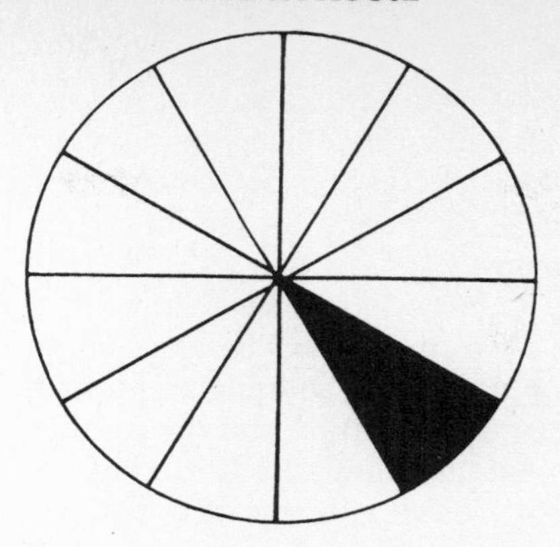

5th

Embedded deep in our psyches, and reverberating throughout the 5th house is an innate desire to be recognized for our specialness. As children, we believe that the 'cuter' or more spell-binding and captivating we are, the more certainly will Mother want to love and protect us. Enslaving and enchanting others with our unique value and worth is one way of ensuring we are fed, protected, cared for, and therefore more likely to stay alive.

Another keynote of the 5th is generativity — which simply defined means 'the ability to produce'. These two principles, the need to be loved for our specialness and the desire to create from inside ourselves, underlie most of the traditional associations with the 5th house.

The 5th house is the area of the chart attributed to creative expression, most obviously with artistic endeavours, although the creativity of the 5th needn't be just painting a picture or performing a dance. Scientists or mathematicians can apply themselves to their work with as great an *artistry* or passion as a Picasso or Pavlova. The signs and planets in the 5th shed light on the possible outlets for creative expression. Mercury or Gemini in the 5th may denote a talent for writing or public speaking; Neptune or Pisces may be absorbed with music, poetry, photography or dance. Cancer and Taurus might exhibit a flair for cooking; while Virgo in this position can be exceptionally adept at sewing and handiwork. However, more than describing which creative outlet we engage in, the placements here suggest the *manner* and *style* with which it is pursued. A piece of music can be an intellectual *tour de force* (Mercury or Uranus) or come straight from the heart (Moon or Neptune). Some people produce spontaneously and joyfully, while others suffer extraordinary birth pangs. Above and beyond purely creative expression, this is the house of the actor, and depicts the way in which we tackle the art of living. One client with an obvious 5th house slant described herself as a 'professional person' — and she did not intend this solely in terms of career.

The creative outlets associated with the 5th also include sports and recreation. For some it is the challenge of athletics, the contest and competition, the joys of winning and coming first. For others, it is the sheer ecstasy of exertion and the pitting of the self against the elements or odds. Similarly, gambling and speculation are assigned to the 5th as well — where we test our wit and imagination against fate and chance.

The 5th house is more broadly associated with hobbies, amusements and spare-time pleasures. These all sound terribly low-key for a house ruled by the Sun and Leo. However, upon examination, they are more important than they first appear. The 5th describes activities which make us feel good about ourselves and make us glad to be alive. Hobbies and spare-time amusements afford the opportunity to participate in what we want and like to do. Through these pursuits we feel the joy of being *fully involved* in something. Unfortunately, many of us have careers or jobs which do not entail this degree of engagement. There is a great danger that our enthusiasm and vitality would run dry unless we had spare-time interests to recharge and reinvigorate ourselves. In this light, hobbies and amusements have an almost therapeutic effect. The word 'recreation' literally means to make new, to revitalize and inspire with life and energy. Planets and signs in the 5th suggest the types of spare-time pursuits we might explore, and the manner in which this is undertaken.

Romance finds its way under the heading of the 5th house. Besides being exciting, passionate, heart-wrenching or whatever, romantic encounters enhance our sense of specialness. We become the main focus of attention for somebody else's feelings and we can display our very special love to someone else. Placements in the 5th reveal the way in which we 'create romance' — the archetypal principle(s) most likely activated in these situations — as well as something about the kind of person who ignites us.

Sexual expression is also linked to the 5th. A good sexual relationship contributes to our sense of power and worth, highlighting both our ability to give pleasure and the capacity to attract others to us. This power to enchant and hold the attention of others is very reassuring and satisfies deeply embedded survival instincts. (Compare this to the 8th — where we seek to transcend our personal boundaries through intimacy.)

All this leads to one of the main representations of the 5th — children, creations of the body and the physical extensions of the self. Most people primarily express their creative drives (and symbolically ensure their survival) through generating offspring. While the 4th and 10th houses indicate how we view our parents, placements in the 5th describe the archetypes constellated between ourselves and our children. Signs and planets here reflect what our progeny mean to us. In line with examples from other houses, placements in this house can be interpreted in a variety of ways. For instance, Jupiter in the 5th may literally produce Jupiterian children — those born under the sign of Sagittarius or with Sagittarius rising or Jupiter conjunct an angle or the Sun, etc. Or we can understand Jupiter in the 5th to mean our predisposition to encounter Jupiter in that area of life: we project Jupiter onto our children or are prone to register their Jupiterian side more strongly than any of their other traits. Planets in the 5th also describe our experience in the role of parent. Saturn there may be terrified of the responsibility of parenting and afraid that they won't be good at it. Uranus' idea of bringing up children may embrace the most new and avant-garde theories on the subject.

More than just describing external children, the 5th house could aptly be called the house of our own Inner Child — that part of us which loves to play and which always stays eternally young. Inside us all is a spontaneous, natural child who craves to be loved for his or her own specialness and uniqueness. However, as children, this part of us is often quashed. Too often, we are loved for conforming and matching up to our parents' expectations and standards, rather than for being who we are. In this way, we lose faith in our budding individuality and become what Transactional Analysis refers to as 'the adapted child'. Invariably, we will project the state of our own inner child onto our actual offspring. We can heal 'the damaged child' in ourselves by giving the love and acceptance we were denied as children to our own progeny or other young people we encounter. However we do it, it is never too late to have a happy childhood.

We augment and enhance our unique identity and exercise our own power through the creative outpourings of the 5th. As a by-product, we may even generate stunning works of art, worthwhile new books and ideas, or interesting children who in some way contribute to society. Benefiting society, however, is not the main concern of this house. Witness the reluctance many people have to releasing either their works of art or their children into the world. In the 5th, we create primarily for ourselves, because the self takes joy and pride in doing so, and because it is in the nature of the self to create.

8.
THE SIXTH HOUSE

A monk told Joshu: 'I have just entered the monastery. Please teach me.'
Joshu asked: 'Have you eaten your rice porridge?'
The monk replied: 'I have eaten.'
Joshu said: 'Then you had better wash your bowl.'

A Zen story

The main problem with the 5th house is a tendency to 'go over the top'. We delight in self-expression, but we don't know when to stop. In the 5th house we no longer believe we *are* everything, but we still think we can *be* or *do* anything. The 6th house follows the 5th and reminds us of our natural boundaries and the need for clearer self-definition. Like the philosophy of Zen, the 6th house asks that we respect and regain the 'perfection of our original nature',[1] that we become what we alone are (no more, no less), and that we live this in our everyday lives. Our true vocation is to be ourselves.

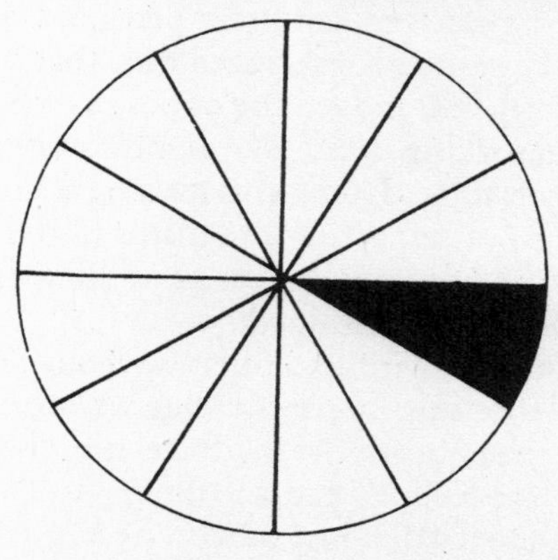

6th

The 6th house shakes a finger at the 5th and retorts:

> Very well, it's wonderful to give expression to your creative flair, but have you really done it that cleverly? That painting is not quite right yet and you've exhausted yourself staying up two nights working on it.
>
> *or*
>
> Sure, you are having quite a sizzling romance, but have you examined the practicalities of this as a long-term relationship — not to mention the fact you can't stand the after-shave he wears?
>
> *or*
>
> Congratulations, you've had a baby girl. Now adjust your schedule and life to her and keep those clean nappies coming.
>
> *or*
>
> Remember that party last week where you really let yourself go? When you look back, don't you think you might have offended that shy boy in the corner who didn't even have a chance to speak because you monopolized the conversation?

The time has come to take stock of ourselves, to discriminate between priorities, to assess the use we are making of our power and capabilities, and above all, to recognize the limits and truth of our own nature and humanity.

Try as it may, a pear seed can never become an apple tree. Nor should it, if we believe as Kierkegaard did, that 'to will to be the self which one truly is, is indeed the opposite of despair.'[2] The 6th house is all about sticking to our plan and blossoming into precisely what we are meant to be. Doing this feels right and good. But the consequences for not respecting the truths of our own nature are stress, frustration and dis-ease: messengers telling us that something is awry and needs to be examined.

'Reality has both a "within" and a "without".'[3] The 6th house explores the relationship between what we are inside and what surrounds us on the outside — the correlation between the inner world of mind and feelings and the outer world of form and the body. The traditional 6th house labels, 'health, work, service, and adjustment to necessity', all stem from this *bodymind connection*.

It is a basic fact of existence that life has to be lived within boundaries. No matter how divine or wonderful we think we are, we still have to eat, brush our teeth, pay bills and cope with the necessities of everyday, mundane reality. Furthermore, each of us has a particular body, a particular mind, and some particular task to perform. We are 'designed' in a certain way to serve a purpose or function specified in our own individual make-up and nature. Nobody can fulfil that purpose better than ourselves. We serve best by being who we are. Through the necessary adjustments and refinements of the 6th house, we become what we alone can be.

Somebody once said that 'work is the rent we pay for life.' For many of us, work is something *we have to do* in order to support daily existence. Daily employment also implies routine and adjustment. We have to arrive there more or less on time, and we cannot be as free and spontaneous as we might like with our lives if we know the alarm clock is set to ring at seven the next morning. We have to structure our time, establish priorities, and make dispensations. In one way, the need to follow a rigid schedule helps to order and pattern life. We escape the existential anxiety which freedom of choice might provoke: we have a job and we know where we must be.

Ideally, however, the work-force is composed of varied individuals each performing the particular skills they have developed best. The end result is a perfectly finished product or the maintenance of the proper functioning of society. Planets and signs in the 6th describe issues relating to work and employment, and suggest the tasks that we can potentially do most well. Placements in this house may reveal the nature of our jobs —Jupiter or Sagittarius could be a travel agent, the Moon or Cancer look after children, and Neptune or Pisces draw pints at the local pub. But much more than describing the type of employment, the placements here suggest the way in which we approach (or should approach) doing the job — not just *what* we do, but *how* we do it. For instance, those with Saturn or Capricorn here may prefer a stable job with clearly defined requirements, at which they can work slowly and steadily; while those with Uranus and Aquarius in this house normally hate to punch a clock and would much rather work without a boss looking over them.

The nature of relationships with co-workers is also shown by 6th house placements. Venus or Libra here may fall in love with someone at work, while Pluto or Scorpio stirs up intrigues and complex encounters. The 6th house is 'naturally squared' the 3rd (see page 121) and 'unfinished business' around sibling and early peer relationships may resurface with co-workers.

Through employment situations, we find ourselves in relationships of inequality. Thirty people may be working under us, and we may, in turn, be subordinate to thirty others. How we cope with dispensing authority, and how we manage in the more subservient position is shown by the 6th. It is a kind of rehearsal for the relationships of equality we form in the 7th house.

The 6th house also describes our relationship to the mechanic who works on our car, our doctor and his or her receptionist, the milkman — in fact anyone who is serving us in some way. Conversely, our own qualities as 'a server' and our deeper feelings and attitudes regarding service are shown by placements here. This is not to be taken lightly, as many people view humility and service as the pinnacle of human endeavour — as the path to God and more enlightened states of being.

The way we use our time and the kind of atmosphere we need in order to function happily in daily life is shown by the 6th. Signs and planets in this house colour the energies we bring (or should bring) into everyday tasks and how we approach the rituals of mundane existence. Mars in the 6th may clean the house like a 'white tornado', while Neptune is still trying to remember where it left the mop.

Pets — who are around us in our everyday life — are also assigned to the 6th house. This may seem a trivial consideration and yet a good number of people are profoundly affected by their experience of caring for animals. Pets can be the 'hook' for any variety of projections and for some people their relationship to their dog or cat is as important as with any human. In certain cases, pets assuage what would otherwise be an unbearable sense of loneliness or feelings of uselessness. The loss or death of a beloved animal can trigger many psychological and philosophical issues.

There is an obvious relation between work and health — the other major concern of the 6th house. Although the dominant work ethic of Western culture may seem extreme or easily abused, nonetheless the need to be productive and useful is somehow basic to human nature. Overwork strains the health, while too little work can leave us listless and lethargic. Redundancy not only deprives us of a source of income, but also a source of a sense of worth and purpose. Studies have shown that the number of reported illnesses increases in areas where the unemployment rate is rising. Conversely, some people will use illness as a way of escaping from a job they hate or which doesn't suit them.

The 6th house concern for craftsmanship, perfection and technical proficiency applies to issues of health as well as work. Optimally the body is a finely tuned mechanism where the different cells work for the good of the larger organism. Each cell is an entity in itself and yet each one is part of a larger system. Each cell must 'do its thing' but each must also submit to the demands of the greater whole. In a healthy person (as in a healthy society) each individual component asserts itself and yet works in harmony with the other components. The 6th house asks that we bring our different parts — that is, our mind, body and feelings — into a harmonious working relationship.

Many individuals with 6th house placements are especially interested in health and fitness, some to an obsessive degree. In extreme cases, special diets and techniques for maintaining the optimal functioning of the body dominate and structure the life, leaving little time for anything else. However, many excellent healers have a 6th house emphasis, and it can be associated with traditional medicine as well as careers in homoeopathy, osteopathy, herbalism, massage, etc.

It has already been mentioned that the body, mind and emotions operate as a unit. What we think and feel will affect the body. Conversely, the state of the body will influence how we think and feel. *Psyche* (mind) and *soma* (body) are inextricably linked. Physiological and chemical imbalances give rise to psychological problems, while emotional and mental turmoil can manifest in physical symptoms. The 6th house may reveal something about the underlying psychological significance of certain illnesses. Saturn could indicate a rigidity in meeting everyday life, as well as arthritis. Mars in the 6th rushes into life, works itself to a frazzle, only to be diagnosed later with high blood-pressure. However, it is an over-simplification to refer to the 6th house only in relation to health. *The American Book of Nutrition and Medical Astrology* by Eileen Naumann (published by Astro Computing Services, San Diego, California) examines medical astrology in great depth, and is highly recommended.

Through 6th house issues we refine, perfect and purify ourselves, and ultimately become a better 'channel' for being who we are. We could be the most wonderfully inspired artist (5th house) but unless we learn the tools of the craft (6th house) — the right use of brushes, paints and canvas — we won't be able to concretize or realize our possibilities. It has been said that 'technique is the liberation of the imagination'. These are true watchwords for the 6th house.

We embark on life unconscious of our unique individuality and by the end of the 6th house we have a much more defined sense of our own particular identity and purpose. Like the 3rd house, the 6th house employs the left brain activity of reducing things to parts. The problem with the 6th is that we end up seeing the world *too much* in terms of 'what is me' and 'what is not me'. When we characterize ourselves by those features which distinguish us from others — our weight, height, skin colour, job, car, house — we are left with the feeling that there is an absolute distinction between who we are and who other people are. While it is the purpose of the first six houses to make us more fully aware of ourselves as separate individuals, it remains for the last six houses (the 7th to the 12th) to reunite us with others again. Otherwise life is awfully lonely.

9. THE DESCENDANT AND THE SEVENTH HOUSE

> Driven by the force of love the fragments of the world seek each other that the world may come into being.
>
> Pierre Teilhard de Chardin

The 6th house is the last of what is known as 'the personal houses', and represents the refinement of the individual personality through work, service, humility and attention to everyday life and the physical body. Taking a microscope to life, the 6th house analyses and categorizes it into different parts, giving each part its appropriate place and purpose. We now know precisely how we differ from everybody and everything else. But, by the end of the 6th house, we have grown as separate from one another as life will allow, and we have a new lesson to learn: that nothing exists in isolation. When we arrive at the Descendant, the westernmost point in the chart, we turn a sharp corner and find ourselves heading back again to the point where it all started. It will be the work of the 7th to 12th houses to reconnect us once more to the lost sense of our unity with all life.

The Descendant is the cusp of the 7th house and the point opposite the Ascendant. Traditionally, the Ascendant is considered the 'point of self-awareness' and the Descendant is considered 'the point of awareness of others'. It describes our approach to relationships and the qualities (along with the planets in the 7th) that we are looking for in a partner. Michael Meyer in *A Handbook for the Humanistic Astrologer* also writes that the Descendant (and the 7th house) denotes the kinds of activities that give the individual the experiences 'he needs in order to realise the significance of others'.[1]

Similarly, the 1st house is traditionally known as 'the house of the self'. The 7th house, which is the farthest from the 1st, is labelled 'the house of the not-self'. It is also known as 'the house of marriage' and curiously as 'the house of open enemies'. Marriage here is taken

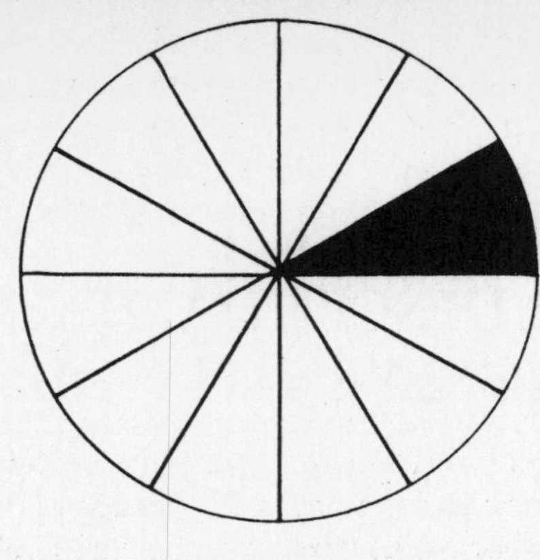

to mean any important relationship based on mutual commitment, legally contracted or otherwise. In the 7th house, two people come together for a purpose — to enhance the quality of their lives by joining with one another, to produce a family and gain greater security and stability, and to assuage loneliness and isolation.

Most astrological textbooks teach that the planets and signs in the 7th house describe the marriage partner, or 'the significant other'. This is true as far as it goes. Placements in the 7th often indicate the kind of partner(s) to whom we are attracted. For instance, a man with the Moon in the 7th may seek a partner who reflects the qualities of the Moon: someone who is receptive, compassionate and caring. A woman with Mars in the 7th may be attracted to a partner who reflects the qualities of Mars: someone who is assertive, direct and forceful. She may be looking for someone to make decisions for her and to tell her what to do.

If there are a number of planets or different signs (as in the case of an intercepted house) in the 7th, the issue can become very confusing because we are looking for so many different kinds of attributes in a partner. For example, should a woman have both Saturn and Uranus in the 7th, she is seeking someone to offer stability and security (Saturn) and yet at the same time she needs someone who is unpredictable, exciting and highly individualistic (Uranus). These two sets of qualities hardly live comfortably together in one person. She may marry Saturn first, become dreadfully restless and bored, meet someone Uranian and file for a divorce. Or she may remain married to Saturn and have an affair with Uranus. Or she may marry Uranus first, divorce him on account of his unstable and erratic character, and then breathing a sigh of relief settle down safely with Saturn. Or, if she is somewhat more psychologically mature, she can marry Saturn and find ways which are unthreatening to the relationship to satisfy her need for Uranus, or even develop it more in herself. Or she can marry a Uranian man and provide the Saturnian security herself in the partnership.

More than just describing the nature of the partner, signs and planets in the 7th suggest the conditions of the relationship: the archetypes constellated by the union itself. Saturn there could indicate a union based on duty and obligation. Mars in the 7th is prone to 'love' at first sight, rushing into marriage, tempestuous battles, passionate reunions, and then more battles again. Arthur Rimbaud, the French poet shot by his lover Verlaine, had explosive Pluto and Uranus both in the 7th house. Rex Harrison, with six marriages to his name, was born with abundant Jupiter there.

As stated earlier, a planet or sign in a house suggests the predisposition to meet that archetypal principle through the area of life in question. Placements in the 7th are what we expect to find in close partnerships and therefore indicate those attributes we notice most in the other person. Invariably, something in our partner's chart will collude with planets and signs in our 7th house, and more often than not, the partner's chart *uncannily* reflects our 7th. For instance, a woman who has Mars, Saturn and Pluto in the 7th may very well find a husband who has Mars, Saturn and Pluto in the 1st or something like an Aries Sun (reflecting her 7th house Mars), a Scorpio Moon (reflecting her 7th house Pluto), and three planets in Capricorn (reflecting her 7th house Saturn).

The psychological mechanism of projection must again be mentioned in respect to the Descendant and 7th house. In *Relating,* Liz Greene suggests that the Descendant and the 7th house planets represent qualities which 'belong to the individual, but are unconscious' and which we try to live out 'through a partner, or through the kinds of experiences the relationship brings'.[2] Let's explore what she means by this.

The Descendant — the westernmost point in the chart — disappears from view as we are being born. In this sense, it describes what is hidden in us, what we feel doesn't belong to us because we can't or won't see it in ourselves. Diametrically opposed to the Ascendant and 1st house, the Descendant and 7th house reveal qualities in ourselves which we have the most difficulty 'owning', being responsible for, and accepting. However, as Jung points out, 'when an inner situation is not made conscious, it happens outside, as fate.' If we are unconscious of something in ourselves then 'the world must perforce act out the conflict and be torn into opposite halves.'[3] In other words, what we are unaware of in ourselves, we invariably attract to us through others. Traditionally the Descendant and 7th house are described as those qualities we seek in a partner; but on a deeper level they represent those qualities hidden in us which we need to consciously integrate into our awareness to become whole — what Liz Greene calls 'the inner partner'. If we have suppressed these attributes in ourselves because we find them disagreeable or unacceptable, then it is not surprising that we won't like them when they are mirrored back to us through another person. Hence, the connotation of the 7th house as the sphere of open enemies.

However, we also tend to inhibit or 'dis-own' potentially positive traits as well and these may be the very attributes which allure or excite us when we meet them in others. We fall in love with those people who openly exhibit these traits because they make us feel more complete. We import these qualities into our lives by marrying them. Ideally, the partner may serve as a kind of role model for these energies, which eventually permits us to consciously integrate them back into our own nature. All too often, though, we remain reliant on the other person to supply them. We polarize with the partner and stay only half a person.

It should be made clear that projection is not something which is purely pathological. A projected image is a potential locked up within the self. When there is the need for this image to make itself known, the first step is perceiving it in someone else. Then, hopefully, we realize that it has something to do with us and we consciously take it back. For example, a woman with Mars in the 7th may not be in touch with her own power and assertiveness. Therefore, she looks for those qualities in a man. She finds a partner with a prominent Mars, one who is dominant and self-centred, and shouts orders at her. Through him, she has brought Mars into her life. However, when she can no longer tolerate him that way, it may dawn on her that she has a right to make demands as well. She begins to fight back, to make a stand for herself, and in this way she discovers Mars in her own nature.

Once we have, to some degree, reintegrated qualities in the 7th house into our own identity, we serve to expose those principles to society at large. Therefore, a person with Mars in the 7th might be someone who rouses other people to action. Someone with Saturn there could function as a teacher or mentor for others. Many people involved in the helping or caring professions have a heavy emphasis on the 7th. They require an almost continual flow of close exchange between themselves and others. It is wiser to 'siphon off' a packed 7th house in this way, and relieve a one-to-one partnership of the full brunt of many planets there.

The 'lower courts' also appears under the heading of the 7th. Social mores come into being to counter-effect the excesses of rampant individuality and to ensure some degree of fairness and justice in the behaviour of members of society. Should these laws be transgressed, then an outside force must intervene to redress the balance. How we fare in courts of this kind is shown by placements in the 7th.

The 7th house, naturally associated with Libra and Venus, is the sphere in which we learn greater co-operation with others. It poses a dilemma with the 1st house: how much do I co-operate (7th) versus how much do I assert my own way (1st)? On the one hand, the danger is giving or blending too much and sacrificing one's own identity. On the other, we could demand that others adapt too much to us, and deprive them of their individuality. The problem was clearly expressed by a Rabbi Hillel: 'If I am not for myself, who will be? And if I am only for myself, what am I?'[4] The 7th house sets the task of encountering another person and balancing both ends of the scale.

10.
THE EIGHTH HOUSE

> If my devils are to leave me, I am afraid my angels will take flight as well.
>
> Rilke

The 8th house has many labels. Since it is opposite the 2nd house which is 'my values', it is commonly called 'the house of other people's values'. This can be taken quite literally. Signs and planets in the 8th suggest how we fare financially in marriage, inheritance or business partnerships. For instance, Jupiter there may marry into money, receive a good windfall through a legacy, escape lightly from the tax inspector, and form beneficial business associates. A poorly aspected Saturn in the 8th, on the other hand, may marry someone who declares bankruptcy the next day, inherit its next-of-kin's unpaid debts, be scrupulously investigated by the tax inspector, and choose disastrous business partners. Nor is it unusual to find people with

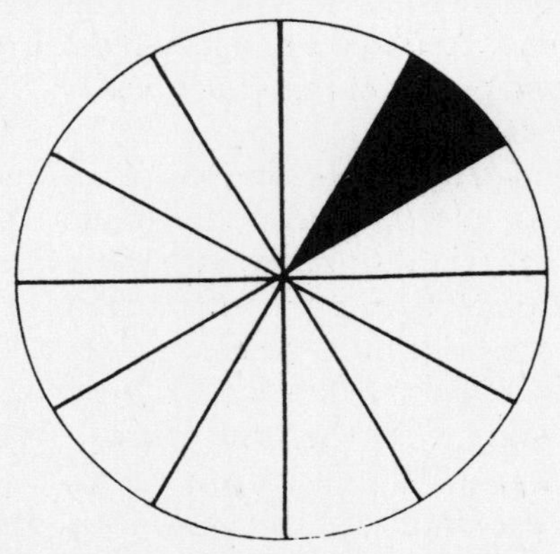

8th

many planets in the 8th in careers involving other people's money: bankers, stockbrokers, investment analysts and accountants.

However, the 8th house is much more than just other people's money. It describes 'that which is shared' and the manner in which we fuse or unite with others. Elaborating and expanding on what has begun in the 7th, the 8th house is the nitty-gritty of relationships: what happens when two people — each with his or her own temperament, resources, value system, needs and biological clock — attempt to merge. A whole plethora of questions and conflicts are apt to ensue:

> I have some money and you have some money. How shall we spend it? How much shall we try to save each month?
>
> *or*
>
> I like sex three times a week and you seem to need it every night. Who wins?
>
> *or*
>
> You believe that to spare the rod is to spoil the child, but I insist that no child of mine is to be hit. Who's right?
>
> *or*
>
> I don't know how you can be friends with that couple. They really irritate me. I'd rather we visit my friends tonight. Whose friends do they end up visiting?

The aisle intended to lead to the path of wedded bliss seems to have forked into a raging battlefield and there is what looks like a funeral procession up ahead.

The 8th house, naturally associated with Pluto and Scorpio, is also labelled 'the house of sex, death and regeneration'. In the myth, the maiden Persephone is abducted into the underworld by Pluto, the god of Death. She marries him there and returns to the upper world a changed person, no longer a little girl, but a woman. Relating deeply with another person entails a kind of death, the letting go and breaking down of our ego-boundaries and tightly knit identity. We die as a separate 'I' and are reborn as 'We'.

Like Persephone, through relationship we are plunged into another's world. In sex and intimacy, we expose and share parts of ourselves which are normally kept hidden. Sex can be considered just a release which temporarily makes us feel better; or through the sexual act, we may experience a form of self-transcendence, a union with another self. In the heights of ecstasy, we forget and abandon ourselves to merge with another. The Elizabethans referred to the orgasm as 'the little death'. Much about our sexual nature is shown by placements in the 8th.

Relationships are the catalysts for change. The 8th house cleanses and regenerates through drawing to the surface (usually via a present relationship) unresolved issues from previous relationships, especially early bonding problems with mother and father. The first relationship in our life, that with the mother or mother-substitute, is the most highly charged. This is not surprising as our survival depends on her. We are *all* born into this world potential victims: unless there is the caring love and protection of someone bigger and more adept than us, our chances of survival are very slim. The loss of a mother's love does not simply mean the loss of a person close to us: it could mean abandonment and death. Many of us continue to project these same infantile concerns onto later relationships. The fear that our partner doesn't love us anymore or is possibly betraying us will trigger or reawaken the primal fears of the loss of the original love-object. It then feels as if our very survival depends on the preservation of the present relationship. Pleas and outcries such as 'If you leave me, I'll die' and 'I can't live without you' reveal the charged undercurrents from early bonding difficulties infiltrating the reality of the current situation. True, as children we might have died if Mother left, but more likely than not, as adults we are quite capable of managing our own survival needs. Through exposing these unresolved and hidden fears, the trials and tribulations in the 8th house help us to shed attitudes which are obsolete and cumbersome. Not every partner is our mother.

In addition to our irrational fears, a good proportion of the anger and outrage we sometimes feel and unleash on our partner can be 'tracked back' to infancy and childhood. Children are not all sweetness, 'goo' and light. The work of the psychologist Melanie Klein has depicted another side to the baby's nature. Because of its extreme helplessness, the small child experiences enormous frustration when his or her needs are not being understood and met. Even the most adept mother cannot always interpret precisely what a screaming baby wants, and invariably the child's frustration erupts into violent hostility. Since early experiences leave such a deep impression, all of us have a 'raging infant' buried inside. A present partner thwarts us in some way and the screaming child may be awakened yet again.

Like Persephone's abduction into the underworld, in very intense relationships we descend into the depths of our being to discover our primordial instinctual inheritance: the envy, greed, jealousy, rage, seething passions, the need for power and control as well as the destructive fantasies which may lurk beneath the most genteel facade. It is only through recognizing and accepting 'the beast' in us that it can be transformed. We cannot change anything we don't know is there. We cannot transform something we condemn. The darker side of our nature must be brought to light before we can be cleansed, regenerated or born again.

Previously, in denying this darker side we may have stifled a vast reservoir of psychic energy. However, acknowledging our vindictiveness, cruelty, or rage *does not* necessarily mean catharting or 'acting out' these emotions indiscriminately. Such behaviour expends the energy and possibly destroys much more than we wish. Rather, the key lies in 'owning' and yet *containing* these explosive feelings. Through reconnecting to the fount of energy expressing itself as outraged instincts and holding on to it inside us, we eventually release this energy from the form in which it has been trapped. Thus diverted, it can be consciously integrated back into the psyche more productively or channelled into constructive outlets. Stewing in the juices of primal emotion until they are ready to shift is not very pleasant, but who has ever said that the 8th house is easy?

The 8th house yields the opportunity to re-examine the connection between present relationship issues and those problems encountered with the mother and father early in life. Based on our perception of the environment as children, we form opinions about what kind of person we are and what life 'out there' is like for us. These beliefs or 'scripts' continue to operate, often unconsciously, far into adulthood. The little girl who believed that 'father was a cad' grows into the woman with a deeply ingrained sense that 'all men are cads.' Due to the laws of psychic determinism, we have a mysterious and uncanny ability to attract into our lives the very people and situations which support these early assumptions. If not, we will probably perceive them that way in any case. The aim of a complex is to prove itself true.

The ruins and rubble from childhood are excavated in the 8th house. Our more problematic and deeper existential life-statements are uncovered 'alive and kicking' in present relationship crises. With the added maturity and wisdom that years of living bestow on us, we can 'clean up' some of the residue from the past, which has coloured and obscured our perspective on life, ourselves and others. The gift of the 8th house is greater self-knowledge and self-mastery, freeing us to continue our journey renewed, less encumbered by unnecessary baggage.

Should we fail at attempts at merging and 'working through' the volatile issues which the 8th house evokes, then we can refer to placements here to gain a sense of what the divorce proceedings might be like. Difficult planetary aspects to the 8th warn of traumatic separations and 'messy' divorce settlements. The two 'raging infants' and their respective lawyers are left to carry out the battle in the courtroom.

All levels of shared experience are described by the 8th house. In addition to the realm of joint finance and the merging of two individuals into one, this house has a broader ecological slant. We all have to share our planet and its resources. The high-powered entrepreneur who indiscriminately levels forests for his own profit is disregarding the inhabitants of the forest, as well as depriving a fellow human being of an area of natural beauty and inspiration. A person's sensitivity to these issues will be mirrored by placements in the 8th.

The house also denotes our relationship to what esoteric philosophers call 'the astral plane'. A strong emotion, though not necessarily visible, will nonetheless pervade the atmosphere around us. The astral plane is that level of existence where seemingly intangible but powerful emotions and feelings collect and circulate. The more rationally minded may doubt the credibility of something which cannot be seen or measured. And yet, almost all of us have had the experience of entering one person's home and feeling immediately 'hit' by something unpleasant, while walking into another person's house and feeling uplifted and spirited. Planets and signs in the 8th show the particular kinds of energies 'hovering' in the astral realm to which we are most sensitive. Someone with Mars in the 8th will more easily 'pick up on' anger in the atmosphere than someone with Venus there who quickly senses when 'love is in the air'. In this capacity, the watery 8th house is akin to the other water houses, the 4th and the 12th. Experiences of the psychic or occult sphere are shown in the 8th, as well as the degree of interest or fascination we have for that which is hidden, mysterious or underlying the surface level of existence.

Death, as shown by placements in the 8th, can be taken literally to mean the manner or extenuating circumstances of our physical death. Saturn there may be reluctant to die, fearful of what lies beyond corporeal existence. Neptune may die from drugs, alcohol poisoning or drowning, or gradually disengage itself in a coma.

Uranus may end it all rather suddenly.

However, in the span of one life-time, we experience many different psychological deaths. If we have been deriving our identity from a particular relationship and it should finish, then this is a kind of death of who we have been. Likewise, if we have gained our sense of vitality or meaning in life from a certain profession and then are made redundant, we also die as we knew ourselves. Childhood dies and adolescence is born. Adolescence passes and we die into adulthood. A birth requires a death; and a death requires a birth. Signs and planets in the 8th indicate the manner in which we meet such phase transitions. Individuals with a strong 8th house slant often experience their lives as a book containing many different chapters, or a long play with distinct changes of scene. These endings and new beginnings may be thrust on us or we might assume a more active role in tearing down old structures to make room for something else.

In mythology, the gods create the world, decide they don't like it, destroy what they have built, and create another. Death is an ongoing process in nature. There is also the image of the dying and reviving god, who is destroyed in one form but then reappears again transformed. Christ is crucified and then resurrected. Dionysus is dismembered, but Athene, the goddess of Wisdom, rescues his heart and he is born again. Like the Phoenix, we may temporarily be reduced to ashes, but we can rise once more, renewed. Form can be destroyed, but essence remains to flourish again in some other form. The German poet Goethe wrote, 'So long as you do not die and rise again, You are a stranger to the dark earth.' On some deep level, any survivor of the 8th house's traumas and tensions knows this.

11.
THE NINTH HOUSE

Mankind is poised midway between the gods and the beasts.
Plotinus

The 8th house invariably implies some degree of pain, crises and suffering. Hopefully, in surviving these difficult times, we emerge renewed, cleansed, and wiser about ourselves and life in general. Having descended into the depths and somehow managed to find our way up again, an overview is gained which allows us to conceive of life as a journey and process of unfoldment. The fiery 9th house, naturally associated with Jupiter and Sagittarius, follows upon the troubled waters of the 8th and offers a broader perspective on all that has occurred up to now. Enough experience has been gathered to attempt formulating some conclusions about the meaning and purpose of our sojourn.

The 9th is the area of the chart most directly concerned with philosophy and religion — questions about the 'whys and wherefores' of existence. It is here that we seek the Truth, endeavouring to fathom the underlying patterns and basic laws which govern life. In one sense, the suffering incurred in the 8th compels us in this direction because pain is more easily borne if we can envision some purpose for having to endure it. In addition, if suffering is in any way linked with a failure to live in accordance to the laws or truths of existence, then discovering and adhering to these guidelines might decrease the amount of pain we need incur.

Human beings seem to require meaning. We apparently need absolutes, firm ideals towards which we can aspire, and precepts which serve to steer our lives. Without meaning, there is often the feeling that we have nothing to live for, nothing to hope for, no reason to struggle for anything, and no direction in life. Many psychologists believe that much of modern-day neurosis is related to a lack of

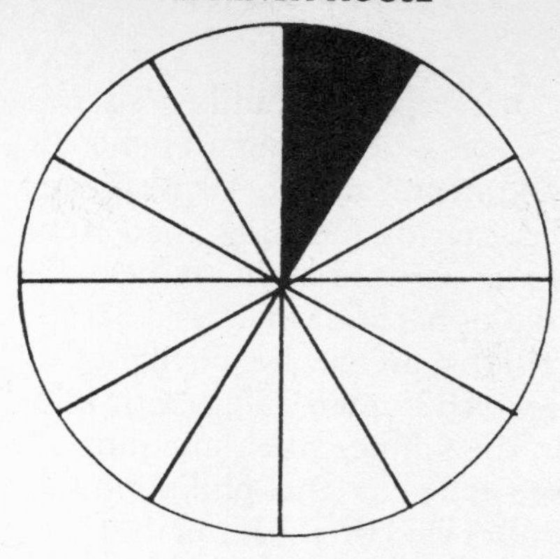

9th

meaning or purpose in life. Regardless of whether it is true or not, we are comforted by the belief that there is something greater 'out there': that a coherent pattern exists and that each of us has some particular role to play in that design. Whether it is ultimately up to us to create our own meaning in life or whether it is our task to discover God's plan and intention, the search for guidelines, goals and a sense of purpose forms the crux of the 9th house.

The 9th house signifies what is known as 'the higher mind' — that part of the mind linked to the faculty of abstraction and the intuitive process — as compared to the concrete mind shown by the 3rd house. Mercury, the natural ruler of the 3rd and 6th houses is a fact-gatherer; while Jupiter, the natural ruler of the 9th denotes the symbol-making capacity of the psyche, the tendency to imbue a particular event or happening with meaning or significance. Facts are collected in the 3rd, but in the 9th conclusions are drawn from them: isolated facts are organized within the framework of a larger scheme of things or seen as the inevitable offspring of higher organizing principles.

While the 3rd and 6th houses are analogous to the analytical and compartmentalizing left brain, the processes associated with the 9th house (and the 12th) correlate to the activity of the right brain. The right brain can identify a shape which is suggested by only a few lines. The points are mentally woven together into a pattern. Synthetic and holistic, the right brain thinks in images, sees wholes, and detects patterns. As Marilyn Ferguson writes, 'the left [brain] takes snapshots, the right watches movies.'[1]

The 9th house often believes that events have a message concealed in them. Jupiter or Venus in the 9th, for instance, may give the feeling that everything that happens is ultimately positive and to one's advantage, as if there were a benign Higher Intelligence at work guiding our unfoldment. Saturn or Capricorn in the 9th could have more difficulty perceiving meaning in an event, or else interpret the meaning in a negative light. Albert Camus, the French existentialist philosopher and writer, had Saturn in Gemini in this house: he believed that events have no higher or absolute meaning other than that which human beings attribute to them.

Placements in the 9th describe something about the style with which we pursue religious and philosophical issues, as well as suggesting the kind of God we worship or the nature of the philosophy in life we formulate. For example, Mercury or Gemini there may lead one to try and grasp God intellectually while Neptune or Pisces predisposes one to embrace the deity through heartfelt devotion, to surrender the self. Mars suggests a dogmatic and fanatical approach to religious pursuits compared to the greater tolerance and flexibility exhibited by Venus in these matters. The God-image is also shown by planets and signs here. Saturn or Capricorn might conceive of a harsh, punishing, critical and paternalistic God, who must be obeyed at all costs. Neptune or Pisces in the 9th, on the other hand, envisions a compassionate and loving God, inclined to leniency and forgiveness.

The 3rd house rules the immediate environment and that which is discovered by exploring what is at hand. The 9th describes the perspective we gain standing back and viewing life at a distance. In this way, the 9th is linked to travels and long journeys. Travelling can be taken literally to mean journeys to other lands and cultures, or it can be understood more symbolically as journeys of the mind or spirit — the broadened horizons gained from extensive reading or the insights gained through meditation and cosmic reflection. Understood more literally, through travelling and mixing with people reared on traditions different from our own, our outlook on life is expanded. The taste and style of some cultures may appeal to us more than others, but nonetheless, other facets of the myriad possibilities of life are glimpsed and compared with our own. Travel enables us to view the world from a different perspective. I may be involved in a complicated relationship in London about which I feel confused and uncertain; yet, when I travel to San Francisco and reflect on this relationship, somehow the added distance of 6,000 miles helps me to understand it more clearly than when the relationship is right in front of me. The epitome of a 9th house experience might be the view of the world afforded the astronaut re-entering the earth's atmosphere. There, at a glance, is the whole picture — our planet seen as an entity in relation to limitless space. One's ordinary, mundane and everyday concerns assume a different proportion after such an experience. John Glenn, the first American to orbit the earth, had both Neptune and Jupiter in his 9th house.

Placements in the 9th designate the archetypal principles we encounter on our travels, and may even reveal something about the nature of the culture or cultures to which we are drawn. For instance, Saturn there may experience difficulties or delays on journeys, or travel more specifically for a practical purpose, such as work or study. Henry Kissinger, the American foreign ambassador under Nixon, has Capricorn on the cusp of the 9th, and Saturn, its ruler, in Libra, the sign of diplomacy. If Pluto or Scorpio is in the 9th, we may attract experiences in another country which profoundly transform us, or we may be drawn to a country with Pluto or Scorpio strong in its national chart. Admiral Richard Byrd, the first man to fly to the North Pole, had innovative Uranus in this house.

Returning much closer to home, 9th house placements indicate relationships with one's in-laws. Just as the third house from the Ascendant describes our own relatives, the third house from the Descendant (the 9th), describes the partner's relatives. Whether such relationships are cordial or stormy will be shown here. An in-law might reflect a planet in the 9th house, or receive the projection of that principle. Some people with Jupiter in the 9th see the universe in a grain of sand, while others might perceive it in their mother-in-law.

Journeys of the mind are described in the 9th, which is also known as the house of higher education. The chosen field of study or the nature of the college or university experience in general is shown by placements here. For example, Neptune in the 9th may concentrate on a degree in art or music. However, that same Neptune could indicate confusion and vacillation in the choice of a course of study or disappointment and disillusionment during the stay at university. Uranus may rebel against traditional systems of higher education, or pursue a degree in some unusual or newly rising field, or be the first person to secure a place at Oxford at the age of seven.

The 1st house is 'I am' while the opposite house, the 7th is 'We are'. The 2nd is 'I have' and its opposite, the 8th is 'We have'. Correspondingly, the 3rd is 'I think' and the 9th is 'We think'. The 9th describes thought structures which are codified on a collective level. These include not only the religious, philosophical and educational systems as already discussed, but also legal systems and the body of law. The 7th house is the lower courts, but the 9th represents the higher courts — the supreme law of the land which governs the actions of the individual within the broadest social context. In the 3rd, we learn about ourselves in relation to those in our immediate environment, but in the 9th a sense of our relationship to the collective as a whole is kindled. The 9th is also associated with the publishing profession, in which ideas are disseminated on a large scale.

Traditionally, planets in the 10th are associated with career and profession. The research by M. and F. Gauquelin, however, has established a correlation between certain planetary placements in the 9th and people who have achieved success in fields related to the nature of these planets. A discussion of these findings is found on pages 118-119.

In the 3rd house, we examine that which is immediate and directly in front of us; in the 9th, we glimpse that which is not only farther away but also 'up and coming'. Strong placements in this house confer an unusual degree of intuition and foresight — the ability to sense the direction in which someone or something is heading. The 9th house 'tunes in' to the pulse of a situation, quickly registering trends and currents in the atmosphere. Jules Verne, the science fiction writer with a remarkable gift for anticipating future discoveries, was born with Uranus in the 9th house. On one level, the 9th gives the prophet and visionary, while on another it denotes the public relations person, or the promoter intent on opening new vistas for others. Energies in the 9th can be expressed through the travel agent picking out 'just the right holiday for you'; the entrepreneur confiding to you the latest sure-fire investment; the proponent of the most recent psychotechnology to hit town which promises instant enlightenment in one weekend; the coach giving his team a pep-talk before the big game; the tipster advising on the winning horse; or the artistic, literary or theatrical agent discovering the next big new talent.

In the 8th, we dug into the past and dredged up the remnants of our primordial and instinctual nature. In the 9th, we look to the future and what is yet to unfold. Depending on the planets and signs there and aspects to these, we may see a future full of hope and new promise or one in which the bogeyman lurks around the corner just waiting for us to be foolish enough to pass that way. In either case, it might be useful to reflect on something which St Catherine once observed, namely that 'all the way to heaven is heaven.'[2]

12.
THE MIDHEAVEN AND THE TENTH HOUSE

> Never measure the height of a mountain, until you have reached the top. Then you will see how low it was.
>
> Dag Hammarskjöld

What the 9th house envisions, the 10th house brings to earth. In Quadrant systems of house-division, the Midheaven — the degree of the ecliptic which reaches its highest point at the meridian of any place — marks the cusp of the 10th house. The Midheaven is the most elevated point in the chart, and symbolically speaking, placements here 'stand out' above all others in the horoscope. The qualities of any sign or planet in this position correspond to what in us is most visible and accessible to others, what 'stands out' in us. Whereas the IC and 4th house (the opposite house) represent what we are like privately and how we behave at home behind closed doors, the MC and 10th house (naturally associated with Saturn and Capricorn) indicate the way we behave publically, the image we wish to present to the world — the kinds of clothes we don when we 'step out'. Liz Greene calls the MC and 10th house our 'social shorthand' — how we would most like to be seen by others and how we describe ourselves to them.

In keeping with the elevated position of the Midheaven, placements in this area of the chart suggest those qualities for which we want to be admired, lauded, looked up to and respected. It is through the signs and planets here that we hope to attain achievement, honour and recognition. Placements in the 10th denote what we would most like to be remembered as having contributed to the world. This is the house of ambition, behind which lurks the pressing urge and compulsion to be esteemed and acknowledged. The ancient Greeks believed that if you performed a truly noble or heroic deed, you were rewarded by being made a constellation in the heavens for all to see for all eternity. Besides the recognition it earns us, being famous means we live in people's minds forever. The isolated ego, so fearful of its own finiteness, finds this idea very reassuring.

The nature of our contribution to society and our status and place in the world are shown by the sign on the Midheaven, planets in the 10th house, and as the Gauquelin studies suggest (see pages 118-19) any planets on the 9th house side of the MC. The planet ruling the sign on the Midheaven and its placement by sign, house and aspect also sheds light on career and vocation. However, other areas of the chart also have considerable bearing on the issue of profession (such as the 6th house, 2nd house, aspects to the Sun, etc.), and the birth map as a whole must be carefully assessed to advise anyone wisely in this respect.

In some cases, the signs and planets in the 10th and on the 9th house side of the Midheaven may literally describe the nature of the individual's career. For instance, Saturn there could indicate a teacher, judge or scientist; Jupiter an actor, philosopher or travel agent; and the Moon a professional childminder or innkeeper. Thomas Mann, the acclaimed German writer, had the communicative sign of Gemini on the MC and Mercury in the 10th. Franz Schubert, the Austrian composer, had musical Pisces on the Midheaven, and Neptune, its ruler, in the 5th, the house of creative expression.

However, it is safer to assume that the positions near the MC and in the 10th suggest not so much the actual profession but rather the approach a person has to the career — the manner in which the work is handled or packaged. The judge with Saturn in the 10th will more

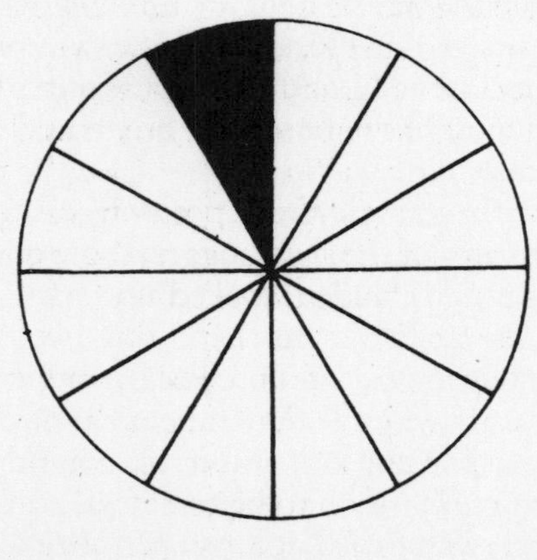

likely follow the letter of the law than the judge with Uranus there, whose readings would be more individualistic, unconventional, and shocking to others.

The kinds of energies we exhibit or encounter in the pursuit of a vocation are also suggested by placements in the 10th. Saturn or Capricorn there may work long and patiently to reach the top; Mars or Aries is aggressive and impatient in this sphere of life, while Neptune or Pisces may be vague or confused as to its role in society.

The 10th house could also describe what we represent or symbolize to others. Mars might be seen as a bully or the pinnacle of courage and strength; Neptune as a saint or martyr, champion of the downtrodden, or the victim himself; and Venus could symbolize the epitome of style, taste or beauty.

If the 4th house is associated with the father, then the 10th house is assigned to the mother. In the beginning of life, she is the whole world to us. Early bonding patterns established with her will be reflected later in life in how we relate to the external world in general. In other words, the nature of what passes between mother and child (as shown by the MC and placements in the 10th) resurfaces at a later stage of development as our way of connecting with society and the world 'out there' as a whole. If we found mother threatening and potentially destructive (such as a difficultly aspected Pluto in the 10th might suggest) then later on the world will seem an unsafe place and we will attempt to defend ourselves accordingly. If mother was experienced as supportive and helpful (well-aspected placements in the 10th), we carry an expectation that the world will treat us similarly — what Erik Erikson calls *basic trust.*

If we associate the 10th house with both mother (the shaping parent) and career, then the choice of vocation may somehow be influenced by our experience of her. For instance, if Mars is in the 10th the mother may have been experienced as pushy and assertive. The child, therefore, harbours resentment and anger against her, and grows up with the desire to actualize a position of power and autonomy in the world so he or she won't be 'pushed around' in the same way as in early life. Fighting with the mother creates a pattern of fighting with the world.

Sometimes it is the desire to win love from the mother (thereby ensuring our survival) which underlies our choice of profession. For example, if Mercury is in the 10th house, the mother may have been experienced as expressive and intelligent. The child then feels that this is what Mother values and appreciates, and so strives to gain her love and support by developing such traits. An expectation is established that excelling in this way earns recognition, and accordingly, later in life, a career is sought which brings Mercurial qualities to the fore.

In some cases, it may be competition with the mother which nudges us in the direction of a certain career. If Venus is in the 10th, the mother may have been seen as glamorous and beautiful. In a sense, Venus has been projected onto the mother. In order to reclaim his or her own Venusian qualities, the child may later seek a profession in which he or she can be admired as beautiful, elegant or tasteful.

At its most simple, the 10th house describes those qualities of the mother (or parent in question) which are in us as well, whether we like it or not. The issue is complicated, however, by the possibility that placements in the 10th often denote aspects of the mother's personality which were 'unlived' — attributes and traits which the mother did not consciously express or represent in the child's growing-up years. Planets and signs in this house may describe the way the mother would have liked to have been if only she had allowed herself the opportunity to do so. A child who is acutely sensitive to the mother's psyche and undercurrents in the home atmosphere will be receptive not only to what she manifests outwardly but also to what she is denying or suppressing. The child may be swayed to 'live out' the mother's shadow side, as if mother is made more whole or redeemed in this way. The mother of a child with Uranus in the 10th, for instance, may have appeared extremely conventional, straight-laced and restrained on the outside, whilst under the surface lurked explosive feelings and the desire for space, freedom and 'busting loose'. In some way this unvented Uranian side is communicated to the child, who grows up with a compulsion to enact just those qualities to which the mother has not allowed expression.

The placement of many planets in the 10th usually suggests someone who is ambitious and desirous of recognition, status and prestige. Men are normally given more permission to pursue these needs than women. It may be easier for a woman with a strong 10th house to seek a partner who is powerful or famous and thereby import a position in the world in that way. She may even be the one who pushes him on to fame and prestige. Ultimately, however, she may feel resentful that it is her husband receiving the acclaim rather than herself, and consciously or unconsciously devise ways of punishing him for this. Likewise, either or both parents with a strong 10th house may displace unfulfilled achievement and recognition needs onto a child. Some children may co-operate with the projection, while others may rebel against it, often becoming the exact opposite of what the parent(s) hoped.

The 10th house extends beyond the mother or shaping parent to designate our relationship with authority figures in general. Early anger or hurt at being suppressed or mistreated by a parent will often distort the reality of later interactions with other symbols of power. The revolutionary may have a true and just cause, but the style, manner or intensity in which he or she espouses convictions may evince, from a reductionist point of view, the contamination of earlier issues stemming from the regime of the parents. This is not to belittle or judge those who object to that which is unfair in society, but they are well-advised to consider their 10th house, and its psychological implications. Throwing a punch at one's boss or eggs at the prime minister is a way of venting the 'angry child' in us but may not be the most effective way to promote even the most needed changes.

Presiding over the top of the chart, the 10th house signifies the fulfilment of the individual personality through the personal satisfaction gained in using our abilities and talents to serve and influence society. Some may even earn applause and public recognition of their great value and worth.

A long way has been travelled from the 1st house to the 10th. In the 1st, we were not even conscious of ourselves as separate entities, not even aware of our own individual existence. By the time the 10th is reached, however, we have developed and 'incarnated' sufficiently not only to have a more solid and concrete sense of who we are, but also to be held in esteem for it.

13.
THE ELEVENTH HOUSE

> In the heaven of Indra, there is said to be a network of pearls, so arranged, that if you look at one you see all the others reflected in it.
>
> A Hindu Sutra

From being oblivious of being anybody, to winning recognition as a somebody: this has been the route from the 1st house to the 10th house. But now that the ego has been firmly established and duly acknowledged, what happens next?

At its deepest level, the 11th house (associated with the sign of Aquarius and co-ruled by Saturn and Uranus) represents the attempt to go beyond our ego-identity and become something greater than what we already are. The main way of achieving this is to identify with something larger than the self — such as a circle of friends, a group, a belief system or an ideology.

According to General Systems Theory, nothing can be understood in isolation but must be comprehended as part of a system. The components of the system and their attributes are viewed as functions of the total system. The behaviour and expression of each variable influences and is influenced by all the others. In what is known as a 'high synergy' society, the goals of the individual are in harmony with the needs of the system as a whole. In a 'low synergy' system, the individuals, in fulfilling their own needs, do not necessarily act for the good of the whole.[1] How we function as part of a system is shown by the 11th house.

In keeping with its dual rulership, the concept of group consciousness implied by the 11th can be understood in two distinct ways. Saturn seeks greater security and a more solid sense of identity through belonging to a group — what psychologists label 'belonging-identification'. Being a member of a particular group, whether it

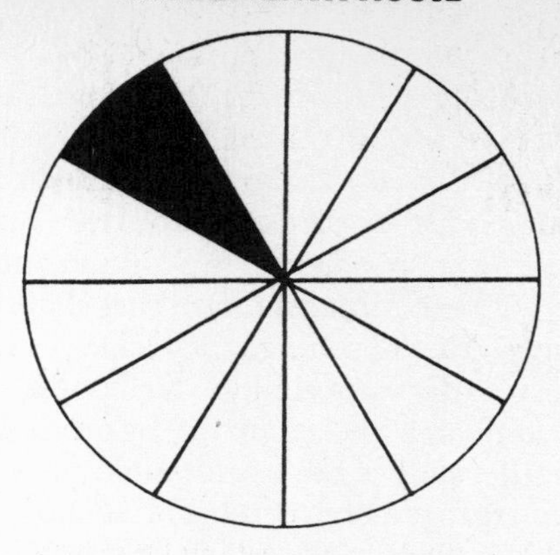

11th

is a social, national, political or religious group, enhances the sense of who we are and gives a feeling of safety in numbers. To some extent, this is exploitive, since the rest of the world is used in the service of augmenting or bolstering the identity. Evidence of this is most clearly seen in those who are overly concerned with having the 'right' friends, being noticed in the 'right' places, and aligning the self with the 'right' beliefs.[2] The most negative face of this Saturn undercurrent of the 11th manifests when a group is threatened by another group — such as blacks moving into a white area, or Jungians moving into a predominantly Freudian neighbourhood.

The Uranian side of the 11th house represents the kind of group consciousness which spiritual teachers, mystics and visionaries from all different cultures and times have repeatedly espoused. Instead of the typical 'me-in-here' versus 'you-out-there' paradigm or self-model, they speak of the individual's unity with all of life, that we are part of a greater whole, interconnected with the rest of creation. Mirroring the mystical perception of the unity of all life, recent scientific breakthroughs demonstrate the web of relationship underlying everything in the universe. For instance, David Bohm, a British physicist, theorizes that the universe must be understood as 'a single undivided whole in which separate and independent parts have no fundamental status'.[3] A thorough analysis of the parallels between modern physics and Eastern mysticism is found in *The Tao of Physics* by Fritjof Capra, an eminent researcher in high-energy physics. Some of the parallels he recounts are so striking that it is almost impossible to determine whether certain statements about the nature of life have been made by modern scientists or by Eastern mystics.[4]

One recent theory proposed by a British plant physiologist, Rupert Sheldrake, is particularly relevant to the 11th house. Sheldrake suggests the possibility of invisible organizing fields which regulate the life of a system. In 1920, William McDougall of Harvard University was studying how quickly rats learned to escape from a maze filled with water; meanwhile, other researchers in Scotland and Australia who were repeating these experiments found that their first generation of rats, bred from a different strain to the McDougall rats, performed the task with the same degree of ability as McDougall's last generation. The skill was in some way 'picked up on' by other rats even though they were in another part of the world. Such occurrences have led Sheldrake to theorize that if one member of a biological species learns a new behaviour, the invisible organizing field (morphogenetic field) for that species changes. The rats who mastered the task made it possible for other rats, many miles away, to do the same.[5] On some deep level, we are all linked together. Sheldrake's theory is nicely summed up in a remark once made by the Jesuit priest Pierre Teilhard de Chardin, born with Mercury, Jupiter and Saturn in the 11th: 'A truth once seen, even by a single mind, always ends by imposing itself on the totality of human consciousness.'[6]

In *The Aquarian Conspiracy,* Marilyn Ferguson writes, 'You cannot understand a cell, a rat, a brain structure, a family or a culture if you isolate it from its context.'[7] Similarly, Carl Rogers, one of the founders of humanistic psychology, once remarked that the deeper the individual delves into his or her own identity the more he or she discovers the whole human race. Our identity has a much wider membership than the 'skin-encapsulated ego' is capable of admitting. In this light, the development of group consciousness as seen in the 11th house is not solely for the purpose of aggrandizing or bolstering the ego-identity. Rather, the awareness of being part of something larger enables us to transcend the limits and boundaries of individual separateness and experience ourselves as a cell in the larger body of humanity. Out of this realization grows a sense of brotherhood and sisterhood with the co-inhabitants of the planet far beyond the obligatory ties of family, nation or church.

Syntropy — the tendency of life-energy to move towards greater association, communication, co-operation and awareness — is the main principle upon which the 11th house operates. Having recognized ourselves as separate and distinct individuals there is the call to reconnect with everything from which we have previously differentiated ourselves. Just as matter organized itself into living cells, and living cells gathered together into multi-cellular organisms, it may be that at some stage human beings will integrate themselves into some form of global super-organism. Even on a Saturnian level, the interdependence and interconnectivity of life on the planet is becoming increasingly obvious. Communications technology has dramatically enhanced the speed of global interaction and Marshall McLuhan's concept of the world as a 'global village' is near to being an actuality. Multinational corporations and conglomerates link the economies of the world inextricably together. The collapse of the monetary system of one country would have a disastrous rippling effect on a host of others. Isolationism and nationalism are no longer practically viable. On another level, small groups, networks, movements and support systems are proliferating all over the world, gathering people together to promote common causes. In short, much in the same way that our own body changes and develops, the larger body of humanity is also growing and evolving. The way in which we might participate in and serve the evolution and progress of this collective Self is shown by placements in the 11th house.

In the 5th house, our energy is used to distinguish ourselves from others, and to augment the sense of our own individual worth and specialness; in the 11th, our energy can be invested in promoting and fulfilling the identity, purpose and cause of any group to which we belong — whether this is understood to be the whole human race or a particular segment of it. In the 5th, we do what we want to do for our own sake. In the 11th, we may choose to relinquish or compromise some of our precious personal urges, inclinations and idiosyncracies for the sake of adhering to what the group decides is best.

Social consciousness is a keynote of the 11th. A society (10th house) is structured on certain laws and principles (9th house). Laws and society easily become both crystallized and turgid, and invariably certain elements of society are favoured by the system while others are oppressed. Groups which feel neglected or betrayed by the existing laws can find a voice through the kinds of reforms associated with the 11th house. Often, those with strong placements here work through humanitarian or political groups to implement needed social changes. However, it is just as common to find others with an 11th house emphasis jockeying back and forth from one social engagement to the next — Ascot this week, centre court at Wimbledon the next, and then a day at Henley's before going off to the opera at Glyndebourne.

In some cases, placements in the 11th may signify the sorts of groups towards which we gravitate. For instance, Neptune could be interested in music societies, spiritualist or psychic groups; Uranus with astrology groups; and Mars with the local rugby club. However, rather than just describing the type of group, it is more likely that signs and planets in the 11th symbolize our style of behaving and interacting in group situations. The Sun or Leo there may have to be the leader, deriving a good proportion of its worth and identity from group involvement. Mercury or Gemini in this house might appear as the secretary of the group or as one of its most clever spokespeople. Someone has to make the tea, and the Moon or Cancer there may be happy to provide not only these services but its home as a meeting place as well. Furthermore, the 11th house gives a sense of how comfortable we feel in group situations. Venus or Libra may blend in easily and make many new friends through joining a group. Saturn or Capricorn is more likely to hold back in the group, and feel awkward or lumpish mixing with the others. Oscar Wilde, who rose to the heights of success in London's artistic and social circles, had the Moon in Leo in the 11th. Paul Joseph Goebbels, the official propagandist of the Nazi party who controlled public communications and the media, had Pluto conjunct Neptune in Gemini in this house.

Friendship clearly fits into the 11th house ideal of becoming greater than what we already are. People are linked together through friendship, personal boundaries are expanded, and both the needs and resources of others become interwoven with our own. We introduce our friends to new ideas and interests and, likewise, we are broadened by what they have to share.

Planets and signs in the 11th often describe the kinds of friends to whom we gravitate. For example, a man with Mars in this house may be attracted to those people who exhibit obvious Martian qualities, such as dynamism, drive and directness. However, placements in the 11th may also show those qualities in ourselves which we 'dis-own', project outwardly and meet externally through friends. If the man with Mars in the 11th has not developed his own 'Mars' side, and lacks that certain 'get up and go', his friends will then provide that energy for him — they stimulate and push him into action. He may even possess an uncanny ability to evoke such qualities in his close associates, who in most other situations and with other people might be normally more placid and withdrawn.

The 11th house also suggests the way in which we make friends. Mars could rush impulsively into friendship, while Saturn is more awkward, shy or cautious in this respect. How we behave and what energies we awaken in friendship is also shown by placements here.

Venus may make friends easily, but prefers to keep things light (although she may expect friends to 'live up to' rather high ideals). Pluto suggests intense and complicated associations which significantly transform us or in which issues of betrayal, intrigue and treachery come into play.

In the 11th house, there is the desire to transcend or move beyond existing images and models of ourselves. We yearn for a more ideal self or a more utopian society. Therefore, this area of the chart has been labelled the house of hopes, goals, wishes and objectives. The desire to become something greater than we are must be accompanied by the capacity to envision new and different possibilities. More than any other species, the large human brain and evolved cerebral cortex endows human beings with the capacity to imagine a wide range of alternatives, choices and outcomes. The manner in which we envision possibilities and proceed toward realizing these hopes and wishes is shown by placements in the 11th. For instance, Saturn there may have difficulty in forming positive images of the future or may encounter blocks, delays or obstructions on the way to finally grounding its goals and objectives. Mars sets a goal and rushes after it, while Neptune may be confused about what it really wants or merely fantasizes and daydreams about unrealistic aims. In this context, it is helpful to remember that the more clearly we can imagine a possibility, the closer we bring it to actualization. Encouraging positive visions of the future aids the process of moving in a more positive direction.

Evolution pushes towards greater and greater levels of complexity, organization and connectivity. In the first air house (the 3rd) we gain the ability through language to distinguish subject from object. Our own mind is developed as we relate to others in the immediate environment. In the second air house (the 7th) we grow through the close encounter of our own awareness with another person's awareness. Subject and object, differentiated in the 3rd, meet face to face in the 7th. In the last air house (the 11th) our individual minds are connected not just to the minds of those close to us but to all other minds. Eleventh house planets sensitize a person to the ideas and thoughts circulating on the level of the group-mind. It is not such an unusual phenomenon for somebody in San Francisco, somebody in London, and another person in Japan to 'flash' on the same bright new idea independently of one another within a relatively close span of time. In the 11th, we discover our relatedness not just to our family, friends, country or loved ones, but to the whole human race.

14.
THE TWELFTH HOUSE

> If the doors of perception were cleansed, everything would appear to man as it is, infinite.
>
> William Blake

Commencing with the 1st house, growth has entailed distinguishing ourselves from the unbounded and universal matrix of life out of which we first emerged. However, as we have seen in the 11th, the distinction between ourselves and others is challenged by the understanding that each part of a system is related and interconnected with the other parts. Mystics and scientists alike tell us that we are not so separate after all. Who we are is influenced by others, and others are influenced by who we are. Our minds are linked and directly affected by one another. The notion that we exist as an isolated entity is quickly losing ground to a more collective or broader sense of self. In the 12th house, the twin processes of the dissolution of the individual ego and the merging with something greater than the self is felt and experienced, not via the mind or intellect as in the 11th, but with our heart and soul. Or as Christopher Fry puts it, 'The human heart can go to the lengths of God.'

The poet Walter de la Mare writes that 'our dreams are tales told in a dim Eden.' On its most underlying level, the 12th house, naturally associated with watery Pisces and the planet Neptune, represents the urge for dissolution which exists in each of us — the yearning to return to the undifferentiated waters of the womb, to the original state of unity. Freud, Jung, Piaget, Klein and a host of other modern psychologists agree that the infant's first structure of consciousness is pre-subject/object, ignorant of boundaries, space and time. Early memories cut the most deeply. On some deep level, every individual intuits that his or her innermost nature is unbounded, infinite and eternal. The rediscovery of this wholeness is our greatest need and

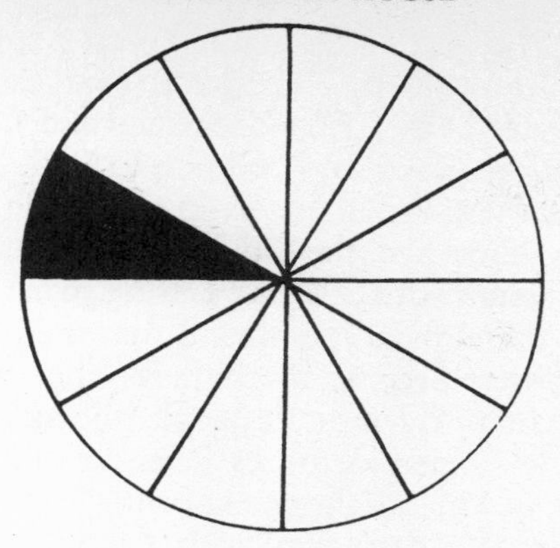

12th

want. From a reductionist psychology perspective, the desire to reconnect with the lost sense of original wholeness can be understood as a regression back to the pre-birth state; but in spiritual terms, this same urge translates into a mystical longing for union with our source and a direct experience of being part of something greater than ourselves. It is a kind of divine homesickness.[1]

In one respect, the prospect of a return to that state sounds blissful, ecstatic and serenely peaceful. And yet, something else in us — the ego's desire to preserve itself and the fear of its own demise — contends with this longing. The ego has fought hard to win a slice of life for itself: why should it relinquish this? In the glyph of Pisces, the sign associated with the 12th house, two fishes swim in opposite directions. Human beings are faced with a fundamental dilemma, with two contrasting pulls. Each person wants to lose a sense of isolation and transcend his or her individual separateness and yet each person is terrified of disintegration and dreads the loss of the separate self.[2] This existential double bind — wanting wholeness and yet fearing and resisting it — is the major predicament of the 12th house.

Because the dissolution of the ego-identity is so frightening, people seek substitute gratifications in an attempt to satisfy the yearning for self-transcendence. One strategy for reconnecting to unity is through sex and love: 'If I am loved, held or included, then I go beyond my separateness.' Another ploy to regain a lost sense of omnipotence and omnipresence is through wielding power and prestige: 'If I can extend my territory of influence over more and more things, then the rest of life is connected to me.' Immersion in alcohol or drugs is another way to break down boundaries and rigidities. Suicidal urges and various other forms of self-destructive behaviour often cloak the desire to return to a more blissful state of non-differentiated being. Others seek transcendence more directly through meditation, prayer and devotion to God. The 12th house may raise any of these issues.

However it is approached, the 12th house 'de-structures', engulfs, absorbs or inflates individual identity. Letting go of the 'me-in-here' versus 'you-out-there' paradigm means that the borders between ourselves and others become blurred. For this reason, a strong emphasis on this house can indicate people who have great difficulty in forming clearly defined identities. They are swayed by whatever they are around, or whoever they make contact with. Others distort their personal identities dramatically out of proportion. Rather than sacrifice the ego to merge with something numinous and divine, a person may try to imbue the ego itself with those qualities. Instead of seeking to reconnect to God, the person tries to play God — a form of inflation related to what Abraham Maslow called 'higher-sidetracking'.

Along with the 12th house confusion about who we are often comes a lack of any concrete direction in life. On some level, there may be the feeling that since everything is all the same anyway, what's the difference? As soon as a clear identity is distinguished or a structure is imposed on the life, something happens which pulls the rug from under the feet and nebulousness reigns supreme again. As soon as the individual thinks he or she has captured something upon which to hang the sense of 'I', it mysteriously slips away or disappears. The capacity to hold things together or further their own personal ends is somehow subservient to a much greater dissolving power over which there is little control.

The obscuring of boundaries between the self and others may create confusion about where we begin and other people end, but it also confers a greater degree of empathy and compassion for those with whom we share the Earth. So overwhelmed by the suffering around them, some people with a strong 12th house will seek any means of escaping or withdrawing from the world altogether. Others who feel the pain 'out there' as their own will naturally work in some way to relieve that pain. To varying degrees, the 12th house describes the helper, 'fixer', rescuer, martyr or saviour who 'takes on' the needs and causes of others.

The original meaning of the word sacrifice is 'to make sacred'. Something was made sacred by offering it to the gods or the higher forces. Rippling through all the levels of meaning of the 12th is the supposition that the individual is redeemed through self-sacrifice, through offering the self up to something greater. This is true in so far as we must, to some extent, let go of a sense of an autonomous and separate self to merge with the all-embracing whole. While sacrifice and suffering often serve to soften the ego and give rise to greater empathy and spiritual awareness, the value of pain and the nature of sacrifice are too easily distorted into 'I have to suffer to find God' or 'Anything that might constitute personal satisfaction must be given up.' However, perhaps it is not things themselves which must be sacrificed, but rather our *attachment* to them. To the degree that we derive our identity or fulfilment from such things as relationships, possessions, ideologies or belief systems, we lose touch with our deeper and most basic unbounded nature.

Some people may even manage to acquire or achieve their 11th house dreams and wishes only to discover, in the 12th, that they still feel cheated of a more complete happiness. What they thought would give them ultimate satisfaction just wasn't enough, or didn't turn out to be everything. The Romans had a saying *'Quod hoc ad aeternitatem?'* meaning 'What is this compared with eternity?' Similarly, the 12th house is a constant reminder that all joys long for infinity.

Traditionally, the 12th house (along with the other water houses — the 4th and the 8th) reveals patterns, drives, urges and compulsions which operate from below the level of conscious awareness and yet significantly influence our choices, attitudes and directions in life. Stored in our unconscious memory, past experiences colour the way we see and meet the world. But from how far back do these past influences stem?

In some cases, planets and signs in the 12th may relate to what psychologists call 'the umbilical effect'. According to this concept, the developing embryo is receptive not just to physical substances which the mother ingests, but is also affected by her overall psychological state during the gestation period. Her attitudes and experiences are transmitted through the umbilical connection to the foetus in the womb. The nature of what is 'passed on' to the child in this way is shown by placements in the 12th. If Pluto is there, the mother might have endured a traumatic time during the pregnancy. The child is then born with a sense of the danger of life and a nagging apprehension that doom is only around the corner. There is no conscious memory of the source of this attitude: only a vague feeling that this is what life is about. For example, I recently came across the case of a pregnant mother who was diagnosed as having a brain tumour. Her baby daughter was born with Pluto in the 12th and the mother died shortly after her birth.

What about further back than the womb? Many astrologers refer to the 12th as the 'house of *karma*'. Reincarnationists believe that the immortal human soul is on a journey of perfection and return to its source that cannot be accomplished in one short lifespan. Definite laws, rather than chance, operate to determine the circumstances of every lifetime or each stage of the sojourn. With each new incarnation, we bring with us the harvest of experience from previous lives, as well as latent capacities awaiting development. Causes set in motion in prior existences affect what we meet in the present one. The soul chooses a certain time to be born because the astrological pattern fits the experiences needed for the present stage of growth. In this sense, the entire chart depicts our *karma* — both what has accrued as a result of past actions and also what we need to awaken to proceed further. More specifically, the 12th house shows what we are 'bringing over' from the past which will operate this lifetime on either the debit or credit side of our account.

Difficult placements in the 12th may indicate old 'trouble spots' and energies which we misused in earlier lives and still need to learn to handle wisely in this one. Positive placements in this house suggest ingrained qualities which will serve us advantageously this lifetime as a result of 'work' done on them in the past. Relative to this theory, some astrologers label the 12th the house of 'self-sustainment or self-undoing'. For instance, if Mars or Aries is there, it could be that selfishness, impulsiveness, or rashness has been a problem in the past and a continuation of such behaviour may be the cause of a 'downfall' in this life. On the other hand, a well-aspected 12th house Mars suggests that positive Mars qualities such as courage, strength and forthrightness have already been learned and will sustain the native through difficult times, coming to the fore just when they are most needed. With mixed aspects to placements in the 12th, the effect of that planet or energy somehow hangs in the balance, as if we are being tested for how we handle that principle. If we use it wisely we will be rewarded; if we run amock with the planet or sign in question, the consequences are likely to be severe.

Whether we refer to 'the umbilical effect' or to the theory of karma and reincarnation, placements in the 12th describe influences which have come down to us from causes and sources which we cannot obviously remember or see. Through the watery 4th we inherit or retain vestiges of our ancestral past. In the 12th, it is possible that we are receptive to an even larger pool or memory — what Jung called the collective unconscious: the entire memory of the whole human race. Jung defined the collective unconscious as 'the precondition of each individual psyche, just as the sea is the carrier of the individual wave'.[3] In some way, as shown by the 12th house, each of us is linked to the past, carrying records of experiences far beyond what we have personally known.

Besides the residue of the past, however, the collective unconscious is also the storehouse of latent potentials waiting to be tapped. Colin Wilson writes that 'the unconscious mind may include all man's past but it also includes his future.'[4] The unconscious mind is more than just a reservoir of repressed or buried thoughts, impulses and wishes — it is also the source of 'potentialities for knowing and experiencing' which the individual has yet to contact.[5] The 12th house, in other words, contains our future as well as our past.

Some people with 12th house placements serve as the mediators and transmitters of universal, mythic and archetypal images swirling about on the level of the collective unconscious. To varying degrees, certain artists, writers, composers, actors, religious leaders, healers, mystics and modern-day prophets tap into this realm and become the vehicles for inspiring others with what they have 'tuned into'. They touch the appropriate chord which then resonates with something inside us, and we are able to share their experience. Numerous examples of charts with 12th house placements illustrate this phenomenon: the composer Claude Debussy with sensuous Venus in Leo in the 12th; William Blake with the imaginative and feeling Moon in Cancer in this house; the poet Byron whose expansive and playful use of word, rhyme and form invigorated the whole Romantic movement had Jupiter in Gemini in the 12th; and the visionary Pierre Teilhard de Chardin with the Sun, Neptune, Venus, Pluto and the Moon all in the 12th, are just a few cases in point.

It is as if energies in the 12th house are not intended to be used solely for personal ends. We may be asked to express that principle for the sake of others, not just for ourselves. For instance, if Mars is there we may take on the role of fighting a battle or cause for other people. In this sense, we give our Mars away, or 'offer it up' to others. Mercury in the 12th may speak other people's thoughts or serve as a spokesperson for others.

Some people, through 12th house placements, lead what might be called 'symbolic lives'. Their individual life issues reflect trends or dilemmas in the collective atmosphere. For example, Mahatma Gandhi, with the Sun in Libra in the 12th, became the living embodiment of a Libran principle of peaceful co-existence for millions of people. Uranus in the 12th house of Hitler's chart rendered him exceptionally open to ideologies which may have been in the air at that time. Bob Dylan has Sagittarius on the 12th house cusp and its ruler Jupiter in the 5th, the area of the chart related to creative expression. Through his music he was both the mouthpiece and inspiration for many of the trends of the 1960s counter-culture. A black woman with Uranus in Cancer in the 12th was born and raised in a part of England where there were hardly any non-whites. In having to integrate herself into the life of the town she was not only dealing with her own personal dilemma but fighting the cause of many other black people as well.

The 12th house has been called the house of 'secret enemies' and 'behind the scenes activity'. This could be taken literally to mean people who plot or conspire against us. However, it is more likely to pertain to hidden weaknesses or forces in ourselves which undermine the realization of our conscious goals and objectives. In brief, unconscious drives and compulsions as shown by the 12th house placements can thwart the achievement of our conscious aims. For instance, if a man has the Moon and Venus in the 7th house, there is a strong urge to be close to another person in an intimate relationship. But if this man also has Uranus in the 12th, it suggests that unconsciously there may be such a strong desire for freedom and independence that he will somehow sabotage any attempt to form binding ties. Generally, in any contest between conscious aims and unconscious aims, it is usually the unconscious which wins. In this case, he may habitually be attracted only to those women who are not free to marry or who, for some reason, do not wish to reciprocate his advances. In this way, the unconscious compulsion to remain independent (Uranus in the 12th) is victorious over the more conscious needs. If we are conscious of urges in ourselves, we can do something to regulate and alter these if we so wish. If we are unconscious of certain patterns or drives, these have a way of dominating and controlling us. What we are unconscious of in ourselves has a knack of coming up from behind and hitting us over the head. Therefore, if no matter how hard we try, some conscious goal is continually blocked, we might examine the 12th house for clues why.

The linking of the 12th house with institutions makes sense in the light of the various connotations of this house discussed so far. The 12th shows what is hidden or in the background just as hospitals and prisons are, in part, places where certain people are 'stored away' from society. Those with difficult placements in the 12th may 'crack' under the strain of life or fall prey to powerful unconscious complexes which erupt to the surface, resulting in the need to be looked after and contained. Others are 'put away' because they are considered dangerous to the well-being of society. In any of these cases, the will of a higher authority is forced on them, congruent with the 12th house principle of the individual submitting to something greater than the self. Hospitalization or a period of withdrawal from life may be needed to re-establish psychological and physical balance, thus making a person *whole* again — another 12th house principle. Experiences in orphanages, hospices and homes for the disabled also appear via the 12th.

It is not uncommon to find people with placements in this house working within such institutions. Serving others less fortunate than the self is the practical expression of compassion and empathy which the 12th house confers. The Church, various charities, or the monastic life will be other spheres which absorb the person who feels it is his or her calling to sacrifice or dedicate the life to God or the welfare of others. Reincarnationists believe that past 'bad karma' can be cleared through goodwill and service of this kind.

As already mentioned, the 12th house gives access to the collective archive of experience passed on generation after generation. Therefore, it is not surprising that the keepers of this storehouse — those who work for museums and libraries — often have 12th house placements.

It would not be appropriate to discuss the 12th house without mentioning again the research done by Michel and Françoise Gauquelin.[6] They analysed the careers of successful sportspeople and found a correlation with Mars in the 12th house sector of the chart. Similarly, scientists and physicians tended to have Saturn there, writers the Moon, and actors Jupiter. Based on their studies, it appears that planets in the 12th (and to some extent the 9th, 6th and 3rd) significantly determine the character and profession of the native. This surprised many astrologers who assumed that placements in the 1st or 10th houses should be stronger in this respect.

However, are their findings so strange in the light of what we understand the 12th house to be? If there is an urge to 'give away' whatever is in the 12th to other people, then it follows that we could make a career out of the principles there. Also, if the 12th house indicates energies in the collective atmosphere to which we are sensitive, then it is likely that our character and expression will reflect these. Sportspeople capture the collective urge to compete and be first (Mars); writers tune into the collective imagination (Moon) and scientists serve the collective need to classify and structure (Saturn).

Since the 12th relates to reconnecting with something numinous and divine, an individual may experience a planet there as the key or path to greatness and self-transcendence. Naturally, he or she would want to develop it. On some level, they may believe that the doors to heaven are opened through excelling at whatever principle is in the 12th. The deep longing for wholeness and immortality which exists in all of us is the enticement which motivates achievement through 12th house planets.

For some people, a 12th house emphasis contributes to the lack of a clear identity, nebulousness, directionless lives, victimization, the experience of being overwhelmed by unconscious drives or undercurrents at loose in the atmosphere, and a distorted sense of the value of suffering and self-sacrifice. On the other hand, the 12th house concept of surrendering the sense of being a separate self gives rise to true empathy and compassion, selfless service, artistic inspiration, and ultimately the capacity to merge with the greater whole.

In the 11th house, we theorize on the unity and interconnectedness of all life. It is acknowledged in principle. In the 12th, the mystery of our oneness with the rest of creation is perceived directly with every cell of the body. All of existence is felt as part of ourselves, just as portions of our body are part of us. With such an awareness, it would be as difficult to heedlessly harm another person as it would be to cut off one of our fingers. Conversely, what we felt served our own individual well-being would invariably serve the good of the whole.

An old story illustrates the positive side to the 12th house. A man is allowed to visit Heaven and Hell. In Hell, he sees a large gathering of people sitting around a long table set with rich and delectable food. And yet these people are miserable and starving. He soon discovers that the reason for their dreadful state is that the spoons and forks provided for them are *longer* than their arms. As a result, they are unable to bring the food to their mouths and feed themselves. Then the man is shown Heaven. He finds the same table set out there, with the same extra-long eating utensils. But, in Heaven, instead of just trying to feed their own selves, each person uses his or her spoon and fork to feed one another. They are all well-fed and happy.

While not *fully losing* our own personal identity or sense of our own unique individuality, we need to experience, acknowledge, honour, and connect to, that part of us which is universal and unbounded. Ultimately, the trick is to swim in the waters of the 12th house without drowning in it.

We emerge out of the universal matrix of life, establish ourselves as individual entities, and then find that after all we are really one with all creation. Whether our connection with the greater whole is consciously experienced or not through the 12th house, it is inevitable that our physical bodies will die and disintegrate. When the body dies, so does the sense of our having a separate physical existence. One way or another, we return to the collective ground out of which we have come. What was there in the beginning is there at the end. We arrive back at the Ascendant to begin again on a new level of the spiral.

15.
GROUPING THE HOUSES

Search for measurable elements among your phenomena and then search for relations between these measures.

Alfred North Whitehead
(*Science and the Modern World*)

The twelve houses can be subdivided and classified under different headings. A knowledge of these groupings enriches an understanding of the meaning of each house and the way in which one house or sphere of life relates to another.

Hemispheres and Quadrants
The line of the horizon divides the chart into the upper (southern)

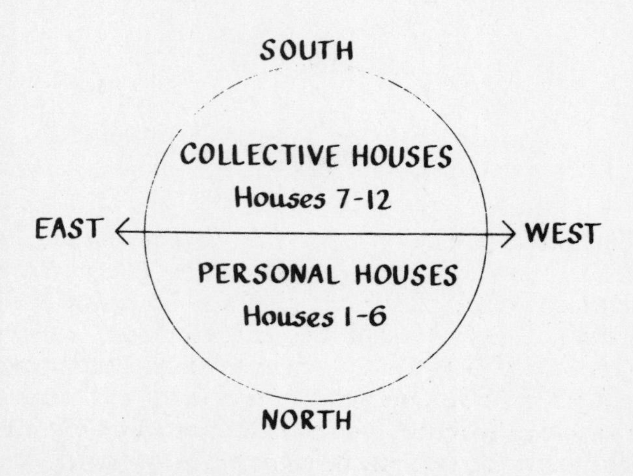

Fig.5

and lower (northern) hemispheres. The houses which fall below the horizon (houses 1–6) are most directly concerned with the development of an individual and separate identity and the basic requirements a person needs to meet life. These are known as the *Personal Houses.*

The houses which are above the horizon (houses 7–12) focus on the interconnection of the individual with others: on an intimate one-to-one level, in terms of society as a whole, and in relation to the rest of creation. These are known as the *Collective Houses* (see Figure 5).

The axis of the meridian crosses the line of the horizon cutting the horizon in half, and spawning another division of the wheel of the houses, the *Four Quadrants* (see Figure 6).

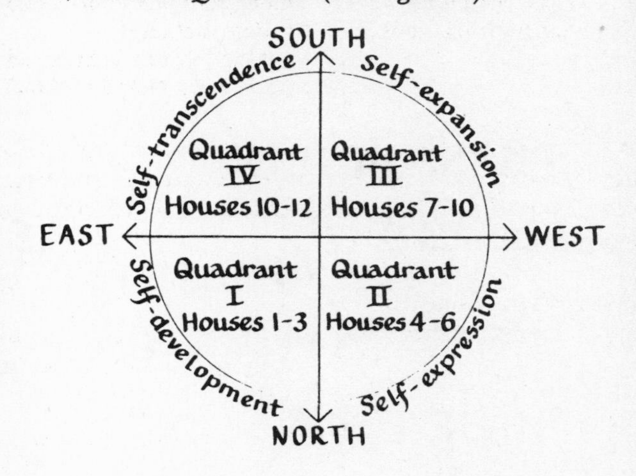

Fig.6

In *Quadrant I* (houses 1–3) the individual begins to take shape as a distinct entity. A sense of a separate identity forms through the differentiation of self (1st house), body and substance (2nd house) and mind (3rd house) out of the universal matrix of life.

In *Quadrant II* (houses 4–6) growth involves the further expression and refinement of the differentiated self. In the 4th house, shaped by the family background and ancestral inheritance, the individual moulds a more cogent sense of his or her own identity. With this as a gauge and base, the 'I' seeks to express itself outwardly in the 5th house, and then further specify, fine-tune and perfect its particular nature, skills and capabilities (6th house).

In *Quadrant III* (houses 7–9) the individual expands awareness through relationship with other people. In the 7th house, there is the close encounter between one person's reality and another person's reality. The 8th house depicts the breaking down of the individual ego-identity through the process of merging with another. The subsequent broadening, reawakening, and re-visioning of the self is shown by the 9th house.

In *Quadrant IV* (houses 10–12) the main concern is the expanding or transcending of the boundaries of the self to include not just one

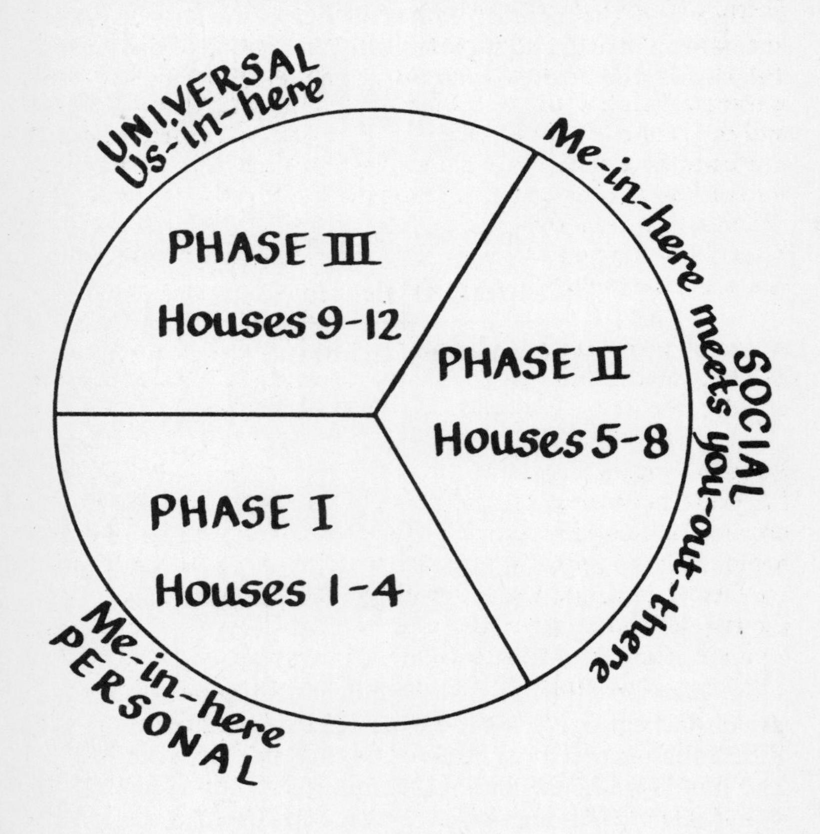

Fig. 7

other, but many others. A person's role in society is described by the 10th house, various forms of group consciousness are explored in the 11th, and an individual's spiritual identity — his or her relationship to that which is greater and yet inclusive of the self — is explored in the 12th.

While the grouping of the houses by quadrants makes sense in terms of the logical boundaries created by the cross of the horizon and the meridian, it is possible to subdivide the wheel in yet another way (see Figure 7). In houses 1–4, the individual is born and becomes conscious of his or her own existence, body, mind, background and feelings. This phase establishes a sense of the 'me-in-here'. Houses 5–8 depict the urge to express and share the autonomous self with others: 'me-in-here' meets 'you-out-there'. In houses 9–12 the task is integration, not just with a few others, but with society-at-large and the greater whole of which we are a part: the development of the 'us-in-here' reality. In this classification, each phase begins with the spark and inspiration of a fiery house (1st, 5th and 9th) indicating the birth into a new level of being; and each phase ends with a watery house (4th, 8th and 12th) describing the dissolution, assimilation and transition which leads to the next stage.

Angular, Succedent and Cadent

The houses are traditionally classified according to whether they are angular, succedent or cadent.

Angular Houses (Figure 8)

In Quadrant systems of house-division, the *Angular Houses* are the ones which follow immediately upon the four angles: the 1st house begins with the Ascendant, the 4th house with the IC, the 7th with the Descendant, and the 10th with the MC. In the natural zodiac, the angular houses correspond to the cardinal signs of Aries (spring equinox), Cancer (summer solstice), Libra (autumnal equinox) and Capricorn (winter solstice). Cardinal signs generate and release new energy. Similarly, the angular houses spur us into action and represent four basic areas of life which have a strong impact on our individuality: personal identity (1st house), the home and family background (4th house), personal relationships (7th) and career (10th).

The signs of the cardinal cross figuratively square or oppose one another. Likewise, the four angular houses represent four spheres of life which are potentially in conflict with each other. An understanding of the paradoxes and dilemmas presented by the different angular houses will help in the interpretation of possible

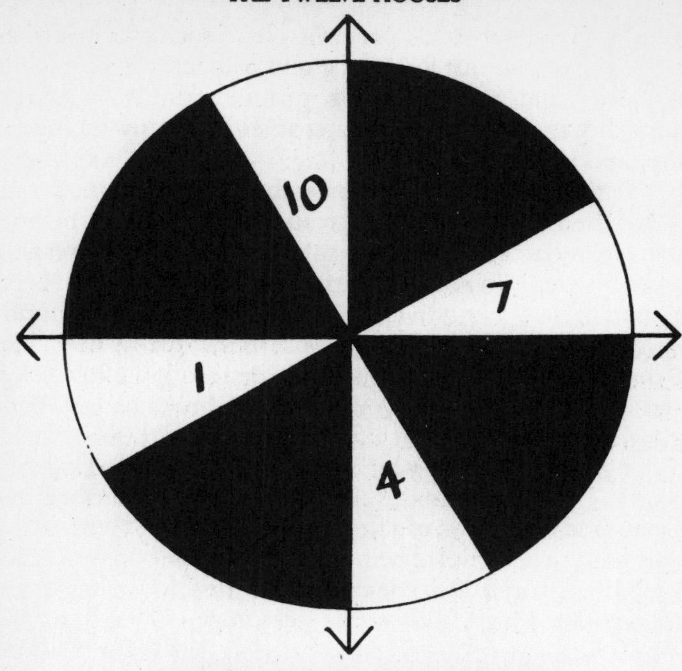

ANGULAR HOUSES
Activating & Generating Energy
Fig. 8

squares and oppositions planets may make to one another if placed in these houses.*

The 1st–7th opposition
Some degree of personal identity and freedom (1st) must be sacrificed to function in a relationship (7th). An opposition between these

* A square is a 90 degree angle between two planets; the opposition is a 180 degree angle. A planet in the 1st may or may not oppose a planet in the 7th. However, if they are in opposition, tension arises between these two areas of life. Even if they do not form an opposition aspect, the pull of one house and the pull of the opposite house could still present a problem. The same applies to planets in those houses which, figuratively speaking at least, square one another.

two houses gives the classic dilemma of will versus love: how much do we assert our own individuality and how much do we adjust to what others need or require. There is a fear that if we adjust too much, then we lose our own separate identity; but conversely, if we are too self-centred and demanding, then others won't love us.

The 4th–10th opposition

Here, one possible conflict is between staying at home and participating in the family unit (4th) versus being away from the family in order to establish a career (10th). The man immersed in career responsibilities does not have the time to be with the family, or spare moments to reflect on the deeper meaning of life. The woman with oppositions between these two houses may be torn between the desire for a profession and her role as a wife or mother. The child-in-us (4th) could conflict with the 'adult-like' behaviour expected in professional life (10th). The businessman, for instance, cannot 'throw a tantrum' in front of a client if the deal threatens to collapse at the last moment.

Our early conditioning (4th) influences how we function later in society (10th). Have we been so denigrated as a child that we feel we have nothing to offer society? Or are we the rejected child who is determined to show 'them' and make a mark on the world? Have we been so spoiled and protected by our parents that we lack the equipment or impetus to venture out of the family home at all? These issues may arise if there are oppositions between planets in the 4th and 10th houses.

The 1st–4th square

We are born separate and unique individuals (1st), but to what degree does the home life (4th) support or quash our budding individuality? I drew up the chart of a young man who had Jupiter in Leo in the 1st squared to Neptune in Scorpio in the 4th. His natural spontaneity and enthusiasm (Jupiter in the 1st) had to be contained and restricted so as not to disturb an ailing father (Neptune in the 4th). We might like to be independent and free (1st), but regressive urges to stay with what is secure and already known inhibit us (4th).

The 4th–7th square

With squares between the 4th and 7th houses, there is a likelihood of projecting 'unfinished business' around a parent (usually the father) onto a partner. Patterns established early in life (4th) often obscure our ability to see other people clearly (7th). Problems in establishing a home (4th) with a partner (7th) could arise if planets in these houses square one another. The capacity to be objective and fair with others is interfered with because of childish needs and complexes.

The 7th–10th square

Conflicts could surface between career (10th) and relationship (7th). If we are so busy pursuing a career, we may have less time for close partnerships. Our attractiveness to a partner (7th) may be contingent on our status in the world (10th). Or a partner may be sought who enhances one's social standing. Issues with our mother can interfere with seeing a partner clearly.

The 1st–10th square

Self-discipline is needed to forge a career (10th) and this invariably limits our personal freedom and spontaneity (1st). What society approves of and validates (10th) may impose restrictions on what we are naturally inclined to do (1st). Something the mother represents (10th) may inhibit the expression of the 1st house planet. One man with Venus in Leo in the 1st squared to the Moon in Taurus in the 10th wanted to be an artist (Venus in Leo in the 1st) but his mother insisted that he choose a more practical career (Moon in Taurus in the 10th). Often, we are labelled solely by what we do in the world (10th) rather than by other qualities we might possess (1st).

Succedent Houses (Figure 9)

The forces set in motion in the angular houses are concentrated, embellished, utilized and developed further in the *Succedent Houses:* the 2nd, 5th, 8th and 11th. These houses are naturally associated with the fixed signs of Taurus, Leo, Scorpio and Aquarius, which consolidate the generative energy of cardinal signs. The succedent 2nd house adds substance to the personal identity (1st) through defining our possessions, resources, shape and boundary. In the succedent 5th house, we affirm and strengthen the sense of 'I' distilled from the angular 4th by expressing who we are and impressing ourselves on others. Through the activity of relating to others (angular 7th house) we increase our resources and delve deeper into ourselves (the succedent 8th). Participating in the maintaining and functioning of society (the angular 10th) enhances the awareness of ourselves as social beings and provides the basis for expanding our sense of identity to encompass bigger and broader boundaries (the succedent 11th).

Like the angular houses, the four succedent houses represent

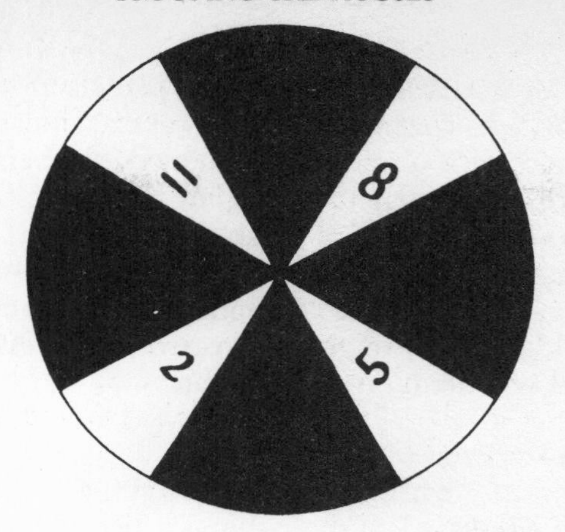

Fig. 9 SUCCEDENT HOUSES

Stabilizing & Concretizing Energy

spheres of life which are potentially in conflict with each other.

The 2nd–8th opposition
Conflicts arise between what one person possesses and values versus what another person holds dear. The 2nd house preserves and maintains forms; the 8th house tears things down to make room for something new. We sacrifice our boundaries (2nd) to merge fully with another (8th). The 2nd house sees the face value of something, while the 8th house looks underneath to detect the hidden significance. The 2nd house tends to indulge the appetites and bodily needs, whereas the 8th seeks to gain mastery over instinctual processes.

The 5th–11th opposition
In the 5th house, we create for our own personal satisfaction, such as designing our own stationery; in the 11th, we devote our energy to something greater than ourselves, such as designing a poster to promote a lecture for a group to which we belong. Another issue might be whether we are willing to release our children or works of art (5th) into the world (11th). A dilemma may arise between 'what I want to do' and the consensus of the group of which I am a member. Do I demand they conform to me (5th) or do I accept the group opinion (11th)?

The 2nd–5th square

A number of conflicts can be stirred if planets in the 2nd square planets in the 5th. The need for security and a regular income (2nd) could interfere with time spent on more creative and recreational activities (5th). Conversely, the struggling artist or 'resting' actor (5th) often suffers from the lack of a stable income (2nd). Some people with squares between the 2nd and 5th derive their sense of power, worth and importance (5th) solely through what they own and possess (2nd). Children (5th) might be treated as possessions (2nd) or experienced as a drain on one's resources.

The 5th–8th square

In the 5th house, we like to be seen as bright, positive, creative and special. Value is placed on those things which enhance the joy and dignity of life. The 8th depicts the darker, more intense and destructive elements lurking in the personality. If we have these two houses accentuated we may be engaged in a fierce battle between light and dark forces in the psyche. The kinds of crises associated with the 8th house can temporarily disrupt the 5th house's spontaneity and enthusiasm for life. Instead of feeling in charge of our lives (5th), we may be driven by unconscious complexes (8th) to act in ways over which we have little control. Sexual conquest could be utilized as a means of affirming our self-importance. Squares between the 5th and 8th houses can sometimes manifest as intense conflicts with one's children. Personal creativity (5th) is associated with emotional tension and frustration (8th). On the positive side, periods of psychological renewal and cleansing (8th) free the life-force to express itself more purely (5th). Creative expression (5th) may be a way of clearing something out of the system (8th). Destructive excesses (8th) may be glamorized (5th) as in the case of the tortured French poet, Rimbaud, who had Saturn in the 8th squared to Neptune in the 5th.

The 8th–11th square

The 11th house may have a vision of a better society, but has it taken into account deep-seated complexes (8th) in people which obscure the ability to relate to others fairly and objectively? The raging and needy infant in us (8th) can wreak havoc in our relationships with friends or groups (11th). The societal reformer with squares between the 11th and the 8th may be fired with such conviction that any means justifies achieving his or her ends. Sexual undercurrents (8th) could intrude on a friendship (11th). In short, highly charged emotions could inhibit the ease with which we relate to the larger unit of society. Conflicts could arise between our own humanitarian, political and social ideals (11th) and those of our partner (8th).

The 11th–2nd square

The 11th house may propose such liberal aims as the equal distribution of wealth, but the 2nd house desire to own things personally could contradict this. The 2nd house need to establish clear individual boundaries conflicts with the 11th house urge for a wider group membership. Eleventh house idealism may be 'out of touch' with the down-to-earth 2nd house. Problems could ensue in financial dealings (2nd) with friends (11th). We could become so strongly attached (2nd) to achieving certain goals and objectives (11th), that excessive force could be used to obtain these. We may cling too tenaciously (2nd) to ideas (11th). More positively, there may be the practical sense and ability (2nd) to realize hopes and wishes (11th).

Fig. 10 CADENT HOUSES
Distributing, Readjusting & Reorientating Energy

Cadent Houses (Figure 10)

The *Cadent Houses* (the 3rd, 6th, 9th and 12th) are associated with the mutable signs of Gemini, Virgo, Sagittarius and Pisces. While angular houses *generate* energy and succedent houses *concentrate* energy, the cadent houses *distribute* and *reorganize* energy. In each cadent house, we reconsider, readjust or reorientate ourselves on the basis of what we have previously experienced in the preceeding succedent house. In the cadent 3rd house, we learn more about who we are through comparing and contrasting ourselves with those around us. As the mental capacities develop, we enter a world beyond that of the bodily senses and biological needs (2nd house). The cadent 6th house reflects on the use or misuse of the outpouring of energy in the 5th, and makes adjustments accordingly. The interpersonal explorations and struggles of the 8th are conducive to the 9th house reflections on the deeper laws and processes which govern existence, and the patterns which weave us together. The perspective of the individual ego, already reeling from the 11th house experience of being part of a group or larger system, finally, in the cadent 12th, topples down altogether from its position as king of the mountain.

Cadent houses have often been described as weak or insubstantial, but the research done by the Gauquelins suggests that placements in these houses are more powerful than previously believed. Michel Gauquelin and his wife Françoise are both psychologists and statisticians who have studied the diurnal distribution of the planets in thousands of accurately timed birthcharts. In particular, they analysed the house position of planets in the charts of certain professions — actors, artists, doctors, business executives, politicians, scientists, soldiers, sports champions, writers and others. The results of their research showed that the planets naturally associated with each of these professions (such as Mars for sportspeople, Saturn for scientists, etc.) appeared more often in the cadent houses than in the angular houses, as traditional astrology would have expected. For instance, Mars in the charts of successful sportspeople appeared most often in the 12th and 9th houses: that is, just *after* the rising and superior culmination of the planet rather than just before in the 1st or 10th houses. The next most frequent house positions of Mars for the sportspeople they tested were the 6th and the 3rd houses. Again, these are just after the setting and inferior culmination of the planet, rather than before in the 7th or 4th houses. The conclusion to be drawn from their survey is that cadent houses are more important factors in determining character and career than previously suspected.

Briefly recapitulated, they found these correlations:[1]

1. Mars appeared most frequently in cadent houses in the charts of physicians, military leaders, sports champions and top executives.

2. Jupiter appeared most frequently in cadent houses in the charts of actors, playwrights, politicians, military leaders, top executives and journalists.
3. Saturn appeared most frequently in cadent houses in the charts of scientists and physicians.
4. The Moon appeared most frequently in cadent houses in the charts of writers and politicians.

In the discussion of the 12th house, I have explained why I don't find these results that surprising (see page 105). A similar rationale can be applied to the other cadent houses. The 9th is where we look for truth and principles to guide our lives — therefore we will be highly motivated to develop and give expression to the planets there as a way of lending greater meaning to our existence. Both the 6th and the 3rd houses describe our efforts to discern how we differ from other people. Therefore, developing the planets in these houses is crucial if we are to differentiate ourselves fully from others and define ourselves as separate individuals. The urge to connect to something greater than the self (as shown by the 12th and the 9th) and the urge to establish and characterize our own specific identities (as shown by the 3rd and the 6th) are the two complementary principles which form the crux of the human dilemma. Seen in this light, the planets in these houses assume a great importance.

As in the case of the four angular houses and the four succedent houses, the four cadent houses figuratively square or oppose one another. Each one represents a contrasting view of life and a different method of acquiring and processing information.

The 3rd–9th opposition

The 3rd house describes the nature of the analytical and concrete mind while the 9th house denotes more abstract and intuitive thought processes. The 3rd house sees the parts; the 9th looks first at the whole. When planets are found in opposition between these two houses, it could signify a good balance and integration between the right and left hemispheres of the brain. However, in certain cases, the opposition might denote a person who gathers facts (3rd) and then draws the wrong conclusions (9th) from them. Mountains are made of mole-hills, or conversely, a person may adhere to some belief or truth (9th) and then interpret everything around them (3rd) solely in the light of these principles. In other words, facts are distorted to prove a point. The 3rd house may labour for many weeks preparing a lecture, making sure that each word conveys the precise meaning intended. The 9th house lecturer may prefer to wait to see what the audience is like, trusting that he or she will intuitively know what to say when the time comes. Sometimes with the 3rd–9th opposition, there is a persistent feeling that the grass is greener farther afield.

The 6th–12th opposition

The 6th house examines the myriad forms of relative existence, scrutinizing in detail how one thing differs from another. The 12th house, however, embraces the essence of a thing — not how much it weighs or measures, but what it 'feels' like. The 6th is discriminating and selective, carefully defining boundaries; the 12th is empathetic and all-inclusive, and a boundary-dissolver. The 6th house is pragmatic, logical and concerned with the everyday realities of life; the 12th aspires to transcend whatever is mundane, and is aware of the elusive, unknowable and mysterious nuances of existence. The 6th house plans life; the 12th flows with it.

Oppositions between these two houses heighten these contrasting approaches to life, but afford a greater chance of achieving a synthesis of the various modes of being. I have seen 6th–12th house oppositions, for instance, in the charts of spiritually-minded people who also have their feet firmly on the ground. One was a dentist with Moon in Capricorn in the 6th opposing Jupiter in Cancer in the 12th, who was a devout follower of an Indian guru. Another was a carpenter who volunteered his services to train people in Third World countries in his skill. He had three planets in the 6th opposing Uranus in the 12th.

Oppositions between the 6th and 12th sometimes manifest in physical ailments which are psychological in origin. Reincarnationists believe that certain health problems (6th) may be the consequences of past-life behaviour (12th). For example, if a man overindulged in food and drink in a previous life, he might be born this life with allergies to certain foods, forcing him to pay more attention to what he put into his body. Or a person who habitually looked down on others in a past life could find himself abnormally tall in this lifetime. Or perhaps he would be born unusually short, so he could experience what it felt like to be the one looked down upon. In any case, with 6th–12th oppositions, the origins of ill health may be difficult to diagnose, stemming from a source which is not obvious to trace.

The 3rd–6th square

Here we have linked together the two houses most directly related to the processes of the logical and rational left brain. The tendency is for the mind to overwork. The 3rd house likes to know a little something about everything, while the 6th house wants to know as much as possible about a few things. Put these two together and we have somebody who wants to know as much as possible about everything. With planets in both the 3rd and 6th, it is possible that something could be analysed out of existence. Taken to extremes, it could be a person who insists that the only real difference between the plays *Othello* and *Hamlet* is that the letters of the alphabet are arranged differently in each play.

More positively, there is generally the pursuit of information (3rd) for the sake of using it practically (6th). There can be a great deal of bickering over details and much discussion about the precise and proper way something should be done. Consequently, those with the 3rd/6th house combination usually do not let others escape with being too abstract, whimsical or vague. If I have someone with these placements scheduled for a chart reading, I will allow an extra half-hour for questions at the end. ('What *exactly* do you mean by . . .?')

With squares between these houses, it is possible that health issues (6th) could affect physical mobility as well as the clear functioning of the mind (3rd). Sometimes unresolved conflicts with siblings (3rd) resurface in the form of problems with co-workers (6th).

The 6th–9th square

The combination of the expansive and truth-seeking 9th house with the mundane and practically-minded 6th can produce a restless soul who moves from one preoccupation to another in a constant search for one thing which is totally fulfilling. The catch is that they will usually find that the thing upon which all the hopes have been pinned somehow falls short of the mark. When that fails, something else is fervently pursued with the same abiding conviction that it should provide 'everything'. Rather than looking to one thing to be the whole truth, they should approach it with the attitude that it may offer some version or angle of the truth. In other words, they take the pressure off one thing to be everything. Then they can find something else to offer another bit of the truth and other kinds of fulfilment. In this way, they are not opening themselves to complete disappointment if one focus of attention doesn't deliver all the nourishment they crave.

The square between the 6th and 9th can be seen historically in the conflict between inductive modes of scientific investigation (6th) and the kind of knowing which arises from religious faith and beliefs

(9th). 6th–9th tension also manifests in the kinds of theological disputes that are concerned with exactly how many angels can dance on the head of a pin. Scriptures (9th) may be interpreted in a fundamentalist way: laws and rituals are to be followed exactly to ensure that even the most humble or ordinary aspects of existence (6th) partake of the sacred or are performed in accordance to higher law (9th). There is also the ability to perceive cosmic significance (9th) in the smallest details of life (6th). On another level, health problems (6th) could occur through travel (9th). Or there may be many differences of opinions with in-laws (9th) over the management of daily affairs (6th).

The 9th–12th square

In this case we have two houses of an expansive nature in relationship to one another. Neither sphere is fond of boundaries and limitations, and those with planets in both these houses may not feel very comfortable within the confines of a mundane existence. Usually an interest in philosophical or religious matters predominates: in extreme cases, they live in a world of symbols, dreams and images, surviving from one peak experience to the next, often totally forgetting about having to go to the dentist. They may have an unending source of transpersonal inspiration but no vehicles for expressing or relating their vision to everyday life. Not inclined to analytical thinking, they may swallow a belief whole and live it fervently until it is spat out again and something new is looked for to swallow. Some sidetrack too far with delusions of being another Napoleon or Christ, landing themselves in mental institutions (12th). More positively, those with a heavy 9th–12th emphasis serve to open other people's eyes to realities beyond the ken of the typical 3rd–6th house thinker.

There are differences in the 9th and 12th house approach to 'higher understanding'. The 9th house believes that the basic patterns and principles which govern life can be known and comprehended. The 12th house feels something which is often unfathomable and beyond knowing. The 9th house is basically concerned with scaling new heights; the 12th finds inspiration not only in the heights, but also in the depths — ecstasy and pain, bliss and suffering, are intimately connected. On a more mundane level, there may be strange and inexplicable yearnings to travel to different countries and a danger of imprisonment (12th) in a foreign land (9th).

The 3rd–12th square

Broadly speaking, the 12th is the unconscious mind and the 3rd the conscious mind. The 12th is the domain of what is hidden and unseen, while the 3rd perceives what is immediate and at hand in the environment. An action or statement can be appreciated at its face value (3rd) or may be felt to be cloaking less obvious feelings or motivations (12th). In psychology, this is known as the *meta-meaning.* The 3rd house observes the actions and makes sense of the words, but the 12th house 'picks up on' and is sensitive to other levels of what is being said or done. The 3rd/12th combination perceives many levels of reality at once. This confers either uncanny insight into people and situations or a great deal of mental confusion. Should they believe what they hear and see or what they sense and feel?

These kinds of mixed messages are not uncommon among siblings (3rd). In general, older siblings feel ambivalent towards the younger child: they know they are supposed to love the new baby, but jealousy and destructive urges are there as well. The younger sibling perceives the older child acting kindly towards him or her, and yet senses something less pleasant passing between them as well. Which level should be taken as real? A case in question is a woman I knew with Saturn and Pluto in the 12th squared to the Moon in Scorpio in the 3rd. Her older sister was outwardly kind to her, but underneath resented the intrusion of the younger child. Later in life, the younger child grew into a woman who had enormous difficulty trusting or believing in what others said to her. Whatever was expressed or done was interpreted in a negative light as if it was intended to threaten her. She mysteriously became deaf in one ear and lived a lonely life in isolation from others. Unresolved past issues (12th) with siblings (3rd) prevented her from relating in a natural way with those around her. With squares between the 12th and 3rd, the capacity for making decisions or the ability to clearly perceive life may be distorted by deep-rooted unconscious complexes. These need to be examined and cleaned up through a conscious analysis (3rd) of the images and fantasies lurking beneath the surface level of the psyche (12th).

Classifying the Houses by Elements

Another way to group the houses is by elements. There are three fire houses (1st, 5th and 9th); three earth houses (2nd, 6th and 10th); three air houses (3rd, 7th and 11th); and three water houses (4th, 8th and 12th). A meaningful and sequential development can be observed as we progress from the first house associated with a particular element, to the second house of that element, and on to the third house of the same element. In general, the first house associated with a particular element brings the nature of that element into focus and personalizes it. The next house aligned with that element further differentiates and defines that principle, usually through comparing our expression of it with that of others. The third house related to a particular element universalizes its expression: that element can be seen to be operating on a broad collective level.

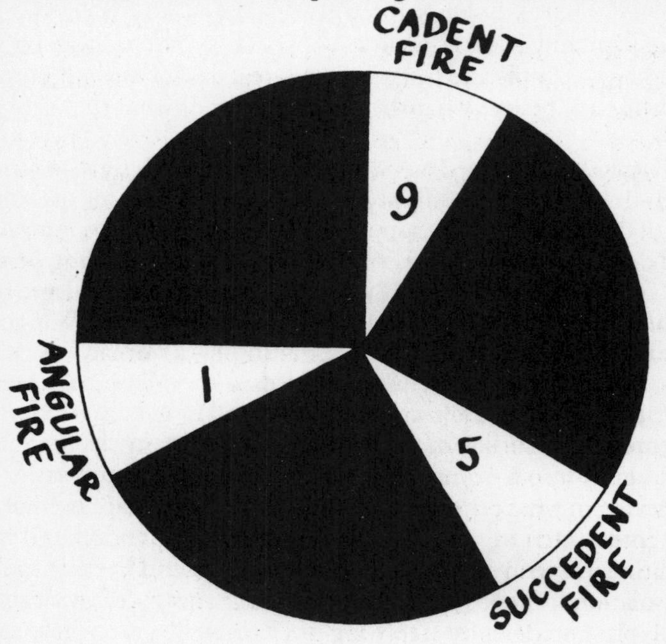

Fig. 11 FIRE: The Trinity of Spirit

The Fire Houses: The Trinity of Spirit (Figure 11)

Fire is the life-force which animates all living forms. It is the element associated with the will-to-be: the urge to express from inside the self.

The 1st house is the first fire house. It is also angular. If we combine the qualities of fire with the nature of angular houses (activity and release of energy) we arrive at a good description of the 1st house

— the activity of releasing the life-force. The 1st house shows the initial stirring of being inside us, the urge to be a separate and distinct person. Developing the signs and planets in the 1st house vitalizes and enlivens us.

The second fire house is the 5th house. It is also a succedent house. Therefore the 5th house combines the qualities associated with succedent houses and the qualities associated with the element of fire. Succedent houses concentrate, stabilize and utilize the energy generated in angular houses. In the case of the 5th house, the pure spirit of the 1st house is given focus and direction. We strengthen our sense of identity (1st) by pursuing those outlets and interests which make us feel more alive, and by stamping our individuality on what we do or create (5th).

The third fire house is the 9th house. It is also a cadent house. Therefore the 9th house combines the qualities associated with cadent houses and the qualities associated with the element of fire. Cadent houses reconsider, readjust and reorientate the way we focus our energy. In the 9th house, we revamp our sense of identity through viewing life and ourselves in a broader context. The fire we recognized burning inside us in the 1st and 5th houses has now spread to everyone else: we now perceive 'fire' or spirit as a universal attribute existing in everything around us. In the 5th house, we explore our own personal creativity, but in the 9th we glimpse the workings of a cosmic creative intelligence which shapes life in accordance with certain laws and universal principles.

In the first fire house (1st) our own identity is sparked. In the second fire house (5th) we strengthen, confirm and express that identity. In the third fire house (9th) the creative nature of fire and the urge-to-be is seen expressing itself impersonally through the archetypal principles which govern and generate all of life.

The three fire houses symbolically trine one another. Planets in the 1st, 5th or 9th houses may literally trine each other — that is, form 120 degree angles to each other (allowing an 8–10 degree orb or so). However, in finding aspects we must always count the actual number of degrees between the two planets, not just the number of houses. A planet in the 1st does not automatically trine a planet in the 5th, and in some cases, due to the unequal size of houses in Quadrant systems, the two planets may even square one another. Nonetheless, it is helpful to understand the basic affinity between placements in houses associated with the same element in the natural zodiac.

The 1st–5th trine

If a planet in the 1st house trines a planet in the 5th, then the 1st house planet finds a creative release through the 5th house planet. For instance, if Mercury is in the 1st house and trine to Jupiter in the 5th, the urge to communicate and exchange information symbolized by Mercury may have an outlet through some form of artistic expression (Jupiter in the 5th). In trine contacts between the 1st and the 5th, there is a natural ease or flow in outwardly expressing who we are. The French author, Victor Hugo, who expressed his humanitarian concerns through literature had sympathetic Neptune in the 1st trine to Mercury in the 5th.

The 5th–9th trine

If a 5th house planet trines a 9th house planet then what we express or create (5th) often influences and inspires other people (the expansive nature of the 9th). It may seem as if creativity flows through us from a higher source of inspiration or 'fired' vision. Lord Byron, the English Romantic poet who expressed his acute sensitivity to beauty through his work, had Venus in the 9th trine Neptune in the 5th.

The 1st–9th trine

Those with trines between these two houses naturally act in accord with a broadened view of life. Their actions comply with trends already in the atmosphere, and therefore less resistance is met in achieving their aims. A wide scope on existence (9th) guides the manner in which they meet the world (1st). The danger with this trine is that it can too easily give rise to the individual identifying the self with the Voice of God, and justifying action on the basis of a higher authority or guiding principle. For example, Francisco Franco, the fascist dictator, had the Moon, Neptune and Pluto in the 9th trine to Saturn in the 1st.

The Earth Houses: The Trinity of Matter (Figure 12)

The element of earth is associated with the plane of material existence: the condensation of spirit into concrete forms.

The first earth house is the 2nd house. It is also a succedent house. Therefore, the 2nd house represents matter trying to make itself more secure or stable: hence the associations of the 2nd house with money, possessions and resources. It shows those things — including the body — which we like to call our own. In economic terms it is capital.

The second earth house is the 6th, which is also a cadent house.

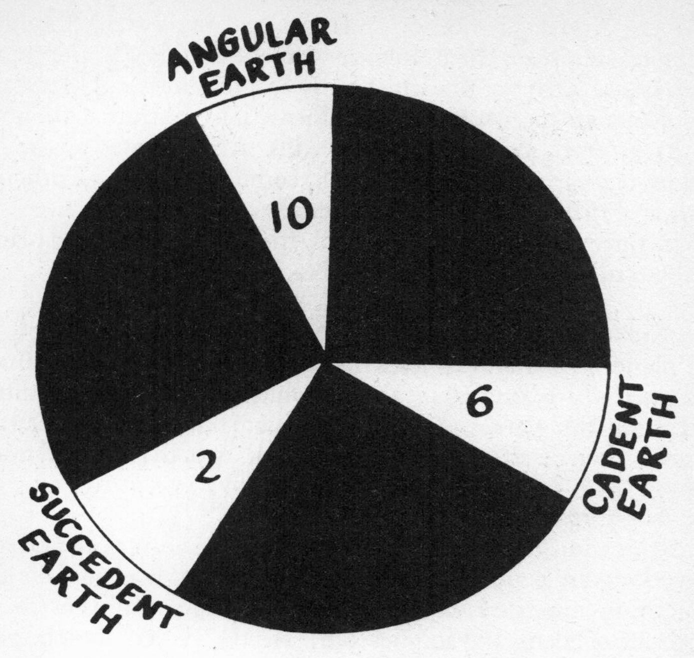

Fig. 12

EARTH: The Trinity of Matter

Therefore, the 6th house adjusts and reconsiders the earth principle. In this house, our resources and skills are compared to other people's resources and skills. Our special abilities are refined and perfected. The body as well needs attention to function efficiently and ill health can be understood as the body trying to readjust itself. In economic terms, it represents the labour force.

The third earth house is the 10th, which is an angular house. In this case, there is the need to generate matter, i.e. productivity. In one sense, the 10th represents the forces of management who actively organize and oversee capital and labour. More personally, it shows how we purposefully structure and direct our energy and abilities for the sake of concrete and definite results. Hence, the association of the 10th with career, ambition and the way we like to be seen by the world. More broadly, the 10th house depicts the role the individual plays in perpetuating and maintaining the body of society itself.

In the first earth house (2nd) the body and matter itself is differentiated from the ouroboric wholeness of life. In the second earth house (6th) our particular body and resources, differentiated in the 2nd, are more specifically delineated. In the third earth house (10th) our own body and practical skills (differentiated in the 2nd and more clearly defined in the 6th) come together with others to form and maintain collective material existence.

The three earth houses symbolically trine one another, and planets in these houses may literally trine each other.

The 2nd–6th trine

If a planet in the 2nd trines a planet in the 6th, the individual is equipped with resources and abilities which he or she can use skilfully and productively, and usually with adequate financial remuneration. There is often an efficient and adept handling of the material world.

The 6th–10th trine

With this trine, there is the likelihood that a person's skills and style of working are conducive to success in a career. It is possible that something inherited via the mother (10th) contributes to the repertoire of talents and abilities (6th). The daughter of show business parents, Candice Bergen makes good use of both her beauty and intelligence in her careers as an actress and photo-journalist. She is born with Venus conjunct Uranus in Gemini in the 6th trine to Jupiter in Libra in the 10th.

The 2nd–10th trine

In this case, the career is usually well-suited to the temperament and abilities. Money and status can be earned from what a person naturally enjoys doing. Something of worth is inherited via the mother or shaping parent (10th). Sir Harry Lauder, the comedian and entertainer, had a wide public appeal and was especially loved for his Scottish dialect. He was born with Mercury (the planet of speech) in the 2nd (resources) trine to Neptune in the 10th.

The Air Houses: The Trinity of Relationship (Figure 13)

Air is associated with the capacity to detach the self and view something objectively with distance and perspective. Once we have separated or distinguished ourselves from the universal matrix of life, then we can start forming relationships with what we find. The element of air correlates to the intellect and the communication and exchange of ideas.

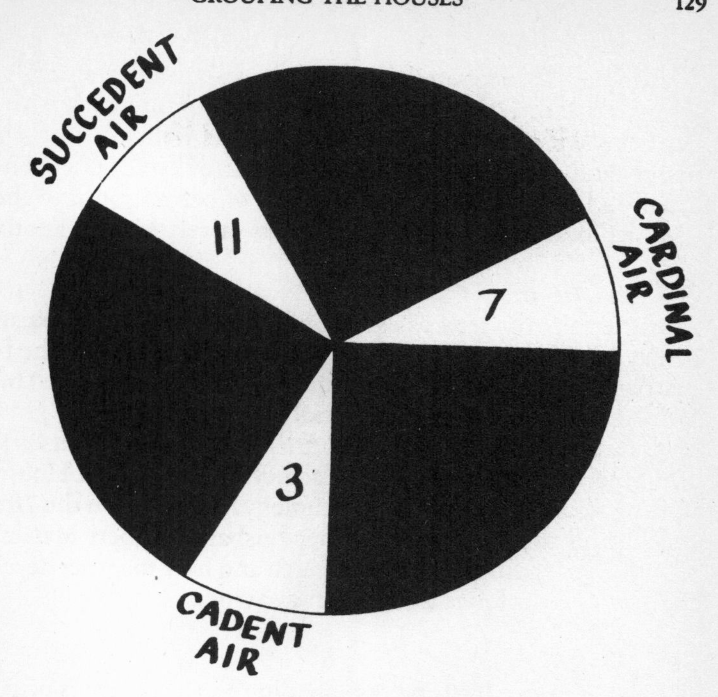

Fig. 13

AIR : The Trinity of Relationship

The first air house is the 3rd, which is also a cadent house. Movement, mental development and the advent of language enable us to readjust and redefine the more concrete sense of self just forming in the 1st and 2nd houses. The second air house is the 7th, which is angular. My mind and perspective on life (3rd) meets your mind and perspective on life (7th). The coming together of two people generates an enormous amount of energy and the failure or success of a relationship may affect how we feel about many other areas of our lives. The third air house (11th) is succedent. We stabilize and strengthen our viewpoints by looking for other people (groups and friends) who share our ideas. Minds come together in the 11th. Ideas are 'fixed' into ideologies and 'isms' which are broadly applied to society and 'taken up' by large numbers of people.

The three air houses symbolically trine one another, and planets in these houses may literally trine each other.

The 3rd–7th trine

The 3rd house is associated with communication and if a planet there trines one in the 7th, there is an ease in communicating with close partners. We can make ourselves heard as well as being able to understand or appreciate others (intellectually at least). There is usually a lively interest and fair degree of perception into the way in which one person or thing interacts or relates with another.

The 7th–11th trine

A partnership may serve as a source of social or intellectual expansion. It may be a friend (11th) who introduces this person to the future marriage partner (7th). Or an important relationship (7th) may be formed with someone the person meets through a group or organization (11th). Usually the partner (7th) shares the person's goals and objectives and is helpful in achieving these. Jean Houston, a leading figure in humanistic psychology has Jupiter in the 7th trine to Pluto in the 11th. She and her husband, Robert Masters, co-founded an institute for mind research and have together developed numerous techniques to broaden awareness.

The 3rd–11th trine

If a planet in the 3rd trines a planet in the 11th, there is usually an ease relating to groups of people. There may be an intuitive grasp of how the individual mind (3rd) is linked to others (11th). The person can speak clearly (3rd) about broad concepts or those things which he or she envisions (11th). Friends or groups (11th) inspire and expand the thinking (3rd), and conversely, the person's point of view or general knowledge affects others. Albert Einstein had Uranus in the 3rd trine to Neptune in the 11th. His new discoveries (Uranus in the 3rd) have led to a greater understanding of the interconnectedness of all life (11th). On another level, a 3rd–11th trine may mean that neighbourhood groups (3rd) can be formed to promote needed social changes (11th), or a sibling (3rd) might introduce the person to new friends, ideas or groups (11th).

The Water Houses: The Trinity of Soul (Figure 14)

Water is the element associated with the feelings. All three water houses are concerned with emotions which dwell beneath the surface level of consciousness. They also deal with the past conditioned responses which are now instinctual, unreflective and inbred.

The first water house is the 4th, which is also angular. It describes feelings active deep within us, as well as the family background and

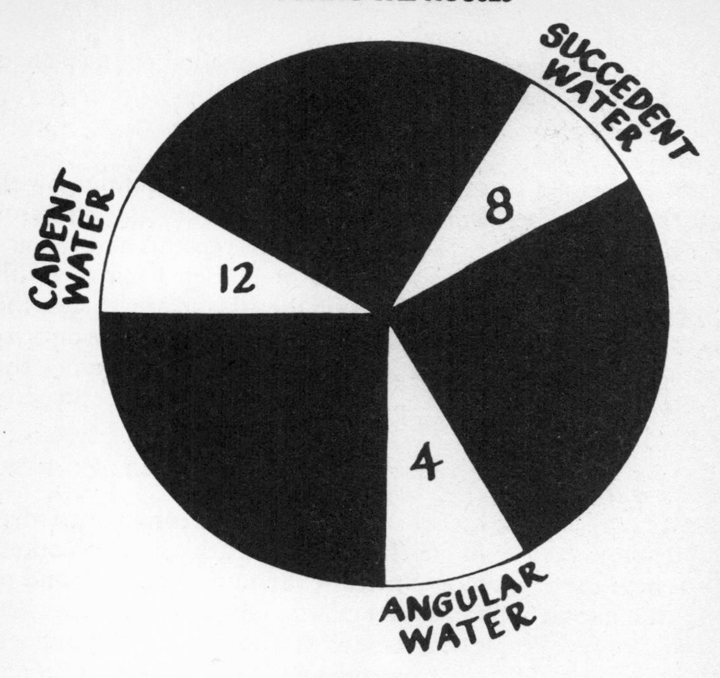

Fig. 14

WATER: The Trinity of Soul

influences within the early home which shape the identity. In the second water house, the succedent 8th, our feelings are strengthened, deepened and stirred through close relationship with another person. Two people, each with their own family backgrounds and emotional make-up attempt to merge into one. Greater security (a succedent quality) is sought through two people linking their feelings together. In the 8th, our own feelings (differentiated and recognized in the angular 4th) flow into another person's feelings. In the third water house, the cadent 12th, we progress from union with a select few (8th) to a sense of unity with all life. We acknowledge the collective unconscious, the collective sea out of which we all emerge, and the background we share with everyone and everything.

In the 4th house we feel our own joy and pain; in the 8th we feel the joy and pain of a close associate; in the 12th, we feel the world's joy and pain. The sequential development of the water houses, as with the houses of the other elements, is a movement from the personal to the interpersonal to the universal.

The three water houses symbolically trine one another, and planets in these houses may literally trine each other.

The 4th–8th trine

This aspect helps a person to share his or her deeper feelings with another person. There will be extreme sensitivity to undercurrents in the home atmosphere. Those with these placements have a knack for sensing another person's motives or hidden feelings. With harmonious aspects between planets in the 4th and 8th, there is the likelihood that a positive early home experience increases the capacity for satisfying interpersonal relationships later in life. Sometimes, the 4th–8th trine is an indication of inheritance (8th) of land or property (4th).

The 8th–12th trine

Aspects between these houses enhance a person's insight into what is subtle or mysterious in life. They see or feel things which others do not have the sensitivity to perceive. Resources can be found to turn a crisis into an opportunity for growth. Often help appears when it is most needed. People with these aspects can guide others through times of upheaval (8th) and may work successfully within institutions (12th). A woman I know with the Sun in the 8th trine Neptune in the 12th has narrowly escaped death three times. She was also employed as a counsellor (8th) for young offenders in prison (12th) and a fund-raiser (8th) for charities (12th). Recently a family inheritance (8th) has freed her to pursue her humanitarian aims more fully (12th).

The 4th–12th trine

Those with trines between the 4th and 12th houses are so sensitive to undercurrents in the atmosphere that they often experience other people's moods and feelings as their own. There is a natural receptivity to collective trends and fashions. Conversely, they are sometimes capable of influencing a group of people through the power of their emotions and feelings. There may be a psychic link with the father (4th), whether he is alive or not. The possibilities of positive experiences through 12th house institutions are increased. Times of rest and retreat from outer life are periodically needed and usually beneficial. Paramhansa Yogananda, an Eastern mystic who founded the Self-Realization Institute, was born with Venus and Mercury in the 4th trine to the Moon in the 12th.

PART 3: A GUIDE TO LIFE'S POSSIBILITIES

16. GENERAL GUIDELINES: THE PLANETS AND SIGNS THROUGH THE HOUSES

In every corner of my soul, there is an altar to a different god.
Fernando Pessoa

Ideally, every factor in the chart should be interpreted in the light of the whole chart; it is only then that the true significance of that placement can be appreciated in relation to the broader pattern of an individual's being and becoming. However, as a step or aid in the process of ultimately synthesizing all the important factors in the horoscope, this part of the book explores the possible interpretations of the different planets and signs through the houses. The suggested meanings are by no means conclusive, nor are they intended to be taken as gospel. It is hoped, however, that the information given (most of which is drawn from personal experience) will generate further thought and insight into the various and numerous ramifications of each placement.

General Guidelines for Interpreting Planets in the Houses

What exactly does a planet (or planets) situated in a house show or suggest? To answer this, we need to recall that the astrological birthchart portrays symbolically how an individual's drives and urges are apt to express themselves. Like the seed of a plant or a tree, it contains a blueprint of what the fully developed person could grow into or become. The chart tells us something about the nature of the seed, as well as offering some general indications about the process of the seed's unfoldment. On this basis, the birth map can be understood as a set of instructions showing how a person can most naturally actualize his or her potential.

Bearing this principle in mind, we can infer three basic guidelines for interpreting a planet in a house:

1. When a planet is located in a house, the function or activity represented by the planet finds its most natural area of expression in the field of experience referred to by that house. The sign in which the planet is placed gives further information about how this activity can be approached.
2. The reverse is also true: the area of life designated by the house in which a planet falls is most naturally dealt with and handled in accordance with the type of activity represented by the planet there.
3. A planet in a house also shows the nature of the archetypal principle we are born already expecting to encounter through that area of life or facet of experience. It is the kind of energy we are innately predisposed to perceive or meet in that domain. It is the *a priori* image of that sphere of life which exists right from birth.

General Guidelines for Interpreting Signs in the Houses

Sign placements are slightly more complicated than planetary placements in relationship to the houses. Firstly, there will always be a particular degree of a certain sign on the cusp or beginning point of each house. In the example shown in Figure 15, 11 degrees of Cancer is on the cusp of the 1st house; 29 degrees of Cancer on the cusp of the 2nd house; 20 degrees of Leo on the cusp of the 3rd house, etc. We would then associate the principles of Cancer with what the 1st house represents; the principle of Cancer will also influence the 2nd house (even though only one degree of Cancer remains in the 2nd it is still associated with that house because of its cuspal position there); the principles of Leo would operate in the 3rd house, etc.

However, if we look closely, we will see that there are a variety of ways in which a sign may appear in a house:

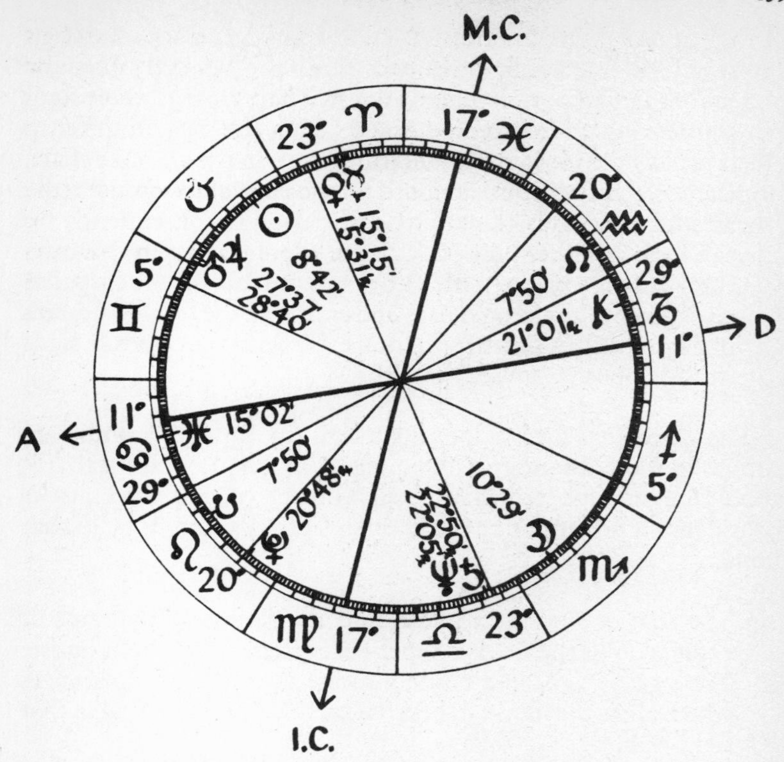

Fig. 15 ELIOT
9.00 a.m., April 29th, 1953.
Florence, Italy.

1. Some portion of a sign may be in a house even if it is not on the cusp of the house. In the example chart, Cancer is on the cusp of the 2nd, but much of the sign of Leo is there as well. Therefore, the 2nd house will be associated not only with a Cancer influence but also with a Leo influence. Usually the influence of the sign on the cusp is considered more important *even if* more of the next sign is present in that house.
2. If, as in the case of the Quadrant systems of house-division, the same sign falls on two successive house cusps, then all of another sign will be *intercepted* in another house. This means that a

house begins with one sign on the cusp, has the next sign intercepted or totally contained within the house, and has the following sign completing the house. There are then three signs influencing an intercepted house (again the sign on the cusp is usually the most important influence). In the example chart, Cancer and Capricorn are both on the cusp of two houses (the 1st and 2nd, and 7th and 8th respectively). Consequently we can look for other houses with intercepted signs. In this case, the 5th house begins with 23 degrees of Libra on the cusp, has all of Scorpio intercepted in it, and ends with the first few degrees of Sagittarius. A similar situation exists with the opposite signs in the opposite house, the 11th.

The guidelines for interpreting a sign (or signs) in a house are similar to those for interpreting a planet in a house, except that it should be remembered that the sign on the cusp of the house is considered more important than other signs that might be in that house:

1. The sign or signs in a house find their most natural area of expression in the field of experience referred to by that house.
2. The sign or signs in a house indicate the types of experiences which allow the native to best realize his or her potential in that field of life.
3. The sign or signs in a house also suggest what kind of archetypal energies the person is predisposed to expect in that area of life.

House Rulerships

There is another factor to be considered in analysing the influence of planets and signs in the houses. When a planet is located in a certain house there is a connection between the affairs of that house and the house or houses in which the sign(s) that the planet in question rules is placed. For instance, in the example chart, Venus is in the 10th house; but because Venus is the ruler of both Libra and Taurus, the 10th house Venus will have an influence on the houses in which Libra and Taurus are found. In this case, Libra is associated with the 4th house (23 degrees of that sign is there) and the 5th house (the 23rd degree of Libra is on the cusp). All of Taurus is intercepted in the 11th. So, Venus in the 10th house (career), through its rulership of Libra and Taurus, will have bearing on the 4th house (home), the 5th house (children) and the 11th house (groups). This man has worked (10th) running groups (11th) in his own home (4th) geared to helping parents relate better (Venus) to children (5th).

To sum up: a planet has an influence on

1. The house in which it is placed.
2. The house on whose cusp is found the sign that planet rules.
3. The house in which any number of degrees of the sign the planet rules is found (even if the sign the planet rules is not on the cusp).

Generally, the weighting of the influence of the various factors can be taken in the order given above.

Empty Houses

Over and over again when teaching astrology to beginners I hear the question 'What does it mean if a house is empty?' Some students are very troubled by empty or untenanted houses — that is, a house in which no planets are found. 'My 5th house is empty — does that mean I won't have any children?'; 'my 3rd house is empty — does this mean I don't have a mind?'

Because there are only ten planets to go around the twelve houses, invariably certain houses will be untenanted. This does not mean that nothing is happening in that area of life. Nor does it necessarily imply that the area of life in question is unimportant.

Strictly speaking it is incorrect to say that a house is empty. Even though there may be no planets in that house, there is still a sign (or signs) placed there which will influence that sphere of experience. Thus, the *first step* in interpreting what is happening in an untenanted house is to relate the qualities of the sign or signs found there to the area of life associated with the house in question. The *second step* is to refer to the planet which rules the sign on the cusp of the 'empty' house. What house is the ruling planet in? What sign is the ruling planet in? How is the ruling planet aspected? In this way, we glean a great deal of information about the house in question. The *third step* is to examine the planet which rules any other signs found in that house (not just the sign on the cusp). Where is that planet by house, sign and aspect?

In the example chart, the 6th house is empty. Following the three steps outlined above, much can be learned about that house. Sagittarius is on the cusp of the 6th house: on one level, this could mean that Eliot should develop skills (6th) of a Sagittarian nature — techniques for expanding or broadening the vision of other people, for instance. The ruler of Sagittarius is Jupiter, which is placed in the 11th house of groups. The group setting could then be an appropriate place to employ his skills (ruler of the 6th in the 11th). Since Jupiter is in Taurus and conjunct Mars, his temperament is suited to leading (Mars) the groups he might establish (Taurus). But we mustn't forget that Capricorn is also in the 6th house. Therefore, Saturn's position in the chart will exert an influence in relation to the 6th house as well. Saturn is in Libra very close to the 4th/5th house cusp. Again, we have the idea that the work (6th) might take place in the home (Saturn in the 4th ruling Capricorn in the 6th). Saturn is so near to the 5th house cusp that it could also have some bearing on that house. One of the associations with the 5th is that of children, so we are back to a connection between work (6th) possibly being linked to children in some way (Saturn near the 5th house cusp rules Capricorn in the 6th). We have previously arrived at the same interpretation through examining Venus in the 10th and its influence (see page 136). Anything which is important in the chart will usually manifest in a number of ways; this is sometimes called 'the rule of three'.

Obviously, a house with many planets in it is very important, but we should not overlook the significance of so-called empty houses. Should the planet ruling the sign on the cusp of an empty house be the focal point for a particular chart shaping, such as the handle to a bucket type chart or the leading planet of a locomotive shaping, then the affairs of the house in question could figure prominently in the native's life. The empty house might also contain the missing element to a T-square and this would increase the relevance of that area of life in contributing to the overall balance of the person's psyche.

Packed Houses

A house may contain more than one planet. Indeed, some houses are 'packed' — that is, three, four or even more planets may fall within one house. In this case, each of the principles, urges, drives or motivations suggested by the different planets will be expressing itself through that area of life. Obviously, should the nature of the planets be contradictory, such as the expansive effects of Jupiter versus the cautious and limiting effects of Saturn, then that sphere of life will be met with greater tension and complexity. Any house containing two or more planets will assume extra significance in the person's life-plan or purpose.

Planets near House Cusps

Generally, if a planet falls a few degrees before the end of a house and therefore close to the cusp of the next house, its effect may be felt in both spheres — in its own house as well as in the house which it is near. The orb of influence can even be slightly increased to roughly five degrees, providing that the sign the planet is in is the same sign as the next house cusp.

The sphere of experience associated with one house naturally leads to the next. A planet at the end of a house and just prior to the cusp of the next, may bring the junction point of these two areas of life into focus. For instance, if Venus is near the end of the 6th house and close to the 7th house cusp, a person may fall in love with and marry (7th) someone he or she has met through a working situation (6th). If Mercury is between the 10th and 11th houses, professional connections (10th) may develop into friendships or contacts with new groups of people (11th).

The astrologer is so often working with an estimated or approximate birth-time that a planet near the cusp of a house might actually belong to the adjacent house. Likewise, given the kinds of discrepancies which occur depending on which house system is used, a planet near a cusp in one system may fall in the neighbouring house in another method. For these reasons, some astrologers believe that a planet placed in the middle of a house has the most reliable influence because it is so firmly established in that domain.

Inequality of Houses and Intercepted Signs

In Quadrant systems of house-division, unless the birth is on the equator, the houses will be of unequal size (especially for births in extreme northern or southern latitudes). Some houses may span sixty degrees while others may be as small as fifteen degrees or less. Many students enquire whether bigger houses are more important. To some extent, this is probably true since transits (the ongoing daily motion of the planets) will spend a longer time in the larger houses than the smaller houses, thereby stirring the affairs of that area of life for a more extended duration. However, a small house, especially if there are two or more planets in it, can still have an important influence. Even untenanted, the ruler of the sign on the cusp of a small house might be significant by placement or aspect and in that way emphasize the affairs of the house in question. Also, though planets transiting through the smaller houses spend less time there, they often 'do their job' in a more condensed and concentrated way, driving lessons home harder and faster.

Students also ask whether signs which are intercepted (not on a house cusp but surrounded entirely by a house) are less important than signs on the cusp of the house. The sign on the cusp is generally more important, but the intercepted sign will definitely be felt in relation to the affairs of that house. The effects of planets in intercepted signs appear to be as strong as planets in the other signs. Some astrologers claim that when a sign is intercepted its nature is introverted or directed inward. I have not found this particularly to be the case.

Bearing these general guidelines in mind, we will now examine more specifically the implications of the different signs and planets in the twelve houses, as well as a discussion of the Moon's nodes and the recently discovered Chiron in this respect. In the main, in order to save space and avoid repetition, except for the Ascendant/Descendant axis (or 1st and 7th house cusps), I have not examined separately the meaning of each sign in a house. However, the reader should remember that the significance of a particular planet in a house is similar to the influence that the sign it rules has on a house. For instance, if you have Cancer on the cusp of the 8th (or contained in the 8th) then you can read the section headed the Moon in the 8th to learn more about the way in which Cancer in the 8th might operate. Or if you have Pisces on the cusp of the 5th, then you can refer to the section headed Neptune in the 5th to glean how the closely related principle of Pisces might evince itself in that house.

Also, there is the problem that any aspects to a planet in a house from other planets in other houses will modify the effect of the planet and house combination in question. For instance, if Venus is in the 7th we might expect an ease and receptivity in partnership. But if Saturn in the 4th, let's say, should square the 7th house Venus, then the expression of Venus will be tempered by the nature of Saturn. Occasionally, I make a distinction between a well-aspected planet in a house or an adversely aspected planet in a house. Please keep in mind that it is not necessarily the case that a difficultly aspected planet will manifest in a negative way, although it may require more effort or struggle to use the adversely aspected planet constructively. For further insight into how stressful aspects can be used productively, the reader is referred to Christina Rose's excellent book *Astrological Counselling* (Aquarian Press, Wellingborough, 1982). As she articulately reminds us:

> Behind every aspect (as with everything in the birth chart) stands the individual himself. His outlooks, philosophies, conditioning and experience so far in his life will all bear upon the way the aspect functions; it is he who lives it, or is seeking to live it, and his *actual* experience may not read exactly like a textbook interpretation. (page 87)

17.
ASCENDANT TYPES

The sign on the Ascendant informs us of the qualities we should consciously strive to manifest in the process of self-discovery and unfoldment. However, it would be misleading to consider just this sign alone, and not take into account the meaning of the opposite sign which will fall on the Descendant or 7th house cusp. While the Ascendant is the point of self-awareness, the Descendant is the point of awareness of others. We find ourselves through the Ascendant, but the Descendant is what we find in others. What rises above the horizon and into the light of consciousness (the Ascendant) is complemented by what sinks beneath the horizon into the dark (the Descendant). When I consciously identify certain qualities as 'who I am', then implicitly there are other qualities which I am identifying as 'not-me'. The qualities I identify as 'me' are shown by the Rising sign; the qualities I identify as 'not-me' are shown by the Descending sign.

But the name of the game is wholeness: what we do not 'own' in ourselves, we will invariably attract to us. The more we develop those attributes on the Ascendant, the more we will meet the opposite attributes of the Descendant in others. The two points of the Ascendant and Descendant form a coupling or polarity which are inextricably linked. None of us exists in a vacuum, and our sense of self (Ascendant) will be reshaped by what we meet through others (Descendant). The nature of the Descending sign will attempt to modify and balance the qualities of the Ascendant until a stalemate, a compromise or a synthesis is achieved. Therefore, in discussing the significance of the Rising sign, some understanding of the implications of the Descending sign are included.

Aries on the Ascendant and Libra on the Descendant

With the fiery sign of Aries rising, the person should meet life in a straightforward and energetic manner: 'Here I am, notice me, now let's get things started.' There is a need to be decisive, take action, and 'own' the power to create and direct the life. The core of Aries rising is finding this creative potency within, not waiting around for things to happen. Life is best viewed as an adventure, quest and challenge. If other placements in the chart indicate a meek or withdrawn nature, there will be more struggle in developing the Aries qualities. If the Aries Ascendant is denied expression, the inner frustration which accumulates could periodically explode in illness, dramatic or wild outbursts, unruly fits of anger, or other forms of self-destructive behaviour. If the rest of the chart is already fairly fiery, the Aries Ascendant allows the assertiveness to flow freely, but with the danger of being too forceful or overly egocentric — which in the end may be self-defeating.

If Aries is rising then the opposite sign, Libra, will be on the Descendant, beckoning the person to balance rampant autonomy with some degree of consideration for another person. However, if those with this Ascendant have to choose one extreme or the other, it is probably wiser that they err in favour of self-assertion and daring rather than hold back too much for the sake of keeping the peace or adapting to the requirements of others. After their own power has been found and the courage to be the self is freed, then they can learn to regulate, adjust and temper the nature accordingly. Ultimately, the Libran qualities of grace, forethought and consideration for another person's case and point of view will need to be included.

Physically, Aries rising may evince a lively, energetic face with intense but darting eye-contact. Movements are usually quick and impulsive, as if the person is ready at any moment to plunge headlong into some new activity. 'Don't stand in my way' may be the message subtly (or not so subtly) communicated to others.

The controversial writer, Henry Miller, author of a number of books which were banned in America, had Aries rising with its ruler Mars in Scorpio in the 7th. Sexual adventures and exploits (Mars in Scorpio in the 7th) were integral to his daring voyage of self-discovery (Mars rules the Aries Ascendant).

Taurus on the Ascendant and Scorpio on the Descendant

If Taurus, a fixed earth sign, is on the Ascendant, then life needs to be met more slowly and steadily. Rather than rushing into things, Taurus rising should plan, structure and work systematically towards its goals. The fixity of this sign on the Ascendant suggests that the person may need to hold onto or remain in one phase of experience much longer than Aries rising types. The danger is becoming too lazy or indolent and staying with something purely out of habit, attachment, and security when it has truly outlived its purpose or usefulness. It will be necessary for the Taurus rising to learn when to hold on and when to let go.

Those with Taurus rising also have a need to feel comfortable with the earthy and material sphere of life, and to see concrete and tangible results for their efforts. A sensible regard for the body and its requirements should be developed. Being too driven or ruled by the instincts is not the ideal, but cutting the self off from the basic instinctual nature is not a healthy situation either.

When Taurus is ascending, then Scorpio is found on the Descendant. This means that strong and intense emotions (Scorpio) will be evoked in the sphere of relationship. Jealousy and possessiveness can be the root of many interpersonal problems, and those with Taurus rising will have to confront, examine and gain greater mastery over the destructive side of their emotional nature. In other words, Scorpio on the 7th house cusp forces them to look inward, to probe hidden motivations and underlying causes in order to transform the way they use their power. The Scorpio Descendant does not allow them to take life at face value. Through relationship problems they are jarred from their lethargy and periodically required to cleanse and eliminate what they have stored up inside, changing old and outworn habit patterns.

I have noticed two different physical types associated with Taurus on the Ascendant. The more usual embodiment of this sign is solid, earthy-looking, and heavy-set: a healthy, 'country' look just right for 'a roll in the hay' or a Falstaffian appearance, often with the characteristically thick Taurean neck. On the other hand, some Taurus rising individuals exhibit a more delicate and chiselled look, emphasizing the aesthetic side of the Venus rulership of the sign. The actress Vivien Leigh (famous for her role as Scarlett O'Hara in *Gone With The Wind*) is an example of this type: she was born with Taurus rising and Venus, its ruler, in Libra.

Percy Bysshe Shelley, the English lyric poet described as fragile and delicate, also had Taurus rising and its ruler Venus in the 5th house of creative expression. Walt Whitman, with his rich appreciation of life and nature, had Venus rising in Taurus.

Gemini on the Ascendant and Sagittarius on the Descendant

If Gemini is rising, life should be met with inquisitiveness, curiosity, and the desire to figure out how people and things work. Versatility and adaptability are two of Gemini's assets, but can give rise to too many diverse interests and the 'jack of all trades and master of none' syndrome. This Ascendant hates to lose alternatives and being committed to just one thing means excluding so many others.

Developing the ability to communicate through writing, speaking or any other form of exchanging ideas contributes to their sense of identity as well as increasing their impact on the environment. In some way, they are meant to distribute information, picking up certain ideas or attitudes in one place and then depositing and applying these in other areas. If the rest of the chart is of an earthy or watery nature, the ability to be analytical, detached and objective is even more of a pressing need. However, if the rest of the chart is already airy and fiery, then this Rising sign adds to the restlessness of the nature and the difficulty in staying in one place long enough to truly deepen the understanding of that sphere or to become a real authority in that area. There is the danger of too quickly 'going into the head' and losing touch with the body and feelings.

If Gemini is rising, then Sagittarius is found on the 7th house cusp. Through a relationship, they are offered another person's philosophical frame of reference through which to understand, explore and interpret life. The best partner is someone who can counter-effect Gemini's tendency to become lost in a maze of ideas or a web of inconsequentials. The broader vision and aspirations of Sagittarius helps Gemini rising maintain a sense of direction and goal, rather than being constantly side-tracked. In short, other people often provide the sense of overall purpose which the Gemini Ascendant cannot find on its own.

Gemini rising is often embodied in a lithe, agile physique with slender hands, which when not busy gesticulating are clever at taking something apart and putting it back together again. The person may literally be 'of two minds' about many situations and even look like different people at different times. Often they are adept at impersonating others.

George Bernard Shaw, who used his acute mind and literary ability to promote his philosophical and social beliefs, is a good example of the Gemini Ascendant/Sagittarius Descendant combination. Vance Packard, the author of *The Hidden Persuaders* and *The Status Seekers* also used his fact-finding Gemini Ascendant to detect and expose the broader trends (Sagittarius) at work in contemporary society.

Cancer on the Ascendant and Capricorn on the Descendant

With Cancer on the Ascendant, greater self-realization is achieved through a sophisticated attunement to the feeling nature. Some people with Cancer rising (especially if the rest of the chart is predominantly watery, or if Neptune is strongly figured) are so emotionally vulnerable and exposed that they learn to protect themselves by developing a hard outer shell. Their task is to find ways of using their sensitivity rather than being overwhelmed by it. Others with Cancer rising (if the rest of the chart shows a great deal of air or earth) may be unaware of just how much is teeming under a cool and collected surface. This type will attract experiences which underline the need to acknowledge, respect and free the feelings.

The nature of the crab provides an apt description of the Cancer Ascendant. Besides being ready at a moment's notice to withdraw back into its shell, the crab has a way of approaching situations sideways, reflecting the non-confronting nature of this Rising sign. The crab is not comfortable all the time in the water, so it ventures out onto land, but then retreats back into the water again. Cancer rising also exhibits a two-steps-forward, one-step-backward dance-like ebb and flow. Cancer on the 1st house should learn to respect and 'go with' an internal and organic sense of their own timing and rhythm. In this respect, they are capable of 'tuning into' the cyclic nature of life. And yet there is a tenacity to the crab; its grasping claws do not easily relinquish what it holds onto. Those with Cancer rising cling to their feelings — be it joy or pain — and won't easily relinquish them until a stronger feeling overtakes. Explanations, reasons and rationalizations, while making perfect sense to an air sign rising, won't get you very far with the crab, and may even be turned against you.

The sign of Cancer is associated with the womb and breasts. The breasts provide the nourishment to sustain new life, and the womb provides the perfect environment in which something can grow. If Cancer is on the Ascendant, the person grows in self-awareness through developing qualities of nurturing and caring. Whether it's through fostering a family, a business project, or a strongly felt cause, Cancer rising blossoms and 'comes into its own'. However, if they shun any active version of the mother role, then they have a way of flipping to the other side: that is, looking for others to play mother to them. An over-identification with the mother, a tendency to stay too long within the womb of the family of origin, or a persistent search for the Ideal Mother they lost or never had, are some of the issues which may manifest with Cancer rising.

The opposite sign of Capricorn will be found on the 7th house cusp, and evokes those qualities which balance the extremes of Cancer. Those with Cancer rising may be flooded and swept away by upsurges of emotion and feeling, but maintaining a relationship demands that they discriminate between which emotions are appropriate and useful and which should be filtered or kept under control. Through partnership, a structure (Capricorn) is built, into which the otherwise random and chaotic feelings of Cancer can flow. They may enact their own need to achieve in the world through helping another person to become successful and established (Capricorn on the 7th). With this placement, a partner is sought who will offer security, strength and stability. At some point, however, Cancer rising will need to find these qualities from within, rather than importing others to provide them.

This Ascendant often has the characteristic 'moon face' — round, receptive and pleasing. Often there is a soft, fleshy appearance with a propensity to put on weight or retain fluids. The upper part of the body may be out of proportion to the rest of the torso.

The Austrian composer Franz Schubert was born with Cancer rising, and its ruler, the Moon, in Pisces in the 10th: an apt configuration for a man who expressed so much feeling through his career in music. Vincent Van Gogh had Cancer on the Ascendant with the Moon square to Neptune, Mars and Venus. His erratic life is a good example of the extremes of sensitivity and emotional chaos associated with this Rising sign.

Leo on the Ascendant and Aquarius on the Descendant

Leo rising creates a world in which the need to develop power, authority and creative expression are requisite to gaining a sense of individual selfhood. The house position of the Sun will designate the specific area of life through which this Ascendant can most naturally discover his or her own unique and special identity. It will be in that sphere that this person will seek love, admiration, applause and effectiveness.

However, for some with Leo rising, being effective is confused with being *a*ffective. Self-display, showiness and extravagant gestures are, in Leo's case, fuelled and prompted by the pressing need to be somebody and to feel important. *Anything* is better than just being ordinary. Those with Leo rising are preoccupied with something with which all of us are at some time concerned — emerging as an individual in our own right.

There is the danger that they might meet the world with too much pride. Some are born expecting to be treated like royalty; but they must be prepared to make an effort to earn the desired respect and status rather than angrily or hastily turning away if glory is not bestowed on them unquestioningly. Sometimes they are afraid or they hesitate to try to prove themselves just in case they should fail. Those who don't manage to develop a healthy outlet for their personal power or creativity sometimes do turn bitter and cynical at the world for not recognizing their genius.

Leo is associated with the heart centre in the body, and the sign has an enormous amount of love to give. Grand gestures aside, Leo rising, like the Sun, can bestow a generous warmth, healing and life-giving energy to those on the receiving end. However, this Ascendant will usually expect something in return, some sort of grateful acknowledgement for all that they have done. A turning point is reached when Leo rising can give without asking for anything back.

While it is crucial for those with Leo on the Ascendant to develop a healthy sense of their own power, authority and worth, Aquarius on the Descendant means that they will be confronted by people or situations which urge that life be viewed from a perspective other than that of the personal self. The individual can still be respected but must consider the requirements of the larger system of which he or she is a part. Aquarius on the 7th suggests that one-to-one relationships are a training ground for the sharing and promoting of common goals, thus neutralizing the possibly overly self-centred or egotistical slant of Leo on the 1st. In order to maintain a lasting relationship in which the personality of either party is not quashed, the fire and passion of Leo rising needs to be cooled and contained (but not extinguished) by the airy objectivity and fairness of Aquarius.

Former world heavyweight champion Muhammed Ali was born with Leo rising and its ruler, the Sun, in the 6th. He achieved his sense of greatness and individual worth (Leo on the 1st) through his skilful technique (6th) in the domain of work. The psychologist Anne Dickson, an adept teacher of assertiveness skills, is the author of *A Woman In Your Own Right,* an aptly named book for someone with Mars conjunct the Ascendant in Leo and the ruling Sun in the 10th house of career.

Physically, Leo on the Ascendant often manifests in a powerful and proud bearing which commands attention. Depending on the aspects to the Sun, there is sometimes the characteristic 'sunny' face and luminous, sparkling eyes.

Virgo on the Ascendant and Pisces on the Descendant

With Virgo rising, the birth into individual selfhood comes through mental analysis, discrimination, self-criticism and the process of defining the self more and more specifically. Often this entails developing greater skill and proficiency in the chosen field of work or area of creative expression. As an earth sign, there is the need to employ knowledge purposefully, to be useful, productive and of service.

Virgo on the Ascendant draws attention to the physical body and the concern for its smooth functioning. The practical management of the mundane necessities of daily life is also an issue for this sign rising.

Virgo in this position can be associated with what might be called 'the proper assimilation of experience'. Experience, like food, needs to be chewed over and then digested. Catabolic processes in the body separate what is valuable and worth integrating from what is toxic and poisonous. Virgo rising should apply this process to the digestion of life-experience. Through analysing the self and life in general, they can extract from experience whatever is most conducive to their well-being. What is not constructive must be acknowledged and recognized but ultimately cleared out and eliminated. Holding onto such things as negativity and resentment for too long means that the psyche, and sooner or later the body, becomes clogged, weakened and poisoned.

With Virgo rising, there is the danger of becoming so obsessive about order, correctness and precision that a person loses touch with spontaneity and flow. Where Virgo boxes itself in and becomes overly tight and rigid, Pisces appears in one form or another to say 'relax, let go, relinquish control, and let yourself indulge occasionally.' Pisces on the Descendant encourages Virgo rising to relate with others more compassionately and with a greater degree of sacrifice and acceptance than judgemental and critical Virgos usually allow themselves. Through the Pisces Descendant, Virgo rising gains the kind of understanding that dawns when the heart is open and receptive. There is more to life than just that which can be measured, compartmentalized and tested.

Virgo on the Ascendant usually gives a neat, wiry body, capable of efficient and economical movements. Often the person looks considerably younger than the actual age, and a youthful appearance is retained even in the later years. The placement by sign, house and aspect of its ruling planet Mercury, will shed more light on the person's appearance as well as his or her major focus of interest. For instance,

Jerry Rubin, a 1960s political activist, has Virgo rising with critical Mercury in the 11th house of social reform. Walter Koch, the astrologer and mathematician who painstakingly developed the complex and intricate system of house-division which bears his name, was born with the Sun, Moon, and Venus all rising in Virgo and Mercury in the 1st house.

Libra on the Ascendant and Aries on the Descendant

Whereas Aries rising calls for wilful, decisive and self-assertive action, Libra on the Ascendant requires deliberation and carefully chosen action based on an objective and fair assessment of any situation. In other words, what others need or want will have to be taken into consideration. Reflective judgement is a keynote for this Ascendant: various alternatives are weighed in the balance, and the most appropriate mode of being or acting is selected. However, the capacity to see another person's point of view as well as the ability to look at any situation from all its sides can be crippling to action. Hence the vacillation, the indecisiveness, and the sitting-on-the-fence reputation of Libra rising.

Choices are more easily made if we have a system of values on which to base them. The responsibility to establish a set of values, standards and ideals upon which action can be gauged rests heavily on the shoulders of this Ascendant. It would be so easy just to let another person decide for them. And even if Libra rising bases its actions on what is believed to be true and just, is there any guarantee that it will all work out beautifully in the end? A friend of mine is an avid sun-worshipper. On those rare days when the sun shines clearly and brightly in England, rather than spending the day at home in her back garden, she acts on her better judgement and dutifully drives to the office. As a reward we might reasonably expect that 'the gods' should smile down on her for such an honourable decision. But why does it always rain on her day off? Libra rising must learn to make choices and then take the consequences for them.

Libra rising also means striking a balance between the 'masculine' and 'feminine' sides of life, between mystical urges and practical notions, between 'head' and 'heart', intuition and logic, and most of all between what we want and need and what others want and need. Libra on the Ascendant searches for the perfect relationship, the ideal philosophy, and for that which is harmonious and pleasing. There is often an interest in the arts and an attraction to such abstract systems as politics or mathematics, which offer symmetry and completeness of concept. Many of Libra rising's beliefs and ideals may be too high-minded in relation to the harsher realities of life. At the same time, this Ascendant can be very critical when something does not meet what is desired or expected. And those with this placement can be very tough: 'In the name of harmony you had better see it my way or else.' (Could this be Aries creeping in?)

Relationships are important to Libra rising, and needed for personal evolution and growth. If Libra is on the Ascendant, then Aries is on the Descendant. In one sense, meeting Aries in the sphere of life associated with the partner elicits Libran qualities. If a partner is strongly self-centred and assertive (an Aries type), then the Libran Ascendant will *have* to learn to adjust and make concessions. However, if the other person becomes too unfair, pushy and demanding, then Libra rising learns to stand up for the self and *demand* the Libran traits of equality and balance. Opposites have a way of turning into one another. If the Libran Ascendant doesn't like the way you are running the show, you will soon know.

Most textbooks attribute Libra rising with physical charm and a well-proportioned body but with the stipulation that there is a tendency to put on weight due to laziness or over-indulgence. Air signs on the Ascendant generally have a refined rather than coarse look about them.

According to baptismal records, Adolf Hitler was born with Libra rising emphasizing the sometimes overlooked ferocity with which Libra will fight for its philosophy or political ideals, quashing whatever doesn't fit into its vision of harmony and perfection. For the sake of balance, I would cite examples of the many positive features of the Libra rising temperament in the charts of the sensitive poet Carl Sandburg with Venus in Pisces in the 5th house of creative expression; and Winston Churchill, with ruler Venus in the 3rd house of communication.

Scorpio on the Ascendant and Taurus on the Descendant

In the eighth labour of Hercules, the hero has to find and destroy the Hydra, a nine-headed monster who lives in a cave at the bottom of a murky swamp. At first, he tries to kill the beast while it is still in the water but every time he cuts off a head, three more appear in its place. Finally Hercules remembers the advice of his teacher: 'We rise by kneeling, we conquer by surrendering, and we gain by giving up.' He kneels down into the swamp and lifts the Hydra by one of its heads out of the water and into the air. Withdrawn from the water, the Hydra immediately begins to lose its power and wilt. Hercules cuts off all the heads, but a tenth one appears in the form of a precious jewel which he buries under a rock.

This story is closely related to the dynamics of Scorpio on the Ascendant. In one form or another, those with Scorpio rising must confront or grapple with that which is dark, taboo, hidden or destructive. Some will see the beast externally and fight what is dark and evil 'out there'. Dr Tom Dooley, the humanitarian dedicated to eliminating suffering in the world, had Scorpio rising, and Pluto, its ruler, in the 8th. For others, the Hydra lurks in the depths of their own psyches, symbolizing such destructive emotions as jealousy, envy, greed, excessive lust or power drives. Sigmund Freud, a Sun Taurus with Scorpio rising, saw the Hydra in the *id* — the raw, primitive, instinctual side of our natures.

Hercules succeeded in slaying the Hydra by lifting it out of the swamp and into the air. Similarly, Scorpio rising must bring into the light of consciousness what is dark and hidden inside. If Scorpionic energy is repressed, it seethes underneath, poisoning the psyche and giving rise to a stench which fouls the atmosphere between people. However, if the full force of these emotions are released in an unregenerate manner, their destructive power may be too much to bear.

A third alternative exists. Rather than either repressing the Scorpio side of the nature or acting it out altogether, it is possible to acknowledge the feelings involved and then transform or rechannel them more constructively. Like the jewel which appears when the Hydra is slain, negative complexes can be changed into something precious. Many artists have produced their best works through redirecting passion, anger or rage into a creative outlet. Goethe, the great German writer who tempted Faust with the Devil, had Scorpio rising.

The snake sheds a skin when growth and pressure from the inside renders the old skin too tight. Volcanic Scorpio rising accumulates internal pressure until an explosion, release and renewal must occur. By choice or coercion, this sign on the Ascendant wipes out and removes old forms and structures so that new ones can be built. Gandhi, Lenin, Mussolini, Stalin and Margaret Thatcher all were born with this Ascendant.

There is a depth to Scorpio rising which compels those who have this placement to burrow their way to the root of an issue in search of underlying meanings and motivations. Nothing is taken at face value. Like Bluebeard's wife, they may open doors which are better left closed. Scorpio rising draws Taurus on the Descendant to itself. Where Scorpio must challenge, attack, destroy and change, Taurus is patient, stable, down-to-earth and preserving. Taurus is equipped to withstand a Scorpio rising's onslaught and then calmly interject, 'Don't forget darling, dinner is at eight.' Those with Scorpio rising need to develop such Taurean qualities in relationship in order to balance the excesses and extremes of their turbulent and strongly felt passions.

The most obvious physical embodiment of Scorpio rising comes in the form of intense and piercing eyes set in a noticeably penetrating brow.

Sagittarius on the Ascendant and Gemini on the Descendant

The symbol of Sagittarius is the archer or centaur, usually depicted as a creature half-human and half-horse. The upper part shows the human torso aiming an arrow into the heavens, while the lower half, the horse, has its hoofs firmly planted on (or prancing over) the ground. Precariously balanced midway between the beasts and the gods, Sagittarius rising evinces this fundamental dilemma in its approach to life. One part of the nature aspires to great heights, noble ideals and lofty achievements, while another side is driven by more basic and instinctual animal urges. Can the animal side emulate the higher vision? The gap between what is and what could be is often painful for Sagittarius ascending to endure: creative ways to resolve the split need to be found.

Another image associated with Sagittarius is that of the Seeker — there is always further to go, always something else to chase after and pursue. With this as an Ascendant, life is best viewed as a journey or pilgrimage. Sometimes the journey itself is more fun than actually getting there: an old motto for the sign is 'I see the goal; I reach the goal and see another.'

As a fire sign situated on an angular house, Sagittarius rising generates heat and needs an outlet or focus for expressing its energy and enthusiasm. Provided they do not put people off by making too great a display of themselves, those with Sagittarius rising have a knack for inspiring others. This Ascendant also has the ability to imbue events in life with symbolic meaning and importance. Therefore something is not seen as existing in isolation but is appreciated in relation to a larger truth or principle.

The dangers of this Ascendant are those of inflation, overdoing and extravagance. Like Icarus, they may fly too high only to crash down to earth later. Some habitually live beyond their means. Others live too much in the realm of possibilities and never succeed in grounding their vision in concrete terms. How much a problem this is will depend on the strength of the element earth or the principle of Saturn in the rest of the chart.

The house placement of Jupiter, the ruling planet of Sagittarius may show the area of life through which they believe fulfilment might come. It is also the domain through which they can broaden or expand others, or where they might be prone to excesses.

The former astronaut John Glenn has Sagittarius rising and Jupiter in the house of long journeys. Bob Dylan, the songwriter and singer who inspired a whole generation, was born with Sagittarius rising and Jupiter in the 5th house of creative expression.

Gemini on the Descendant is the necessary counterpoint to Sagittarius on the Ascendant. In the context of a partnership, those with Sagittarius rising can observe at close range the basic laws and patterns of existence which they have intuited. A Gemini-type mate is ideal for them. The Geminian mind can find the precise words to give expression to the broader concepts and feelings of Sagittarius. Gemini can analyse and question the conclusions of Sagittarius and thereby force the latter to think things through more thoroughly. Gemini provides Sagittarius with the immediate practical steps which can be taken in order to realize goals and aspirations. Sagittarius decides it must get away on holiday, but it is the Geminian part of the self which reaches for the telephone directory and finds the number of the travel agent. Again, as with the other Ascendant-Descendant combinations, the Descendant qualities can be imported via another person or they can be developed within the self in the quest for wholeness.

On the physical level, Sagittarius rising may exhibit a high degree of restlessness. Sometimes there is the characteristic broad mouth or 'horsey' grin, as if it must be that large to allow room for all they have to say. Because of the expansive nature of this sign, there can be weight problems when it is placed on the Ascendant.

Capricorn on the Ascendant and Cancer on the Descendant

Saturn, the ruler of Capricorn, has a split personality in mythology. On the one hand, we hear about him castrating his father and eating his children. In this sense, he represents a repressive principle — critical, cold and harsh. On the other hand, however, in Roman mythology he ruled over the Golden Age. The Saturnalia was a festival of licence, sensuality, abundance and indulgence — the time of the cornucopia.

The qualities of Capricorn on the Ascendant reflect the dual nature of Saturn. Remembering the general principle that we find ourselves through developing the qualities of the Ascendant, Capricorn there suggests that an appreciation of these two sides of life are needed.

The first side of Capricorn is well documented. With this sign rising, there is often the sense that a stern father watches over them expecting obedience and certain achievements from his children. The energy and enthusiasm of the previous sign, Sagittarius, must be used practically and productively and within defined limits. They cannot just flow or float with whatever comes along or allow themselves to be swept away by every whim or passion. In order to meet the requirements of the *father-in-oneself,* Capricorn rising has to cautiously plan and structure the life, building logically and slowly towards achieving goals and ambitions. Energy must be carefully measured out and this calls for discipline and control. Capricorn rules the knees and sooner or later those with this Ascendant must bend in submission to a higher authority — internal or external — which expects something of them. Like Job, it is often through hardship and frustration that Capricorn rising is humbled and learns to accept certain laws, limits and structures. Like Christ, there may be doubts at the last minute whether the sacrifices were all worth it.

In short, Capricorn rising needs to 'make something of the self' and achieve some degree of collective validation and respect. They may rebel and try to escape lessons and responsibilities, but eventually it dawns that they simply feel better if they face obligations, whether to themselves or others.

What about the other side of Saturn — the deity who ruled over the Golden Age? As a cardinal earth sign, Capricorn has the capacity to operate very efficiently in the material world. Through developing their potential adeptness in handling and organizing practical affairs, Capricorn rising experiences a sense of fulfilment and accomplishment. Next to Virgo, no other Ascending sign is better capable of creating order out of chaos than Capricorn, or taking a vision of possibilities and making it real. And we mustn't forget the Pan or Satyr side of earthy Capricorn — the capacity to enjoy the physical senses and the natural world. Perhaps it is because Capricorn rising is so aware of the harsher realities of life, that they can, by contrast, savour that which is sensual and beautiful.

Capricorn rising has the feeling and watery sign of Cancer on the Descendant. The soft-edged, fleshy and rounded image of Cancer opposes and naturally moderates the rigidity and inflexibility of Capricorn. Capricorn rising may look so tough to the world, but often runs home to be pampered and mothered by its mate. In spite of an external hardness or diffidence, those with Capricorn on the

Ascendant are unusually sensitive to the feelings of those close to them and often adapt themselves to meet their partners' needs. The stern and judging Father is mediated by the all-accepting and protective Mother. If in one sphere of life we go too far in one direction, life compensates for it in other places.

Many astrologers believe that Capricorn rising, like good wine, matures or ripens well, becoming better and happier with time. Physically, Capricorn on the cusp of the 1st often appears fairly wiry and lean, and there is usually something distinctive about the bone structure in the face. Sometimes, like Pan and his followers, they look a little devilish.

Machiavelli is an example of the harsher and more stringent side of Capricorn rising. He used his sensitivity to other people (Cancer on the Descendant) as a means of better manipulating and controlling situations to his gain. Yehudi Menuhin, the great violinist, is an example of the side of Capricorn rising which will work hard and discipline the self to bring gifts and talents to the world (ruling Saturn in the 7th conjunct Neptune, the planet of music).

Aquarius on the Ascendant and Leo on the Descendant

Ironically, those with Aquarius on the Ascendant (the point of self-awareness) gain a clearer sense of their own unique and particular identity through standing back and taking an objective and impersonal look at life. Viewing events, people, circumstances and even themselves from a detached perspective affords them a more global or complete picture of the plan of things. A greater awareness of 'the group' and a heightened sense of the social context in which they function supersedes a purely subjective or personal frame of reference.

As discussed under the 11th house, Aquarius is co-ruled by Saturn and Uranus. The Saturn side of Aquarius rising may look to a group to enhance its own sense of identity or importance. Along with this comes concerns about belonging to the 'right' group, doing the 'right' things, etc. The more Uranian side of Aquarius on the Ascendant, however, may feel it is inappropriate to conduct the life solely for augmenting or bolstering personal security or power. Something larger than the individual self needs to be considered.

On this basis, more than any other Ascending sign, Aquarius rising can act in accordance with what he or she feels will support or improve the functioning of the greater whole. The sign of Aquarius has been associated with the myth of Prometheus. Believing that humankind could be better off than it already was, Prometheus stole fire from the gods to give to man. Similarly, Aquarius rising can best meet life with a sense of hope and vision of a new future: a belief that with the application of the right theories or concepts, circumstances could be improved. But just as Prometheus is punished by the existing powers for his defiant deed, some modern-day Prometheans may be condemned, mistreated or even imprisoned for theories or actions which transgress or threaten the established authority. And yet, it is the nature of life that old structures and paradigms, when outlived or past their usefulness, give way to fresh patterns and ideas. Aquarius rising is often in tune with the latest trends and new ideas in the atmosphere.

Usually the ideals associated with Aquarius rising are egalitarian — brotherhood, sisterhood, solidarity, fairness, equality and justice for all. For these ends, Aquarius on the Ascendant may assume the cause of segments of society which the existing system condemns or oppresses. (Abraham Lincoln, reputedly born at sunrise, is believed to have had Aquarius on the Ascendant.) Sometimes the vision of this Ascendant is too idealistic and underestimates the force of the more greedy, territorial and acquisitive nature of people. Similarly, those with this Rising sign are often ill at ease with irrational and self-centred emotions in themselves or others which conflict with their noble and utopian theories. Immanuel Kant, the German philosopher who wrote on ethics and aesthetics, had Aquarius on the 1st. The clear-eyed mystic philosopher Krishnamurti was born with Aquarius rising and Uranus in the 9th house of higher understanding.

Leo on the Descendant is the shadow side of Aquarius on the Ascendant. Beneath the cool objectivity and the egalitarian ideals of Aquarius may lurk the Leo urges for personal power and recognition. Those with Aquarius rising, with all their love of equality and freedom, are often attracted to prestigious and influential people. There may even be a tendency to use others as a means of gaining strength, power and importance (Leo on the 7th). For all their lack of self-centredness, they may sulk for hours if somebody makes them look silly at a party. (The other person will probably get the cold shoulder for days.) Leo feels passionately and intensely and uses its own sense of self, honour and prestige as a primary frame of reference. To avoid some form of Leo backlash, either from within or without, Aquarius rising is well-advised not to overly denigrate the Leo approach to life. With Aquarius, there is the danger that the needs of the efficiently functioning system will take precedence over the uniqueness, human-ness and creative individuality of those who must fit into it. Taken to extremes, the Aquarian dream could too easily turn into an Orwellian nightmare.

Physically, Aquarius rising tends towards a broad build with clear, refined, light and open features. Often there is an electric or magnetic charge in the aura.

Pisces on the Ascendant and Virgo on the Descendant

Pisces rising can embody any of the various manifestations associated with this complex and elusive sign. Like the two fishes swimming in opposite directions in the glyph, the urge to form a concrete and solid sense of ego-identity conflicts with those forces which encourage the dissolution and transcendence of ego-boundaries. The resolution to this dilemma requires that the person with Pisces rising develop an identity which does not exclude the awareness of being part of something greater than the self. Too rigid a personality would make this impossible, and yet too diffuse an identity would create difficulties in effectively dealing with life. In the former situation, nothing beyond the ego-boundaries could filter into the awareness, while in the latter case, the person is overwhelmed by his or her sensitivity and openness. The dangers are inflexibility on the one hand and chaos and disintegration on the other.

Pisces on the Ascendant may manifest on any of the three levels traditionally associated with this sign: the victim, the artist or the healer/saviour. The victim does not cope well with the more difficult realities of the world and seeks an escape route or crutch — perhaps turning to drugs or alcohol as a way of release. Vague and confused, Pisces rising may flow with whatever is happening, letting other people make choices for them. Some may try to escape the net of daily tedium and entrapment within traditional societal frameworks, turning to crime, underground activity and villainous behaviour.

However, another expression of this sign on the Ascendant is the artistic type. Inspired by the imaginal realms of the psyche, the artist channels his or her perceptions through some sort of medium. The third level, the healer or saviour, dedicates the life to serving others, endeavouring to make real a vision of life glimpsed in a more expanded state of consciousness. Pain 'out there' in the world is felt as their own pain. On all three levels, to varying degrees, this Ascendant is taken over by something which obliterates or supersedes a more mundane existence or limited view of life.

A keynote for Pisces rising is the sacrifice of the personal will. However, if taken to an extreme, those with this Ascendant may repeatedly set up situations through which others take advantage of them. Besides being trampled on like the proverbial doormat, a lack of clear prohibitions and boundaries often means abandoning the self to emotions and appetites which in the long run are excessive and self-destructive. Virgo on the Descendant provides the balancing principles of discrimination, common sense and a healthy respect of caution and limits. Others may need to provide these qualities but ultimately those with Pisces rising are much better off if they can find such traits within themselves. Some with this configuration will be so absorbed in spiritual ecstasies or high-flown missions that they will require partners to manage the more trivial and mundane necessities of everyday life (Virgo on the 7th). Sometimes the Pisces rising type will be so idealistic and romantic, that unconsciously they are highly critical and condemning of others (Virgo Descendant) for not living up to their expectations. Others with Pisces rising derive their identity solely through rescuing or serving others (Virgo on the 7th).

Physically, Pisces on the 1st may have a dreamy, romantic or mysterious quality in the face. The eyes may be large and almost like liquid. Often the overall features are soft and rounded. Like plastic, they can mould their looks into different shapes. In their manner, they may exude a receptivity and willingness-to-please allure which charms and seduces others. Sometimes they exhibit such a degree of helplessness that others are inspired to come to their rescue.

The famous conductor Leopold Stokowski was born with Pisces rising and Neptune, its ruler, in Taurus in the 2nd House. Pisces on the 1st gives the openness to music, and Neptune in earthy Taurus in the 2nd enabled him to concretely channel or literally 'conduct' his inspiration. Swinburne, the dissolute English poet whose poetic voice in many ways articulated the Pre-Raphaelite movement, had Pisces rising and Neptune in the 11th house of groups.

The Ascendant Complex

It has already been mentioned that a number of factors influence the workings of the Ascendant in addition to what sign is on the 1st house cusp. These include:

1. The ruling planet of the sign on the Ascendant, and its placement by sign, house and aspects.
2. Planets near the Ascendant (within ten degrees of the cusp either in the 1st or 12th houses).
3. Aspects to the Ascendant itself.

The Ruling Planet

The planet which rules the sign on the cusp of the 1st house, known as the ruler of the Ascendant and sometimes referred to as the chart ruler, suggests how the sign on the Ascendant may seek expression. Its position by sign, house and aspect should be carefully scrutinized.

For example, if Aries is rising, then Mars is the ruling planet. The elemental placement of Mars shows what stimulates the Aries rising. Mars in a fire sign is aroused by something it envisions or intuits. In a water sign, Mars is stimulated by emotions and feelings. Mars in air is excited by something it contemplates or thinks, while Mars in earth is motivated by a sense of something practical or concrete to be gained by action. If Mars is in watery Cancer or Pisces, the physical vitality of the Aries rising is less obvious than if Mars is in the fiery signs of Aries, Leo or Sagittarius.

The house placement of the ruler of the Ascendant suggests the area of life where important experiences which directly influence growth and self-discovery are met. Continuing with Aries rising as an example, the house placement of its ruler Mars will elaborate on the field of experience which requires the Aries need for action and decisiveness. If Mars is in the 2nd house, the person should develop greater potency handling money and the material world. If Mars is in the 3rd house, enhancing self-expression, communication skills and developing the intellect yield a fuller sense of self.

Aspects to the ruling planet shed light on the way a person functions as well as the manner and direction the expression of the Ascendant takes. For example, the quality and direction of energy exhibited by an Aries rising with Mars conjunct Jupiter will be very different from the Aries rising with Mars conjunct Saturn.

The size of the 1st house will depend on whether a sign of long ascension or short ascension is rising relative to the hemisphere in which the person is born, and also on the house system chosen in setting up the chart. Some people will have a very large 1st house, sometimes an arc of as much as sixty degrees. They may have one sign on the Ascendant, another intercepted, and a portion of a third sign leading into the next house. All of the qualities represented by the signs there will need to be developed in some way, although the sign on the cusp will carry the most weight. The placement of the ruling planet of any sign in the 1st house can be examined in the same way as the ruler of the Ascending sign.

Planets near the Ascendant

Planets on or near the Ascendant (within ten degrees either in the 12th or the 1st) enhance or modify Ascendant qualities. If Aries is rising, but Neptune is conjunct the Ascendant, the urge to assert the self is affected by the sensitivity and diffuseness of Neptune. However, if Jupiter or Uranus should be there instead, the person's will-power and directness are increased.

Aspects to the Ascendant

Planets aspecting the Ascendant itself will show whether other qualities in the person are in harmony or conflict with the type of expression required by the sign on the Ascendant. For instance, Saturn *squaring* an Aries Ascendant might suggest that the person's fear, caution or reserve (Saturn) inhibits the full force of the Rising sign. If Saturn *opposes* the Ascendant, the person may feel restricted by others. Saturn *sextile* or *trine* the Aries Ascendant suggests that the person knows just the right amount of effort to apply in a given situation and also possesses a good degree of discipline and practicality to further achieving objectives. In short, both the nature of the planet and the nature of the aspect need to be taken into consideration to judge its influence on the Ascendant in question.

18.
THE SUN AND LEO THROUGH THE HOUSES

The symbol for the Sun is a circle with a dot in the middle. The circle, which has no beginning or end, stands for unboundedness and infinity, and the dot represents the individual as a separate entity — who has his or her own personal identity and yet is part of that greater whole. The Ascendant is the path we follow to find who we are, but the Sun is what we discover or what we seek to become. Through developing the qualities of the sign the Sun is in, and through encountering the sphere of life designated by its house placement, we gain a greater sense of our power, purpose and direction in life.

Very simply, the house position of the Sun indicates where we need to distinguish ourselves in some way — to radiate our influence, shine forth, stand out and be special. It is the area of life through which we separate from the archetypal Mother, recognizing our own individual identity rather than remaining fused with the rest of creation. While the Moon is swayed by deeply embedded instincts and habit patterns from the past, the Sun has the power to provoke change, to implement choice, and to create fresh alternatives in the area of the chart in which it is found. Just as the Sun in the heavens is the centre of our solar system and influences the planets to revolve around it, the position of the Sun in the birthchart shows where we ought to develop the power to be self-generating and causal rather than merely reactive.

Like the hero in the world's myths, the Sun's house placement is where we have to fight dragons, confront life, and overcome obstacles and forces which hinder our advancement and unfoldment. Expanding and developing in the Sun's domain usually involves a struggle, which, if successful, enables us to emerge forth with a more solid and coherent sense of 'I'.

The significance of the Sun in a house is similar to the influence that Leo has on a house — whether Leo is on the cusp, intercepted, or completing a house which has Cancer on the cusp. In the following analysis of the Sun through the houses, a sense of the meaning of Leo in each house can also be gleaned. (For instance, if you have Leo on the cusp of the 2nd, or contained in the 2nd, then you can read the section headed the Sun in the 2nd to learn more about how Leo in the 2nd might manifest.)

Also note that the house with Leo on the cusp (or some or all of Leo contained within it) will somehow be related to the house in which the Sun is placed. For example, the French poet Jean Cocteau was born with the Sun in the 3rd house ruling Leo on the cusp of the 5th. In an effort to communicate his ideas to others (Sun in the 3rd) he explored a wide range of artistic media (Leo on the 5th) including film, verse, novels, theatre and set design. He kept experimenting with his creative style (5th) in order to express himself as fully as possible (Sun in the 3rd).

Sun in the 1st

Those born with the Sun in the 1st are born just before sunrise when the creative forces of day and light are gaining supremacy over the darkness of night. As the Sun edges its way over the horizon, the planet wakes up — hidden things become visible, greater activity commences, and people drag themselves out of bed and into the world. The Sun in this position has an obvious stimulating effect on life and those born at this time should have a similar impact. These people are meant to influence and catch the attention of others, to radiate their power in such a way that others are attracted to their energy and warmth. They should meet life with vigour, enthusiasm and the determination to make something of themselves. Rather than relying on the family background to feel important and gain a sense of identity, they need to forge their own 'place in the Sun' and be appreciated and respected for what they themselves can do, create or make happen. These people should not go unnoticed. They require a position in life which exercises their natural authority and fulfils their desire for recognition.

The constitution should be strong if the Sun is in the 1st, although this will very much depend on the sign it is in and aspects to it. When the Sun and the Ascendant are in the same sign, astrologers say that the person is a double Aries, double Taurus, etc. In this case, they usually clearly exemplify and embody the qualities of that sign. For instance, the great emancipator and advocate of personal freedom, Abraham Lincoln, was born with the Sun rising in egalitarian

Aquarius. The American television star Ed Asner (formerly the lead in 'Lou Grant') was born with the Sun rising in Scorpio. In courageously speaking out against what he felt were political injustices he could not tolerate (Sun in Scorpio in 1st) he upset the show business establishment and gravely disrupted his life and career (Scorpio Sun rules Leo on the 10th of career and reputation).

If the Sun is well-aspected in the 1st, the influence of the early environment is likely to be supportive of the person's desire to express his or her individuality. Usually their birth will draw much attention, as if to corroborate their need to feel important. A negative expression of the Sun in the 1st may be an overbearing personality, extreme egocentricity, and excessive pride. Those who do not manage to express or develop a healthy outlet for their power and authority may turn bitter and cynical. Rather than being resentful if their worth is not acknowledged unquestioningly, they should recognize that admiration and appreciation from others must be earned first.

Sun in the 2nd

If the Sun or Leo are in the 2nd house, this area of life should be met with vitality and forcefulness: there is a pressing need to develop personal skills, values and resources to achieve a sense of individuality. They need to find and define what constitutes security for them, rather than relying on other people to provide safety, money or resources. A sense of power and self-worth can be gained through acquiring money and possessions and through the ability to manage and organize the material world. Some may incline towards status-seeking, showiness and extravagance to prove their value and enhance an insecure internal identity. They can be generous with money and possessions but usually expect some sort of recognition in return. Wherever the Sun is, is where the personal ego is seeking acknowledgement. The impeccable, internationally loved singer and actor, Maurice Chevalier, had the Sun in Virgo in the 2nd: he was born in a slum and died a millionaire.

The nature of whatever planet is in the 2nd house is valued because those qualities offer us security. Therefore, with the Sun in the 2nd, security comes through developing and possessing such attributes as strength, nobility, authority, a sense of specialness, and courage. People with this placement will feel safer in life if they foster these traits, regardless of how much money is in the bank.

Sun in the 3rd

Rather than just absorbing and reflecting attitudes and influences from the environment, these people should develop and honour their own thoughts, views and perspective on things. A sense of value, worth and power comes through strengthening the intellect and communication abilities. Often they feel the most alive when they are learning something, or when they can be sharing and exchanging their ideas and knowledge with others. Those with the Sun in the 3rd (or Leo in this house) need to feel heard and to be noticed in the immediate environment. Consequently, rivalry with siblings and competitiveness among peers could be issues worth investigating. Some may project their own need for power and authority onto a brother or sister. Or knowledge itself is worshipped like the Sun. Difficult aspects to the Sun in the 3rd could indicate problems with early schooling. These will need to be examined if learning is to proceed unfettered. No matter how clever or articulate the 3rd house Sun appears to others, those with this placement normally feel that they could still know more or communicate better. The American writer Philip Roth, author of many best-selling books and known for his repartee and quick wit, was born with the Sun in the 3rd. The Nobel prize winning author George Bernard Shaw, who espoused his personal philosophy through his writing, was born with the Sun in Leo in this house.

Sun in the 4th (Leo on the IC)

Those with the Sun in the 4th need to delve deep inside to find themselves. What is achieved in the outer world is perhaps less important than what is accomplished in terms of soul-growth and inner spiritual development.

The struggle to define the self rages on the home front. They need to distinguish their own individual identity as distinct from the family background without denying that they are also part of the family. On one side, the danger is deriving the identity too much from the ancestry and becoming just a replica of what it represents or how it has shaped them. On the other side, however, there is the danger of totally rejecting the background altogether as a means of freeing themselves from its imposition. The first instance denies their own uniqueness and originality; the second denies their 'fate' — their biological and psychological roots. The task at hand is somehow combining the two: acknowledging their heredity and links with the family of origin, and yet as the same time developing an identity in their own right. They may carry something of the tradition of the family, and yet do it in their own way.

If the 4th house is taken to be the father, energies here may be experienced through the father or projected onto him. Those with the Sun in this house might have experienced the father as so powerful and authoritative that they subsequently cannot surmount a crippling sense of their own smallness or inferiority. They may have to do battle with the father to sever the hold he has on them. In other cases, the father may have been physically or psychologically absent. For the boy-child this could mean that there wasn't a clear sense of a father upon which to model his own masculine qualities. These would have to be found from within the self. For the girl-child, the experience of the absent father could entail a lifetime search for the lost father. She, too, would ultimately need to 'find' father qualities inside.

There is a strong need to own their own homes where they can exercise authority and influence. Sometimes there is a prolonged search for the right place to root.

The Sun in the 4th suggests that they come more into their own in the second half of life. A renewed sense of creative potency, vitality, and the joys of self-expression are potentially available in the later years.

The nature of the Sun in the 4th is similar to Leo on the IC. A deep need to express their own unique and special identity is the foundation upon which much of the life is built.

Sun in the 5th

The Sun is strongly placed in the 5th, its natural domain. For those with this placement, a sense of identity, power and purpose in life is found through wholeheartedly engaging in activities which make them feel good about being alive. The need to give expression to the self is vital to physical and psychological health and people become ill and depressed if they have nothing to live for. Of course, they also fall sick if they are trying to pack too much in. It is not a case of how much the 5th house Sun can do, but rather the *quality* of the involvement and the degree of satisfaction which is obtained from it.

Some form of artistic expression is advised — not necessarily in order to be another Mozart (Sun in Aquarius in the 5th) or Matisse (Sun in Capricorn in the 5th), but more for the sake of freeing the spirit, releasing emotions and feelings, and having the opportunity to create from inside the self. The richness of life is also enhanced through hobbies, sporting events, recreational pursuits, trips to the theatre, art galleries, etc.

The 'playful child' is alive and well in someone with a 5th house

Sun and struggling to be free. No matter how creative people with this placement may appear to others, they usually feel they could be better at whatever it is they do. The Sun by nature is expansive and in the 5th it seeks to express itself more and more and continually increase its territory of influence. A good example of the spirit of the Sun in the 5th is Sir Richard Burton, the scholarly English explorer who wrote about his adventures in exotic lands. His 5th house Sun ruled Leo in the 9th and 10th houses of long journeys and career.

For those with the Sun in the 5th, love affairs and romance heighten their sense of participation in life as well as embellishing their feelings of specialness. Producing children is another way they can bolster their sense of identity as well as extending their power and influence. There is a danger, though, that a parent with this placement could attempt to 'live out' his or her life too much through a child, projecting unfulfilled needs for fame and glory onto the offspring. The child might be exhibited like a work of art in the hopes that what has been 'produced' will be praised.

The need to be the centre of attention is very strong with the Sun in the 5th and these people may be unable to tolerate situations in which all eyes are not focused on them. A difficultly aspected Sun in this house could resort to devious, manipulative or exaggerated ways of gaining attention: even negative 'strokes' are better than no 'strokes' at all.

Sun in the 6th

With the Sun in the 6th, the experiences needed to develop a solid ego-identity revolve around health, daily ritual and work. Without becoming unduly obsessive, those with this placement should pay particular attention to matters of self-improvement. Physical and psychological weaknesses and imperfections are often highlighted in some way so that necessary adjustments can be made.

First and foremost, they need to form a good relationship to the body — respecting the physical vehicle is a lesson they sooner or later must learn. Unfortunately, for some, the recognition of the importance of caring for the body only registers when the consequences of neglect and ill-treatment have gone too far and manifested in illness. And yet, even if difficulties do arise in this area, the quest back to health and wholeness will serve the larger process of individuation more appropriately than other paths. They also have the ability to enlighten and illumine other people about better ways to participate in maintaining good health.

Those with the Sun in the 6th should strive to develop skills and abilities which secure them a useful place in the employment market. A sense of personal worth, value, and distinction is obtained in this way. They 'find themselves' through being of service to others.

There is a need to organize effective daily rituals and routines which ensure a smoother running of the life. Learning to function efficiently in practical matters strengthens the sense of identity. This is not the placement of someone who should just sit and meditate all day. It is surprising what poignant realizations can dawn scrubbing the kitchen floor or washing your socks. With the Sun in the 6th, accepting boundaries and routines empowers a person to perfect and refine the art of living. The end results of this attitude are not necessarily glaring, but show ever so subtly and tastefully in all the person does, recalling a Zen saying: 'Before enlightenment carry water, after enlightenment carry water.'

Sun in the 7th

When the philosopher Martin Buber wrote that 'Man becomes an I through a You,' he could have been referring to those with the Sun in the 7th. Almost paradoxically, a sense of their own power, purpose and individuality is found through partnership and relationship. Participating in joint activities raises issues which enable them to define who they are more clearly. Through the ups and downs and entanglements encountered in the attempt to form vital, honest and life-supporting alliances, the identity is shaped and strengthened. It is a fact of life that something exists more clearly if it can be seen in relation to something else; likewise, a personality has more meaning when seen in relation to other personalities. When the Sun shines in Libra's house, the 'I' needs a 'Thou'.

However, it doesn't always work this way. In some cases, those with the Sun in the 7th may try to abscond with another person's identity by finding someone who will be big and strong for them or who will tell them what to do with their lives. Or they may be preoccupied with gaining prestige and authority through aligning themselves with an important or influential figure, or by looking for a hero or heroine they can serve, worship and forever adore. In a man or woman's chart, the Sun here can indicate a search for a 'daddy' figure. In short, an attempt is made to 'live out' the solar principle through projecting it onto the partner. This is different to discovering the self via the help of another. It is also less productive, and often doesn't succeed for very long.

The 7th house also depicts how we interact with society in general. For the sake of the individuation process, those with the Sun in the

7th need to be involved with people. Princess Diana of England, whose marriage to Prince Charles became the focus of world attention and made her a celebrity in her own right, has the Sun in the 7th. Some may even find a vocation which deals with the issues of interpersonal relationships — marriage guidance counselling, for instance, or work which requires skill in arbitration and diplomacy. Leo on the Descendant is similar in meaning to the Sun in the 7th.

Sun in the 8th

On a deep level, we all yearn to reconnect with something greater than the self. Although often oblivious to such underlying motivations, those with the Sun in the 8th seek to expand themselves and transcend their personal limitations and separateness through some form of union and interchange with other people. This can be achieved in a variety of ways and on many different levels. For instance, some people with the Sun here augment their identity, value and worth by drawing to them other people's money and possessions. At worst, this is premeditated and conniving (not unlike a formal invitation to a midnight feast at Count Dracula's castle). More often, however, it just happens that other people naturally want to help those with an 8th house Sun — shower them with gifts, leave them inheritances, bestow grants upon them, etc. Frequently the urge to invest their energies in joint or collective enterprises brings them into the realm of business, banking, insurance and anything to do with other people's money and resources.

But money and possessions are just the surface level of what is shared and exchanged between people. Feelings and emotions circulating in the invisible undercurrents which connect one person to another also demand the attention of an 8th house Sun. Although these may appear to be the brainchild of a sadistic god who has watched too many soap operas on television, relationships which expose hidden passions and trigger the primal emotions of unresolved childhood complexes also serve the solar processes of growth and unfoldment. Releasing psychic content from the bondage and repetition of patterns established years before in the nursery, intimate partnerships act as catalysts for breakdown, regeneration and change. For those with the Sun in the 8th, relationships are not something to dip a toe into for refreshment every once in a while; they must learn to swim in these waters. Some may try to avoid real intimacy altogether, but in doing so they cheat themselves of transformation.

The 8th house Sun usually bestows an interest in that which is hidden, occult, or mysterious in life. Sometimes there is a fascination or preoccupation with death or any subject which society considers taboo. The daredevil Evil Knievel who constantly tests his strength and power performing death-defying stunts was born with the heroic Sun in this house. The film director, Sam Peckinpah, whose movies expose the more violent undercurrents of life, has the Sun in Pisces here. Hugh Hefner, the founder of *Playboy* magazine, one of the first widely circulated publications to write openly on sex, has the Sun in Aries in the 8th.

Sun in the 9th

Those with this placement should strive to broaden their understanding and perspective on life. This can be achieved through travel, extensive reading, flights of the imagination, or through philosophical enquiry into the 'whys and wherefores' of existence. The capacity to perceive deeper meanings and patterns which operate in the collective and personal spheres of life, vitalizes and empowers the Sun in this house.

As with any Sagittarian emphasis, life is best viewed as a journey or pilgrimage. In fact, some may come to believe, like the Spanish writer Cervantes, that 'the road is better than the inn.' Rather than swallowing whole any one belief system, insight gained through the exploration of different groups, philosophies or religions can be distilled into a personal vision of the truth. Sharing and exchanging their insights with others helps them to distinguish themselves.

There is the danger of becoming so overly concerned with 'the big picture' and abstract issues of life that they lose touch with everyday reality. Obsessed with what the future might bring, an immediate here-and-now participation in life is somehow lost in the shuffle. They may be so busy planning life and mapping out the future that they forget to live it. Sometimes they abound with good advice and counsel for others, and yet never quite manage to apply it to their own predicaments.

This placement suits a variety of vocations. They may excel at public relations work where they promote a concept or vision to inspire other people. They are adept at 'selling trips' — extolling the virtues of an African holiday, for instance, even though they may have never been there themselves. They make excellent managers and coaches, directing and organizing others towards achieving some common goal. They fire others with their enthusiasm and vision, and often spread knowledge through teaching, writing or publishing.

The philosophical German writer Thomas Mann was born with the Sun in the 9th. He believed that human beings were 'a great experiment . . . the failure of which would be the failure of creation itself'. He added that even if this point of view were not true, it would be better 'for man to behave as if it were so'.[1] The Sun in the 9th *needs* something to believe in.

Sun in the 10th (Leo on the MC)

With the Sun in the 10th, the identity is bound up with career and professional achievements. The 10th house describes the qualities in ourselves which we wish others to notice: in this case, the Sun strives to be seen as emanating power, strength and authority in respect to the sign in which it is placed. The Sun in Gemini there, for instance, wants the power of its intellect acknowledged; the Sun in Pisces craves recognition for its power to heal, enchant, or inspire, etc.

The Sun in the 10th has a deep urge to be admired as 'a Somebody'. Some degree of ambition should be 'owned' and satisfied if they are to fulfil their life-purpose. Examples of people born with this placement include the business executive John DeLorean (Sun in Capricorn) who tirelessly worked to make a name for himself; the actor Mickey Rooney (Sun in Libra), a childhood star who made his way 'to the top' and stayed there; and General Rommel (Sun in Scorpio) whose cunning as a field-marshal earned him the nickname 'the desert fox'. Women with this placement who do not satisfy their own need to achieve through a career may be drawn to prestigious or successful men as partners (the 'Hollywood wives' syndrome). For either sex, conflicts between the home and personal life versus achieving publicly and professionally are shown by oppositions from the 4th house to the 10th house Sun. The kind of self-exertion, dedication and perseverance required to ascend the ladder of success often limits the freedom and spontaneity to move in other directions. Another danger with this placement is that the sense of identity or worth could rely too much on their title or position in the world. Should that be lost, they are left totally bereft and annihilated.

If the 10th house is taken to be the mother, then the Sun in this position makes her very important. The child with the Sun here could project his or her own identity and power onto the mother: her needs and wants become the child's needs and wants. Conversely, this placement sometimes indicates a mother who requires that the child mirror her, imposing her own individuality onto the offspring, as in the classic example of the 'stage mother'. ('I'm a frustrated actress, so my child is going to learn to act.') Usually there is a collusion here: the child worships and adores the mother and offers the self up to her — 'You want me as your showpiece and I want to be that for you.' At some point, those with the Sun in the 10th must examine how much they are doing something for themselves, and how much it is being done to win Mother's love. Leo on the MC or contained within the 10th house implies some of the same meaning as the Sun there.

Sun in the 11th

Those with the Sun in the 11th establish a more cogent sense of identity through social, humanitarian or political activities. The phrase 'no man is an island' is commonplace, but it still has particular significance for this placement.

In some way, the identity should be linked to a larger unit than the individual self. Personal recognition could be gained through group involvement, and it is not unusual for someone with the Sun here to rise to a position of prominence or wield influence within various kinds of organizations. The nature of the experiences encountered through group situations — how easily a person functions or adjusts in this sphere — can be seen by aspects to the Sun in this house. The person may be a channel through which new currents or trends entering the collective could manifest. The American 'muck-raking' writer Upton Sinclair, who fought for new legislation protecting the work-force against the evils of big industry was born with the Sun conjunct Mars in Virgo in the 11th.

There is a danger that the identity could be bought wholesale by aligning the self with a group, belief system or cause. In this instance, it's not a case of you are what you eat, but you are what the group feeds you. Those with the Sun in the 11th need to distinguish carefully between what they believe and what the group tells them they ought to believe. (Gay black vegetarians don't all have to think alike!)

Friendships are important to the full development of the Sun in this house. Those with this placement could have a marked impact on close friends and conversely friends could open new vistas and be helpful in the achievement of goals and objectives. As with groups and belief systems, taken to an extreme, some sort of divine potency could be projected onto friends.

It is wise for people with the Sun in the 11th to make a conscious effort to set themselves feasible goals towards which to aim. Somehow, their efforts to realize these will contribute towards the formation of a more solid and concrete sense of identity, purpose and power. One of the most vital ingredients in the self-healing process is having a reason to live.

Sun in the 12th

There is a basic archetypal discrepancy between the solar principle and the essence of the 12th house. The Sun's task is to establish, clarify and perpetuate a separate identity while the 12th house dispatches forces which threaten to dissolve, undermine, de-structure and overwhelm the boundaries of the individual ego. Resolving the conflict requires that the person's sense of 'I' extends in scope beyond the more normal or usual reaches of consciousness. With the Sun in the 12th, the ego must play its part as a servant of the soul.

Those with the Sun in the 12th need to learn how to straddle the borders between personal and universal, conscious and unconscious, individual ego and collective self. This is challenging: the personal ego needs to be flexible enough to allow entry to these elements and yet not so weak that it is overwhelmed by them.

In the effort to maintain a solid and firm identity, the person may reject the existence of a personal or collective unconscious altogether. In the name of clarity and reason, barriers are erected to prohibit the entry of anything fuzzy, vague, irrational, mystical or transpersonal. The daytime border patrol follows the orders of the ego with the utmost alertness and alacrity, but the nightwatchmen are notoriously inefficient. As soon as they fall asleep on the job, what has been hidden or kept out of consciousness slips through and invades. (It was Robert Frost who wrote 'Something there is that doesn't love a wall.') The next morning the day patrol is back at work and the intruders are driven out once more. And so it goes on — vast reserves of psychic energy are spent keeping one part of ourselves away from another part. Alienated from aspects of our own make-up, it is not surprising that we suffer so much conflict and disease, not to mention the feeling of being cut off from other people. The Sun in the 12th, however, is given the opportunity to join the two sides of the self — personal and universal, conscious and unconscious — in an attempt to help these make friends with one another.

The coalition between the forces of the ego and the hidden, deeper realm of the psyche is potentially very fruitful. Those with the Sun in this house can act as channels or mediums for the expression of mythic or archetypal images in the collective unconscious, whether it is through art, poetry, dance, music or some form of psychic work. Their sensitivity and openness to that which is beyond the requirements of the personal self make them effective servants and healers who respond to the needs of others. They may be used as vessels for invoking changes on the level of the collective. In some way the personal identity meets and incorporates something larger and more universal.

In line with traditional 12th house associations, those with the Sun here may need to spend a good deal of time on their own. So receptive to others, they continually absorb influences from the environment. Periods of withdrawal and retreat help them to shed what they have 'picked up' and regain a sense of their own boundaries again. Sometimes, crisis and confinement precede an experience of awakening and illumination. Others may be so confused and undermined by unconscious forces or outside elements that leading an ordinary day-to-day existence is severely hampered.

Various forms of institutions may play a part in their lives. The vocation could involve work in hospitals, prisons, museums, libraries, etc. Certain astrological texts suggest that those with the Sun in the 12th have used their will-power too selfishly in a previous lifetime. Now they must employ their power for the sake of other people, or have the experience of being at the mercy of somebody else's authority. Hidden pride and arrogance or the unconscious belief that the world owes them a living and should without question recognize them as special could cause problems.

The Sun is a 'male principle' and in the nebulous 12th it could mean some confusion around the father or other males in the life, or sacrifices to be made regarding them. Sometimes, there is a strong psychic link with the father.

19.
THE MOON AND CANCER THROUGH THE HOUSES

The Moon in the heavens has no light of its own — it only reflects the light of the Sun. Unlike the Sun which shows where effort is required to become a conscious individual, the Moon is that area of life in which there is a natural tendency to blend in and adapt to what is given. The Moon's house is where we are sensitive and responsive to the needs and influences of other people. It is where we are more easily moulded, shaped by habit and past conditioning, and likely to be bound by the notions, expectations, values and standards of our family or culture. Some of these inbred patterns may be worthwhile and constructive, while others might hinder or retard progress in new directions. The domain of the Moon is the area of life into which we retreat when we need a rest, pause or sanctuary from the struggle of individuation and consciousness raising.

We are drawn into the sphere of life that houses the Moon out of a need for belonging, comfort or safety. It is where we find *or play* Mother: we look for security, containment or an anchor in its domicile or else we offer others nurturing or support in that specturm of experience.

The Moon in the heavens goes through phases and cycles — sometimes it is full and open and at other times it is closed and hidden. Similarly, the house position of the Moon indicates where we are likely to encounter fluctuating circumstances, where we 'go through phases' depending on our changing moods — sometimes open and vulnerable, and at other times closed and withdrawn. We may exhibit regressive, childish and insecure behaviour in that area. More positively, it is where we keep in touch with the emotional and instinctive side of life, and where useful inclinations and memories which support existence are exhibited. Women may play an important role in our lives through the house placement of the

Moon, a basic feminine or *anima* principle.

The house with the sign of Cancer on the cusp or contained within it carries a similar influence to the Moon in a house. Also, the house with Cancer in it will in some way be connected to the house in which the Moon is placed. For instance, the philosopher Bertrand Russell was born with Cancer on the cusp of the 9th house and the Moon in Libra in the 11th. His philosophy and world view (9th) strongly sympathized with and supported (the Moon) the cause of humanitarianism and freedom of thought (11th house).

Moon in the 1st

Any planet in the 1st house is amplified as if the volume has been raised on that principle. According to its sign placement, the Moon there energizes the emotional, instinctive and feeling responses of the individual. Unless strongly modified by other aspects in the chart, the person will radiate lunar qualities — sensitivity, receptivity and a kind of child-like openness to which others are naturally drawn.

While the Sun in the 1st wants to exert a dynamic impact on the environment, the Moon in the 1st is more inclined to stay fused with mother and surroundings. All little babies instinctively know that winning the love of the caretaker helps to ensure survival and therefore they adapt to what the mother likes or wants. But those with the Moon in the 1st — even later in life when survival is not dependent on the presence of another person — may habitually act as if their lives depended on being what others want them to be. Consequently, they exhibit a radar-like ability to pick up and read signals emanating from those around them. However, the interpretation of these signals is often distorted by a high degree of subjectivity. They can be so swaddled in their own needs, feelings and emotional complexes that they are sometimes incapable of viewing life or others at all objectively. In extreme cases, all they care about is what they want and can't easily give another person anything unless it fits in with that.

Nonetheless, the Moon in the 1st bestows an almost animal-like intelligence — instinctively knowing what to do in certain situations. They can 'sniff out' opportunity, 'feel' danger, or 'hear' trouble.

The house with Cancer on the cusp or contained within it will be connected in some way to a 1st house Moon. For instance, Derek Jacobi, whose subtle and sensitive character portrayals have made him one of the most respected of English actors, was born with the receptive and naturally creative Moon in Libra in the 1st and Cancer intercepted in the 10th house of career.

Moon in the 2nd

Whereas the Sun in the 2nd enhances its sense of identity and power through money and possessions, the Moon in the 2nd is content with the emotional security these things bring. The Sun must find its own value system, but those with the Moon here might swallow whole the value system of the family of origin or those around them. The Sun projects prestige onto possessions; the Moon projects feelings onto what it owns. There can be a sentimental attachment to objects, especially those inherited from the family or linked with the memory of key people or situations in the life. Often there is an interest in heirlooms and antiques — anything from the past.

Like the changing Moon in the heavens, financial circumstances might fluctuate. Money can be earned through professions related to the Moon such as those which serve public needs, careers in catering, pub or hotel work, child-care, housing and real estate, or even work at sea. This position suggests inner resources of adaptability, sensitivity and the ability to instinctively know what others want or need.

Moon in the 3rd

While the Sun in the 3rd bursts in on the scene and wants to create an impression on the immediate environment, the Moon in this house reflects and is shaped by the surroundings. As there is the ability to 'feel' what others are thinking, those with this placement may have some difficulty in distinguishing between their own thoughts and the ruminations of others around them. At times, they may believe that they are being objective and rational when in actual fact they are reacting on the basis of some emotional complex. Situations will be coloured according to their moods and sensitivities. If they are in a positive frame of mind, then they will interpret everything positively. If they feel touchy and vulnerable, the same environment will be interpreted quite differently.

The mind is imaginative and there is usually a retentive memory. The Sun in the 3rd believes that knowledge is power; the Moon in the 3rd craves knowledge for the security it brings to truly know how something works. Since the Moon is associated with influences from the past, there may be a fascination for such subjects of study as archaeology, genealogy and history. This placement gives a certain adaptability to changing environments, but the mind may wander or fluctuate from one interest to another. The relationship to siblings — especially female relatives such as sisters, aunts or girl cousins — is worth examining for clues to the psychological make-up of those with this placement. Comfort and security is sought through a sibling or a relative, or they may have had to be 'mother' to others around them during the growing-up years. The actual mother may be related to more like an older sister than a parent.

The Gauquelins found that this placement confers some degree of writing talent. Unless the Moon were in an air sign, the writing would likely display heartfelt emotion or describe personal memories and experiences. Public speakers with the Moon in the 3rd should be able to sway the feelings of the audience. Teachers with this placement can relate to the deeper feelings and needs of their students.

Moon in the 4th (Cancer on the IC)

Whereas the Sun in the 4th struggles to free itself from too great an identification with the family, the Moon in the 4th finds security and a sense of belonging within this structure. Refuge from life's battles is sought by withdrawing back into the home. Even when they have a family of their own, those with this placement may pack their bags and run back to the family of origin when difficulties arise. They need the home to be a kind of retreat and sanctuary, and therefore they are highly attuned to the undercurrents and changes of atmosphere in that environment. Nonetheless, they may not always make their own feelings obvious to others. Often they regress into their early childhood behaviour patterns when the struggles of life become too much. I know one person with this placement who whenever he is upset has an intense craving for chocolate chip cookies because that is what his mother gave him to make him feel better as a child. It is as if there is a mechanism in the psyche which says 'Alright, I've had enough growing up for now, I'm going backwards for a while.'

A child normally looks to its mother for security and containment but with the Moon in the 4th it is possible that the father emanated a safer feeling than the mother. Some with this placement may still be searching for a father to make life secure for them. In the long run, the parent needs to be found on an archetypal level from within the self. Depending on the aspects to the Moon in this house, qualities of caring and nurturance might have been learned from the father rather than the mother.

Sometimes the 4th house Moon wanders restlessly in search of the home or even the country in which it feels the most safe or has the greatest sense of belonging. Sometimes it is the conditions within the home itself which fluctuate. Often there is an interest in family lineage, real estate or archaeology and perhaps a strong desire to live by water. The conditions surrounding the end of life may be shown by the aspects to the Moon in this house.

With Cancer on the IC, a deep and persistent longing for peace, safety and tranquillity is the foundation on which the life is built.

Moon in the 5th

The Sun in the 5th stresses and strengthens its individuality through tackling hobbies, romance and creative pursuits; those with the Moon in this house, however, engage in such outlets in the search for comfort, security and relaxation. While 5th house Suns struggle to be creative, 5th house Moons feel most 'at home' when creating. Often artistic expression is innate and natural. An inborn sense of importance and specialness allows them to enjoy themselves — they don't have to prove anything. Of course, aspects to the Moon must be examined in this respect to see with what degree of difficulty or ease this principle is operating.

Unless the Moon is difficultly aspected by Saturn or the outer planets, there is normally a desire to produce children. We meet the mother in whatever house the Moon is in. In this case, patterns established with the mother during the growing-up years may be re-enacted through their own children. For instance, if they felt that mother didn't like them when they were small, they may then fear that their children won't like them or they may be afraid that they won't like their children. The Moon in any house evokes old memories and associations. Similarly, issues around the mother could be relived through romantic entanglements.

Very often, those with 5th house Moons have a great appeal to the public in general. Their way of presenting themselves is pleasing, engaging and usually non-threatening to most people, as if there is something vaguely familiar about them. Sir Laurence Olivier, known for his ability to portray so impeccably such a wide range of characters, was born with the inherently discerning and skilful Moon in Virgo in the 5th.

Moon in the 6th

Those with this placement find security and comfort attending to daily routine and administering to the needs of the body. Daily rituals like making the morning coffee, taking tea at four, and the bath last thing at night give them a feeling of continuity and well-being.

Physical health and their ability to function and cope with everyday contingencies will vary according to moods. Aspects to the Moon in this house reveal how successfully a person can contain the kinds of anxieties that crop up from day to day. A trine from Saturn could indicate, for instance, that the physical vessel is a hardy container, remaining steadfast in situations to which others might overreact. A square to Mars though, suggests that the person 'acts out' every little anxiety — the body just cannot contain or support the stress that quietly. There may be a connection between how the mother coped with daily tensions and the way in which this person does the same. Those kinds of illnesses which can be inherited or which 'run in the family' should be noted and preventative measures are worth taking. They should be careful about diet — eating problems or overindulgence in alcohol could arise at the onset of emotional difficulties. The body has an instinctual wisdom of its own which they can learn to respect and recognize without too much effort. If they take the time to notice what their bodies register when they walk into a room or meet someone for the first time, they will realize just how much can be intuited through bodily sensations.

There is a need to feel emotionally engaged in work. Usually a job which involves interaction with other people is better than working in too isolated a situation. Sometimes they find themselves entangled in the personal life of co-workers or servants. Those with the Moon in the 6th are adept at fulfilling the practical and emotional needs of others and are well suited to any employment in which they can play 'Mother'. Unresolved mother issues may be projected onto the dog or cat. More seriously, a pet to love and care for and who is there when they come home could contribute to both psychological and physical health.

Moon in the 7th

Those with the Moon in the 7th may be over-sensitive or over-adaptive to the needs of the partner, deriving their identity too much from what the other person wants them to be.

Conversely, they may be looking for a mother in a mate. Early emotional patterning around the mother might be projected onto the partner, clouding an objective perception of the here-and-now reality. A host of problems arise if a partner (male or female) is confused with the mother in this way — not to mention the fact that even the thought of sex with the mother is taboo. Marriage may be sought for the security it offers and the promise of a cosy home and family which provide the person with a sense of belonging. The Moon is not that concerned about being a separate individual. Getting married is what most people do — so why shouldn't they follow suit? Hard aspects to the Moon from Saturn or the outer planets may render the fulfilment of these basic desires more difficult: while the Moon in the 7th is definitely inclined towards relationship, other parts of the self may not be so co-operative.

The partnership itself may need the kind of nurturing and caring that a small baby would be given. The fluctuating nature of the Moon could manifest in a number of ways. Those with this placement might experience many moods and changes of feelings in connection to the relationship. In some cases, the Moon in the 7th describes a restless, unstable or emotionally idiosyncratic partner. As with any planet in the 7th, the person is advised to reflect on why he or she has attracted those particular qualities in another person. What is the other person 'living out' for them?

Moon in the 8th

This position gives an innate openness and attunement to hidden forces operating personally or collectively, which might express itself as the ability to sense evolving social currents, especially subtle economic or business trends. However, those with the Moon here could, at times, be confused or 'taken over' by powerful unconscious complexes which grip and overwhelm them. As children, they would have been extremely sensitive to undercurrents in the home environment, especially the mother's deeper feelings, moods and frustrations, which they may still be 'carrying around' inside them. Present relationships will reawaken earlier emotional patterns and there is the need to delve into the past to uncover the roots of these problems.

Early experience with sex or death may have strongly affected the character. Sex or intimacy could be sought primarily for emotional security or as a way of forgetting the struggles of the world. This placement is usually very responsive to the sexual or emotional needs of the partner and will probably not find it difficult to adapt to these. Very often, there is a natural capacity to help others discover a greater sense of their value and worth. They may literally 'care for' other people's money, or nurture others through times of trauma and transition.

If the Moon is difficultly aspected, divorces, endings or separations may be messy and fraught with more than the usual degree of anxiety, although hitherto untapped resources and strengths could be discovered through such breakdowns and crises.

On a more mundane level, there is the possibility of inheritance of land or property, most likely through the mother or the partner.

Moon in the 9th

The Moon in the 9th often exhibits an uncanny ability to foretell the outcome towards which events are leading. There is a natural receptivity to the realm of philosophy and religion and an intuitive grasp of concepts and symbols. The feelings give access to what the mind cannot rationally comprehend. Although those with this placement may rely on a faith which has been inherited via the family or culture, they have the ability to adapt the philosophy to changing influences and conditions.

Ninth house Moons may reside in a foreign country for periods in the life. Travel is connected to the emotional life — some people yearn for their spiritual home or feel a special link to a particular culture other than their own. Travel, adventure, fanciful dreaming or philosophical pursuits could be used as a means of escaping from stressful situations or the struggles of everyday life. They may feel most 'at home' when contemplating the meaning of life, praying in church, or when they are about to board an aeroplane or embark on a new venture or enterprise.

Their way of caring for others may be through sharing philosophical or spiritual insights, or inspiring potential disciples with new hope, vision, meaning and direction. The image of God may have a matriarchal slant, although this will be strongly coloured by the Moon's signs and aspects.

In men's charts, there can be close relationships with foreign women, or women who somehow broaden or expand their horizons. Difficult aspects to the Moon in the 9th could indicate problems with female in-laws. The Gauquelins found a correlation between the Moon in the 9th (just after culminating) and writing as a profession.

Moon in the 10th (Cancer on the MC)

As children, our well-being depends on our mother loving us. Those with the Moon in the 10th project the 'mother' onto the world: their safety and security needs are linked to issues of profession and status. They are extremely sensitive about their reputations, standing before the public, and what people think about them in general. No matter how mature and self-sufficient they appear, inside is a little boy or girl looking up to the mother/world and asking to be loved. Squares and oppositions to the Moon in the 10th denote other parts of the person which frustrate or do not necessarily gel with what winning that approval requires. One gruelling example of this is Richard Speck, born with the Moon in Cancer in the 10th but with Mars in Aries squared to it, who murdered eight nurses in June 1966 when transiting Jupiter was conjuncting the Moon and bringing out the Mars square.

The person with the Moon in the 10th often exhibits, through gestures and movements, a close identification with the mother. As children, they are exceptionally responsive to her physical and emotional life. The acclaimed musician Van Cliburn first studied the piano at the age of three and was taught by his mother who had been a concert pianist herself: he had Cancer on the 10th house cusp and the Moon in Leo in the 10th. Later on, some people with this placement may even become like mothers to their own mothers. At some point, they need to sort out just where mother ends and they begin by defining their own space and physical reality.

The career or profession may reflect mothering qualities: serving and catering to other people's needs, feeding them, housing them, nursing them, etc. Career issues will elicit and expose their feelings and emotions. Bosses or authority figures may be the target for unresolved problems with the mother or parents in general.

Some may look to the world to mother them via the welfare state. There will be a sensitivity to the moods of the public and a potential to sway the feelings of the masses.

Cancer on the Midheaven or in the 10th house carries a similar connotation to the Moon there.

Moon in the 11th

Those with the Moon in the 11th seek security, comfort and a sense of belonging through friends, groups and organizations. They could be very impressionable and should exercise some discrimination in the choice of people or circles with whom they associate. Unless the Moon is strongly fixed, they have the capacity to blend in with many different crowds.

They may like to 'mother' friends and likewise expect a fair degree of support and nurturing from others when needed. Some may keep friends from as far back as childhood. If the Moon is in a mutable sign there may be many changing acquaintances and fewer lasting friendships. Early hurts or disappointments with friends are worth exploring if the Moon is difficultly aspected as problems may have established patterns which need to be examined and cleared. Women with hard aspects to the Moon in the 11th often complain about trouble getting along with other women. It is possible that 'unfinished business' with the mother could be projected onto female friends. For either sex, a well-aspected Moon here usually implies beneficial friendships with women. The mother may be experienced more as a friend than an actual mother.

Many people with the Moon in the 11th involve themselves in group activities and social outings as a way of relaxing and unwinding from the struggles in other areas of life. Others join groups which promote causes about which they feel very emotional. Some may play 'mother' in the group, making sure everyone else is comfortable or they may even open their own home as a meeting place. There is the potential to stir the feelings of large groups of people.

Goals and ambitions could fluctuate with moods, and are perhaps too easily influenced by other people's opinions about what would be best for them.

Provided heated emotional issues don't cause too many problems with others, this placement is an indication of those who could accumulate a 'family of friends' with whom they share ties as strong as those of blood.

Moon in the 12th

Like the Moon in the other water houses, this placement suggests an innate psychological openness and vulnerability. A thin line exists between what they are feeling and what others around them are feeling. Like psychic vacuum cleaners, they 'suck in' what is circulating in the atmosphere. They may believe they are experiencing their own emotions, when, in actual fact, they have absorbed those of someone else. Without foregoing their inborn receptivity, they would be wise to develop ways of strengthening their ego-boundaries in order to protect themselves from being too invaded. They need to master and use their sensitivity rather than be overwhelmed by it. Some may require periodic seclusion to re-establish their inner peace and equilibrium.

The root of emotional problems is deeply embedded in the unconscious and not easily accessible to the conscious memory. Psychological difficulties could stem from very early infancy or even pre-natal experiences. Reincarnationists would maintain that hard aspects to the Moon in the 12th suggest that present life problems are directly connected to unfinished emotional business from past lives. These could manifest in difficulties with the mother, children, and women in general, or may reveal themselves in the house with Cancer on the cusp or contained within it.

In any case, the Moon in the 12th often indicates a complex or unusual relationship with the mother. The 12th house knows no boundaries: the child would have been very receptive to the mother's feeling life and would continue to be so even when physically separated. Through dreams, mediumship and visions, many people with 12th house Moons are still closely linked with mothers long departed from the world.

While those with this placement have vivid feelings and dreams, they may carefully conceal their emotions and exude an air of mystery. In certain cases, there are secret love affairs or emotional liaisons which are kept hidden for any number of reasons.

There is a natural capacity to care for those who are limited or afflicted in some way. As with the Sun in the 12th, some may be so overwhelmed by deep seated phobias and complexes that they have great difficulty in leading an ordinary day-to-day existence. In some cases, an institution may have to 'mother' them. Sometimes early experiences in hospitals or childrens' homes would have affected the character significantly.

In general, the Moon in the 12th indicates a fairly prevalent desire to regress back into the bliss of a womb-like existence. Those who had difficult pre-natal experiences or who were deprived of the mother at an early age may need to heal these wounds before they can accept incarnation and say 'yes' to life.

More positively, the Moon in the 12th often indicates direct access to a storehouse of wisdom available to the individual at those times when insight and inner resources are most needed. Some will act as vessels to mediate mythic and archetypal images for others. William Blake, with the Moon in Cancer in the 12th, is a supreme example of this. He believed that the artist, not the priest, was our closest link with God. Blake elaborated on his role as mediator in his poem *Jerusalem*: 'I rest not from my great task! To open the Eternal Worlds, to open the immortal Eyes of Man inwards into Worlds of Thought.'[1] The Gauquelins also found a correlation between 12th house Moons and careers in writing and politics.

20.
MERCURY, GEMINI AND VIRGO THROUGH THE HOUSES

Each planet has certain associations with the gods and goddesses of Greek and Roman mythology. The characteristic activities of the Greek Hermes and the Roman Mercury shed light on the function and meaning of this planet and the way it expresses itself through the different houses.

Mercury was the messenger of the gods — a fact-gatherer and distributor of information. Likewise, the planet Mercury in the chart is associated with the workings of the mind and intellect and with various forms of exchanging information, such as writing, speech, teaching and travel. The myth tells us that as soon as Mercury was born he was bored with just being safely tucked away in his cradle; in fact, he abandoned it as quickly as he could in order to find something more interesting to do. Similarly, Mercury's house position in the birthchart, indicates an area of life in which we are restless, curious and inquisitive. Like a growing child fascinated by all the different things in the world to touch, name and discover, we embark on a quest to figure out how life works. In myth, Mercury was always portrayed as young, and never as an old man. By house, this planet defines that sphere of life where we can stay eternally young, maintaining an open and fresh outlook.

Mercury was an arbitrator and maker of deals. He pleaded different cases for the various gods. One of his first actions after birth was to make offerings to all of the twelve great divinities of Olympus. He was also a notorious thief who stole a little something from all the other gods (such as Apollo's cattle and Aphrodite's girdle). In this sense he was a kind of cosmic mimic able to partake of some of the qualities of each and every god. Likewise, Mercury, by house, shows where there is a high degree of adaptability and versatility on the one hand, and a changeability and fickleness on the other. Just when you think you have nailed him down, he slips away and turns up somewhere else with a different point of view. The mind itself, like the god Mercury, is a kind of trickster. The intellect enables us to be objective and analytical but very often it can trick us by twisting facts to suit any case we wish to justify. As someone once said, 'there are lies, damned lies, and statistics.'

The medieval alchemists wrote of a figure they called Mercurius. He was defined both as 'the world-creating spirit' and 'the spirit concealed or imprisoned in matter'.[1] Paradoxically, he was responsible for creating the world and yet he was trapped within his own creation. Many years laters, a twentieth-century German scientist, Werner Heisenberg, researching into the field of atomic physics, disclosed his 'Uncertainty Principle' in which he showed that 'the act of observation itself affects that which is being observed.'[2] Somehow, our minds play a part in determining the world.

Mercury delivered messages from the gods to mortal humans. In this sense, he represents a process in all of us which allows a bridge to be built between higher understanding and everyday reality, between consciousness and unconsciousness, and between ego and environment. The mind can divide us from other people, but it is also through the mind that our consciousness can be expanded to a broader awareness of the interconnectedness of all life. The mind can *sever* or it can *unite*, and the house position of Mercury shows where we can box ourselves into a corner *or* reach out to touch and understand other people and our own selves better. It is worth reflecting on something the philosopher Epictetus said almost two thousand years ago: 'We are not troubled by things, but by the opinions which we have of things.'[3] In Mercury's house, we may not always be able to change the world but we can always do something about the way we are looking at it.

Mercury is associated with two signs, Gemini and Virgo, which represent two complementary functions of this planet. The Gemini side to Mercury is clever at piecing bits of information together and relating different aspects of life to one another; Virgo, on the other hand, dissects and pulls things apart, analysing each component in detail.

Gemini contained in a house elicits Mercury's changeable, communicative and restless qualities. It is where we tend to be 'on the go' and often spread somewhat thinly. Like the proverbial butterfly, we may be hard to pin down in that area.

Virgo on the cusp or contained in a house evokes that side of Mercury which is precise, critical and attentive to detail. While Gemini likes to know a little bit about a host of different things,

Virgo prefers to know a great deal about a few things. In Gemini's house we pursue knowledge for knowledge's sake, but in Virgo's house we acquire knowledge in order to use it practically and constructively.

The house Mercury is in will be connected in some way to any house with Gemini in it, and also with any house where Virgo is found. For instance, the writer Oscar Wilde was born with Mercury in Scorpio in the 3rd house and Gemini on the cusp of the 10th, relating the house and planet of communication (Mercury in the 3rd) with profession and career (10th). But his 3rd house Mercury is also linked to his Ascendant, because Virgo is on the cusp of the 1st house. He met life (1st house) equipped with a razor-sharp intellect and a threateningly incisive wit (Mercury in Scorpio in the 3rd).

Mercury in the 1st

Those with this placement become conscious of themselves and life in general by being curious and asking questions. They are meant to be spokespeople — distributors of ideas and information or channels through which one discipline is linked to another. They are usually highly analytical, both of themselves and others.

Mercury is a mimic and will take on the qualities of the sign it is in and any planet it closely aspects. Therefore, these need to be carefully examined. For instance, Mercury in a fire sign or conjunct Mars in the 1st gives rise to impulsive speech, action and behaviour. Things pop out before they know it. Mercury in an earth sign or conjunct Saturn is more prone to cautious assessment prior to committing the self to activity. Things have to 'sit' right with them before they can act. Mercury in a water sign or aspected to Neptune will evaluate the perceptions through the feelings and emotions, unlike Mercury in air or aspected to Uranus which will speak and act from a more purely objective stance, having (often in a flash) computed the bigger picture.

Those with Mercury in the 1st imbue the world with significance on the basis of what they *think* about it. If they don't like what they see, rather than blaming the world 'out there', they should try changing their own attitudes and then take another look at what they find. This same important idea was clearly expressed by the deep and independent thinker Albert Schweitzer, born with Mercury conjunct the Sun in Capricorn in the 1st, who wrote: 'The greatest discovery of any generation is that human beings can alter their lives by altering their attitudes of mind.'[4]

Those with Mercury in the 1st often maintain a youthful appearance throughout life. Sometimes there are frequent changes of environment in the early years, as if they are forced from a young age to view life from different angles.

Mercury in the 2nd

If well-aspected, Mercury in the 2nd can be a skilful manipulator of money or finance, especially adept at arbitration and making deals with others. Money can be earned through such professions as selling, writing, lecturing, teaching, secretarial work, the transport industry, etc. They may be concerned with the movement or distribution of goods, with devising new techniques of production, or with ways of improving the quality of existing products. Innate values to be developed include inventiveness, dexterity, flexibility and a talent for using words.

On a broader level, there is a curiosity and urge to understand the nature of the physical world. A small pebble found on the beach or the intricacies of a hair follicle found on the body are endlessly fascinating for a minute or two. A sense of security is found through knowledge and learning how something works. However, unless Mercury is in a fire sign, it may take some time before experience is fully transmuted into understanding when placed in the earthy 2nd house.

Gemini in the 2nd suggests more than one source of income or way of earning money. Cleverness and ingenuity are marketable assets. Sometimes the person may work with relatives.

Virgo on the 2nd emphasizes precision and attention to detail as inborn resources worth developing. Shrewd and cautious with money and possessions, they may place more importance on quality than on quantity. Some with this placement come to value the healthy functioning of the body as the most important possession in life.

Mercury in the 3rd

Mercury is strongly placed in the 3rd, since in the natural zodiac this is one of its own houses. The sign placement and aspects to it will describe the way a person thinks, learns and digests experience. A 3rd house Mercury in fire or air or in aspect to Mars, Jupiter or Uranus indicates a more extroverted and speedy mind than when Mercury is placed in an earth sign or in aspect to Saturn, which slows down and deepens the thought processes. Mercury in water or aspected to the Moon or Neptune learns more through osmosis, absorption and aesthetic and emotional appreciation than in an analytic, step-by-step mode. A 'good mind' is normally defined as one that can think rationally and logically, but an examination of the 3rd house may reveal other kinds of minds — *just as good* — which operate differently from the standards of traditional educational systems. Learning difficulties may be shown by aspects of Uranus, Neptune, or Pluto to a 3rd house Mercury and often stem from the fact that this person's mind is not the type that is favoured by conventional teaching techniques.

In general, however, Mercury in the 3rd, unless adversely aspected, reveals a lively, witty, observant intellect, adept at communication and repartee, with good attention to detail. Those with this placement are unusually clever at selecting those facts which justify or support the case they wish to present. (Oscar Wilde, with Mercury in Scorpio in the 3rd once wrote, 'Truth is rarely pure, and never simple.') Those with Mercury in the 3rd normally have at least a little something to say about everything. If you don't think so, ask them and wait a minute.

The nature of the relationship with siblings and neighbours will be shown by the aspects to Mercury in this house. Mercury in difficult aspect to Saturn or Pluto, for instance, could indicate some deep-rooted problems stemming from sibling issues. These are worth examining as they often illuminate patterns which may still be operating much later in life. I drew up the chart of a woman with Mercury conjunct Pluto in the 3rd house whose younger brother died when she was only six years old. At the age of twenty-eight, she was still walking around believing that something she had said or done was the cause of his death.

Gemini on the 3rd usually gives a quick and alert mental style. An innate ability to master languages is indicated. However, there may be a tendency to mouth opinions before all the facts are known, thus landing a foot in it.

Perhaps due to an anxious disposition, Virgo on the 3rd attempts to handle everyday affairs and interactions with efficiency and caution. Critical and analytical abilities are increased with an aptitude for selecting just the right word or phrase to precisely express a concept or sentiment.

Mercury in the 4th (Gemini and Virgo on the IC)

Mercury in the 4th sometimes indicates an intellectual or academic home background, where the emphasis was on being sensible and rational, perhaps at the expense of feelings, warmth and physical closeness. Intelligence may be inherited through the family line. If the 4th house is taken to mean the father, then in some way he would have carried the Mercury projection: he might have been experienced as expressive, articulate, critical or possibly tricky and elusive, someone who 'comes and goes'. Mental attitudes could be mixed up with those of the father. There may even be more than one father — the actual father and a stepfather or another person who fills the role of a father-figure.

Early changes of residence may bring to the surface underlying qualities of flexibility and adaptability. Some with this placement might prefer a nomadic lifestyle. If Mercury is difficultly aspected in the 4th, there could be more than the usual amount of bickering, arguments and back-biting within the early home or later home environments. Mental and educational activities could be carried on in the home. Even well into the second half of life, the person would benefit from further learning or studying.

Gemini on the IC describes a curious and restless soul, often with a strong dual nature. Dane Rudhyar compares this placement to a palm or sequoia, which has many roots, though none reach very far below the surface.[5] The person could 'lose the self' in a web or maze of ideas, thoughts, or a mass of inconsequential, or contradictory bits of information. More positively, there is a persistent urge to order and understand the self and the environment. The home may be used as a place where ideas are exchanged and neighbours congregate. Sometimes there are two homes, perhaps one in town and the other in the country.

Virgo on the IC indicates a highly self-critical nature. A desire to refine or improve the self is the foundation upon which much of the life is built. This is exteriorized into a preoccupation with improvements around the home, or the maintenance of an efficiently functioning household. Virgo on the 4th house cusp may use the home as a base of operation for work. Attention should be paid to health problems which run in the family.

Mercury in the 5th

Creative pursuits, hobbies and recreational outlets are the means of becoming more conscious of the self and the environment. Some form of artistic expression may be the medium through which this person sees, thinks, feels and communicates. The incomparable Mozart, the expressive symbolist poet Verlaine, and the learned Renaissance painter Raphael all had Mercury in this house. For those with this placement, experience is more richly understood and better digested if it can be described in poetic words, drawn, sung about or danced. Knowledge is passed down from generation to generation in this way.

Expanding the mind through knowledge and developing the ability to communicate and convey ideas contribute to greater self-fulfilment with Mercury in this position. Mental amusements such as chess, scrabble and other games of strategy and wit might be typical 5th house Mercury pursuits. Gymnastics, track and field events, and those sports which involve precision teamwork such as basketball (Wilt Chamberlain of the Harlem Globetrotters had Mercury in Virgo in the 5th) also come to mind.

Mercury's restlessness and need for variety can manifest itself in an active romantic life. (Virgo here will go for quality, but Gemini in the 5th, in the tradition of great French farces, may juggle a few at a time.) The flame of romance is probably kept burning longer if the other person is mentally stimulating. Flattering those with Mercury in the 5th about the acuity and breadth of their knowledge or their brilliant way of putting things will get you everywhere.

Parents with this placement normally foster the intellectual abilities of their children and both probably have a lot to learn from one another. The parent-child relationship may blossom when the child is older and increasingly able to communicate and exchange ideas. Mercury in the 5th makes a good teacher or educator of young people and I have often seen this placement in the charts of those who work especially well with adolescents.

Gemini on the cusp or contained in the 5th enhances writing, speaking, and mental and physical agility. Virgo there often indicates practical creative skills — carpentry, gourmet cooking, making their own clothes, pottery, etc.

Mercury in the 6th

Knowledge is acquired in the process of managing the affairs of everyday life and maintaining the health and well-being of the body.

With Mercury here, a great deal can be learned from the body — especially when little things go wrong. But those with this placement must learn to ask the right questions at the right time, such as, 'Why do I always get this pain in the neck when you walk into the room?' Or, 'Why does my backache get worse on Saturday nights?' In its own domain of the 6th, Mercury dispatches messages from the unconscious mind to the conscious mind via those minor aches and pains which most of us interpret as cues to reach for the aspirin. Information about the environment is also available through the barometer of the body if we only learn how to read the instrument. Carl Jung, who often used his intuition in this way while treating patients, had Mercury in the feeling sign of Cancer in the 6th sextile the equally receptive Moon in Taurus in the 3rd. The psychologist Arthur Janov promoted a form of treatment called Primal Therapy, in which patients were encouraged to discharge their deepest feelings and emotions through expressing these physically by crying, screaming, kicking, biting, etc.: he was born with Mercury in Virgo in the 6th ruling Virgo on the 6th house cusp and Gemini on the cusp of the 3rd house of communication.

Health problems may be connected to nerves, excessive worrying, too much activity and not enough rest. Yoga, relaxation techniques, meditation and attention to breathing can help reduce the stress of an overwrought mind and body. Mercury in the 6th is sometimes a case of mind (Mercury) over matter (the earthy 6th): positive mental images of the self affirm health, foster the healing process, and may even serve in the cause of prevention.

The 6th house describes how we make use of our time, and with Mercury here, the overriding need is to keep busy. Check priorities: how much of the time is frittered away in an endless number of pursuits and activities which in the end don't really lead anywhere?

It is helpful if the work is mentally engaging and allows for some movement and mobility (especially if Gemini is on the 6th house cusp). Virgo in the 6th excels at those jobs which require precision and attention to detail and may perform daily routines with a ritualistic fanaticism (and even a fetishistic obsession for one particular brand of soap powder over another). If Mercury in the 6th is difficultly aspected, watch out for gossip, slander or back-biting among co-workers and a tendency for unresolved issues with siblings to resurface in the office.

Mercury in the 7th

Mercury's dual function of gathering information and then distributing it again operates clearly when this planet is housed in the 7th: there is an enormous amount to learn through being with other people but there is just as much to teach and share with them. Mercury in the 7th naturally desires to communicate and exchange ideas with many different types of people. Assessing and understanding how and what others think is a favourite pastime. Telling them one's own thoughts and opinions runs a close second.

Mercury in the 7th shops around for a partner who is intellectually stimulating. Of course, they may find so many people who are interesting in different ways, it is difficult to settle on just one. Then again, there may be no one ever interesting enough. Nor is Mercury in the 7th immune to the pitfalls of projection: some may try to import another person to do their thinking, talking and decision-making for them. Or they may attract someone who is non-commital, unreliable, or tricky to pin down. As hurtful as this might be, there is the secondary gain of having escaped being pinned down themselves.

While being careful not to approach the whole delicate and mysterious area of relationship too much 'from the head', some degree of objectivity and detachment is required to sustain a long-term involvement. With Mercury in the 7th, many problems can be 'worked through' if they are discussed and analysed. Some people with this placement may be fairly (or should I say unfairly) critical and judgemental about 'those little things' which their partners do that annoy them. Fortunately, the antics of the god Mercury remind us that a sense of humour about such things is the great balancer.

Gemini on the 7th sometimes indicates more than one important close relationship in the life — or one relationship which undergoes such a transformation that it is almost like an entirely new one. Virgo is more cautious and discerning about its choice of partners, although anyone who 'needs saving' or likes to save others is fair game.

Mercury in the 8th

The 8th house entices curious Mercury to explore and learn from what is hidden and less obvious in life — to ferret out secrets, and probe into mysteries in search of the bottom line. This is the detective-like mind, with eyes that can see in the dark. Bordering on a voyeuristic preoccupation, Mercury in the 8th watches the kinds of exchanges that go on between people — at the bank, the stock market, in the bedroom or behind any closed door. They may penetrate the world of money and finance, or turn their attention to psychology and the occult, with a fascination for the mysteries of sex and death. Although often adept at communicating and sharing with others anything which is obscure, subtle, deep or profound, they prefer to keep their own thoughts and motivations secret. For those with Mercury in the 8th, experience is not fast-food grabbed hastily between appointments, but something to be savoured and thoroughly digested.

Many astrological texts advise those with Mercury in this house (especially if difficultly aspected to Neptune) to examine all contracts for possible misunderstandings before signing. What one person believes is being said or promised may be different from how the other person reads it. The same note of caution applies to wills and inheritances — problems with Mercury in the 8th sometimes manifest as entanglements with relatives over such things. Any difficulties stemming from childhood or adolescent sexual explorations with brothers, sisters or neighbours are worth considering, as well as early encounters with the death of anyone close to them. Their own death could be related to diseases of the respiratory or nervous system, so attention should be paid to these areas.

With Mercury, Gemini or Virgo in this house, the mind is suited to investigative exploits and research work. Those with such a placement can be cool and detached about subjects which often arouse other people's passions and fears. For Virgo, the sex drive may be targeted into some quite specific area of focus, while Gemini is curious (and perhaps opinionated) about almost everything in this respect.

Mercury in the 9th

When Mercury wanders into the 9th, he takes his wings along with him, for this is an expansive territory to cover. An 8th house Mercury burrows deep down and peers closely into things; in the 9th, Mercury gains his perceptions and awareness by 'zooming up' or standing back and looking at it all from a distance and a higher perspective. Believing that life and the cosmos can be 'figured out' intellectually, those with Mercury in this house attempt (or should attempt) to discover and understand the laws and principles which govern existence by scrutinizing the larger patterns at work. A natural urge to expand and broaden the mind through study, reading and travel keeps those with this placement as busy as ever in this domain.

Usually, there is a desire to teach and share what they perceive and discover, and to inspire others with what has inspired them. This placement suits philosophers, clergymen, writers, publishers, educators and public relations people.

Adhering too fanatically to their own beliefs or version of the truth is the danger of a difficultly aspected Mercury in this house. Facts which support the cherished belief system are readily received, but the others are handily overlooked.

In some cases, relatives who live abroad may figure in the life or a long journey might significantly influence how the person thinks. Problems with Mercury in the 9th can also mean bickering and gossip among in-laws.

Gemini on the 9th may have to explore many different philosophies and cultures in order to satisfy a thirst for knowledge and experience. Virgo here inclines the person to explore particular philosophies and cultures more in depth. With Virgo, the letter of the law may be taken too literally in an attempt to live the daily life in accordance with a rigid interpretation of the scriptures. Virgo believes in that which can be seen and tested and may have trouble card-cataloguing the inexplicable mysteries of life.

Mercury in the 10th (Gemini and Virgo on the MC)

The qualities and principles associated with Mercury are usually reflected in the choice of career when it is in the 10th house. The work may involve writing, teaching, printing, lecturing, selling, the media, telecommunications, administrative or secretarial skills, forms of manual dexterity, and the transport of goods or people from one place to another. While pursuing career and professional ambitions, they can learn about themselves and the environment. Those with this placement like to be seen as bright, intelligent and capable, and will want to be remembered by others for these qualities.

If the 10th is taken to mean the mother, then Mercury will colour the image of her. If she was seen as clever and articulate, then the child emulates those traits and tries to develop them. The mother might have emphasized the importance of a good education and the need to be intelligent and expressive in life. She also could have been experienced as fickle and changeable — not always present — as if her body was there but her mind was somewhere else. I have seen difficult aspects to Mercury in the 10th in the charts of some people whose mothers were mentally unstable. If besieged by hard aspects, this placement could also indicate communication problems between parent and child and a difficulty in understanding or appreciating one another.

Gemini on the cusp of the 10th may indicate more than one important career in the life. The work may be linked with siblings or other relatives. Sometimes there may be two people who have shared the mother's role. Virgo on the 10th emphasizes a pride in the impeccability or exactness of one's work. In this case, the mother may have been experienced as hardworking, critical and orderly, depending on the aspects to Mercury.

Mercury in the 11th

Awareness of the self and life in general is expanded through friendships and group contacts if Mercury is in the 11th. Rather than just pursuing something alone, Mercury here enhances its knowledge by seeking other people who share a similar interest. For instance, you can study astrology on your own at home with some books, or you can gather together with other people interested in it. Through doing so, other people's attitudes, points of view and experiences of the topic enlarge your own scope and appreciation. Helpful hints can be shared and your own opinions aired: 'Oh yes, I hadn't seen that before, but did you ever consider . . .' Problems with Mercury in this house could indicate trouble communicating or being understood in groups.

Mercury in the 11th also joins organizations which promote a common belief, concept or cause. One voice becomes many: a group of people thinking something is more powerful than just one person thinking the same thing. Mercury's thoughts might dwell on the ways in which society can be improved or advanced. Mercury in the 11th feels a kinship with like minds or with other group members and sometimes acts as the group spokesperson. Then again, they may be the one that everyone else tells to shut up so that other people can get a word in. The nature of the group itself may be 'mercurial' — debating clubs, writing societies, or networking groups which link or refer one person or group to another.

Much of the same applies to friendship. If Mercury is projected onto companions, then those with this placement may seek a friend to do their thinking and decision-making for them. Or a friend may turn out to be unreliable, gossiping, or the type who says one thing and then does another. An actual brother or sister may be their best friend, or a friend is sought who can be like a brother or sister to them.

The 11th house is the house of goals and objectives and Gemini on the cusp may have some difficulty in choosing one particular goal or aim on which to focus. Dithering, what they think they want one day is not what they think they want the next. In groups, Gemini makes friends easily and usually has a great deal to say. Virgo in this house is more discriminating about its choice of groups or friends, but once having chosen probably finds it easier to make a longer commitment. Goals and objectives are achieved in a more logical step-by-step fashion than Gemini in this sphere. Virgo offers practical services to friends or organizations with which they associate.

Mercury in the 12th

Mercury doesn't exactly wander into the 12th house — he falls into it. And, like Alice, he finds himself in a strange land, encountering things that are awesome, helpful and fascinating.

Primarily, a 12th house Mercury attempts to build a bridge between the conscious and unconscious minds — to integrate into conscious awareness what is operating in the hidden depths of the psyche. This involves a twofold process. First, those with this placement must venture into the imaginal realms of the unconscious, although if they don't choose to take that initial step, it doesn't matter — what is down there will sooner or later come up to get them. Secondly, once in that realm, they must look around, take notes and then come back up again. If they get stuck down there, forgetting to return up again or unable to do so, then someone else will have to be called in to rescue them.

What does this all mean? Those with Mercury here — through introspection, soul-searching, psychotherapy, good literature, or dreamwork — need to explore the unconscious to find out what makes them tick. Depending on the aspects to Mercury, some of what is stored there will be useful and productive and well worth bringing to the surface. However, other stuff may need to be sifted through and sorted out — especially learned impressions and memories from the past which, consciously remembered or not, distort and obscure how information received in the present is being interpreted. In order to see what is in front of them more clearly, they will have to clean up some of the early life (or previous life?) debris cluttering their immediate perception and awareness.

After a while uncollected rubbish starts to stink. If they don't take some of that 'garbage' and convert it to compost, then the dissolving action that the 12th house has on any planet in it begins to take effect: in this case the mind (Mercury) breaks down. I mentioned that if Mercury doesn't go down there, what's down there comes up and gets them. Mercury in the 12th could suffer occasionally from intrusive thoughts of an obsessive or disturbing nature. If difficultly aspected, paranoia and the fear that others are talking or plotting against them could result. Innocent facts and people will be distorted to give support to these fantasies.

Planets in the 12th house are not sure of their boundaries. The question for Mercury there is, 'whose mind is it anyway?'. An openness to thoughts and undercurrents in the atmosphere makes it difficult to know what thoughts are their own and which belong to other people. In fact, some people with Mercury in the 12th may be so afraid of 'losing their mind' that they compensate by being super-rational, only believing in what can be statistically proven or tested. This placement also gives a secretive mind, which hides what it is thinking from others. However, if Mercury is not too badly aspected, there are psychic abilities, a vivid imagination and access to the accumulated wisdom of the past.

The imaginative Pulitzer prize winning author, Ernest Hemingway, was born with Mercury in Leo in the 12th ruling Virgo on the

Ascendant and Gemini on the cusp of the 10th, the house of career. The film-maker and actor Orson Welles is another brilliant talent with an expansive imagination: he was born with Mercury in Taurus in the 12th exactly sextile Jupiter in Pisces in the 10th. The often divinely inspired actor, Lord Olivier, also has Mercury in the 12th, ruling a Gemini Ascendant and Virgo on the cusp of the 5th house of creative self-expression.

I have met some people with Mercury in the 12th who are insecure about their mental abilities. It may be that they understand much more than they are able to put into words, or suffer from learning or educational difficulties. Conversely, those with Mercury here are sometimes involved in helping others who have problems with speech, reading, hearing or mobility. Whatever is in the 12th house is not just there for our own consumption — we can often use these energies to help or serve other people. There may be sacrifices that have to be made for brothers or sisters, or something unusual about the relationship with them.

The 12th house has been referred to as 'the house of self-sustainment or self-undoing'. With Mercury here, negative thinking could be the root of many problems, while learning to use the mind and imagination more positively may be just the needed ingredient to transform obstacles into blessings.

Gemini on the cusp of the 12th warns that clear thinking could be obscured by unconscious emotional complexes which should be examined. On the positive side, they can usually talk themselves out of difficulties or like Odysseus manoeuvre cleverly through tricky situations. Virgo on the cusp of the 12th is prone to obsessive-compulsive thoughts. Stemming from a fear of looking silly or appearing foolish, they may be afraid to relax and let go. Often they judge themselves against too rigid ideals of perfection and harbour feelings of inadequacy. This sensitivity to what is weak or flawed can be turned around and used to help themselves or others where it is needed most.

21.
VENUS, TAURUS AND LIBRA THROUGH THE HOUSES

The planet Venus associated with the Roman goddess of love and beauty with the same name and with the Greek goddess Aphrodite, symbolizes the desire in all of us for union and relationship. Like the Moon, she is, in Jungian terms, an *anima* principle representing the urge to balance, harmonize, merge and cherish. By house, Venus indicates a sphere of experience through which we can most naturally attain a sense of peace, equilibrium, well-being and satisfaction. Our ability to appreciate, to value, to love and be loved is stimulated in her domain. It is where we are pleasing and open to being pleased and where we exhibit some of our best style, taste and consideration for others.

Sounds nice — but before you rush to look where Venus is placed in your chart, keep in mind that this goddess had other sides to her nature which were less pleasant. First of all, she couldn't bear it if life or other people didn't measure up to her idea of what they should be. Because of such high expectations of perfection and harmony, the house of Venus may denote where we suffer some disappointment and disillusionment when life fails to meet these ideals. However, motivated by such dissatisfaction, Venus could also indicate the area of life in which we feel impelled to do something which will make the world (or ourselves) slightly more just, fair or beautiful.

Secondly, Aphrodite hated competition. She subjected the beautiful young mortal Psyche to extremely humbling lessons because she felt that Psyche had overstepped her place in receiving a degree of attention which only befitted a goddess, i.e. Aphrodite herself. Also, when Paris had to judge whether Aphrodite, Athene or Hera was the most beautiful goddess, Aphrodite unabashedly stripped off to bias his opinion. By house, Venus may show the area of life in which we feel rivalry or envy towards those who might be better endowed than ourselves. It is also where we will use seduction, sweet deceit and other such wiles to secure our aims. Reputedly, Aphrodite wore a magic girdle which had the power to enchant and enslave men.

As a further bribe to influence Paris to select her rather than the other goddesses, she offered him the ravishing Helen as his wife. It didn't seem to matter to Aphrodite that Helen happened to be married already: winning the beauty contest was more important. As a result, the Trojan War was started, bringing misery and upheaval to the lives of thousands. Aphrodite (Venus), the goddess of love and beauty, sometimes makes a mess of people's lives.

Finally, Aphrodite occasionally functioned as a kind of redresser of imbalance. For instance, by encouraging her son Eros to pluck Pluto with one of his famous arrows, she gravely disrupted the life of young Persephone, whom she felt was just too innocent and virginal for her own good. At times, in the house of Venus, a certain degree of pain, strife or suffering is needed to bring us into better harmony or balance if we have swung too far in any one direction.

Venus rules two signs, Taurus and Libra. Taurus represents the earthier and more sensual side of Venus. The house with Taurus in it is where we most directly seek to satisfy desires of a physical or instinctual nature — appetite indulgences like food or sex and basic needs for comfort and security. Libra's house, however, is where we want to fulfil romantic and aesthetic ideals of love, fairness, symmetry and proportion in a quest for the good, the beautiful and the truth in life.

The house Venus is in will influence any house with Libra or Taurus on the cusp or contained within it.

Venus in the 1st

If we understand the 1st house to describe the way in which we best realize our own special and unique identity, then Venus here suggests that life should be met with open arms. A natural urge to relate to others with sensitivity, refinement and goodwill is indicated. Although they find themselves by being harmonious and accommodating, there is a danger that in attempting to be all things to all people, they actually lose themselves. Venus in the 1st suggests that we should love and respect *our own selves* as well.

In fact, a feeling of self-worth and self-esteem is crucial to loving and seeing other people more clearly. If we appreciate our own worth, then we can appreciate the worth of other people. If we accept ourselves, then we can more easily accept others. If those with Venus in this house don't learn to love and accept themselves first, they may manipulate other people to do so in order to fill the gap. Like the proverbial coquette, they are out to get as much flattery and attention as possible to prove their value and worth. Some people with Venus in the 1st never take Aphrodite's girdle off: they display an obvious seductiveness which can be used for their own benefit. They may even be downright treacherous.

Venus in the 1st often exhibits physical beauty or a 'certain something' which draws others to them. They may literally embody the best qualities of the sign in which the 1st house Venus is placed. Even without traditional good looks, an appreciative and admiring disposition will make them attractive and appealing.

In the 1st house, we need to make our presence known. Venus' sweet dalliance can be very charming but taken too far borders on laziness — someone who sits and waits for things to come to them. If well-aspected, this placement is an indication of a harmonious early upbringing which endows the person with a positive sense of self and optimistic outlook on life.

Venus in the 2nd

Obviously, Venus in this house has a love of money, not just for the security it brings but because it allows them to purchase all those things they find beautiful and worthwhile. A sense of well-being is attained by surrounding themselves with that which they consider stylish and tasteful. They have an eye for beauty in the physical and material world. Some may shun anything considered ugly or inharmonious, while a more finely developed 2nd house Venus has the insight to perceive beauty, reason and purpose in those things which others might scorn.

Their innate resources include a sense of fairness and diplomatic tact. They have a knack for attracting what they need or value, so money, unless extravagantly spent, should not be too great a problem. An income could be earned through 'Venusian' professions: artistic endeavours, modelling, the selling or marketing of beauty or beauty-products, the diplomatic service, etc.

Taurus in the 2nd is sometimes too possessive of people and objects. Usually there is a deep love of the natural world, physical comforts, and the sensual side of life, as well as practicality in money matters. Libra in the 2nd values gentility, refinement and social niceties. The style and finesse with which an appetite is satisfied is more important than the quantity which is consumed. Libra on the 2nd has a greater concern for the fair and equitable distribution of money and possessions than Taurus there, who is worried about having enough for itself.

Venus in the 3rd

Those with this placement have the ability to communicate in an easy, fluent and non-threatening manner if Venus is not hampered by difficult aspects. They are sensitive to the needs of those around them although some may try a little too hard to speak only what they think will please others. People generally find it easy to communicate and 'open up' to someone with Venus in the 3rd as if they sense the atmosphere of loving receptivity this placement bestows. There is usually a fondness and appreciation of brothers and sisters and benefits through them, although certain aspects to Venus (from Pluto for instance) suggest an intense sibling rivalry or incestuous urges. Unless Venus is difficultly aspected, the educational experience should be fairly enjoyable. There is often a love of words, knowledge and languages, or the capacity to express the self through some form of artistic medium. Weekend jaunts here and there are likely to give pleasure and these people normally fit easily into different situations and environments.

Taurus in the 3rd may slow down the thought processes but when something is learned it will sink in deeply and remain with them. It may be easier to digest experience through the senses — how something 'feels' or 'touches' them rather than what they actually think about it. Libra on the cusp or contained in the 3rd enhances the ability to be persuasive, influential, and yet tactful in dealing with the immediate environment. In the name of harmony and fairness, they will 'weigh up' what others say or do. Libra here can see beauty in something which another person might overlook.

Venus in the 4th (Taurus and Libra on the IC)

The 4th house indicates qualities deeply embedded within the person. Those with Venus there basically value and desire peace and harmony in their surroundings. They cannot easily live in an atmosphere of strife, tension or discord, and in the end will do all that they can to reconcile problems or smooth over differences. Satisfaction and fulfilment can be found in making a home and in such domestic pursuits as cooking, decorating and gardening. If not too badly aspected, Venus in the 4th suggests a comfortable situation in the later years of life.

Venus carries with it the image of the beloved and all that is beautiful. One possible interpretation of this planet in the 4th is that the father (or 'hidden parent') catches this projection — he is made into the beautiful one. The boy-child may feel some rivalry or jealousy. How can he ever be as good as Daddy, who has all the charm and grace, and Mummy as well? The little girl may fall in love with such an enchanting father, in which case the mother becomes the rival. Nonetheless, Venus in the 4th suggests a positive family inheritance, both psychological and material. Sometimes good taste runs in the family or there has been an artistic influence in the early upbringing. Often, there is an interest in exploring the genealogy or family tree.

With Taurus on the IC or in the 4th house, the need for security is the foundation upon which the life is built. A deep-seated, instinctive territorial nature expresses itself in a powerful urge to have a home of one's own. Regardless of how flipppant the rest of the chart might look, underneath there is a basic caution and conservatism. Those with this placement are unlikely to disrupt or change situations unless there is an organic sense of 'rightness' about doing so. Time is needed to fully assimilate events and experiences. Any opportunity to spend more time relaxing in nature and just watching the grass grow and feeling the soil under their feet strengthens and stabilizes them.

With Libra on the IC or in the 4th house, a person's sense of balance and well-being hinges on a good home environment and fulfilling relationships. The atmosphere in the home can be one of sharing and creative exchange. There is a deep need to establish a clear set of values, ideals and standards upon which to base action in the world.

Venus in the 5th

With Venus in the 5th, there is a natural urge to express the self in a creative or artistic fashion. Even if a career in the arts is not pursued, some sort of creative outlet brings greater personal fulfilment and well-being. In times of stress, picking up a paintbrush or sitting down to write something may restore a sense of equilibrium and balance. The motto of those with Venus in the 5th might be 'If it's worth doing, it's worth doing in style.' Unless very difficultly aspected by the outer planets, the personal style and flair is usually of a type which most people will find pleasing and endearing. For example, the actor Richard Chamberlain and the singer Glenn Campbell, who both claim a wide public appeal, have Venus in the 5th. The glamorous actress Ava Gardner, born with Venus in Scorpio in the 5th, literally got to act out (5th) her Scorpionic Venus. In a 1948 movie called *One Touch of Venus* she played a statue of the goddess come to life, who brought love and havoc into the affairs of everyone she met.

Those with this placement are often 'in love with love' and romantic pursuits will be high on the list of priorities. Some will only feel alive if they are in the throes of a great romance with (of course) the *most divine* creature on earth. Hobbies, recreational activities and trips to the theatre, cinema or art gallery help to 'round out' the personality. In short, they love to play.

If Venus is well-aspected, children are likely to be a source of pleasure and fulfilment. Parents with this placement will usually encourage any sign of their children's budding creativity — especially if their own artistic promise was stifled when they were young. Taken to an extreme, the child may be shuffled off to dancing school on Monday, acting class on Wednesay and piano lessons on Friday whether the poor kid wants to or not. Parents with Venus in the 5th need to be careful about unconsciously setting up situations of competition or rivalry between children or between themselves and their children in an attempt to find out just who is the fairest or most talented of them all.

Taurus on the 5th emphasizes the enjoyment of the sensual side of life, creative talents of a practical nature and hobbies like gardening and cooking. There may be some difficulty letting go of children or creations. Libra enhances the appreciation of the fine arts and the pursuit of all which is beautiful and aesthetic. Usually there is a good relationship with children and young people.

Venus in the 6th

By house, Venus indicates those things we care about, are attracted to and appreciate. The 6th house is concerned with the running of everyday affairs, issues of work and service, and attending to the proper functioning of the body. Combining Venus with this house we come up with someone who actually enjoys vacuuming the sitting room, has a tendency to fall in love with co-workers, and derives great satisfaction from the daily rituals of mundane life. Even brushing the teeth can be done with style.

Frivolity aside, Venus in the 6th takes pleasure in developing and fine-tuning their talents, skills and abilities. It's not good enough to just do a job, it must be done beautifully. I have done quite a few charts for people with Venus in the 6th who have careers in the field of health, beauty and fitness, and many others who put their artistic talent to practical use as designers and draughtsmen. One in particular was concerned with designing kitchen products which were both functional and beautiful. More generally, there is the desire for a harmonious work atmosphere and the capacity to bring good feelings into this area.

Normally, the person feels the importance of developing a good relationship with the body. If health problems arise, these could be due to over-indulgence or some imbalance in the diet or life in general that needs consideration.

While Venus in the 6th enjoys the more mundane and everyday tasks of life, some may become obsessive about things — such as not being able to make love if the ashtray is too full. They are usually able to apply themselves to work involving precision and detail. The image of the beloved (Venus) might be projected onto servants, co-workers, milkmen, telephone repairmen, dental hygienists, and even pets. (I did a chart for a woman with Venus in the 6th who took her poodle to the hairdresser every third Friday.)

Taurus in the 6th enhances the stamina and gives a practicality and determination in meeting everday life. There is a natural enjoyment of the physical body and the diversity of the natural world. Libra on the 6th emphasizes the capacity to be tactful and diplomatic in dealing with colleagues. They may, however, antagonize others if they demand the same kind of perfection from fellow workers that they ask of themselves. Ill health might result if the work environment is too stressful.

Venus in the 7th

For those with Venus in the 7th, the image of the beloved and that which is beautiful 'lands' on close partners and the whole arena of partnership in general. They only feel alive, happy, satisfied or complete if they are involved in a relationship. They can most easily see their beauty and value when it is reflected back from someone else. In other words, Venus in the 7th hands Aphrodite's girdle over to their partners to slip into: seeing the beloved as perfect and beautiful helps them to feel good about themselves.

As usual, there are both pluses and minuses. If we perceive someone in a very positive light, then we increase the likelihood of getting back what is best in that person. However, no partner can always live up to the expectations which Venus in the 7th might place on them. The other person is not *all* Venus: sometimes he or she will do something which isn't that beautiful or graceful and then the 7th house Venus is disappointed or turns critical. The same applies to the relationship itself: it can't always be all hearts and flowers and Venus in the 7th (especially if aspected by Saturn or Pluto) will have to learn to accept the hard work entailed as well.

The 7th house describes how we interact with society in general, and Venus there would be very at home in the opulent drawing rooms and salons of early twentieth-century Paris (Marcel Proust had Libra on the 7th house cusp). What we bring to others is also shown by the 7th, and Venus offers gifts of art, beauty, diplomacy and fashion. This placement also promotes success in legal matters.

Taurus on the 7th emphasizes constancy, fidelity and devotion in relationship with a tendency to possessiveness and jealousy. Marriage may be sought for the security, financial gain or physical closeness it offers. Libra in the 7th has a very strong urge for relationship and the need to develop tact and make adjustments for it to work without going along too much with others just for the sake of being included. (Don't forget, with Libra on the 7th, Aries is on the 1st.) The partner is more likely to be idealized or there may be an endless search not just for Mr or Miss Right, but for Mr or Miss Flawless.

Venus in the 8th

Venus in the 8th 'cares about' what happens between people, and wants to ensure that anything which is shared or exchanged is beautiful, appropriate, beneficial and valuable. It favours business partnerships and the accruing of money and possessions through marriage or inheritance.

In the bedroom, Aphrodite's magic girdle transforms into a provocative corselet (possibly black leather if Venus is aspected to Pluto). Her seductive charms find no better mode of expression than in the intimate whispers and caresses of love. Venus in the 8th has a way of receiving and responding to others which relaxes them, making partners feel secure enough to loosen inhibitions and restraints. In this sense, those with Venus in Scorpio's natural house, whether innocently or not, entice others to give to them. Hearts open, secrets are exposed, and bank accounts are put in their name.

There is also a love for that which is mysterious or esoteric and a desire to probe for anything hidden or subtle as if what is found on that level will make them more complete. (Seance parlours are probably filled with people with Venus in the 8th contacting their dear and departed wherever they might be.)

Taurus on the cusp or contained in the 8th has a flair for handling money and making business deals. There are usually concrete financial gains through marriage. Sex could be used as a way of manipulating or entrapping others. Libra on the 8th draws beauty out of people. There is a natural urge to relate closely with others and to treasure and value what others have to give. Both Libra and Taurus in this house give a sixth sense in partnerships which enables those with these placements to use tact and timing advantageously.

Venus in the 9th

For many of us, sitting down to contemplete the meaning and purpose of existence results in a headache. But rather than just struggling endlessly with religious and philosophical issues, those with Venus in the 9th usually derive greater happiness, peace and well-being from their belief systems. Somehow it wouldn't be right for a 9th house Venus to project anything too nasty onto God: in Venus' eyes only that which is fair, just and equitable deserves to be worshipped. Whether their God manages to live up to these high expectations will be shown by the aspects to Venus and other placements in the 9th. (For instance, the brilliant, influential *and* tormented German philosopher Nietzsche had Venus in the 9th *but* Leo on the 9th house cusp and its ruler, the Sun, opposed to Pluto and squared by Saturn.)

There is usually a love of travel and adventure and the promise of beneficial and pleasurable experiences to be had through them. Possessing a natural appreciation and fascination for the diversity of life expressed in the customs of different cultures, they might fall in love with a country other than their own, emulating its taste and style. Some may even marry someone foreign or a person met on holiday or abroad. This is also a good placement for teachers and educators who will be able to communicate the love of their subject to their students. Venus in the 9th easily and graciously enthuses about those things which they find valuable. Writers and artists with this placement invariably share their philosophy of life through their creations. Among those born with Venus in the 9th are the adventure writer Jack London, the controversial author Norman Mailer, and the lyrically profound Thomas Mann.

On a lighter note, relationships with in-laws are usually favoured if Venus is well-aspected in the 9th. If we understand a planet in a house to indicate the way in which we should meet the affairs of that house, then Venus here suggests that in-laws can be handled with tact and diplomacy.

Taurus in the 9th probably seeks some practical justification for philosophical beliefs and needs a philosophy which works in the everyday life. Because of the discomforts often entailed in being away from the home base, there will have to be some good reason to travel. Libra on the 9th has a strong sense of justice and fairness and may require a philosophy which has love of others as its main premise or which envisions humanity living up to some rather high ideals. Those with Libra on the 9th might also be fatally attracted to anyone with a foreign accent.

Venus in the 10th (Taurus and Libra on the MC)

If we understand the 10th house to be how we wish to appear to others, then Venus here is not likely to go out of the house looking too dishevelled (or without her trusty girdle on). Those with this placement want to be seen for their beauty, taste, grace or style. Professions are sought which afford them the opportunity to look beautiful or exhibit these traits: the artistic field, the entertainment business, the diplomatic service, the fashion world, etc. Two examples of Venus in the 10th in the field of show business are Jack Nicholson who has become a kind of middle-aged male sex symbol with a reputation of knowing how to enjoy himself; and Brooke Shields, the teenage star who portrayed the lead in an appropriately named Venusian vehicle, *Pretty Baby*. Regardless of the chosen career, Venus in the 10th needs and desires a harmonious working situation doing a job they value with people they like. Aspects to Venus may show other parts of the character which render fulfilling this aim more difficult.

Venus in the 10th suggests a warm, close tie with the mother, although certain difficulties may present themselves. If Venus is projected onto the mother, then she is experienced as the one with a monopoly on sexual power, taste and style. The little girl with this placement may feel inept or awkward next to such a mother, or turn her into a rival with whom she competes for attention. The boy-child may be as receptive to the mother's sexuality as he is to her maternal qualities. Mother then carries the image of the beloved and other women will have to compete with her.

Taurus on the MC or in the 10th may like outward displays of status and power. They can be possessive of their position and authority, showing great determination in the pursuit of career once they get going. Of the charts I have seen with this sign on the MC, some work as landscape gardeners, architects, builders and along the lines of massage and therapeutic body-work.

Those with Libra in the 10th or on the MC often work best in partnerships or in joint efforts with other people. They have much to offer in any work situation, but may be too exacting in demanding that others equal their service, precision and dedication. This sign shows up on the MC in the charts of certain diplomats, lawyers and politicians which I have seen as well as those who work in the arts, beauty and fashion fields. Those with Libra in this house are usually sensitive to how others might help them further their own social and career ambitions.

Venus in the 11th

A planet's house position instructs how the person can best approach life in that area. Those with Venus in the 11th, then, should encourage and develop a natural inclination to unite and co-operate with others in friendship and group situations.

They have the capacity to bring positive influences into any group they join and receive the same back in return, although aspects to Venus will show if other things get in the way of this happening. Usually there will be a fondness for social life and cultural outings. If Venus is difficultly aspected by Jupiter or Neptune, too much energy may be dissipated in social situations and greater discrimination is required.

The image of the beloved and that which is beautiful might be projected onto a friend or a group. Some people with Venus in the 11th only feel beautiful if they are seen with and accepted by the 'right' group or crowd. There may be an eye to personal social advancement through choosing groups or friends who are helpful in achieving their goals and objectives in life. Unlike Neptune, Venus doesn't always put on her girdle for nothing back in return.

For others, however there is an interest in those groups or organizations which propose to better or improve life in some way. Venus in the 11th gives and expects quite a high standard of friendship or group involvement and may be disappointed if others don't share or live up to these ideals. Sometimes, issues of rivalry and competitiveness may surface with friends or in group situations.

Taurus on the cusp of the 11th or contained in this house could cling too closely to friends and exhibit an overdependence which is suffocating to others. They tend to be loyal, and once given, their friendship lasts a long time. A sense of security is gained through their friends and any groups to which they might belong. Services offered are often of a practical nature.

Libra in the 11th loves to entertain and be entertained by others. They are drawn to friends with whom they share similar tastes and have an intellectual rapport. Unlike Taurus here, they are more careful to allow others the same degree of space they want for themselves. A friendship may turn into a romance or vice versa. Either Venus in the 11th or Libra there may fall in love with someone they meet in a group situation or who has been introduced to them by a friend.

Venus in the 12th

According to Greek myth, Aphrodite had a rather unusual beginning to her life. Saturn castrated his father Uranus and cast the dismembered phallus into the sea. The severed genitals floated on the waters and produced a white foam from which Aphrodite rose. At first it seems strange that the goddess of love and beauty is born as a result of such a ghastly and despicable conflict, but it is this side of Venus which is often evinced in the 12th. Sometimes it is through pain, wounding, suffering and loss that we grow more beautiful, tender, poised and loving.

Also rippling through the 12th house is the urge to transcend separateness and merge with something greater than the self. Venus in this houses suggests a love of letting go, of abandoning the self to something numinous, unbounded and divine. (Plato once said that 'Love is the pursuit of the whole.') In the 12th, Venus thirsts for an undefinable and immeasurable kind of beauty, something which offers total fulfilment, or perhaps a rememberance of a bliss long past.

Trying to quench this thirst by looking for this kind of love and beauty with another person, those with Venus in the 12th yearn to give themselves to a lover as one would to a god or goddess. Besides being a lot to ask of anybody, something deep inside still nags that adoration of just one person is not enough. With Venus in the 12th, a love is needed that knows no boundaries. Roberto Assagioli, the founder of Psychosynthesis, once said something which might help Venus in the 12th out of her predicament. 'If you appreciate everything, you remain free.'[1] In that case, if you lose a person or it is not opportune to have the thing you love, there is always something else you can enjoy. Perhaps this is the task of Venus in the natural house of Neptune and Pisces — to love everything.

Venus in the 12th also suggests the love of anything subtle, hidden, intangible or hard to grasp. Spend a rainy afternoon listening to Debussy (Venus in Leo in the 12th) and you will glimpse something of the nature of this placement. Some may literally fall in love with a person who isn't free and in true 12th house fashion the relationship may have to be kept hidden, lived within restrictions, or ultimately given up. (In the 12th, Venus loves to make sacrifices for love.) Venus in the 12th also denotes the love of what other people reject; the love of the downtrodden, the underdog, the criminal who really has a heart of gold, the person nobody else understands, etc.

On a more mundane level, Venus in this house favours associations with institutions. Some may work in art galleries or museums, while others administer to those less fortunate in hospitals. In two instances of Venus in the 12th I have seen, one worked as a drama therapist and the other as an art therapist helping people to recover after severe breakdowns. In another case, I did the chart of a woman with Venus in the 12th who said her three years recuperating in a mental home were some of the happiest in her life. Sometimes it is within the confines of prison walls that people discover a talent for painting, writing or sculpting. Venus in the 12th can also work behind-the-scenes designing sets or costumes, or putting on the star's make-up.

Any energy in the 12th house hangs in the balance — how we use that principle may determine what degree of joy or pain we meet in life. If Taurus is on the cusp of the 12th, being too materialistic or stubborn can cause problems, but not enough practicality or down-to-earth common sense could also be the tragic flaw. Libra on the 12th suggests that over-sensitivity to other people might give trouble, but not taking others' needs or points of view enough into consideration is also a danger. If a 12th house Taurus can learn to hold fast when necessary but let go when appropriate, an important lesson in life will be learned. Similarly, Libra on the 12th needs to learn to love and include others and yet keep their emotions in balance, and a little space to themselves.

22.
MARS AND ARIES THROUGH THE HOUSES

The planet Mars is associated with the Roman god of the same name and the Greek god Ares. In Greece, Ares, the god of war was thought of with terror and generally disliked for his furious and unmanageable disposition. The story goes that Hera was so outraged that her husband Zeus had given birth to Athene on his own (she sprang forth fully grown from his head) that she then produced Ares without recourse to him. In this sense, Ares (Mars) is born out of anger and spite, an image of his mother's fury and rage. In battle, he was accompanied by his squires Deimos (Fear), Phobus (Fright), and Eris (Strife). Not a very jolly band. Contrary to what you might expect, he was hardly ever victorious in battle and often made to look very silly. When Athene effortlessly knocks him over with a stone, the wounded Ares clumsily falls to the ground screaming and crying like ten thousand men. Even two ordinary mortals manage to capture Ares and hold him prisoner in a bottle for thirteen months (not unlike the way we 'bottle up' or repress our own anger). Not only made to look ridiculous in battle, he fares just as badly in love: when seducing Aphrodite he is embarrassingly caught in the act and entrapped in a net set by her husband Hephaestus. Invited to watch the spectacle, the other gods come to mock and laugh at the mighty Ares' plight. (Had the Greeks spoken Yiddish they would have called Ares a 'klutz'.)

By contrast, the Roman Mars was respected and honoured, and assumed an even more elevated position in the pantheon than the great god Jupiter. The Romans worshipped Mars not only as a god of war, but also a god of vegetation and fertility, a god of spring. The Latin root of his name is associated either with *mar* or *mas*, words which signify 'to shine' and describe the generative force. He was called Mars Gradivus, from the Latin *grandiri* — to become big, to grow. This time he is accompanied by his squires Honos (Honour) and Virtus (Virtue).

The Grecian disapproval of Ares as coarse and brutish and the Roman reverence of Mars as honourable and virtuous is indicative of two aspects of aggression: those forms we deplore and those forms we must not disown if we are to survive and grow. Mars can represent brute force, blind rage, impetuosity and a recklessness which makes us look stupid, but it can also be understood as a kind of healthy aggression — the positive impulse to comprehend and master the external world. Healthy aggression is the drive in living matter to express itself, the power which impels a seed to germinate. A positive Mars enables us to achieve independence, gives us the ability to stand our own ground and make choices which are self-directing. A healthy Mars provides the impetus to learn new skills and is the very basis of achievement in life (we *grapple* with an issue, we *attack* a problem, we *master* a difficulty).

The house position of Mars indicates where either one or both these forms of aggression and assertiveness will be operating. The distinction between the two may not always be clear: the child who rebels angrily against authority is being aggressive but is also manifesting a drive towards independence which is a vital and necessary part of growing up. By house, Mars shows where we need to attack life, take risks, be daring, and affirm our initiative, freedom and independence. It is also that area of life in which we may be prone to belligerence, passionate over-stimulation, accidents, too great a degree of competitiveness, violence and an insatiable drive for power. If Mars is 'bottled up' in a house, this may give rise to a sense of hopelessness, helplessness and subsequently depression via that sphere of experience. We also might provoke others into anger in that domain.

Aries on the cusp of a house or contained within it is similar to Mars in a house. The individual should meet that area of life with courage and vigour in order to unfold his or her unique potentialities and fulfil the life-plan. If we are depressed or psychologically down, we might try turning our attention to the house with Aries on the cusp as a means of 'getting things started again'.

There will be a relationship between the house with Aries on the cusp (or within it) and the house containing Mars. For instance, if Mars is in the 12th house and Aries is on the cusp of the 10th, the person might develop his or her enterprise and power through a career (Aries on the 10th) which involved work within an institution (Mars, rules of Aries, in the 12th).

Older astrological textbooks assign Mars co-rulership of Scorpio; therefore any house with Scorpio in it may be influenced by the placement of Mars in the chart. Personally, I feel Pluto suitably serves as the sole ruler of Scorpio.

Mars in the 1st

According to the myth, Ares (Mars) sprang forth fully grown from the body of the outraged Hera. Similarly, those with Mars here may find that their anger, fury or actions 'leap out' before anything can be done to stop them. At worst, they can be impatient and furious with the slightest obstacle blocking their way and exhibit a constant need to prove their power. Rather than turning their own bodies into a battlefield or taking out their aggression on whoever comes along, they will benefit from some sort of regular physical exercise or competitive sport. The disciplines of tai-chi, yoga, karate or the various body-therapies (which allow, and work creatively with, the cathartic discharge of anger and tension) are also recommended.

At best, those with Mars in the 1st are authentic, spontaneous and refreshing. Without appearing too blunt or rude, they can be honest and self-directing, possessing the courage to respect their own priorities rather than playing a role for somebody else. They are meant to meet life 'head on'. Rather than waiting for something to happen, people with this placement should take the first step.

Mars in the 1st is most noticeable in a fire sign but even if placed in watery Cancer or Pisces, they will still evince a strong presence whether they speak up or not. If those with Mars in this house appear shy and withdrawn, then other aspects in the chart are impinging on its expression and these should be examined. In some cases, they may need to be reminded that it is permissible to ask for what they want in life, rather than covertly manipulating others into giving it to them.

The urge to be the masters of their own destiny is usually strong and they will grapple against all odds to satisfy their desires. The Duke of Windsor, who abdicated the crown to marry the woman of his choice, was born with Mars in Aries in the 1st. Ernest Hemingway, obsessed with proving to the world that he was the epitome of a 'real man' had Mars in Virgo in the 1st. Another good example of this placement is the French existentialist writer Jean-Paul Sartre, born with Mars in Scorpio in the 1st house. He based his whole approach to the world (1st) on the premise that we are entirely responsible for our own lives — not only for our actions but also for our failures to act. For him, the individual alone was the creator and nothing in the world had significance except in terms of how one constituted it.

Mars in the 1st often calls for a fair degree of stamina, strength, fight and independence even very early in life.

Mars in the 2nd

If we understand a planet in a house to define the way in which a person can best approach that area of life to unfold the potentiality, then Mars in the 2nd calls for aggressive, assertive and daring action in the pursuit of money and possessions. They may have to take risks and chances to attain what they so desperately want. Unfortunately, this 'go out and get it quality' may prove counter-productive if their manner is too rash, impatient and abrupt. Machiavelli is reputed to have been born with Mars in the 2nd.

More generally, this placement describes a strong desire nature, with an urgency to enjoy the material world and the realm of the senses. While Venus in the 2nd turns on her seductive charms to allure and entice others to give her what she wants, Mars in this position operates more on the premise that 'I want what I want and I want it now.' If those with Mars in the 2nd don't take the initiative to go after what they want themselves, then they reach in the cupboard for their favourite whine: 'Give me, bring me, buy me, take me!' They also might take out their aggression on objects, smashing a prized vase to underline a point during an argument.

On a more positive note, their innate inner resources are characterized by courage and initiative and they could excel at any work which required these qualities. They will defend and fight for what they value, although they could also force what they value onto others.

For them, money and possessions are concrete symbols of their power and strength. In fact, we can understand these people better if we realize that they are basically trying to assert and affirm their individual existence, 'alive-ness' and vitality (Mars) by showing the world just how effectively they can go out and get what they want (2nd). (Even so, I would still keep my distance from them on the first day of the Harrod's sale.)

Mars in the 3rd

By asserting themselves on the environment (usually through their words, opinions, knowledge or points of view) people with Mars in the 3rd affirm their power, vitality and existence. Although many of us are afraid to say what we really think, this is precisely what those with Mars in the 3rd must do — if possible, of course, with tact, the universal antidote to a bad case of Mars.

Some may be afraid that being clear and direct is too rude or blunt. As a result, instead of saying what they really want to say, they resort to dropping large hints and heaving great sighs. Unfortunately, in any house containing Mars there appears to be a kind of storage tank which can accommodate only a certain amount of unexpressed thought, feeling or action before it blows up and makes a huge mess. Ultimately, with Mars in the 3rd, it is better to say what one is feeling or thinking rather than suppressing anything for too long.

There is usually an active, eager mind with quick repartee. A piercing intellect, a strong vocabulary or sharp verbal ability may be stockpiled as the necessary weapons with which to mount any advance. Although sometimes those with a 3rd house Mars may 'ram' their thoughts down another person's throat, their words also have the capacity to arouse others to action. Then again, they may spend as much time fighting their own thoughts as challenging those of other people. They can attack any subject of interest with zeal, and there is a natural desire to talk or write about whatever excites them. Some may 'blow off steam' through writing down their thoughts and feelings. A good form of self-therapy might be composing an angry letter to someone with whom they are furious, and then ripping it up.

Those with Mars in the 3rd find their own initiative and learn how to assert themselves by constellating power games with others in the early environment. Therefore this is one of the prime placements for conflicts with siblings, teachers and neighbours. However, when caught for something they shouldn't be doing, rather than owning responsibility, they may exclaim that it was their brother or sister, something they read, or a video nasty which put them up to it.

Because of a restless and highly strung nervous system, these people should strive to develop some degree of control and caution, especially on any form of journey or travel. Mars in the 3rd may also need to 'siphon off' excess energy through sport and exercise. Some may find tinkering with the car or other mechanical things relaxing.

It is an old adage that 'thoughts have wings'. Mars in the 3rd is powerful on the mental plane and any strongly felt thought could affect the environment whether or not it is directly spoken or acted upon. In a sense, the mind is like a sharp instrument or tool, which if handled in the right fashion can be highly effective in cutting through anything; but if employed incorrectly it can be dangerous and destructive, both to the self or others. Regardless of the aspects to Mars, it is ultimately this person's choice which way the implement is used.

Mars in the 4th (Aries on the IC)

Anything in the 4th house may be hidden from view. But, sooner or later, the drive to express the self latent in a 4th house Mars can no longer remain underground. And like anything which has been locked away for any length of time in the basement, it is not likely to be very pretty when you finally let it out. This placement suggests a hidden aggressiveness and anger that needs to be brought to the surface, analysed, re-integrated into the personality, and consciously directed to constructive ends. At first Mars may appear as intense fury and rage, erupting volcanically all over the place, surprising both those who spew it and anybody within close range. Once the Mars is 'freed', however, those with this placement eventually grow more adept and graceful at expressing and honouring everything that is going on inside them — the nasty bits as well as the good. Reconnecting to a 4th house Mars, like drinking a well-known beer, enlivens the parts other planets can't reach. A kind of juicy vitality which wasn't there before pervades much more of the life.

When most people come home to roost after a hard day's work, they just want to take off their shoes, mix a drink, put their feet up and watch television. But for those with Mars in the 4th, it is after they've 'clocked off' that their day begins. It is within the home sphere and personal life that they are likely to evince their greatest drive and enterprise, not to mention their domineering and aggressive streaks. In this respect they are not unlike a certain type of creature called a cichlid fish. These war-like fish need other fish on whom they can vent their aggression. If a pair of them are isolated from a tank containing other fish, then the male will turn his aggression towards his spouse and offspring. Similarly, those with Mars in the 4th may displace the anger they feel but don't express to other people onto those innocently waiting for them back at home. Well-mannered and docile at work, they may come home spoiling for a fight. Aggression can be displaced in other ways however: digging in the garden, building an extension on the house, provoking someone to get angry at them, or falling down the stairs, etc.

The father (or hidden parent) may be experienced as powerful and masterly, or as pushy, argumentative, sexual and potentially violent. Those with this placement may have to do battle with the father in order to reclaim their own sense of autonomy and freedom of expression. They may not succeed in this until they establish a home of their own and there is usually a strong urge to do so. Often they are descended from a background of 'survivors', and they, too, possess a mighty resilience — they can only be held down for so long before they bounce back fighting.

With Aries on the IC or in the 4th, there is a deep need to find the self in one's own right rather than to rely on the tradition or patterns of the family of origin. As those with Mars or Aries at the Nadir probe further into themselves, they will discover untapped reserves of energy and creativity yearning for a purposeful outlet. Sometimes it is not till later in the second half of life that they are free enough from ties and restrictions to fully attend to the question, 'But what do *I* want?'

Mars in the 5th

The 5th house is the house of play. And when Mars plays, there is no doubt who is boss of the sandbox. The competitive spirit is very great, and if you build a bigger or better castle than your friend with Mars in the 5th, watch out — you may end up with sand in your eyes. Who said it's not whether you win or lose, but how you play the game that counts? Not likely somebody with Mars in Leo's natural house.

And the same applies to life, love and creativity. It's not good enough just to *do* something — it must be done dramatically and with all the heart. On the plus side, there is a natural vitality and enthusiasm which stamps the individuality on everything those with Mars in the 5th undertake. They may not be another Picasso, but the picture they paint is very special — at least to them. And who's to deny it, if even for just a few days or moments the act of creating from inside themselves has given them a greater feeling for who they are or enhanced their sense of power, identity and vitality.

Often there is a love of competitive sport or feats involving some degree of daring, risk or strenuous physical exertion. And with the same zestful and impulsive spirit, they pursue the greatest sport of them all, the game of love and romance. Nor are they just looking to make a match; nothing short of a whole forest fire will do. Provided those with Mars in the 5th don't frighten others off with their intensity, how soon the flames of love are extinguished or whether the fire quickly spreads somewhere else will depend, to a large degree, on the aspects and sign placement of Mars.

Children will catch something of the Mars projection. The initial enthusiasm to produce a family will probably be very strong; but the daily drudgery and sacrifices involved may be much less appealing. How can they paint pictures, take tennis lessons, make love, go to the opera, and have the time to raise children as well? It's not surprising that people with this placement bear offspring with strong independent streaks. The children would need to learn to stand on their own fairly quickly and develop strong enough wills to combat and compete with the demands of the parent's 5th house Mars.

Mars in the 6th

The possible manifestations of Mars in the 6th house become clearer if we compare and contrast the ways in which the Greek Ares and the Roman Mars would approach the affairs of this house.

First, picture Ares mounting an attack on the housework. Within ten minutes he would have whizzed through every room and nearly all the corners as quickly as possible, hopefully not knocking over too many things in the process. His motto might be 'A job worth doing is a job worth doing in a hurry.' Or after losing yet another battle with his sister Athene, he might immediately take out his rage 6th-house fashion by furiously scrubbing the kitchen floor, yelling at a servant, or kicking the dog.

Ares would push his body hard. Besides exhausting himself continually chasing around from one thing to another, he could attract accidents due to recklessness and inner discord.

Although it is not like Ares, if he did hold in his anger, he would probably suffer regularly from headaches or more generally turn his aggression against the body. (With the planet Mars in the 6th, feelings and impulses register very strongly in the body and must find some sort of expression if it is not going to short-circuit and blow a fuse.)

Of course, Ares would be a big hit at the office. Unlikely to tolerate someone lording over him and probably exhibiting a tendency to run roughshod over co-workers, it's fortunate that he prefers to attend to his job independently.

In striking contrast, the Roman Mars handles the affairs of the 6th house very differently. Seeing every little thing he does as a reflection of who he is, he would take fastidious pride in his work down to the last detail. Concerned with achieving independence and self-sufficiency in the running of everyday affairs, he would welcome the opportunity to learn new skills, and gain great satisfaction mastering tasks which challenged him.

Although he could be obsessive at times about the body's smooth functioning, much energy would be directed into caring for and maintaining the body. He recognizes the body as the vehicle through which he can express himself and prove his power, and naturally he wants to keep it in good shape.

Somewhat reminiscent of his Greek counterpart and due to a strong belief about how something should be done, the Roman Mars (in the 6th) may experience difficulty and impatience with co-workers, although in the right situations a joint effort could prove stimulating. But usually Mars in the 6th wants to run the show himself. He might, however, fight battles for workers' rights or stand up for a colleague whom he believes is being mistreated. Mars in the 6th might equally support an animal rights group.

In general, a well-aspected Mars in the 6th tends to act like the Roman Mars. But difficult aspects to Mars in this house (hard angles to it from the Sun, Jupiter, Uranus and Pluto especially) are more likely to manifest, initially at least, as the Greek Ares.

Mars in the 7th

By house, Mars shows the area of life in which we need to take action and assert ourselves. In the 7th, this gives rise to a strong urge to define the identity and gain a sense of power through relationships with other people. I have seen many instances of this placement in the charts of young men and women who rush haphazardly into marriage — often inspired by the first taste of sexual passion or partially motivated by the desire to escape from the restrictions of a difficult or oppressive family background. Through marriage they believe they will find themselves in their own right. More often what they do discover is that they have replaced one form of tyranny with another. The initial sexual attraction may die down, but the power games are still there.

Some people with this placement come on so strongly at first that they frighten others away. Conversely, there may be an attraction to someone with obvious Mars qualities — the bold, straightforward, dynamic hero or heroine who can relieve them of the burden of making their own decisions in life. After a while, they may become angry or resentful at the bossiness of the other person and attempt to take back the power they once so freely handed over. But it is unfair to condemn Mars in the 7th only to relationships filled with strife and contention, although some people seem to thrive very well on a diet of fireworks. There are many examples of Mars in this house which manifest in lively, stimulating relationships where the partners positively 'spark off' one another, while still allowing the mate to maintain personal freedom. However, there is the danger of taking their aggression out on those closest and most dear to them, or not so subtly arousing other people to anger and thereby conjuring a justifiable excuse to vent their own. Those with Mars in the 7th also appear to need fairly constant reassurance of their worth in the eyes of other people. They are also likely to be the first to stand up and defend another person if they believe that he or she is being unjustly accused.

Mars in the 8th

Those with Mars in the 8th come alive in joint enterprises where they can give and receive all they can. Usually there is a shade more subtlety to Mars in this house than in his other domains, although the clumsy Greek Ares may evince his characteristic impetuosity by rushing into hastily conceived financial deals. Some people with Mars in the 8th will gain a sense of honour and virtue by standing up for their deeply felt beliefs, and will try to challenge and convert others who don't share the same values. Others with Mars in the 8th find the prospect of appropriating the values and possessions of another person much more rewarding and enticing. A difficultly aspected Mars could indicate fights with the marriage partner over joint resources, battles over legacies and inheritances, trouble with a belligerent tax-inspector, and conflicts with get-rich-quick business partners, so some degree of caution is advised in these areas.

But it is in the more intimate arena of the bedroom that an 8th house Mars most clearly exposes itself. Their passions are strong, but sexual expression may be more than just a means of relieving built-up physical tension: for many, sex is a contest and Mars is determined to be the victor. Again, we can understand these people better if we realize that in acting this way they are attempting to affirm and define their identity and power. The principle of the Sun distinguishes us from others, but we need Mars to prove our point; and whether, in the 8th house, the point is given or taken, Mars here likes to be in charge. With a little bit of thought it's not hard to appreciate that there is more to a person's sexual taste than meets the eye; and fortunately or unfortunately for some, Mars in the 8th may take out their aggression in the bedroom. Or due to guilt and ambivalence, Mars in the 8th may resort to its second favourite battle-cry: 'They made me do it,' blaming others for forcing them into situations they somehow help to contrive.

By meeting it in others or through their own selves, those with Mars in the 8th often discover and have to grapple with the darker emotions of blind lust, envy, greed, jealousy, etc. The need or ability to transmute these seething feelings into a more constructive expression depends, to a large degree, on the aspects to Mars. If Mars is difficultly aspected by the outer planets, it is usually most pressing that the raw, primordial side of Mars be rechannelled in other ways.

Sometimes there is a burning interest in the esoteric or the occult.

Caution should be taken when exploring or experimenting in anything mediumistic in nature: there is the danger of projecting their own anger and aggression onto something 'out there' and then experiencing the disowned quantity as turning around and pursuing them. Although Mars can hardly be defined as covert, in the 8th he does have a kind of detective-like ability to probe subtly and persistently into what is hidden or secret. If those with this placement sense something wrong or askew in a relevant person or situation, for better or for worse, they are not easily able to let it rest.

The Scorpio Dylan Thomas wrote, 'Do not go gentle into that good night.' In deaths and transformations of a physical or psychological nature, Mars in the 8th will usually follow that advice.

Mars in the 9th

We might think there is a chance to breathe some fresh air when we enter the realm of the 9th — the house of religion, philosophy, long journeys and higher education. But history has shown that in many respects this is the stickiest and bloodiest battlefield of them all.

With Mars in the 9th, God is not just sought after, but hunted. Those with this placement usually pursue and stand by strong philosophical or religious beliefs. Believing that their version of the truth is the only one, they might promote and defend it with a crusader-like zeal. And some might say why shouldn't they, since it is probably formulated in such a fashion as to support and justify their deepest desires and passions in life anyway. Although the image of God may be an angry and fiery one, He is probably cast enough in their own likeness to understand and indulge those occasions when they may have to break His rules. For a few with this placement, God even manages to accept killing, raping and pillaging provided that these things are done in His name. In this way, some people with Mars in the 9th are culpable of displacing responsibility for acting out their own cruel drives onto God. Generally, before they undertake something they like to have the justification of some higher law behind them.

However, others may express a 9th house Mars by being angry at God Himself. Like Tevya in *Fiddler on the Roof*, they shake a fist at heaven or go even further, and start telling God how He should run the show.

There is often a strong urge to travel, and sometimes they may just 'pick up and go' at the spur of the moment. A woman with Mars in this house might develop a powerful attraction to a foreign man, or someone who offers to broaden her horizons in some way. In like manner, there may be a passion for one particular culture.

Mars in the 9th will also influence the sphere of higher education. Expansive knowledge on one or two subjects gives them a sense of power and authority. The Mars may be projected onto an institution of higher learning or one particular professor with whom they do battle.

Careers which offer a chance to preach — such as writing, teaching, publishing or the ministry — may attract those with Mars in this house. The Gauquelins found Mars in the 9th prominent in the charts of champion sportspeople, top executives, military leaders and physicians.

Finally, on a more mundane level, Mars may describe something about their relationship with in-laws. This, like the proverbial mother-in-law, speaks for itself.

Mars in the 10th (Aries on the MC)

Mars is one of the most ambitious of all the placements to be found in the 10th. There is a need to be seen as powerful, strong and assertive, and a career which brings these qualities to the fore may be sought. Those with this placement want to be remembered as having done something worthy of attention — honourable, if possible, but otherwise if there is no other way. Examples of Mars in the 10th include Tracy Austin, the American tennis pro with Mars in Leo in the 10th ruling Aries on the 6th house cusp, clear placements for someone esteemed for athletic prowess; and Roman Polanski, with Mars in Libra in the 10th, noted as much for his ill-fated relationships as for his creative talents. In some cases, the ambition of Mars can turn into a ruthless clawing to the top or a situation where the means justifies the ends: John Mitchell, one of Nixon's cabinet indicted in the Watergate affair has Mars in Gemini (the sign of communication) in this house.

If the 10th house is taken to be the mother (or shaping parent), then the archetypal principles symbolized by Mars would have passed in some way between her and the offspring with this placement. In a positive light, the mother could have been experienced as masterly and powerful, thereby modelling to the child how to be strong in the world. Difficult placements to Mars, however, suggest a more turbulent relationship. The mother might have been seen as pushy and contentious, and the child, therefore, may have grown up loathing her power or fearing her wrath. Later in life, the way this person relates to the world will be influenced by the early experiences with the mother. The world may be seen as a place in which one has to fight to get along or a position of autonomy is sought so that one is no longer in such a subservient role. At some stage in life, children with this placement may have to battle with the mother to free themselves from her control. Some may succeed to such a degree that roles are reversed and they end up the ones running their own mothers' lives. Later problems with bosses and authority figures in general are often evinced with Mars in the 10th.

Aries on the MC or in the 10th is similar to Mars there. In this case, the house position of Mars will reveal more about the kinds of qualities a person brings into public view. Work which allows for initiative, leadership and a fair degree of autonomy is recommended.

Mars in the 11th

In the 11th, an active participation with friends, groups and organizations provides the outlet for the passion, energy and assertion of Mars. The aspects to Mars in this house, though, will reveal just how welcome this involvement is.

Mars, the essence of personal initiative, is curiously placed in the group-minded 11th. While those with Mars in the 11th may extol the rhetoric of teamwork and co-operation until they are red in the face, they often have a difficult time adjusting or compromising their own strongly felt ideas and opinions with others. While friendly Venus effortlessly blends and harmonizes for the sake of peace and love, Mars is concerned with imposing *its* way despite all odds. Good old Mars, spoiling for a fight as usual and in this case choosing one of the most appropriate houses in the chart to find it.

Mars in the 11th represents a dilemma which is actually inherent in all of us. By nature, we are social beings (11th) and yet we all strongly feel the urge to assert our identity as autonomous individuals (Mars). We form groups on the basis of common interests, ideals and aims, but it is precisely in those groups where there is a close identification among members that the most bitter disputes arise. (The early Christian Church is one example.) As soon as we grow too closely identified, our autonomy is threatened and the urge to split, differentiate and disrupt naturally makes itself felt. And Mars, schooled in the arts of aggression and self-assertion, is just the man for the job. In the end, however, the trick for Mars in the 11th is to unite with others for a common purpose and yet not lose its individuality.

Mars in the 11th can play other roles as well. Those with this placement often have the ability to arouse the group to action.

Conversely, being a member of a group or crowd may give Mars the exact justification needed to do something he might never allow himself to do on his own. In this sense, Mars in the 11th might displace personal responsibility onto the group. Those with Mars in this house may take up a cause which they feel will improve society in some way or champion the downtrodden. Care should be taken that such crusading is not done so belligerently that more harm than good is done.

The possible interpretations of Mars in relation to groups also applies to personal friendship as well. Mars may be the first to stand up to defend a friend, but in the name of autonomy he may be the first to attack or fend off that same person. Some with this placement could try to run and direct the lives of their friends in an overbearing manner, while others will accuse friends of trying to manipulate and boss them. Other examples of the likely effects of Mars in this house have been covered in the general discussion of the 11th house in Part 2 of the book, and the reader may wish to refer to page 96 to review these.

If well-aspected, Mars in the 11th is usually quite clear about achieving its goals and objectives in life. Problems occur if Jupiter or Neptune, in particular, cloud the judgement, influencing Mars to aim unrealistically or dispersing his energy unproductively. Saturn and Pluto aspecting an 11th house Mars may also set up stumbling blocks which Mars may have to learn to work his way around.

Mars in the 12th

Mars is at his most manic and inconsistent in the 12th house. Sometimes, as the Gauquelins found, he is out there in full gear for all to see; at other times, he is just nowhere in sight. And if this isn't enough to confuse you, he reappears now and again behind different masks. It's not like Mars to be so elusive — somewhere along the line he's picked up a trick or two from Neptune.

In the 12th, the natural aggression of Mars may sometimes be disguised as a vague and passive dissatisfaction with life: nothing feels right but he can't put his finger on what's wrong. At other times, Mars resorts to one of his favourite disguises, The Incredible Sulk — whining endlessly about everything that's wrong but refusing to do anything constructive about it. Having driven everyone around the bend, he miraculously snaps out of it as soon as he has managed to make someone else express his rage for him. Mars in the 12th may consciously deny his anger and assertion and yet vicariously enjoy violence and have dreams or fantasies of a destructive nature. Hidden somewhere in his psyche is an incendiary device which can flare up in sudden episodes of uncontrolled behaviour. To complicate matters, Mars in the 12th may be the one to act out the unexpressed stirrings and anger of those around him: the battles he ends up fighting may not even be his own.

Mars needs to affirm his sense of personal power and identity: in the 12th this is sometimes paradoxically achieved by giving over his will to another person or higher cause. Although the study of successful sportspeople has shown that it is in this house that Mars comes first and wins his gold, there is no other domain in which Mars can so graciously put himself aside for other people. The 'me-first' attitude associated with this planet may be replaced by a sense of 'You-first and I'll help you' or 'Rather than just doing it for me, I want to do it for everyone.' While this sounds noble, and often is, sometimes the abnegation of personal responsibility to serve a greater purpose inspires disastrous consequences. Adolf Eichmann, with Mars in the 12th helped by Pluto in the 1st, is a case in point. John DeLorean, the untiring business executive apparently determined to promote his large-scale schemes at all costs, was born with Mars in Aries in the 12th.

The problem with Mars in the 12th is not really a lack of fight but the fact that the troops are sometimes deployed in the wrong direction. Rather than using their energy to face life 'head on', Mars in this house frequently devises highly effective strategies for retreating from it altogether through escapist or self-destructive behaviour. In whatever house Mars is placed, he has the urge to go out and get what he wants: in the 12th house, the desired goal may be the dissolution and transcendence of life's limits and boundaries. And just as Venus in the 12th can't love enough, Mars in this house feels that he can never do enough. According to Lois Rodden in *The American Book of Charts*, the actor George Sanders (Mars in Cancer in the 12th) featured in *ninety* movies in thirty-six years but killed himself because he was bored.

Those with Mars in the 12th might benefit from actively investigating and interpreting the meaning of their dreams. As with Mars in the 4th and the 8th, there is also the ability to perform actions in a covert manner or for reasons not immediately obvious to others. Sometimes institutions will play an important part in their lives, although anger and hostility may be unleashed on nurses, prison wardens or some poor librarian who can't find the book they want. Other possible effects of Mars in the 12th can be found in the general discussion of this house in Part 2 of the book.

23.
JUPITER AND SAGITTARIUS THROUGH THE HOUSES

The planet Jupiter is associated with the Roman god of the same name, and the Greek god Zeus. In Greek mythology, Zeus was the majestic god of the heavens, ruling limitless and expansive space. Residing in the upper ethers of the air and on mountaintops, Zeus was believed to be omniscient, a god who knew and saw everything. From his high perspective, he viewed life on earth and dispensed both good and evil, although he was mostly thought of as compassionate and benevolent. His daily rounds included protecting the weak and innocent, unleashing thunderbolts on the wicked for their own good, averting any catastrophies which might come up in heaven or on earth, and squabbling with his jealous wife Hera, whom he felt restricted him too much. Somehow, he also managed to make room in his already busy schedule for an extraordinary number of extra-marital affairs. Acting on the spur of the moment and with a zest equal to 6,000 i.u.'s of Vitamin E a day, he enthusiastically chased after various goddesses, mortal women, and the occasional smooth-skinned young boy. While not always successful, he nonetheless appeared to take great delight in the pursuit of his ever-changing objectives, transforming himself into a bull one day, a swan the next, and a shower of gold another. A consummate actor, he loved playing roles. While producing numerous children as a result of these escapades, he left the job of raising them to other people.

The question is: how do we squeeze all this and more into any one house? Needless to say, the house in the chart containing Jupiter is an area of life in which we require a great deal of room to grow and explore. It is where we are not content with that which is routine or humdrum, but rather where we are propelled to experience life more fully and completely. Whether or not a Hera is there to restrict us, we are not necessarily unhappy with what we already have in that domain, but we still want more and there always seems further to go. Jupiter is ultimately more interested in what might be around the corner than the reality at hand.

As you might imagine, problems in Jupiter's house generally stem from over-extending ourselves in that area. Wherever Jupiter is in the chart, we never know what is enough until we know what is more than enough. Also, because Jupiter viewed life from so far up, he didn't always examine things as closely as he should have. A difficultly aspected Jupiter in a house could indicate where we take action based on misguided judgement or perspective, usually as a result of being overly optimistic or too enthusiastic about what is possible. And like the promiscuous god, it is also the sphere in which we may sow many creative seeds but not always stay around to attend to their growth. We start something, but before we know it something else has caught our attention.

We mustn't forget Jupiter's important role as the guardian of law and religion and the noble protector of the people. The populace prayed to him for help, guidance, inspiration, benevolence and preservation. His presence in a house makes us hopeful, positive and expectant in that area of life as if with him there we are charmed and protected. And if we entertain such positive feelings and good vibrations as these, it is not surprising that we usually are successful in Jupiter's sphere. A danger exists, however, that we might sometimes feel betrayed if it happens that what we enthused over doesn't turn out to be as wonderful as we had hoped. But usually, even if we are let down in Jupiter's house, he still makes sure that we land on our feet.

The planet Jupiter represents the symbol-making capacity of the psyche and we normally imbue the events and experience of the house Jupiter is in with great significance. While this may give rise to histrionics, it is also through Jupiter's house that we glimpse a larger pattern, order or meaning to life. In his domain, we search for the higher rules and laws upon which existence can be based and by which it can be guided. Consciously or not, we look for God there, or endeavour to find within that framework of experience 'the Truth' with a capital 'T'.

Jupiter was prayed to as the Great Preserver of life and the Deliverer from battles and plagues. Sometimes our very survival may depend on being able to give some sort of symbolic meaning to an event or perceive its significance within a larger perspective. The humanistic psychologist, Viktor Frankl, confirmed this function of Jupiter for himself on the basis of his experience in a concentration camp: while interred in Auschwitz, he observed that those who could impart some sense of meaning to the agony they were having to endure were the ones most likely to survive.

Although aspects to Jupiter may distort just how clearly or reasonably we see the 'truth', the affairs of the house this planet is in offer us the belief in something greater, the hope for something better, and the sense that life is not just a collection of random events, but has meaning and purposeful intention. When our faith in life begins to falter, it is by looking towards Jupiter's domain that we may gain the inspiration to travel on.

Jupiter will influence any house with Sagittarius in it. Likewise, the effect of Sagittarius on a house carries much of the same meaning as Jupiter in a house.

In older textbooks, Jupiter is given co-rulership with Neptune of Pisces. Therefore, Jupiter may have some bearing on any house with Pisces in it. I personally feel that Neptune serves the job as sole ruler of Pisces very well without needing Jupiter's help.

Jupiter in the 1st

Accompanied by a fanfare and a drum roll, Jupiter in the 1st house appears on the scene. The house placement of Jupiter indicates where we are open to higher inspiration. Those with Jupiter in the 1st house of the self are natural philosophers who attempt to answer some of the 'big' questions of existence. In whatever they do, they have the ability to inspire and arouse new life and interest, throwing themselves into something with great initial enthusiasm. Sometimes they are important social, educational or religious thinkers, while others with this placement play out the more sporty side of Jupiter, living the life of the adventurer or gambler. Some are the 'trendies' who are up on the latest styles and seen in all the right new places. There are also the nature-loving 1st house Jupiters, who climb mountains to glimpse even more expansive vistas. For some the world is their playground as they rove here and there, encountering others, sharing what they have with them, and then moving on.

If we understand a planet in a house to indicate the best way to meet life in that area, then those with Jupiter in the 1st should seek to expand themselves in ways associated with its sign placement. For instance, Jupiter in Pisces should explore ways of opening up the feelings; Jupiter in Aquarius will grow through expanding its understanding; and Jupiter in Leo through increasing the capacity for self-expression. For instance, the almost mythic and larger than life superstar Mick Jagger was born with Jupiter in Leo in the 1st. Radiating his being through his music and creative expression (Jupiter in the 1st rules Sagittarius intercepted in the 5th house of creativity), he fills vast concert halls with his powerful presence.

While Jupiter in the 1st wants to go further and faster and can envision far-reaching goals, aspects to Jupiter might indicate other parts of the personality which hold the person back or hinder the progress. It's probably still best for them to view life as a journey, even if they have to move along at a pace which is much slower than they would like.

In some cases, an inflated sense of identity is one of the dangers of this placement. Innately believing that they have so much to offer which is valuable, expansive and worthwhile, there are those with Jupiter in the 1st who hold nothing back. An exaggerated opinion of themselves may lead them to over-reach or extend beyond their capacities. Sometimes there is a marvellous vision and inspiration but insufficient discipline and concentration to follow something through to completion. Because they so dearly want to free themselves from all restrictions, they may look for the easy way out if the going gets tough.

If Jupiter is well-aspected, it is likely that the atmosphere in the early environment was conducive to growth and positive self-development, enhancing their creativity and playfulness. Sometimes it indicates travel or many changes of residence while still young. Since Jupiter's tendency is to inflate and expand, weight can sometimes be a problem for these people.

Jupiter in the 2nd

Those with Jupiter in the 2nd may seek to expand their resources and possessions as a means of gaining greater joy and fullness of life. Taken to an extreme, it could mean the god Mammon is worshipped as the be-all and end-all of existence, or a religious or numinous value is bestowed on monetary and material success. Some might see money and possessions as a symbol of their worth and value. Certain objects may be treasured because they inspire, communicate or symbolize something significant for them. The value system in general (2nd) may be linked to their philosophical and religious beliefs (Jupiter). Some with this placement perceive God's touch in all the manifestations of nature, glimpsing the underlying patterns and laws expressing through the form world.

The acquisitive instinct is heightened for those with Jupiter in this house and with such a strong motivation, they usually succeed in the material realm. However, what is earned may be spent as quickly as they make it. While they are usually generous, difficult aspects to Jupiter suggest a wastefulness with money and possessions, or a tendency to invest recklessly and unwisely. But should they fall flat on their faces, they generally have the ability to 'drum up' money again — just when they are most 'down and out', an opportunity comes along which saves them.

The 2nd house represents what constitutes security for us. With Jupiter there, personal safety could be sought through abundance on the material plane; while, for others with this placement, security might mean possessing higher knowledge or sound religious beliefs. Paradoxically, some may feel most secure if they know that at any moment they are free to get up and go. Innate resources include a natural enthusiasm, an ability to inspire other people, and the capacity to impart practical meaning to life. The desire nature is strong and usually they will believe that there are 'higher' justifications for their having what they so urgently want. Therefore, they don't feel too guilty satisfying their endless appetites. Money could be earned through Jupiterian pursuits such as teaching, travel, the law, import-export trade, spreading religion, etc.

Jupiter in the 3rd

In the 3rd house, Jupiter has a great deal to say. At best, the energy and inspiration which give rise to thoughts or words can be communicated and channelled to others, who are then 'fired', enlivened and expanded by what those with Jupiter in this house have shared or made accessible. At worst, they waffle on endlessly, more concerned with the quantity of what they have to say than the quality, pausing now and then to savour the rare genius of their insights.

Jupiter in the 3rd also expands the mind. While this may yield an over-abundance of thoughts on any one topic or a mind which is literally all over the place, it also gives an awareness broad enough to fit any one particular thing happening around them into a larger framework or perspective. While focusing on something specific, they do not lose sight of what is going on in the background and all around it. Some may hurry through a book thinking that the sooner they are done with it the more quickly they can read the next; while others may find that just one sentence is enough to transport them on a journey to other worlds — and hence they never finish the book at all. Similarly, there can be a tendency to 'read too much' into another person's passing comment or glance, and they end up making a Mount Olympus out of a molehill.

One of Jupiter's main concerns is finding greater fulfilment. In the 3rd, knowledge can be worshipped as a god who offers them increased joy and mastery over life, inclining those with this placement to exhibit an almost insatiable need to learn things. Sometimes this position is referred to as that of 'the perpetual student'. For them, life is a huge jigsaw puzzle, and the more pieces they can find to fit together the better. Each time two parts click into place a kind of mental orgasm is experienced. Some may think that they have to travel the world sixteen times over to achieve the ultimate release, while others learn sooner or later that there is more than enough just happening between the front door and the nearest travel agency.

Since those with Jupiter in the 3rd are expanded by whatever is around them, this placement normally indicates a good relationship with brothers, sisters, neighbours, etc. Sometimes there are a large number of siblings. However, difficult aspects to Jupiter can manifest in fierce sibling rivalry or the hero-worship of an older brother or sister, and later disappointments if too much has been expected of them. People who have travelled or changed residences many times during childhood and adolescence often have this placement of Jupiter as well. Usually, early schooling is not found too threatening, but welcomed as an opportunity to broaden the horizons beyond what the family has to offer. Writing, teaching, lecturing, study, travel and knowledge of languages should all be encouraged.

Jupiter in the 4th (Sagittarius on the IC)

At first, the hidden and insular 4th house seems an ill-suited domain for a sky-god like Jupiter. However, true to his nature, he manages to make a very comfortable life for himself in this sphere — provided that his home life does not fence him in too much.

I have seen many charts with Jupiter in the 4th in which the people were born into aristocratic families or had a few well-known ancestors. Through the father's line, there is often the influence of a foreign culture in the blood. But even if they can't claim descent from Louis XVI, the last Czar of Russia, or the king of the gypsies, they inherit a religious, philosophical or travelling nature through the background or early home conditions. Like the genie in the bottle, residing deep within those with Jupiter in the 4th is a powerful and expansive spirit wanting to be freed.

They can invest a great deal of energy in establishing the home of their dreams, but they had better ensure there is enough room in it to satisfy their need to move around. Often they benefit from living out of the crowded conditions of the city, and in the more natural and open setting of the country where views and vistas are unobstructed. (I always picture them living on a ranch.) Some may travel from country to country looking for their spiritual home. Rather than aiming for public or professional recognition, they might devote themselves to work on the soul and inner growth. A woman I know with Jupiter in Sagittarius in the 4th is a good example of this placement. Born into an aristocratic home and a lady by birth, she now lives on a spiritual commune in Canada. At first caught between the values of her family and those preached by her guru, she moved back and forth from tea at royal garden parties to washing pots at the ashram. But later, she realized that the best of these separate worlds had something to offer each other. She has brought a renewed sense of spiritual vision to her family while helping her fellow disciples to appreciate those more solid, earthly values of the English tradition.

Jupiter in the 4th may colour the paternal relationship. In some cases the actual father is confused with the image of god: he is seen as noble, majestic and larger than life. Reflecting some of the other qualities of Zeus, the father might be experienced as a promising figure full of potential and inspiration, but with an incorrigible roving eye and bags full of wild oats. Sometimes the father will suppress the Jupiterian side of his nature for the sake of providing the kind of structure and security expected of him; in this case, the child with this placement may grow up with an irresistible urge to enact what the father has not played out.

If Jupiter in the 4th is well aspected, there is an underlying optimism and faith in life which will come to the fore as the person grows older. Generally, it favours a promising old age filled with many interests and pursuits. Contemporaries may lag behind while Jupiter in the 4th is still lively and progressive.

With Sagittarius at the IC there is usually the attempt to build the life on a clear moral or philosophical framework. Sometimes they travel in childhood or grow up in a religious family. If life comes to a standstill, they can renew themselves by strong acts of faith or envisioning some new goal towards which to aim.

Jupiter in the 5th

William Blake, a Sagittarian with Sun conjunct Jupiter in the 5th house wrote that 'the road of excess leads to the palace of wisdom.' For those with this placement, more is definitely better than enough.

The 5th house always enjoys expressing itself; but with Jupiter here, it has to be done with panache and thunderbolts. Through any form of creative self-expression, those with Jupiter in the 5th step into something more spacious, perhaps replicating in their own creativity a sense of Divine creation itself. In other words, by being creative they find 'God' in themselves.

The 5th house is the house of play and nobody plays quite like Jupiter. It's hardly likely that the sandbox is large enough (Malibu beach would do better), but their castles must be bigger and more imaginative than the next fellow's. Unlike Mars, who chases you out of the sandbox altogether if you get in his way, Jupiter in the 5th is willing to co-operate on joint ventures with his playmates, provided that he is the one to direct the show. After all, his vision is really the most interesting and if he likes it then it has to be best for everyone. Even if a friend slips him an idea or two, Jupiter will expand and elaborate on it until it is totally his own.

Those with this placement should have no trouble filling their lives with hobbies and artistic outlets which they find exciting and satisfying, provided that they stay with these long enough to develop a fair degree of expertise. They like to test themselves against life, and there is sometimes a taste for adventurous sports, games of chance, and playing the stock market. For them to feel most alive, each new hurdle must be that little bit bigger than the last.

With Jupiter in the 5th, a love of the amorous chase is highly evident. Naturally romantic, they seek outlets in relationships and affairs. A case in question is Prince Andrew, with Jupiter in Sagittarius in this house — who between flying helicopters, pursuing actresses, blessing new ventures and dodging reporters is as good a modern-day equivalent to Zeus as can be found. However, if Jupiter is difficultly aspected, their perspective in respect to 5th house matters may be impaired by their own subjectivity, excitement and over-enthusiasm.

Usually this placement indicates a good rapport with children, who grow up with a philosophical or spiritual outlook or a strong desire to broaden their horizons through travel and adventure. Some parents with this placement may project their own unlived-out yearnings and wanderlust onto their offspring. In certain cases, this may spur the child on to greater achievements; while in other instances, in an attempt to be a person in his or her own right, the child may have to betray some of the parent's ideals. Nonetheless, the parent-child relationship usually survives intact. Jupiter was prayed to as the protector of the people, and it is interesting to note that Princess Anne, the patron of the Save the Children Fund was born with Jupiter in Pisces in the 5th. (Jupiter rules horses and her equestrian abilities are shown by this placement as well.)

Jupiter in the 6th

Jupiter may seem a little cramped in the 6th house of health, adjustment to necessity, and the management of mundane affairs. But regardless of what he does with his time, he always manages to make something significant of it. Those with Jupiter in this house seek (or should seek) to experience meaning in life through work and service to others. Self-purification and the refinement of their skills and abilities afford them a greater sense of well-being and satisfaction.

As in the 3rd house, Jupiter may manifest in different ways. In a bid to do as much as possible for themselves or others, some might hurry through one task in order to move quickly onto the next. Others, however, will apply themselves to any small matter with the utmost concern and diligence. As in the traditional Japanese tea ceremony, a tiny detail can assume cosmic importance.

Pride will be taken in their work and they usually have a great deal of energy to contribute to any employment situation. Although Jupiter is prone to believe that his way of doing things is best, they will normally have good relationships with co-workers. This position could indicate work of a Jupiterian nature — involving travel, public relations, educational activities, the promotion of art, culture, sports, religion, etc.

Some may burden themselves with too many duties in life and not leave the time to care for their own bodies. Others may become almost obsessed with health or making the body a better vessel for the spirit. These people might undertake any new diet, technique or exercise which promises heaven on earth. In fact, the whole day may be strewn with such activities: waking up at seven, taking six deep cleansing breaths, a two-mile jog, a hot and cold shower, some yoga, meditation, and then a breakfast of bran, grapefruit and one walnut. Although Jupiter in the 6th is normally associated with excesses of food and drink, I have noticed the extremes of Jupiter just as frequently operating the other way — week-long fasts eating nothing but grapes, for instance.

In a number of instances I have run across Jupiter in the 6th in the charts of people who developed cancer, but in a good proportion of these cases they have overcome the disease. By nature this planet represents over-production and in these cases, it is the cells in the body which proliferate. There is an intimate relationship between mind and body, or psyche and soma, and any planet in the 6th has an influence to bear on this coupling. For instance, if too much time is spent serving others then a hidden resentment could build up in the person: 'When is it my turn?' or 'What about me?' Sickness may be the only way the person can justify getting some attention for the self. Jupiter asks that we grow, expand and develop in different areas of our life and if for any reason we are avoiding doing so, then the cells in the body may assume the job for us, and they start growing and expanding. Fortunately, it is not difficult for people with Jupiter in the 6th to understand illness symbolically and see it in the context of their lives as a whole. In the pursuit of a cure, they make significant alterations and changes in their entire lifestyle and philosophy of living. Those with Jupiter in the 6th could be the people who inspire others to participate more positively in their own self-help. By contrast, a poorly aspected 6th house Jupiter is sometimes an indication of the kind of person who falls ill on holidays or trips abroad.

Jupiter in the 7th

Examining Zeus' own married life will help us to understand how Jupiter works in the 7th. He had a number of marriages before settling down (in a manner of speaking only) with Hera, the wife officially associated with his sovereignity. One account relates the story of their courtship in this way. It was the middle of winter and Zeus appeared before Hera in the form of a cuckoo. The bird was so frozen by the cold that Hera took it to her breast to warm it. At that moment, Zeus, eager as always to take advantage of an opportunity, changed back to his usual form. Resisting at first, the shrewd Hera finally consented to give way if he promised to marry her. Those with Jupiter in the 7th may resort to all sorts of tricks or disguises to capture the partner of their choice.

The marriage was not an easy one, mostly due to Zeus' philandering and Hera's passionate jealousy. This dynamic often replays itself in the relationships of those with Jupiter in this house. One partner gets to be the faithful and obedient one while the other justifies running free-range. Sometimes the roles will reverse overnight. In the few cases in which Hera decided to enjoy herself, Zeus was instantly back at home complaining about his wife's absence. Similarly, Jupiter in the 7th suffers from a classic freedom-closeness dilemma. They want their independence to explore different facets of life, and yet they want their security as well. (On an archetypal level, spirit as symbolized by Jupiter yearns to be free of the restrictions of matter represented by Hera, and yet spirit needs matter through which to express itself.) Ideally, those with Jupiter in this house do best with partners who share and understand their urge to have other interests outside of the relationship.

Jupiter in the 7th can manifest in other ways. They may project Jupiter onto a partner and look for somebody to play God to them. In this sense, they are prey to anyone who promises them the world, and liable to disappointment when they only get Blackpool. The partner can reflect Jupiter in other respects — he or she may be foreign, prestigious and influential, religious or philosophical, spendthrift, or a loveable rascal who perpetually says one thing and does another. Most positively, the partner can bring warmth, generosity, good faith, material wealth, optimism and an expansion of awareness into the life of those with this placement. Conversely, the person with Jupiter in the 7th can offer these same qualities in return and more often than not the relationship is beneficial to both people's lives. Even if a partnership fails, there is the abiding hope of a better one just around the corner. If those with Jupiter in the 7th never marry, it is usually because they are reluctant to be tied down and lose alternatives.

The 7th house describes our relationship to society in general. Jupiter there favours social and communal interaction as a natural means of broadening and expanding the horizons in life. Well-aspected, Jupiter in this house inclines towards success in legal matters.

Jupiter in the 8th

Jupiter in the 8th can translate literally into expansion through other people's money. One woman I knew with Jupiter in Leo (conjunct Pluto) in the 8th worked as a 'go-go' dancer in a Hollywood discotheque in the early 1970s. A middle-aged self-made millionaire who attended the club took a genuinely fatherly interest in her. Absolutely no sex was exchanged, but he bought her a home of her own in fashionable Laurel Canyon. Jupiter protects and looks after us in whatever house he is placed. In the case of the 8th, he does this through other people's resources.

Jupiter in the 8th can indicate a financially beneficial marriage, good business partnerships, windfalls through inheritance, and a tax inspector you regularly play golf with and allow to win. If Jupiter is not too badly aspected, those with this placement can trust their sensitivity to future trends in the market place and follow successfully any intuitions they may have about the direction in which a venture or event is heading.

Less mundanely, people with Jupiter in the 8th seek expansion and greater meaning in life through sharing and exchanging what they possess, believe in and value with what other people have and hold dear. They can sometimes see a kind of truth or beauty in another person which somebody else might miss. Naturally other people will respond to Jupiter's faith and openness by feeling comfortable relaxing and letting themselves go with them.

With Jupiter in Scorpio's natural house, partnerships may be sought as a way of transcending individual boundaries and self-limitations. For Jupiter, sexual intimacy can be understood symbolically as two people merging to become something greater than what each one is individually. However, hard aspects to Jupiter can show excessive sexual appetites and a certain Don-Juan-like constant need for new experience in this area. On the other hand, I have seen difficult aspects to Jupiter in the 8th reveal a person who has trouble reconciling his or her philosophical and religious beliefs with the sexual drive. Jupiter in this house may also have such high expectations of what sex should be that they are disappointed if bells don't ring and mountains don't move every time they make love.

In the 8th, Jupiter looks for meaning in what is hidden, taboo or mysterious and their religious and philosophical beliefs may be tinged with the metaphysical or occult. They will push open a door that others prefer to leave shut just in case the answer to life lies behind it.

Periods of breakdown and transition are usually weathered in good spirit, often bringing their innate faith and optimism to the fore. A crisis can be seen in the broader context of the whole life, and understood as a potential turning point or opportunity for change and growth. Like Peter Pan, they may believe that even to die must be a great adventure.

Jupiter in the 9th

According to myth, Zeus' first wife was Metis, the goddess of Wisdom. She was pregnant with Athene when Zeus was warned that he would be dethroned by any child of his which Metis bore. In order to save himself, he swallowed both Metis and the unborn Athene in one gulp. As the saying goes, 'we are what we eat,' and in this way Zeus came to embody supreme Wisdom in himself. Later on, after a splitting headache, he safely gave birth to Athene on his own and she became not only one of his favourite children but also a goddess of Wisdom in her own right.

The story offers insight into how Jupiter can best function in the 9th, his own house and the natural domain of Sagittarius. Metis, the first goddess of Wisdom is a threat and cannot be allowed to give birth to anything. Only when she is taken back into the self — that is, digested and well thought over — can Jupiter in the 9th give birth to a greater wisdom which it is safe to love and allow to exist.

In other words, with Jupiter in the 9th, a little knowledge, not properly integrated with the rest of the personality, can be a dangerous thing. In extreme cases, some people with this placement think they know all there is to know and will justify whatever they wish to do on the basis that 'if God didn't want me to do it he wouldn't have put that thought into my head.' James Earl Ray, the assassin of Martin Luther King, was born with Jupiter in Aries in this house. The mass murderer Richard Speck (see page 181) had Jupiter in Gemini there. Jupiter in the 9th is also found in the chart of someone known as 'the Mayfair Boy', who robbed Cartier of London as a kind of joke. In short, those with Jupiter in its natural house may get carried away by what they think, and fanatically worship their own philosophy and beliefs as a kind of law unto themselves.

Because Zeus swallowed Wisdom, he came to embody it and those with Jupiter in the 9th also often exhibit the kind of knowledge which can attribute meaning and significance to even the most unbearable agonies they may have to endure. They will travel far and wide in search of basic laws and truths upon which to guide their pilgrimage through life. Provided they do not lock themselves up in an ivory tower of mental abstractions, they will inspire others with their vision and insight. Those with Jupiter here can journey to the furthest reaches of the mind or even into outer space but what they discover is of little use to anyone unless they come back down again and use what they have learned practically.

Along with philosophy and religion, travel and higher education will be seen as the ways of expanding awareness and finding meaning in life. It would make sense to encourage a person with this placement in any of these directions. If other aspects in the chart help to ground the Jupiter, they make excellent teachers, writers, lawyers, managers, coaches or public relations people. The Gauquelins found Jupiter on the 9th house side of the MC in the charts of successful actors who can convey experience vividly and clearly to others. Vivien Leigh, William Holden and Robert Redford all have Jupiter in this house. If well aspected, a beneficial rapport with in-laws is also suggested.

Jupiter in the 10th (Sagittarius on the MC)

The ancient Greeks believed that if Zeus appeared to a mortal dressed in all his splendours and bedecked in his full array, then the poor earthling would be turned to ashes just at the sight of the god's radiance. Similarly, those with Jupiter in the 10th want to be seen for all their power, brilliance and leadership abilities. When they step out of the house and into the public eye, they don't intend to slip by unnoticed.

It is through career, status and recognition that they seek meaning and fulfilment in life. In some cases, fame itself is worshipped as something numinous and divine. Often they can rise to good positions in reputable professions such as law, education, banking, politics, corporate management, etc. Their careers may involve travel or international connections. Others may be actors or exponents of religion and philosophy. The choice is varied but no matter what occupation they are in, they bring with them a high degree of energy and enthusiasm, vision, insight and the capacity to organize others. They can work well with people, but probably do best if they have a fair degree of authority and a lot of room in which to manoeuvre. Usually, they are sought after for posts and will not find too many obstacles in the way to being successful. Arthur Schlesinger Jr, the historian who won two Pulitzer prizes, was born with Jupiter in clever Gemini in the 10th. Franz Schubert, the Austrian composer, had Jupiter in musical Pisces there. Other examples of internationally successful 10th house Jupiters are Victor Hugo, the French writer noted for his humanitarian philosophy, with Jupiter in Leo in this house; the gifted sculptor Rodin, whose work *The Hands* inspires us to look upward to heaven; and Herman Melville, with Jupiter in Aquarius, who led a life of travel and adventure, and epitomized the quest for God and wholeness in the hunt of the great white whale Moby Dick.

The image of the mother will be reflected by Jupiter in this house. In certain cases I have seen, she has been experienced as dramatic and theatrical, adept at manipulating others through her emotional dramas. Sometimes she has a far-reaching interest in religion and philosophy which makes her seem as if she is not really of this world. She could be foreign or from an influential or well-known family background. The child may experience and worship her as something larger than life and some daughters with this aspect may feel competition and rivalry with such a mother. On the positive side, the mother could be a source of inspiration and guidance, with helpful advice about meeting life and yet not saccharine and over-protective. With this kind of mother, the child feels confident about encountering the world and those in authority in general.

Sagittarius on the MC or contained in the 10th house is similar to Jupiter there.

Jupiter in the 11th

The god Zeus had the task of looking after the well-being of the populace. Similarly, the planet Jupiter, extending our awareness beyond the self-centred concerns of Mars, reminds us of the larger social context in which we exist and have a part to play. In this respect, Jupiter is quite at home in the 11th house.

The people prayed to Zeus for help, guidance and protection against harm, and those with this placement may be sought by friends and groups to provide the same sort of inspiration and support. Conversely, their own horizons and understanding of the meaning of life are broadened and expanded through social interaction. They may assume the role of a guru, hero or heroine in the eyes of friends or groups, or find themselves looking to a friend or group to be their protection and salvation.

Jupiter in the 11th will normally join clubs or organizations which promote humanitarian and egalitarian causes or which promise growth and expansion for everyone involved. Usually they are in tune with new currents and progressive social trends. Difficult aspects to Jupiter may indicate high expectations and ideals, and disappointment when the group fails to solve all their problems or doesn't succeed soon enough in eliminating the woes of the world. Undismayed, however, they will move on to the next cause or organization in the hopes that a new-found formula will be the key.

Jupiter in this house suggests an ever-expanding circle of friends, often of varied cultures and nationalities. For some, life's significance only comes to fruition if their diaries are fully booked and they are having to choose between Mick Jagger's birthday party or an invitation to St Moritz for the weekend. Sometimes an over-involvement in social activities or too great an entanglement in the lives of their friends may dissipate their energy and detract from applying themselves in other areas of life.

Both Jupiter and the 11th house are concerned with becoming more than we already are — therefore, these people are usually not short of goals and objectives in life, and can almost always be seen looking ahead. As soon as one objective is attained, another one appears in its place. A narrowing down of goals or more discrimination in choosing which ones are worth following may be necessary if they are not to spread themselves too thinly. If they shoot their arrows too high, these may come back down on them; if they aim in too many different directions at once, they don't know where to shoot first. It's dizzying just watching them. However, because there is usually such a strong faith that they will and should achieve what they want, life can't help but support them accordingly. Often, friends or groups share this faith in them and their goals, and will be helpful in their realization.

Jupiter in the 12th

The poet Hölderlin wrote that 'where there is darkness, the saving powers also rise.' This is one of the most important ramifications of Jupiter in the 12th — just when things seem the most hopeless and bleak, Jupiter arrives out of nowhere and salvages the situation. Those with this placement may feel as if they have a guardian angel, who appears in the nick of time with a shiny new 'get-out-of-gaol-free card'.

But should we put this down just to luck and good fairies? What really sustains and rescues those with Jupiter in the 12th is a deep faith in the benevolence and significance of life, and an openness and willingness to receive whatever it has to bring them. In any house in which it is placed, Jupiter is looking for meaning in life; but in the 12th, that meaning is not found in any outer event or external reality, rather, it exists nascently within the self. Through the meaning and significance they choose to attribute to an event, those with Jupiter in the 12th can turn negative experiences into positive ones, and obstacles into blessings.

Jupiter's house is where we are looking for the truth. In the 2nd, this may be sought in values, money or possessions and in the 7th through partnerships; but in the 12th, the truth is found within the self, on the level of the unconscious mind. A willingness to turn the attention around 180 degrees and explore the inner imaginal realm of dreams and symbols will help those with Jupiter in the 12th find the kind of truth they are seeking, and contact the inner 'wise person' inside each and every one of them. The breadth and scope of infinity, that bigger picture Jupiter craves to see, can be found in the vast interior recesses of the psyche — a world beyond time, space and all boundary. Meditation, stillness, prayer, retreat, music or art may be the path into that world. Imagine Jupiter's joy when he finally arrives there.

Running around desperately hunting for their joy in all other directions, many people with this placement will look everywhere else but inside for their fulfilment. Reckless behaviour, over-indulgence in alcohol and drugs, manic theatricality, hypocrisy, general imprudence and other such negative traits may be the 'self-undoing' of a 12th house Jupiter.

Jupiter in the 12th can be the channel through which inspiration and healing flow and therefore those with this placement have much to offer working within hospitals, prisons and various charitable institutions. The expanded vision which dawns in times of trouble not only provides hope and inspiration for themselves but will guide others through difficulties as well. I have seen this placement in the charts of a number of gifted counsellors, psychics and healers. Flowing aspects to Jupiter in the 12th also bode well for those who are institutionalized for any reason. Benefiting from the care and protection they receive, they can turn the experience into a positive one, or else they will probably not have to stay confined for any longer than necessary.

24.
SATURN AND CAPRICORN THROUGH THE HOUSES

Whereas Jupiter evokes a sense of expansion and optimism in the house in which it is placed, Saturn elicits almost the polar opposite experience. Rather than feeling that life is essentially benevolent and trustworthy in that area, we anticipate difficulty, disappointment and restriction in Saturn's domain — and consequently approach this area with fear and caution. We often revel in a sense of freedom and limitless possibilities in Jupiter's sphere, while Saturn's domicile is where we face restrictions and boundaries and a nagging sense of duty, responsibility and the 'oughts' and 'shoulds' of life.

The old tyrant is one of the faces of Saturn. Afraid that his own children might overthrow him, Cronus (the Greek equivalent of Saturn) ate them. In this respect, Saturn's house placement is where, due to conservatism or fear, we don't allow our own creative impulses to have free reign. Dreading the unknown, the untried and anything new, we maintain the status quo in that area of life, even if what already exists there is not all that wonderful. Self-critical and self-effacing, we worry so much about making a wrong move in Saturn's domain, that for safety's sake we restrict our actions severely. Like Cronus, by inhibiting, judging and censoring ourselves we devour the offspring of our own creative expression.

Cronus wielded a sickle, bringing to mind the proverb 'as ye sow, so shall ye reap' of which his own life is an illustration: having castrated and dethroned his father Uranus, Cronus himself was toppled later in a coup led by his own son Zeus. Similarly, in the chart, the planet Saturn represents exact and undeviating justice. We squirm and suffer if we neglect or avoid what Saturn requires; but he duly rewards us for any effort, hard work, persistence and patience we do put in. We may attempt to disguise or alleviate the pain associated with a lack of fulfilment in Saturn's house by denying the importance of that area of life. Sooner or later, however, our sense of inadequacy or incompletenes there hits us squarely where it most hurts.

More than a tyrant, Saturn is also associated with the archetype of the Wise Old Man, a kind of Celestial Schoolteacher, who employs pain as a messenger to inform us of those aspects of ourself which need attention and development. Running away from that sphere increases rather than diminishes the discomfort; but listening to what Saturn is trying to teach or show us gradually transforms our sense of inadequacy into feelings of increasing completeness, solidity and worth. By facing Saturn's challenge, we strengthen ourselves and are rewarded with greater knowledge and fulfilment. As a result, we later become teachers in the very area of life we have had the most difficulty mastering. The incomparable German poet Goethe (born with Saturn rising in Scorpio) grasped the true essence of this planet in a single line: *In der Beschränkung zeigt sich erst der Meister*: 'It is in self-limitation that a master first shows himself.' Saturn, like a thorn in a donkey's side, spurs us on to develop certain qualities and characteristics which we probably would not have bothered developing unless forced by internal or external pressures to do so.

The mountain goat is another symbol of Saturn and we are turned into one in the house where Saturn is found. In its laborious efforts to ascend to the top of the mountain, the goat encounters many ups and downs, but eventually it reaches its goal. Before taking each new step, the goat makes sure it has a solid footing in the one before. Positive qualities such as careful and cautious thinking, tact, perseverance and a healthy acceptance of reality, duty and responsibility are all to be found in Saturn's terrain.

Saturn in a house is similar to having Capricorn on a cusp or contained within a house. The house where Saturn is sited will influence any house with Capricorn in it. For instance, Dr Elisabeth Kübler-Ross was born with Saturn in Scorpio in the 8th house and Capricorn on the cusp of the 11th. She is renowned for her in-depth workshops (11th) about coping with death, dying and bereavement (8th).

Saturn is a co-ruler of Aquarius and may also have an influence on any house with Aquarius in it. In Dr Kübler-Ross' chart, Aquarius is found on the cusp of the 12th house — her pioneering work has been done primarily within hospitals and institutions. However, in general, the influence of Uranus appears to be stronger on Aquarius than Saturn.

Saturn in the 1st

Those with Saturn in the 1st house are reluctant about approaching life at all. They cautiously venture out expecting the worst and are invariably worried that they won't meet the mark. And yet they have to challenge themselves. It's like having a little man on their shoulders who repeatedly reprimands: 'I'm sorry, that's just not good enough — you know you can do better.' They imagine that others are constantly judging and assessing them, when in actual fact it is their own self-criticism which gives the greatest problem.

Saturn in the 1st may experience the physical body itself as awkward, gross and uncomfortable. Or they feel that their personalities are inadequate and lacking in social graces. Because of their difficulty in feeling easy and relaxed, they may present themselves in an austere or withdrawn manner. Or fearing that unless they are careful they might look silly, they develop a most dignified stance and posture in all they do. Even if they appear frothy and superficial on the outside, they are likely to be masking something insecure and problematical. Others may interpret their lack of confidence and reticence as cold and unfriendly.

Usually they have (or can develop) a good sense of responsibility and a willingness to work hard in life. This may stem from a need to prove their worth to the world — a desire to receive some sort of collective validation of their 'okay-ness'. For these reasons, they may be ambitious, exhibiting a steely determination to make something of themselves.

Very often, the early life has been experienced as difficult or restricting. They may have felt the childhood environment as unsafe or unsupportive of their free expression and personal creativity, as if they were squashed every time they stepped out of line. Others may have been lumbered with worries and responsibilities inappropriate to their young age. Later on in life, they can usually make up for the fun and spontaneity they missed as a child.

Physically, those with Saturn rising are sometimes on the lean side, and often have a distinguishing facial bone structure. If Saturn is within a few degrees of the Ascendant, the birth may have been a difficult one as if the person was actually resisting incarnation. All new phases in the life may be met with the same degree of caution, trauma and fearful expectation. And yet, if they set their goals sensibly and realistically, they usually manage to achieve their objectives in life.

Saturn in the 2nd

Saturn's placement in the chart indicates where there is the expectation of difficulty, limitation and testing. In the 2nd, insecurity and feelings of inadequacy are experienced in the sphere of money, possessions, values and resources. Believing that their sense of worth or security cannot be provided by others, they have a pressing need to 'make it on their own'. Even if they marry into or inherit money, they still gain greater satisfaction from what they earn themselves. As in the case of Prince Charles with Saturn in Virgo in the 2nd, some may be born into money and yet feel 'watched' or tested for their stewardship: that is, how wisely and effectively they put the money to use.

Although financial stress is not a very pleasant situation, sometimes it does serve as an impetus to force people to develop more of their skills and potentials than if money were no problem. I have also seen cases where those with Saturn in the 2nd accumulate an enormous amount of money and possessions and yet still feel anxious and threatened about their security. For this reason, this position of Saturn might indicate 'the hoarder' — everything needs to be guarded and kept in vaults for fear that it might be snatched away.

On a deeper level, those with Saturn in the 2nd are often unsure of their own innate worth and value, or lack confidence in their ability to deal effectively with the material world. Some may compensate for this by endeavouring to prove themselves through conventional outer hallmarks of success: 'I must be okay — I've got a nice house in the right neighbourhood and two cars in the garage.' Others disguise their concern about these things by belittling the importance of money and the material sphere of life in general.

The inner resources of Saturn in the 2nd are those of cautious planning, tact, perseverance and patience. Developing these qualities will prove productive. Wherever Saturn is in the chart is where we have the potential to turn difficulties into strengths. Through facing the challenges of the material world and finding their own worth and value in this way, those with Saturn in the 2nd are spurred on to greater achievements and a deeper appreciation of life in general.

One example of this placement is Guru Maharaji, who came to the United States from India at the age of fourteen. Saturn is in Sagittarius in his 2nd house and he earned his money through teaching his religion and philosophy in a foreign country (Sagittarius).

Saturn in the 3rd

One of the main issues for those with Saturn in the 3rd is expressing themselves to people in a way that can be understood. The early environment may have felt inimical or dangerous to their safety and therefore not conducive to easy and open exchanges with others. As a result, they may walk around harbouring the belief that nobody understands what they are talking about, or hold back feelings and thoughts for fear of being misinterpreted or having these used against them. They might appear shy, aloof, arrogant or stupid when really they are just uncomfortable communicating.

Such insecurities about their articulateness and intelligence have various repercussions. Compensating for a sense of inadequacy in this area, they might try to prove themselves by developing a precise and exact verbal or mental style: Saturn in the 3rd often manifests the kind of serious and orderly thought processes linked to the logical and rational left brain. Others disguise their awkwardness in 3rd house matters by becoming anti-intellectual, and putting others down who are too 'stuck in the head' as uptight or 'pseudo'. They may have great difficulty making 'small talk' or constantly engage in babble in order to avoid revealing what is really going on inside their heads.

Whereas those with Jupiter in the 3rd operate happily and easily within the immediate environment, eager to see what waits for them around the next corner, Saturn in the 3rd limits a person's free expression of movement. This may stem from an early childhood experience of an environment that didn't feel safe or allow such flexibility. Sometimes they have suffered a crippling sense of restriction or loneliness while growing up. If children are kept too much in harness during certain stages of development (the primate phase) their natural curiosity and desire to explore, imitate and learn skills will be greatly diminished. [1] Those with Saturn in the 3rd may benefit from therapies or techniques which enable them to re-experience the early kinds of movements and mobility denied them for one reason or another.

I have seen many instances of Saturn in the 3rd where a lack of siblings gave rise to feelings of deprivation and isolation in childhood. At the same time, some people with this placement report experiencing their brothers and sisters as burdens and restrictions. In the case of those with Saturn in the 3rd being the older child, they may have been lumbered with the responsibility of looking after their younger siblings or setting a good example for them.

On the basis of any of the reasons given above, those with Saturn in the 3rd may have problems with early education and a difficult adjustment to school in general. For some, the boarding school experience may be felt as a kind of exile or banishment. There also may be delays, obstacles and challenges encountered on short journeys or travel in general. While Jupiter will just 'pick up and go', Saturn will want to make sure that everything is booked in advance. Jupiter arrives at a friend's for the weekend to discover a party in full swing. Saturn comes to the same house the next weekend to discover his friend's father has just been taken ill.

Again, the whole point of Saturn in the 3rd is not that one is condemned to a life of inarticulate misery hobbling around on crutches missing trains. Rather, this placement is an invitation to develop the potentials of a deep and steady mind, to refine the capacity to communicate more clearly with others, and to discover the kind of joy that learning about something brings. Those with Saturn well-aspected in the 3rd may naturally exhibit these traits or have less problems coming to terms with Saturn than others with the same placement.

Saturn in the 4th (Capricorn on the IC)

The 4th house represents the base of operations from which we meet life: this usually means our home, but can also apply to the family background, roots and race. Saturn in this house implies difficulties and restrictions with respect to these areas.

The child with Saturn in the 4th may not have experienced his or her early environment as a very supportive place, and the atmosphere in the home may have seemed cold, unloving or depriving in some way. In certain cases I have seen, the family of origin was impoverished or struggling materially as the child was growing up. In other instances, money wasn't the problem, but rather a lack of emotional closeness in the family which obscured the child's sense of belonging and well-being. One way or another, children with this placement may feel unwanted or that life is not on their side. Certain basic requirements of love and security are not being met, and consequently they begin to wonder what is wrong with them. They are hungry and not being fed or they want to be held closely and reassured of things, but nobody seems to be around when most needed. They begin to feel that they must be inadequate, flawed, or failing in some way, and their sense of who they are deep down inside is coloured by these misgivings. The 'me' residing inside those with Saturn in the 4th is a 'not-good-enough-me'.

In short, for children with this placement, their sense of security or 'okay-ness' is not easily found from outer sources. Instead, they will have to discover their own strength, solidity, support and lovableness from within themselves. If this is achieved, then Saturn in the 4th is truly a blessing in disguise: because once we establish our sense of value and worth from within, then the outside world can never take that away from us. This is the precious gift of a 4th house Saturn.

In general, there is trouble with the father. Sometimes he is not around at all. In other cases, he is physically there but psychologically absent. He might be experienced as cold, conventional, critical, materialistic and rigid or a burden and responsibility due to ill health, personal problems, etc. Children with this placement may feel that they have failed the father in some way, or what's worse, that they have transgressed not just him, but the whole family, race and background, and even God as well. They grow up not only with a nagging sense of guilt that they are not good enough, but also with a great deal of suppressed anger and resentment directed at those they feel are unappreciative and judging of them. Untangling this kind of knot is never easy and will take a long time, if done at all. A major step is achieved when they ask themselves 'What do I really need?' They may find that this is not all that dissimilar to what they believed the harsh parent was trying to shove down their throats. Or once they discover what it is they need, they can proceed to build it in or provide it for themselves and let the depriving father or whoever off the hook for not giving it to them. More positively, a well-placed Saturn in the 4th could indicate a father who models qualities of strength, depth, patience and a commonsense adaptation to the rigours and joys of the material world.

Those with Saturn in the 4th are in a tricky position. They often feel deeply inadequate and mistrusting of others and yet they yearn for something permanent and stable in their life. Some may compensate for their sense of insecurity by acquiring land or property. On a more mundane level, Saturn in the 4th suggests duties and responsibilities in the domestic sphere and problems setting up a home. As usual, wherever Saturn is, hard work, persistence and making the most even of a limited situation pay off in the end.

People with this placement may take a long time to establish their inner strength and identity, but once found, it is solid and enduring. In doing the charts of older people with Saturn in this house, I have observed that in the second half of life they often discover what they feel is their true work or mission and pursue a project or study with great commitment.

Capricorn on the IC is similar in many respects to Saturn in the 4th. The life is built on a deep need for stability and the search for an authentic sense of their self-worth, purpose and value. Looking for these things from the outside may prove uncertain and disappointing.

Saturn in the 5th

While Mars and Jupiter rush into the sandbox to get started on their castles, Saturn in the 5th hesitantly steps into it with a worried look on his face. 'What if my castle is no good? I'm sure other people won't like it at all. Do I have to do one? I really should — all the other kids are. Everyone really liked Johnny's castle, maybe I'd better do one just like that?' Meanwhile Mars has finished his and Jupiter's is nearly done (it's bigger than Mars'). Saturn is still ruminating. 'Is this the best shovel to use? What are the basic principles of sandcastle building? I must get everything organized first.' Jupiter and Mars have now left the sandbox and are playing on the swings as the sun sets on Saturn firmly fixing the foundation of his castle into place . . .

Later in life, those with Saturn in the 5th have the same difficulty freely expressing their individuality and personal creativity. They desperately want to be loved for their specialness and originality and yet feel that it is precisely their differentness which will put others off. What's gone wrong?

For one reason or another, they have had 'the playful child' inside them rebuffed. The psychologist Karen Horney believes that in the same way a pear seed develops into a pear, human beings naturally grow into their intrinsic potential provided various adverse circumstances don't stand in the way of this happening. Very often, however, children only feel loved and acceptable when they are living up to what their parents desire them to be. Rather than risk revealing who they are in themselves, they will hide their own uniqueness for the sake of conforming to their parents' expectations. Their energy is then directed into this image of what they should be, rather than freely unfolding in its own right. A kind of alienation from the real self occurs and the spontaneous flow of the self is blocked by rigidity, doubt and insecurity. They end up watching themselves watching themselves, while their real light stays hidden behind a cloud. The discrepancy between their real selves and their contrived identities leaves them unhappy and uncertain with what they produce. Ultimately the challenge of Saturn in this position is to find ways to free their trapped creative spirit. Mother and Father are no longer there watching over them. What those with Saturn in the 5th need to do is to give themselves permission to allow the spontaneous and playful child hidden inside to come out once in a while.

Often they lack hobbies and spare-time amusements which would serve to add that extra something to the enjoyment of life and through which their individuality is further defined. Similarly, they are insecure in affairs of the heart: romance adds spice to life and makes us feel important and special, and yet those with Saturn in the 5th aren't sure enough of themselves to fully enjoy a piece of the cake. Afraid of rejection, they are too guarded and fearful of looking silly to feel relaxed in these situations. For Saturn in the 5th, having fun is hard work.

They also fear that what they give birth to will be unacceptable. Hence, this placement is often associated with a reluctance to have children, or problems with offspring. They may fear that their children won't like them or, conversely, that they won't like their children. The tests and restrictions imposed by raising children will be strongly felt with this placement so it is probably wise if they carefully plan the timing of when to start a family. It is likely that they will learn as much from their children as their children learn from them.

Curiously, I have done charts for quite a few professional artists and actors who have Saturn in this position — as if they must make work out of creative expression. Others may have careers in the organization or administration of the arts, or in professions which deal with children or young people.

Saturn in the 6th

This position normally confers organizational and administrative ability as well as the capacity to pay close attention to detail. At the same time, a compulsive need to order the environment in this way may denote some deeper fears and a mistrust of life which ought to be acknowledged and examined.

With this placement, daily life and its routine requirements can be felt as oppressive and exceptionally demanding. Managing mundane affairs such as paying the electricity bill, running the car and keeping the flat tidy may become as complex and pressing as planning the execution of a major military strategy. They need routine and ritual and yet there is the danger of being frustrated and trapped by the structures they create.

Issues arise in the area of health and the efficient functioning of the body. For some, health problems curtail or limit individual freedom — such as special diets or certain physical exertions which must be restricted lest disastrous consequences ensue. With Saturn in the 6th, symptoms of ill health should be examined as symbols or messages forcing themselves into the awareness, offering awakening and change. The body concretizes the system's imbalances in the form of illness and disease in an attempt to show us where there is something awry happening in the whole pattern of the life. Particular health problems may come through Saturnine areas — the skin, bones, knees and joints. Some medical and health practitioners have observed that those people who want to do something but continually hold themselves back (Saturn) may be the ones most prone to arthritis and rheumatism. In some cases, Parkinson's disease has been tracked back to suppressed fear, another Saturnine trait. Those with Saturn in this house can participate in their health not only in direct ways such as diet and exercise, but also through adjusting and examining overly rigid or fearful psychological attitudes. If these challenges are met, they will grow not only stronger, but also much wiser. This placement might also describe 'health freaks' who are exceptionally cautious about what they eat or take into their bodies. Some may make a career in the health or healing professions.

With a difficultly aspected Saturn, problems could arise in the area of work. There can be over-criticism of those with whom they work, or a fear of being unacceptable or inadequate in the eyes of co-workers or bosses. Shadowy and unintegrated parts of their own psyches can be projected onto those they meet at work or people they employ to do various jobs for them. Those with Saturn in the 6th find their place in the scheme of things by developing and fine-tuning their marketable skills and abilities. This will not necessarily come without dedication and effort or a menial and humble apprenticeship.

Although it may sound trivial, their relationship to pets and small animals may assume some importance with this placement. The death or loss of their trusty dog or beloved cat can open up a Pandora's box of psychological and philosophical issues.

Saturn in the 7th

Relationships are not that easy for people with Saturn in the 7th and yet this is precisely the area through which they will be challenged to grow and examine themselves. Trying to wriggle out of the hot seat, they might complain that the right man or woman has just never come along, or moan that some flaw in the partner is the root of the trouble. However, rather than just blaming fate, bad luck or poor choice it is by searching inwards that they will unearth reasons for the dispiriting state of affairs.

Wherever there is Saturn, there is fear. Very often these people obstruct relationships because they are frightened of becoming too deeply involved with others. They may be afraid of the degree of commitment a relationship requires, and terrified of becoming too dependent on someone else. Dreading and half-expecting to be hurt, they cannot risk the vulnerability of true intimacy. As is often the case with the 7th house, in order to trace the origins of these kinds of complexes, earlier relationships will have to be examined.

Did they open to a parent and then experience hurt, rejection and misunderstanding? If so, they may still anticipate being unlovable or unacceptable to others. Was the parental marriage so atrocious as to obliterate the very idea of a happy union? If so, can they not learn from their parents' mistakes? By seeking answers and solutions to these kinds of questions, they grow wiser about themselves, relationships and life in general. This is the gift of Saturn in the 7th.

I have seen many instances of people with Saturn in the 7th house who complain that their partners are too limiting and restricting — if it only weren't for their spouses, they would accomplish so much more. Sometimes this is true because they have chosen, unconsciously or not, ostensibly tyrannical men or women as partners. However, the belief that the partner is holding them back is a form of self-deception: in actual fact, what they have done is to project their own internal blocks and fears of stretching themselves onto the partner. Even when they are free of their supposedly restraining husbands and wives, many of those people with Saturn in the 7th will just find other reasons for not venturing forth and expanding themselves. Why not examine these inner obstacles first?

Saturn in the 7th may look for a partner who is safe. Sometimes the least risky ones are those who do not engender an enormous amount of passion. Or as a kind of self-protection policy, they may deliberately choose partners whom they feel are inadequate or lacking in certain respects. Therefore, if the relationship fails, and the other person walks out the door, they can reassure themselves that they are better off without that no-good lame duck. Others seem to select partners who have the same weaknesses as they do, and then proceed to batter the other person for those things they feel unhappy about in themselves.

Saturn in this house also manifests in the search for a partner who will provide security and stability for them. For these reasons, this placement has often been associated with marriage to an older person, or a mother-figure or father-figure. This may work, but at the expense of keeping them small and dependent. Should it fail, it may be a blessing in disguise because they are forced to develop their own inner source of strength and support. While this is not easy, it is invariably a worthwhile achievement.

Saturn in the 7th may marry later in life or not find more complete fulfilment in a union until somewhat older — as if Father Time must teach them a thing or two before a truly mutual and healthy relationship can be formed.

More mundanely, lawsuits may be long and drawn out, and it might be advisable to try to settle out of court.

Saturn in the 8th

Saturn in the 8th gives apprehensions and difficulties in the area of intimacy, sharing and joint resources. They may feel insecure about what they have to give or experience some difficulty receiving what another is offering. More generally, there is the fear of letting go, of merging and blending with another person. To truly merge with someone else means the death of the self as a separate individual. This is a frightening prospect for those with Saturn in the 8th who want to hold onto what they value and possess. In addition, letting themselves go in a relationship entails the possibility of being overtaken by feelings that they have attempted to keep under rigid control — rage, jealousy, envy and passions of a primitive and instinctive nature. They desperately crave a close union and yet withdraw from it for fear of being overwhelmed by such eruptions. Subsequently they may have difficulty relaxing and being open and trusting with others, all of which could give rise to sexual problems. (In mythology, Eros and Thanatos were brothers and the sexual union is a kind of death of one's individuality.) Investigating the root causes of inhibitions in this area deepens and enriches their self-knowledge and understanding.

Besides possible sexual hang-ups, there are conflicts pooling resources and making personal adjustments in relationships. The partner's beliefs or values may differ from and contradict their own, or they may choose a mate who is a burden in some way. And yet, helping out with the welfare of others may be precisely what Saturn in the 8th needs for their own personal development. There can be trouble over inheritance, taxation and business contracts, and the possibility of drawn-out divorce proceedings. Some will make a career dealing with other people's money — bankers, investment consultants, stockbrokers and accountants may have this position of Saturn.

Generally, they hesitate to probe beneath the surface of life and yet this is what is needed for greater depth and maturity. Obviously, people who attempt to maintain rigid controls over themselves are likely to be very frightened by the prospect of physical death and what looms in the hereafter. These apprehensions could provoke them to a serious pursuit of more knowledge in these areas. A supreme example is found in the chart of Dr Elisabeth Kübler-Ross, with Saturn in Scorpio in the 8th; through her pioneering research, she has helped thousands face death with nobility and peace.

Saturn in the 9th

Those with this placement encounter the serious, methodical, conservative and apprehensive Saturn in the sphere of religion, philosophy, higher education and travel. Usually they have an interest in religion and philosophy and the need to find definite answers to basic questions concerning the meaning and patterning of existence. Unlike Jupiter here, who can justify almost anything he wants to do, with Saturn in this house the sense of the divine is tinged by the attributes of the old tyrant himself — God is judgemental, stern and liable to punish them for the slightest mistake. Often they have been brought up under the yoke of conventional or orthodox forms of religion, and their 'spiritual superego' is very strong and inhibitive. Saturn in the 9th may feel that what God likes and dislikes is clearly defined, and that there are strict rules and laws which designate how life should be lived. To transgress these spells disaster. Consequently their philosophy is practical and utilitarian. Some may be caught in the outward trappings of religion, obsessed with observing the exact letter of the law, and forgetful of the inner meaning behind these forms.

Conversely, there are some people with Saturn in this house who are so frightened of anything which smacks of universality or bigger principles that they hide behind sceptical and cynical attitudes. They will believe only in that which can be seen, tested and proven. Others may undertake serious studies of philosophy, theology or metaphysics in an attempt to concretize, specify and 'pin down' higher truths. The Gauquelins found this placement in the charts of scientists, who literally make a career of 'knowing' and classifying the laws and principles which govern life.

While those with Saturn in the 9th may fear that they are not good enough for God, they also worry that God is not doing His job very adequately, and could try to take up the burden. (They might also experience similar kinds of feelings about their in-laws.)

Saturn in this house can also give rise to what Erica Jong called 'the fear of flying'. While Jupiter in the 9th is ruminating about all the things he can and will do, Saturn here is frightened of its own potentials and afraid of taking risks. For those with this placement, every time they lift their arms to reach for the sky they feel a cramp. Such negative expectations do not augur well for the success of such ventures. And yet, slowly and with persistence, they can sort through the doubts and hesitations and arrive there in the end — sometimes even before Jupiter, who has changed his mind and veered off in another direction entirely.

Correspondingly, on a mundane level, Saturn in the 9th will encounter some difficulties or feel uncomfortable with a great deal of travel. Some may reside abroad out of necessity or travel in connection with their work, but their idea of fun is usually not wandering around the world seeing what will happen next. They find it much more reassuring to have the future planned. Ironically, however, those times when the diary is empty and they have to trust and believe in whatever the next day brings may be their most opportune periods of breakthrough and growth.

Saturn in the 10th (Capricorn on the MC)

In his own home and elevated by position, Saturn operates powerfully in the 10th. Whether they acknowledge it or not, these people are extremely sensitive about how other people see them. Saturn in the 10th, like the personal ego itself, wants to be seen as strong, solid and enduring. Success is normally judged in terms of traditional values and roles — the career status, the kind of house they own, the respectability of the marriage, etc. Usually (and there are exceptions) there is the need to achieve position and recognition through some sort of work which is socially acceptable. They may be judgemental and condemning of others who venture to live outside of that which 'straight' society validates. If they must constrict themselves, why shouldn't others — and they may be both envious and angry at those who don't.

They will probably have to work hard to achieve the respect and status they want. If well-aspected, they can realize their career aims through dedication and logical step-by-step progression up the ladder. However, if Saturn is difficultly placed, there may be many delays and obstacles along the way. Some may feel that any means justifies winning their ends — thereby compromising themselves or using others for their own gain. They may reach a certain plateau, and then feel stuck and thwarted in their efforts to go further. Others may rise fairly quickly, misuse their power, and then topple just as fast. We usually land on our feet in Jupiter's house, but in Saturn's domain we may be brought down to our knees if we aren't careful. A contemporary example of a 10th house Saturn is John Mitchell, one of Nixon's cabinet, who was indicted and sent to prison for his part in the Watergate affair. Famous historical examples of this placement of Saturn include Hitler and Napoleon.

Some people with Saturn in the 10th may actually rebel against their over-sensitivity to society's codes and values by trying to break the rules. (We musn't forget that Cronus started out in life by transgressing the existing authority — i.e. his father.) A case in point is seen in the chart of Nathan Leopold, born with Saturn in Aquarius in the 10th, whose story was related in a book and film entitled *Compulsion*. Although he came from a wealthy and respectable family, his compulsion was to commit the perfect crime, and together with his friend Richard Loeb, he carefully planned the sadistic murder of an innocent young boy. Like the hero of Dostoevsky's *Crime and Punishment,* Leopold challenged the restraints of Saturn and society in an attempt to prove that he was above the law. Because of the pressure of social propriety that they feel, those with Saturn in the 10th may do all they can to kick against it. Bob Dylan summed up this placement nicely in a song with these words: 'To live outside the law you must be honest.' Or, as the saying has it, 'Liberty is the luxury of discipline.'

And of course there is the mother: with Saturn in this house, she is often experienced as a strict socializing force, the law-giver who decides what is acceptable and proper. Children with this placement may internalize her rules or later believe that the kind of obedience Mother wanted is the same that should be given to society. The mother may be felt as critical, cold, demanding and unloving. Whatever the child does is never good enough. Or the mother may seem more like a burden and responsibility — someone the child has to care for, rather than the more usual way around. On a more hopeful note, the mother could serve as a model of positive Saturnine qualities, exemplifying patience, discipline, durability, pragmatism and determination.

Saturn in the 10th is similar to Capricorn on the MC. Those with this planet or sign there are often excellent organizers and administrators, executives, managers, scientists, builders and teachers.

Saturn in the 11th

Saturn is by nature ambivalent about the main thrust of the 11th — the urge to become more than we already are. On the one hand, Saturn is attracted by the lure of anything which offers greater security and prestige; on the other hand, he is terrified at the thought of having to open up and expand his carefully guarded boundaries.

While those with Saturn in the 11th may experience a pressing need to join with others and be part of a group or circle of friends, they often feel awkward or threatened in such situations. Some may react accordingly by avoiding these kinds of social contacts, and yet, in doing so, forfeit the opportunity to grow and learn in this important area of life.

Even if they only form a few carefully selected friendships, somehow problems still arise. Friends may be the catalyst through which they have to face issues which are most challenging for them. For example, one man I know with Saturn in the 11th loves to flirt with any woman he meets and yet he invariably chooses friends who are very possessive about their wives. As friend after friend broke off their association with him, the man in question was forced to reflect on the causes and reasons for his compulsive behaviour. He could blame his friends for being such jealous types, but why did he repeatedly set up the same situation, and what was this fatal fascination for married women all about anyway?

People with Saturn in the 11th will usually have to work hard at developing those qualities which earns a person the 'good friend' label. Unlike the example above, some may be too rigid and formal with a friend, as if they are afraid of putting a foot wrong or being taken advantage of by an associate. Sometimes friends can be felt as a burden, restriction or responsibility. They may worry that a friend will reject or criticize them; or they, themselves, might be the ones who feel cold and judgemental at times. They sometimes choose older or more mature associates who have had greater experience in this area and can serve as models or teachers for how to behave. Or Saturn in the 11th may suffer a sense of loneliness and isolation because of a lack of companions. However, if difficulties are faced and examined, Saturn in this house has the capacity for loyal and enduring friendships.

Similar experiences can occur in groups, clubs or organizations. Although those with Saturn in the 11th don't always feel easy in group situations, this is precisely where they can learn the most about themselves and others. They might belong to a group which limits or restricts their freedom in some way or they may assume heavy duties and administrative responsibilities within a club or organization. Whereas Saturn in the 5th needs the permission to be different, a difficultly aspected 11th house Saturn needs lessons in how to work jointly with other people. What is their place and purpose in the human family? How can they promote the growth and evolution of society in some way?

Some with this placement may be trapped by their own rigid ideals of what they should be. Others might be afraid to commit themselves to any particular goal, feeling that this would be too binding or limiting. At times, frustrated by blocks to their progress, they will want to give up entirely. While it's wise to periodically review, reassess and even re-choose our objectives in life, Saturn in the 11th shouldn't forget their mascot, the goat — who reaches his goal by patiently and persistently taking little steps at a time. He isn't an overnight success, but he arrives there in the end.

Saturn in the 12th

Like those with Saturn in the 8th, people with Saturn in the 12th are often afraid of what lurks beneath the surface level of consciousness. Should they relax their controls over themselves, they fear that they might be engulfed by overwhelming emotions.

The neo-Freudians believe that in the name of security and social adaptability, we repress certain drives, impulses and appetites which others (or our own egos) would find unacceptable. But some with Saturn in the 12th go a step further. In divorcing themselves from what is in the unconscious, they also inhibit a very positive and pressing desire which exists in all of us — the urge to reconnect to our at-one-ness with the rest of life. Instead of experiencing joy at the prospect of merging with something greater than the self, they recoil in horror at the thought of dissolution of their individuality. Robert Desoille, a French psychotherapist, coined a term for this, calling it 'the repression of the sublime.'

In certain cases, they suffer a type of guilt or despair — something inside tells them that they are not all they could be. Or they are beset by paranoia, a feeling that someone or something is out to destroy them. Traditional textbooks interpret Saturn in the 12th as 'undoing by secret enemies'; but more often than not, the enemy is an aspect of their own unconscious selves, angry with them for having been brushed aside. When they make friends with what they have rejected, a sense of peace settles over the psyche, and they rest more easily at night. If they don't reconcile themselves with parts of themselves they have denied, then they protect themselves against invasion by double-locking their doors, keeping to themselves, and remembering to forget their dreams.

Deep psychological fears which are difficult to trace may contribute to a pervading sense of self-doubt and lack of confidence. Sometimes their problems may stem from pre-natal difficulties. The womb is a place where we are meant to swim in a sense of the totality of life.

If for any reason those waters were troubled, then we may later resist anything which resembles that kind of experience. It may be worthwhile for those with Saturn in the 12th to investigate what the gestation period might have been like. Perhaps the mother wasn't sure about having a child at that time. Or she could have been worried about money or the state of affairs with the father. For whatever reasons, the developing embryo, through the umbilical connection, registers that life is not all right. The child grows up vaguely anxious about almost everything, guilty about being alive, and in poor relation to the rest of life.

Either due to this sense of guilt or partly motivated by an innate feeling of being responsible for other people's problems, they may feel that they owe a debt to society which can be paid off through service. They sometimes work in hospitals, prisons, charities or governmental agencies dealing in any number of ways with those in trouble or need. Others with Saturn in the 12th may live out their all-pervading sense of unacceptability behind bars or hidden away in a hospital ward.

Some with Saturn in this house are terrified of intimacy. This could stem from a fear of being engulfed, or a dread of losing their identity as a separate individual. They may believe that they can only maintain their autonomy by withdrawing from people. Or they fear that no matter what they do, all things will come to a bad end. Thus, they shun attachment or commitment to people or things. This underlying sense of futility needs to be brought to the surface and explored. Until they do this, they may fear the whole realm of emotions and feelings (12th house) and take refuge by living mainly 'in their heads'.

Any principle in the 12th house can sustain us or undo us. Positive Saturn qualities such as recognizing their natural limits, the acceptance of duty and responsibility, and plain common sense may help them through difficult situations. Some exhibit a deep inner wisdom which can guide them through the most difficult times. However, too great a sense of separateness from the rest of life, an overly materialistic outlook, or a refusal to examine psychological problems could be the cause of pain and suffering. Sometimes there is a voluntary withdrawal from activity or a compelling need for privacy and seclusion to recollect the pieces of the self which have been shattered by a stressful encounter with life. At times, they may be driven to seek the support or aid of caring agencies or turn to 'something up there' for help. As hard as this might be, a crisis which precipitates their asking others for help may enable them to discover that they are not as alone in the world as they believed. The German poet Goethe, born with Saturn in Scorpio in the 12th, lyrically expressed a similar sentiment when he wrote: 'Who never ate his bread with tears, who never sat through the sorrowful night, weeping on his bed, does not know . . . heavenly powers.'

In conclusion, Saturn in the 12th asks that the whole realm of the unconscious be taken seriously. Those with this placement may be afraid to explore these waters and yet this is precisely what they need to do. Should they overcome their fears and embark on the path of psychological self-investigation, their efforts will be amply rewarded. They will not only reconnect to severed parts of themselves but regain a lost sense of relatedness to the rest of life in the process.

A Note on the Outer Planets in the Houses

In whatever houses they are placed, the three outer planets — Uranus, Neptune and Pluto — bring experiences of a more disruptive, radical and transforming nature than the other planets which might occupy that sphere. Rather than just living the affairs of the house in an ordinary, routine or uncomplicated way, we are somehow catapulted into a more complex relationship with that dimension of life.

Saturn, by house, makes us aware of what is weak, inadequate or incomplete in ourselves and in this way highlights those areas which we need to work on and strengthen. However, the outer planets go a step further by periodically challenging the very existence and viability of the kinds of structures which we have created in the spheres of the chart where they are found. Besides complicating the affairs of the house, they symbolize certain kinds of conflicts, paradoxes, tensions and traumas which cry out for some sort of major change or shift on our part whether we like it or not. Hopefully we break down in order to break through — and the end result is a broadened, deepened, refined and expanded awareness of ourselves and life in general.

The sign positions of the outer planets remain the same for all people over long durations of time. Therefore, the more personal influences of Uranus, Neptune and Pluto are shown by the houses in which they are placed.

25.
URANUS AND AQUARIUS THROUGH THE HOUSES

Not a great deal is written about Uranus in mythology. The first sky-god, he ruled the limitless expanse of space and had the job of inventing and designing Nature. He accomplished such creative feats as fashioning the wings of butterflies, each one stamped with its own uniqueness and individuality. By house, Uranus in the chart is where we are capable of fresh and original thought and action. In his domain, it is not necessary to conform to traditional and conventional patterns of behaviour.

He was married to Gaea, Mother Earth. Every night the Sky lay down on the Earth, and as a result they kept conceiving children. The prolific couple gave birth to the race of giants known as the Titans; to a few one-eyed Cyclopses; and a host of other monsters each with one hundred arms and fifty heads. Disgusted at the sight of his own offspring, Uranus refused to allow them to exist. Instead, as soon as they were born, he shoved them back into Gaea's womb, the very bowels of the earth itself. Astrologically this implies that in Uranus' house, we may conceive what we believe are some very good ideas, but when acted upon and concretized, they may not turn out so well. What in theory seemed highly desirable can in actual fact disappoint us when put into practice. And like the god Uranus, we sometimes have to bury our original ideas and try again.

Obviously, Gaea, her womb gorged with these banished children, was not amused. Reaching into her bosom, she produced some steel, fashioned a sickle, and then implored her children to castrate their father with it. Her youngest son, Cronus (Saturn), already exhibiting a well-developed sense of responsibility, volunteered to undertake the task. Some of the blood from Uranus' dismembered phallus spurted back into Gaea's womb and gave birth to the Furies. When the organ was cast into the sea, it merged with the foam and Aphrodite (Venus) was born.

This myth suggests the complexities which characterize Uranus' sphere of influence. That part of us which is more earthy or Saturnian — our reserve, caution, conservatism, respect for tradition, and fear of the unknown — can literally 'cut off' the creative impulse of Uranus. The inhibition of Uranus in a house can give birth to the Furies, whose names translate into 'envious anger', 'retaliation', and 'never-endingness'.[1] If we cling too long to old and outworn 'scripts' and patterns of behaviour in Uranus' domain, then the Furies will pursue us. Resenting the state of affairs in that area of life, we often blame others for our unhappiness, causing a poisonous and bitter residue to build up in the psyche. An awesome amount of energy is required to hold back a change when it is really needed, and we may end up exhausted, diseased or alienated as a result. Or, perhaps we courageously undertake the new action and explore other provocative and independent ways of being in that house. Even so, we may still evoke the Furies — this time unleashed on us by those who feel challenged, transgressed and threatened by our behaviour. On either a personal or collective level, Uranus' house is where we may have to deviate from conformity, experiment with new trends or currents of thought, and risk disrupting ourselves and everything around us in the name of progress and evolution.

Thankfully, Aphrodite is also born out of this struggle. Her presence suggests that while respecting and working within some of the limits and confines of Saturn, we can attempt to find the most harmonious and creative ways (Venus) to bring forth new life. In some cases, we may not be able to totally overthrow the old structures, but we can endeavour to make room within these for new ideas and interests, and in this way give some sort of expression to change. This is the challenge Uranus presents in the area of the chart he inhabits.

Uranus was discovered relatively recently in 1781, during the period of the American and French Revolutions, and on the eve of the Industrial Revolution. Synchronously, this planet is associated with ideals of truth, justice, liberty, fraternity and equality as well as any progressive collective trends which challenge the status quo. Uranus wants us to transcend the limits of our past, our background, our biology and if possible our fate: just because we are born into a poor family doesn't mean that we have to be a peasant. In pure form, its vision is of many individuals grouped together, each expressing his or her own uniqueness and yet supporting the larger whole of which each is a part.

However, Uranus is prone to certain distortions. By house, it is where we have a need for truth and freedom as well as an inordinate fear of being trapped or imprisoned by our own creations. If we are too attached to change for the sake of change, then nothing will ever take root in this area. Or wavering on that fine line between madness, eccentricity and genius, we may persistently feel the need to be different for no other motive than causing some disruption or drawing attention to ourselves. Uranus' house may show where we rashly disrespect the limits of our 'human-ness'. Presuming we can automatically transcend the restrictions of the physical body or rise above the instinctual components of our nature, we commit the sin of *hubris* and invite punishment to fall on us. With the same finesse that inspired Dr Frankenstein to make his monster, we unleash horrors on the world in the name of advancement and progress. Or when utopian ideals (as in the French Revolution) don't take into account the realities of human nature, they convolute and turn in on themselves, sometimes strangling almost everyone in the process.

Aquarius on the cusp or contained within a house will have a similar flavour to Uranus there. There will be a connection between the house containing Uranus and any house with Aquarius in it.

Uranus in the 1st

Those with Uranus in the 1st best meet life by having the courage to determine their own truths for themselves. If there is no path, they should make one. Highly original and inventive, they offer new insights or ideas into their various fields of interests. Alexander Graham Bell who patented the telephone was born with Uranus in Aries in the 1st. Mary Baker Eddy, the founder of the Christian Science Church and the only woman to ever establish a religion, was born with Uranus in Capricorn in this house. Nikola Tesla, a Yugoslavian-born scientist and inventor whose life is recounted in a book called *The Prodigal Genius,* had Uranus in Taurus in the 1st. Traditionally, Uranus is associated with electricity, and Tesla was the first man to effectively utilize the alternating current. Obviously, those with Uranus in the 1st are better in leadership roles — they just can't cope very well being followers. Nor should they, with the highly individualistic Uranus in the natural house of Aries and Mars.

Talk about electricity — they usually have it. Often this can be seen in their eyes, face or around their hair — something about them crackles and buzzes. If Uranus is difficultly aspected, they can be extremely obstinate and unreasonably dissenting, revelling in being different simply for the sake of it.

Nonetheless, they must be given a great deal of personal freedom to find themselves. Most of us derive our sense of who we are from being somebody's wife, mother, child, boss, lover, etc. However, for those with Uranus in the 1st, these traditional collective representations of identity are just not enough. There is always something better or different that they could be and therefore they have great difficulty settling into any one definite sense of who they are. Others may find this wonderfully exciting or painfully irritating.

Basically, they just want to be left alone to get on with what they want to do without people bothering them. It's no use trying to stop them anyway. Unwilling to adhere to conventional forms or standards of behaviour, they 'cut through' anything which is phony or stifling with laser-like alacrity. To others, they sometimes appear shocking.

If Uranus is close to the Ascendant, there may be something unusual about the birth or early upbringing. One extreme case which Lois Rodden (*The American Book of Charts*) cites is a Brazilian boy with Uranus in Virgo in the 1st and much of Aquarius in the 6th house: he was born with two heads, each of which ate and breathed separately. I also know of a child born with Uranus in the 1st house on the Ascendant who was taken away from his teenage mother one day after birth and put up for adoption. One way or another with Uranus in the 1st, life is not going to be ordinary.

Uranus in the 2nd

Those with Uranus in the 2nd will have to approach the whole area money, possessions and resources in a different way from the ordinary. This position represents a challenge to rise above the collective's traditional value systems and the more usual ways of viewing the material world. Not wishing to be bound by the need for material security and possessions, some may shun attachment to those very things which most people are seeking. If valued at all, money will be appreciated for the freedom it offers them to pursue what it is they really want to do.

Sometimes there may be unusual ways of earning money or the income can be gained from newly developing fields, modern technologies, or some highly individualistic endeavour. Some people with this placement may support more radical economic or political systems which organize the distribution of wealth differently from their native regime. Uranus in this house is also associated with sudden material and financial ups and downs. Intuitively acting on a hunch, they may take risks with money. Depending on the aspects to Uranus, these may 'pay off' admirably or land the person penniless.

Those with Uranus in the 2nd often experience some sort of change, disruption or de-structuring in the area of personal security which forces them to re-evaluate this whole sphere of life. For instance, even if they are trying to pursue a more orderly or conventional approach to the material world, they may find themselves the victim of some larger collective influence or upheaval which disrupts their source of income or security. The company they work for may do a re-shuffle, or due to a recession they find themselves on the redundancy list. Or for reasons beyond their control, they have to flee their country of residence, leaving everything behind to face the prospect of starting anew. At some time in their lives, they might have to develop different skills to support themselves unlike those which they have previously used.

Very often, it is their own strong unconscious urges which coerce them to break with past attachments. If they are unconscious of their deep need for freedom, they may choose situations which they believe offer security but which ultimately turn out to be unstable. (In any battle between conscious desires and unconscious ones, the unconscious usually wins.) Some may believe in the principle of 'mind over matter': that there is a higher plane which can affect and shape the happenings on the material level of existence.

The innate resources which should be developed are those of originality, inventiveness, openness to new currents and progressive trends, and an often crystal-clear insight into situations. It may be that those with Uranus in the natural house of Taurus can *materialize* their 'genius' more easily than when this planet is in other houses. For example, Yehudi Menuhin, who was giving public recitals from the age of seven, earned his money through his musical genius (Uranus in Aquarius in the 2nd). Guglielmo Marconi, the inventor of the wireless and radio magnetic detector, was born with Uranus in Leo in this house. Michelangelo, 'the universal genius', is reputed to have had Aquarius on the 2nd house cusp.

Uranus in the 3rd

Those with Uranus in the 3rd keep looking for their own ways to understand what happens around them, rather than adhering to how they have been educated to see things. In other words, they are inventive, original and intuitive thinkers. The Uranian mind grasps concepts whole, and has revelations and sudden insights into life, people, events and situations. Somehow they perceive the environment from a slightly different angle to others. Very often they exhibit a kind of detached clarity which enables them to solve problems quickly. While others are grappling with solutions and establishing research projects to comprehend an issue more fully, Uranus appears on the scene and immediately knows the answer — 'It's obvious, you ought to try it this way.' A more rational and logical mind will be baffled by the Uranian ability to 'pull answers out of the air'. Sometimes, their ideas are slightly ahead of their time. Others simply will not be able to fathom them immediately. But days, months or years later they begin to understand what Uranus had computed instantly and naturally. It won't come as a surprise to learn that Albert Einstein was born with Uranus in the 3rd ruling Aquarius on the 9th (the house associated with the laws and principles which govern existence).

People with Uranus in the 3rd may be restless and highly strung. They need to move around, explore and experience a wide variety of life's facets. Their minds may change course so quickly that others are left totally confused about what is happening. They are mental gymnasts: it appears that they are changing the subject or talking in *non sequiturs* when actually they have made a quick connection between one topic and another which a slower thinking mind may fail to perceive. Uranus' thinking is often non-linear or 'lateral'.

Uranus in the 3rd can describe a disruptive early environment, possibly one in which significant changes in residence produced upheaval for the person. Even at an early age, they may have felt separate or different from others in the immediate environment. The relationships with siblings may be unusual, as in the case of blended families — where there are step-sisters or brothers from a previous marriage of one or both the parents. I have seen this placement in the charts of people who are considerably older or younger than the other siblings. A brother, sister, aunt, uncle, etc., may exhibit obvious Uranian characteristics.

Uranus in the 3rd might have a hard time adjusting to traditional educational systems. Any course of study may be subject to some chopping and changing. Often, they make highly original contributions to any branch of learning, and I have seen this placement in the charts of individuals who stand out in the fields of education and communication.

The 3rd house rules short journeys, and with Uranus here, unexpected happenings are to be expected. My favourite example of someone who travels from *A* to *B* in the most unusual ways is the daredevil Evil Knievel, with Uranus in the 3rd ruling Aquarius on the Ascendant.

Uranus in the 4th (Aquarius on the IC)

Dane Rudhyar writes of Uranus in the 4th that it 'points to the possibility of becoming constructively uprooted'.[2] Whether through personal choice or unavoidable external circumstances, those with Uranus in the 4th are not meant to be bound by the traditional biological family unit. They may feel like outsiders, strangers or outcasts from their families of origin; or for some reason, the early home life was disrupted and the family scattered. This placement of Uranus implies a need to find where they truly belong as their family or racial roots don't seem to provide this kind of containment. Often deeply restless, they require the space and freedom to search for their true 'spiritual' home or family.

Fearing the loss of alternatives, they are sometimes reluctant to put down any roots at all — maybe there is some place better or more appropriate around the corner. In certain instances I have seen, this disruption has been attracted externally as if by fate — something from the outside compels a move or the need to uproot. Or everything seems to be perfectly secure in the home until Uranus in the 4th is 'triggered' by progression or transit and suddenly, out of the blue, they pick up and leave or the family breaks up or changes in some way.

This placement could also describe an unusual home life. The home could be used as a meeting place for groups or organizations where different ideas are exchanged. They may live in a utopian community, or a housing venture based on something slightly unconventional. The father (or hidden parent) may bear some of the characteristics of Uranus. He may have been unconventional or erratic in some way or literally kept appearing and disappearing from the home scene. He might have felt trapped by being a parent. Sometimes he is physically present but remains an unknown quantity with whom a close emotional rapport is difficult. Occasionally, I have seen Uranus in the 4th in the charts of people who, as they were growing up, watched their fathers' suffer mental breakdowns. More positively, it can be a father who is highly original, inventive, free-thinking, and loving without being smothering.

Although this may not be revealed until later in life, those with Uranus in the 4th are often deeply unconventional. In some cases, they may live in a certain way until mid-life and then radically change their lifestyle when Uranus opposes its own place. An interest in metaphysics and in philosophical and political systems may surface as they grow older.

Uranus in the 4th is similar to Aquarius on the IC or in the 4th house. An identity needs to be found which is based on something other than just the personal family unit. At some stage in the life, they may want to participate in an activity which benefits or advances the family of humanity.

Uranus in the 5th

Rather than relying on conventional or traditional modes of self-expression, those with Uranus in the 5th should let their individuality shine through whatever they do. Similar to Uranus in the 1st, they almost can't help being innovative and different. Elvis Presley, who combined a whole new trend in music in the 1950s with a way of moving his body that many people found shocking, was born with Uranus in Aries in the 5th. Those with Uranus in this house may never be totally satisfied with what they create, always thinking it could have been better or more ideal. Sometimes creative inspiration comes in a flash, like a bolt of lightning charging the body.

We have personified some of the other planets in the 5th as children playing in a sandbox — what would Uranus be like there? True to form, it's hard to predict. He would probably join the others at first, but eventually get bored. Castles are a 'cinch' and so dreadfully banal, besides it's very frustrating trying to construct a model of the Houston Space Center in something as one-dimensional as sand. Doesn't anyone have a new video game he hasn't mastered yet? Having persuaded Mars and Jupiter to come with him to practise a few new stunts on his recently acquired BMX bike, he can't resist a passing comment to Saturn on how to improve the castle he is still putting the finishing touches to (see Saturn in the 5th).

Later in life, Uranus is more interested in what others find weird and eccentric and may pursue hobbies which are out of the ordinary. The same goes for love affairs and romances — which may be unconventional and with sudden beginnings and endings. Uranus becomes bored when the initial excitement and enthusiasm wanes, or if the affair becomes too known or constricting. At that point, justifications are sought for an abrupt finish.

Most people create on the ordinary biological level by producing children, but those with Uranus in the 5th have to find other ways than the purely biological to express themselves. Even if they do have children, their creative needs won't be totally satisfied by just being a parent. If they cling too closely to offspring or try to turn them into vessels to 'live out' their unused potential, the children will probably react by breaking away from home as soon as possible. In certain cases, it may be the parent who leaves the child. I have seen a few instances of women with Uranus in the 5th who have very little desire to be mothers, or who have been separated from their children for various reasons. Uranus in this house seems to ask people to find additional ways of fulfilling the need for creative outlets rather than *only* through bearing progeny. As parents, their views on raising children are likely to be progressive or contrary to what society upholds. The English poet, Percy Bysshe Shelley, had Uranus in Leo in the 5th ruling Aquarius on the 11th. After the death of his wife, he was denied custody of the children because of his atheistic beliefs.

Uranus in the 6th

Those with Uranus in the 6th are meant to explore in a deeper way the intimate relationship between the inner world of the mind and feelings and the outer world of form and the body. A connection exists between what we are inside and the kind of everyday reality we create for ourselves. Uranus in the 6th has a chance to learn that in order to change the outside, the inside must be altered first. Any problems which they face in their daily lives or physical bodies can be met with the questions: what patterns in me produced these difficulties and how can I change them? Self-examination, based on the liberating idea that we create and are responsible for our own reality, is the key to a positive experience of Uranus in the 6th. Otherwise they are prone to minor or major upheavals in the life — such as falling ill to avoid going to a job they don't like, rather than admitting first they are feeling trapped by the work and acting accordingly to change the situation.

In fact, the whole area of work and employment can be approached in a non-conventional way. Rarely suited to a repetitive nine-to-five routine, they will usually find it difficult to stay in a job purely out of a sense of duty or for the sake of security. Their minds need to be continually engaged and interested in the tasks before them and it's best if their work allows scope for change, variety, inventiveness and movement. Often there is difficulty working under others because they need to approach any job in their own way — even if it has never been done in that fashion previously. However, if Uranus is not too badly aspected, exchanging ideas with co-workers can be lively and stimulating.

Often, they are interested in the new technologies as well as subjects like astrology or other related metaphysical or psychological systems — anything which gives them a frame of reference from which to observe and meet life. They might suit a 'think-tank' situation.

In general, they do not like to be bound by the little everyday necessities and routines of existence and may create upheavals to make life more interesting and exciting. Again, life might become easier if they consciously acknowledge what they don't like, and do something to change that area rather than subtly provoking external forces to disrupt it for them.

Interested in the relationship between mind and body, they might explore various forms of alternative and complementary medicines, sometimes experimenting with unusual diets and various exercise routines. Health problems can stem from too much stress and nervous tension which weakens the body's defences. An overly inhibited 6th house Uranus attracts the Furies (see pages 264-5), which may lodge themselves in the body, creating havoc in the system. In charts I have seen, there appears to be a connection between Uranus in the 6th and various forms of allergies. Interestingly, some medical researchers have linked allergies with unexpressed anger and resentment, suggesting that people with 'short fuses' are more prone to allergic conditions. (In her book on medical astrology, Eileen Nauman associates Uranus with 'the actual impulses that leap from one nerve synapse to another'). [3] Obviously, those with Uranus here will benefit from any form of activity which helps them unwind — physical exercises, yoga, meditation, etc. On the positive side, Uranus offers the possibility of a speedy recovery or release from illness, helped enormously by the right mental attitudes.

If we take the combination of Uranus and the 6th house to its logical conclusion, then there may be the possibility of unusual pets. One woman I know with this placement keeps rats as pets in the house — uncaged, of course.

Uranus in the 7th

The attitude towards relationships needs to extend beyond a wholly conventional framework if Uranus is in the 7th. While many people remain in a relationship because of a need for safety and security or out of a sense of duty, those with Uranus here will find it hard to endure a lifeless or outworn partnership just for those reasons. If a relationship is not creative, exhilarating, open and honest, they may disrupt it for the sake of finding something better.

One or both partners might require more space and freedom than is found in the typical marriage or close union. Rather than simply being categorized as somebody's mate, they need other interests outside of the relationship from which to gain a sense of identity and vitality.

If those with this placement are not the prime movers in acting out the urges of Uranus, they may attract or select a partner who perpetrates this for them. If they don't acknowledge their restlessness or need for a less conventional structure, then they might provoke the other person to somehow alter the state of affairs. The general rule with Uranus in any house is that the more we acknowledge its presence there and internalize its nature, the less likely it is that external situations force upheaval on us.

Problems occur when planets which by nature crave security, convention or closeness — such as the Moon, Venus or Saturn — are in hard aspect to a 7th house Uranus. In such cases, one side of the person yearns for the intimacy and safety of a relationship while another bit of them is frightened of losing their separate individuality or being too confined by the partnership. As with Jupiter in this house, a possible resolution is finding a partner with the same conflicts — keeping an awareness of the dilemma in the open and structuring the relationship accordingly. An atmosphere in which the two people can freely exchange and discuss their feelings and moods without the other taking it too personally will facilitate this arrangement. They will need to recognize that each person is an individual in his or her own right, and not someone who exists solely to fulfil whatever one or the other requires at any particular moment. Obviously, a fair degree of maturity will be needed to accomplish this, and their best relationships usually come when they are older and wiser about themselves and life in general.

Those with Uranus in the 7th sometimes experience revelations and sudden changes in outlook and attitude which render a present relationship obsolete. New ones are sought which reflect the changed state of mind. In general, there is the need to periodically re-stimulate or reinvigorate an existing relationship, usually when Uranus is triggered by progression or transit.

The 7th house describes what we are seeking in a partner, as well as qualities which might be latent or undeveloped in ourselves. Those with Uranus there seek a highly original, spirited, dynamic, inventive, magical and charismatic partner — someone who wakes them up and offers change or new vistas. However, a person of this nature is not likely to be the kind who brings a great degree of stability and security to a relationship.

Our society places a lot of pressure on people to marry — to such a degree that those who are not married or in a close conventional relationship may feel that there is something dreadfully flawed about them. Those leading a single lifestyle may need to remind themselves that they *are worthwhile* whether they are in a relationship or not. The 7th house also refers to social interaction in general and the principles of Uranus will apply here, possibly indicating those who are meant to bring new ideas, insights and breakthroughs to society in general, by virtue of their work or who they are.

The actress Elizabeth Taylor was born with Uranus in Aries in the 7th ruling Aquarius on the 5th house cusp. The disruptive marriages and their sudden beginnings and endings reveal the handiwork of Uranus. Perhaps, in some cases, she is unsuccessfully trying to apply the traditional structures of marriage too readily with whoever she is romantically (5th) involved with, rather than respecting the open mode in which Uranus prefers to operate.

Uranus in the 8th

The 8th house, the natural domain of Scorpio, engenders those kinds of emotions and feelings so often awakened by the agony and the ecstasy of love — passions like lust, jealousy, rage, envy, possessiveness and vindictiveness. Uranus seeks to approach this sphere somehow differently from the way most people go about it. Often those with Uranus in the 8th have a compelling urge to free themselves from the restrictions of the basic instinctual nature, and to overcome being ruled by such emotions. They may continually expose themselves to situations which challenge them to rise above and develop detachment from these primal instincts in order to forge a broader and more tolerant understanding than such messy feelings allow — for instance, the concept of a communal marriage or even husband and wife swapping. In some cases they may try this sort of liberality and fail miserably.

Similarly, they may seek to express the instinctual nature in other ways than merely for the purpose of mating and procreation. Hence, the reputation of this placement for some degree of sexual curiosity and experimentation. Others might look for techniques and systems which enable them to transcend the realm of libidinal desire through re-directing the sex drive into other outlets.

In cases I have seen, Uranus in the 8th alternates between the extremes of excessive passion and inhumane coldness. For instance, believing fervently in a certain cause, they may not think twice about planting a bomb in a department store if this would promote their mission. Adolf Eichmann, the Nazi who exterminated millions of Jews, was born with Uranus in Capricorn in the 8th ruling the 11th house of goals and objectives. Another Nazi leader eventually hanged for atrocious war crimes, Joachim von Ribbentrop, had Uranus in Scorpio in the 8th ruling an Aquarian Ascendant.

Those with Uranus in the 8th often have a desire to probe beneath the surface level of existence to discover the more subtle laws of nature operating in life. Astrology, psychology, alchemy, the occult, magic, sub-atomic physics or modern chemistry might interest them. One man who literally explored the potentially transformative and explosive possibilities of the deeper strata of life was Enrico Fermi. Born with Uranus in Sagittarius (the sign of the explorer) in the 8th house, he not only discovered uranium fission but also produced the first nuclear chain reaction. Along similar lines, Uranus in the 8th may be fascinated by what death is all about, and attempt to understand it in a less conventional framework. Psychic and telepathic experiences are not uncommon for people with Uranus in this house, although some may not have too much control over them when they occur.

On a more mundane level, sudden reversals of fortune could come through marriage, inheritance and business partnerships. Also, phases of the life may end suddenly and irreversibly: seemingly overnight, one chapter finishes and another begins, or an unforeseen event drastically alters the direction in which the person is heading.

Uranus in the 9th

Uranus is always searching for 'the truth' and what better house to do it in than the 9th, the natural abode of Sagittarius. Rather than adhere to traditional or orthodox views, they must independently find a meaningful set of beliefs or a philosophical system by which to order life. But in true Uranian fashion, they will keep on destroying systems they have created for the sake of discovering or trying out new ones which might be broader or more inclusive.

The image of God may be cast in the likeness of Uranus — the starry heavens — vast and very difficult to grasp. And yet, just as there are laws which guide the movement of the planets, somewhere in it all, there must be a system. (Einstein, who had Aquarius on the 9th house cusp once remarked 'I cannot believe that God plays dice with the cosmos.') Those with Uranus difficultly aspected could, at certain times, adhere to quite odd or fanatical cults. Too abstract, their philosophy may not translate easily into everyday life. Occasionally, they might have flashes or insights into what they believe are the workings of the Divine or Universal Mind. Lois Rodden gives the chart of Guy Ballard with Uranus in Leo in the 9th squared to Pluto in Taurus in the 6th. Ballard founded a religious movement called 'Mighty am I', and reportedly received messages from 'the Ascended Masters', and glimpsed his previous lives from seventy thousand years back. A more down-to-earth use of this placement is shown in the chart of Mohandas Gandhi with Uranus in Cancer in the 9th ruling Aquarius on the IC (the homeland). On the basis of his strongly felt philosophy (Uranus in the 9th), he led his people from colonialism to freedom (Uranus rules Aquarius on the 4th). The profound sage and mystic, Krishnamurti, was born with Uranus in Virgo in the 9th ruling an Aquarian Ascendant. Interestingly, he preaches that people should find the truth on their own (9th house Uranus rules the 1st house of self) rather than trying to follow the teachings of any particular guru or sect.

Often those with Uranus in the 9th will hold progressive views in the field of education. They may seek an alternative rather than traditional academic structure — such as an independent study programme or the Open University in England. At any time in the degree programme, they may decide to make an abrupt change in their course of study. A 9th house Uranus can bring new ideas, concepts, and insights into any field.

Unusual and unexpected experiences can come through travel. They might, while visiting another country, encounter people or ideas which wake them up and shatter old structures. An in-law may even be the catalyst for inspiring new vision.

If Uranus is not too adversely aspected, they will probably have an uncanny insight into future trends, as if they can feel the pulse of society. The science fiction writer Jules Verne, who often anticipated the course of the future, was born with Uranus in Capricorn in the 9th.

Uranus in the 10th (Aquarius on the MC)

Those with Uranus in the 10th need to contribute something original and progressive to society. They don't want to be seen as ordinary, but rather as forces for change, rebellion or innovation. Because the 10th is Capricorn's natural domain, there is the ability to channel their new ideas or insights through concrete vehicles. Often, they will hold fairly liberal or even radical political views. Karl Marx, who inspired others with his vision of a new world was born with Uranus in Sagittarius in the 10th ruling an Aquarian Ascendant. The artistic genius and gifted inventor Michelangelo was born with Uranus in Scorpio in the 10th ruling Aquarius on the 2nd. Disraeli, the only Jew ever to be Prime Minister of England also had Uranus in the 10th. With Aquarius on the cusp of the 3rd, he was noted for his extreme speech and dress, and even wrote a few novels.

I have known a number of people with this placement who have resigned from jobs because they didn't agree with how things were being run. Others I have come across, constantly change their work in search of something more meaningful to do. Like Uranus in mythology, they destroy their creations and start again. Edmond Rostand (Uranus in Cancer in the 10th ruling Aquarius in the 5th) was first a lawyer, then a journalist, before he finally became a poet and playwright and author of *Cyrano de Bergerac*. Sometimes, those with Uranus in the 10th have unusual jobs. (One woman with this placement headed a research project into the effects of dance and high protein diet on body fat in women.) Or they wake up one morning with a revelation which renders their present work obsolete. Sometimes events seemingly out of the control will disrupt the status quo in the career. Again, if they have not acknowledged their restlessness or need for a change in this area, they may in some way provoke this to happen. Others will simply fall prey to collective trends which shatter or alter their course of direction, such as redundancy or changes of political power.

The mother may be cast in a Uranian light. She might be viewed as eccentric or unconventional in some way. She might have had outside interests which interfered with the mothering role, or felt trapped as a parent. The child could have sensed a degree of restlessness in her, as if she really wanted to be somewhere else. If the mother was very erratic, then the child would be forced to develop more independently, not being able to rely on the mother as most children do. At first, children may resent this, but later reflect thankfully that they had a chance to grow freely and learn how to meet the world on their own. Sometimes the mother is conventional on the outside, but underneath is bursting with a desire to break loose. Children sense this and later 'live out' the mother's unfulfilled wishes — they carefully avoid getting hemmed in by too much maternal or familial responsibility. Sometimes, Uranian mothers feel guilty about their lack of typical maternal instincts, forgetting their good traits — loving without being smothering, they mirror and represent free-thinking for the child. Women with Uranus in the 10th may be happier raising children after they have satisfied some of their need to contribute to society.

Uranus in the 10th is similar to Aquarius there. With Aquarius on the MC, work is needed which benefits as many people as possible, and which allows scope for the inventive and idealistic side of the person's nature to come to the fore.

Uranus in the 11th

Powerfully placed in its own house, Uranus in the 11th can expand the concept of being part of a group to its broadest dimensions. Their main task is a far-reaching one: to widen their individual identities to include all living creatures. This goal may never be realized completely, but it is liberating just striving to accomplish it.

Ultimately, those with Uranus in this house are capable of feeling a sense of kinship with the whole human race. Rather than just seeing the world as an assortment of people and nations attacking and accusing one another, they have the ability to view the whole planet as one family struggling to resolve its problems and conflicts. The difference in these two perspectives is subtle but profound.

Those with Uranus in the 11th should seek others with whom they can link together in the pursuit of a common goal. Generally we form friends with neighbours or people we meet at work; but people with Uranus in this house feel most connected to those with whom they share a similar vision. They don't have to be geographically close to each other to be part of the group — what is important is that they are dedicated to the same ideals and objectives. Someone once said that 'the group is the self of the altruist' and this may ring true for Uranus (or Neptune) in the 11th. Obviously, many people with Uranus in the 11th won't even begin to see it this way; nonetheless, such possibilities do exist for this placement.

More generally, Uranus in the 11th enjoys mixing with like-minded people, whether it's a group of scientists or astrologers. They may serve a 'Uranian function' within any group: presenting challenging and radical ideas, playing the devil's advocate, or sparring with other members to make the debate more lively. If Uranus is difficultly aspected, they might promulgate revolutionary ideas which could be too hard-hitting and drastic. They may also fall out with other members of the group over a matter of principle. Like Mars in the 11th, on one level Uranus may be ambivalent in a group. They enjoy sharing and being part of something larger, and yet are threatened by losing their individuality and freedom in the process.

On a personal level, they will generally have strong feelings about the meaning of friendship and expect others to live up to these. Sometimes their high ideals may be unrealistic given the more selfish and instinctive side of human nature. This placement could indicate friends who serve as important catalysts for change. Likewise, they could be the agents who bring fresh experience to their friends. Some people with Uranus in the 11th may have a fascination for slightly eccentric people, who express sides of their natures that those with this placement are not acknowledging in themselves. Sometimes they have many different types of friends who wouldn't mix easily with one another.

Their goals and objectives in life could change radically in a relatively short span of time, as if they wake up one day with a new vision which they must follow.

Uranus in the 12th

The 12th house represents the collective sea out of which we all emerge. Those with Uranus in the 12th need to take a deep breath and jump in, not forgetting to bring along their best diving equipment and research apparatus. Through exploring the unconscious it is possible for them to regain a sense of continuity with evolutionary and historic processes and glimpse the guiding patterns on which their lives are based. It's not everyone's cup of tea, but in whatever house Uranus is placed, we have to take risks and be different.

People with Uranus in the 12th can approach the whole unconscious realm in an inventive, original and intuitive way. They have access to the mind's storehouse of ancestral wisdom — experiences accrued in the past and inherited through previous generations. Some find the key to unlocking this treasure through drugs, others through meditation or any form of artistic expression which allows them to 'tune into' these ancient records of experience.

The philosophy and radical psychology of R. D. Laing form one of the clearest expositions of what a 12th house Uranus is all about. Laing, who was born with Uranus in Aries in the 12th ruling Aquarius on the cusp of the 12th, wrote that 'the need to know who one is appears to be the most deep rooted in humanity.'[4] Sceptical of almost every social institution in existence (including the family) he believes that the mystical state of consciousness is the only salvation left for the oppressed individual. He maintains that if people could go deep into their unconscious psychoses, in their own way and at their own pace, they would eventually re-emerge from their regression repaired and more whole. On this basis, he established his own institution (Uranus in Aries in the 12th) — homes in which people could go on a 'voyage within the self'.[5]

Dr Arthur Janov, born with Uranus in Pisces in the 12th ruling Aquarius on the cusp of the 11th, is another well-known and controversial psychologist. Like Laing, he also set up his own institution. At Janov's Primal Therapy Institute in Los Angeles, people are encouraged to delve deeply into their unconscious (12th) and relive painful experiences from early life. During primal therapy, patients are helped to feel what they were too frightened to feel when they first had the experience. By reconnecting to and abreacting the pain stored up in the psyche, they aim to free themselves from tensions and symptoms they have been carrying around for years. Again, similar to Laing, the principle is that by freeing what is in the unconscious (Uranus in the 12th) a person can be renewed and liberated.

Uranus in the 12th can also give a close attunement to movements within the collective, often before these actually manifest (the 12th house contains the seeds of the future as well as the remnants from the past). In a collection of her essays on the outer planets and their cycles, Liz Greene points out that Uranus in this house often has 'a very strong interest in political movements and ideologies, but in a rather compulsive as opposed to reflective way'.[6] Adolf Hitler, born with Uranus in Libra in the 12th ruling Aquarius on the cusp of the 4th (the homeland) is a case in point. His vision was not rationally and logically thought out, but rather 'appeared in his mind full-blown'.[7] Uranus gets the rumblings of something even before it happens.

From what I have observed, if Uranus is well-aspected in the 12th, these people have a wealth of good advice to offer others — as if insight and knowledge are there on tap. However, if Uranus has many hard aspects, then their vision is sometimes impaired by their own personal neuroses and complexes. These will have to be 'cleaned up' before the positive benefits of this placement are felt. They are also more likely to be thrown off course by negative feelings in the atmosphere. Regardless of how Uranus is aspected, there is often an interest in parapsychology and spiritualism.

A deep-seated reluctance to relinquish their independence can make it difficult for them to settle down or take root. One part of them might desperately want closeness and security but somehow they manage to thwart this happening. Exploring their own unconscious motivations can free them from this conundrum and help alleviate a lingering sense of loneliness and isolation.

Some join secret societies or engage in 'behind-the-scenes' work for groups. They may align themselves with institutions of a progressive or unusual nature. Acting as a channel through which new ideas and trends are established, they could revolutionize or disrupt the workings of any institution with which they are involved.

Periods of confinement or incarceration may produce surprising effects. In a few cases I have seen, they have not acknowledged a need to temporarily retreat from life and consequently attracted 'accidents' or illnesses which forced them to do so. Sudden reversals of fortune are possible: something which seems ominous and threatening may turn out to be completely different from what they expect, and vice versa.

It could be fruitful to enquire about anything unusual which might have occurred to the mother during the gestation period — in some way, this may have impressed itself on the psyche of the developing embryo.

26.
NEPTUNE AND PISCES THROUGH THE HOUSES

The planet Neptune is associated with the Roman god of the same name and the Greek Poseidon. Personifying water, Poseidon was the god of the seas, lakes, rivers and underground streams. Although inhabiting a vast palace at the bottom of the ocean, he resented Zeus' sovereignty and thirsted for more wordly possessions. Poseidon wrestled with Athene for Attica and lost; unsuccessfully, he battled with Hera for Argolis; and he failed to capture Aegina from Zeus. Angry and forlorn, he flooded the lands he couldn't win, or dried up their rivers in spite. Like Poseidon (Neptune), our volatile emotions often yearn for things we can't have.

The astrological element of water, associated with the realm of the feelings, acts similarly to Poseidon in other ways. When he emerged from the sea, one of two things happened. Sometimes the water opened joyfully and magnificently around him. At other times, however, his appearance was signified by wild tempests and furious storms. Likewise, when our feelings come to the surface, they can be full and divinely inspired or they can sweep over us like a tidal wave.

The planet Neptune, like the Moon and Venus, is another *anima* energy — representing that part of us which fuses, adapts, mirrors and seeks union with others. While Mother Moon gains her identity by reflecting another, and charming Venus gives with the intention of receiving a little back in return, soulful Neptune wants to lose his identity by merging with something greater than himself.

Whereas the main task of the isolated ego (Saturn) is self-preservation, the planet Neptune symbolizes the yearning to dissolve the boundaries of the separate self and experience unity with the rest of life. We've encountered these two principles already in the general discussion of the 12th house, and if you remember, they are not the best of friends. In fact, Saturn (representing the structuring principle of the ego), afraid that he would be overthrown by Neptune, swallows him at birth. For many people, the prospect of disintegration of the individual identity is frightening, and they will relegate Neptune — the urge to reconnect to the wholeness of life — to the unconscious. But (to borrow Liz Greene's analogy), whatever is shoved into the basement has a way of burrowing itself out from under the house and appearing on the front lawn. If Neptune is suppressed, it doesn't go away — instead, it disguises itself and sneaks up on us. In Neptune's house, we may unwittingly 'set up' circumstances in which we have no other alternative than to sacrifice our personal wants and desires in obedience to forces which we cannot change or do anything to alleviate. In this way, the individual ego is cleansed of its sense of almighty superiority and separateness. Purified, we are welcomed into the arms of something bigger than ourselves.

Actually, it was Jupiter who rescued Neptune from Saturn's tyranny: the individual ego's own desire to expand itself (Jupiter) eventually undermines its very separateness by allowing Neptune to run free. Likewise, many people, rather than dreading the disintegration of the ego, actively encourage it, in a pursuit of the expansion and bliss associated with an unbounded existence. This can be constructively achieved through meditation, faith and worship, artistic creativity, and a selfless devotion to another person and cause; or more dangerously attempted through drugs, alcohol or an unbridled abandonment to the passions.

Some people, vaguely remembering a lost Eden of the past, look for heaven on earth in Neptune's house. In the belief that Neptune should give us everything, we may pin great hopes on the affairs of his domain, as if our very redemption lay there. Having bargained on nothing less than absolute ecstasy, we are invariably disappointed when the external world fails to deliver the goods. Wounded and embittered, we may look elsewhere around the house for comfort — often in the liquor cabinet or medicine chest. However, for some of us, the disillusionment entailed in not obtaining what we desire from Neptune is an entry point into another dimension of experience: rather than searching for our happiness solely in the outer realities of life, we turn our attention inward. And eventually we may discover that the bliss we were looking for was already there, inside ourselves, hidden away in Neptune's indestructible golden palace under the sea.

It took Jupiter to rescue Neptune, and very often in the house in which Neptune is placed, we are looking for a saviour. Playing the victim or the underdog (at the same time abnegating personal responsibility and effort), we hope somebody will appear to take care of that area of life for us. Conversely, some people invert this dynamic and attempt to be a saviour for others in that domain. Unlike Saturn, this is not undertaken because of the pressure of an 'ought' or 'should', but much more out of a sense of empathy for the other person's pain. In some cases, we may even become the living embodiment of some sort of popular image or ideal in Neptune's sphere — anything from a neo-god or goddess, or a superstar, to a public scandal or convenient scapegoat.

As might be imagined of the god of the sea, Neptune is rather slippery. Something we are chasing in this area of life may mysteriously evade us. Often, instead of facing up to the facts, we will act like Blanche Dubois and create the illusion that everything is wonderful. We may choose to see only that which supports our fantasy. Sooner or later, reality will probably crash down on us. Then again, maybe not: we can never be sure with Neptune.

Neptune is associated with the things of the etheric world, which cannot necessarily be grasped, measured or seen. It is the essence underlying form, rather than the form itself. Through Neptune's house we may glimpse a higher or altered state of consciousness, a view of infinity and eternity and that which transcends normal boundaries of space and time. On another level, Neptune is fog, mist and nebulousness; and by house, it may show where we are perennially confused, vague and unclear about our aims and goals or inclined to drift and float with whatever comes along. If (as Neptune believes) everything is All One, then, whatever happens, it shouldn't make that much difference to us anyway.

Two figures associated with Neptune are Dionysus and Christ. Both preached relinquishing the separate identity and the need to merge with something numinous and divine. Dionysus gathered a group of followers and with the help of the intoxicating effects of wine, they were transported via feeling and ecstasy to another realm. Oblivious to the mundane realities of life, they simply abandoned themselves to something greater than the self — not bothering if their cars were parked on a double yellow line, or if they were meant to be at home putting dinner on the table for their husbands. In this sense, they transcended time, boundary and form.

Christ is considered by some to be 'the Neptunian Master'. Both a victim and a saviour, he taught 'the giving up' of the self to the spirit. The establishment — ordinary ego-consciousness — found it difficult to recognize either Christ or Dionysus as gods. Both of them suffered forms of dismemberment. Both died, but were born again. The house position of Neptune is where we may share, to some degree, the experience of these divinities. In this domain, we may fall apart, so that we can come back together again in a different way, opened up to something beyond the ego. Attitudes of willingness, acceptance and faith aid the process. Sometimes, in Neptune's house, we have no other viable choices.

Pisces on the cusp or contained within a house is similar to Neptune there. The house with Neptune in it will influence any house where Pisces is found. For instance, Marilyn Monroe was born with Neptune in the 1st house and Pisces on the 8th house cusp. She came to symbolize an idealized image of feminine sexuality (Pisces on the 8th) and sacrificed much of her own identity in the process (Neptune in the 1st house of self).

Neptune in the 1st

In the 1st house, Neptune diffuses the boundary between a sense of the self as a separate entity and other people. In extreme cases, those with Neptune in the 1st are like mirrors — they just reflect who or whatever is in front of them. Because they often derive their identities from what other people want or need them to be, others may look to them for their salvation: 'At last, here is a person who really understands and appreciates me, and who is just naturally everything that I need in another person.' However, the honeymoon is over when they observe that Neptune in the 1st opens up, adjusts and adapts in a similar fashion to whoever is around, not just to them. We might rightfully praise 1st house Neptunes for their exquisite sensitivity to other people; but we might also concern ourselves with their lack of a clear or well-defined sense of their own identity and direction in life. Not having crystallized a sense of self, they appropriate someone else's.

In general, the 1st house thrust to distinguish the self as a distinct and unique individual conflicts with Neptune's tendency to dissolve and merge back into a state of non-differentiated wholeness. Just when they build up something or establish a more solid footing, events seemingly conspire to erode or undermine the foundations — and down comes the structure. For whatever reasons, a person with Neptune in the 1st is being asked to sacrifice or let go of the sense of being a separate self. This kind of selfless or egoless state is the goal of many mystical seekers, and this placement of Neptune may be 'a natural' in this respect. But one might rightfully enquire whether or not Neptune in this house ever had a self to relinquish in the first place.

The problem may stem from the early bonding with the mother. We cannot grow separate and self-reliant unless another person has loved us enough to make us feel that we are worthy of being 'a somebody'. A symbiotic closeness to Mother is the first stage of this process: in the early years, we need a close, caring, good-enough mother in order to develop the courage and strength to grow into an autonomous individual. If this does not happen, we are not only afraid to be ourselves, but we will keep searching for that 'perfect fit' with another person which we didn't have as children, adjusting ourselves all out of proportion to achieve this. But the problem is that *if we are not enough, then nobody else is ever enough either.*

However, if as children we are secure with mother's love, we eventually begin to feel that we can do with a little less of it. Besides, we want to explore more of the environment, venturing out and experimenting with things. At this stage, Mother must be willing to let go of us — otherwise we may be made to feel guilty about our need for separateness.

With Neptune in the 1st house, something could have gone askew at either of these two important stages of symbiosis and separation. If there was not a secure enough tie with the mother, then they might be afraid to develop a strong, individual identity. But if they were forbidden by her to separate, they may never have had the chance to find out who they are in their own right. With the help of therapy or any of the many forms of self-exploration available today, it is never too late to start.

With Neptune in the 1st, the personality or style may embody any of the possible connotations of Neptune. While their diffuseness may make them appear mysterious or enigmatic, some wander aimlessly through life. Many too easily slip into the role of martyr and then feel resentful if others take advantage of them. Some are fair game for anyone who offers to save or rescue them. A few may turn to hard drugs and alcohol in an attempt to alleviate the harsher realities of life and find themselves worse off in the end.

However, there are many positive ways to embody Neptune. Because they can encompass realms beyond the ordinary ego-borders of existence, they may be able to give expression to collective feelings and images through some sort of artistic medium. Their vision may be truly inspiring to other people who are unable to see so easily in those dimensions. And this placement often appears in the charts of excellent counsellors and healers: the diffuse boundaries of Neptune enable them to 'tune into' and help other people. Some dedicate their whole lives to uplifting or redeeming the planet.

If Neptune is close to the Ascendant, the person may never really have wanted to be born in the first place. They will need to learn to say 'Yes' to life to counter-effect a persistent longing to return back to the oceanic totality of the womb. Alternatively, these desires may be projected forward in a spiritual direction, giving rise to the mystical longing for higher states of consciousness.

With Neptune in the 1st, some confusion may attend the birth and early years of life. I have seen this placement in the charts of people whose actual births were shrouded in mystery or kept secret from others. Early conditions may not contribute to their sense of trust and security in life, as if they are called upon to sacrifice the degree of love and attention that is normally bestowed on the newborn infant. Illness at an early age could further accentuate the tenuous hold they have on life in their bodies.

Neptune in the 2nd

Like Uranus in this position, Neptune in the 2nd requires a deeper understanding and feeling for the whole sphere of money, possessions and resources. Neptune has a dissolving effect wherever it is placed in the chart, and in the 2nd, any tangible or outer forms of security may be subject to this influence. Unconsciously, the person may feel guilty about acquiring money or holding onto possessions, believing that what belongs to one should belong to all. Conversely, they may feel that the world owes them a living — what is other people's should rightfully be theirs as well. Whether they like it or not, watery Neptune creates fluidity in the 2nd house sphere.

I have seen a variety of manifestations of this placement. Sometimes, it indicates general confusion and nebulousness in the handling of finance and investment. Unforeseen forces undermine speculation — what seemed safe turns out to be a fraud. In some cases, thieves come in the night and claim what they feel should be theirs. Or they may receive a large cheque in the first post and a bill for the same amount in the second. Or, generous to a fault, they are a soft touch for any hard luck story, continually reaching into their pockets to give spare change away, or getting out the cheque book to donate to a worthy cause.

Poseidon had great riches under the sea and yet he still longed for the earthly power of Zeus. Those with Neptune in the 2nd may be dissatisfied with what they already have and always want more — especially if someone else has it. They may worship money and possessions as the key to heaven on earth, or value money because it allows them to live out their fantasies. Even if they achieve the material status they hope to gain, they may discover that it isn't all that they imagined it would be. Something is still lacking.

Ultimately, rather than seeking security and well-being from outside of themselves, they might need to reconsider their value systems and look inward to what some call the 'higher spiritual planes' for fulfilment. They might even unconsciously provoke this by 'setting up' losing what they have gained or dearly value as if they sense that giving everything away is their path to rebirth and redemption.

I have observed that these people are often unsure of their own inner value and worth. They may not be appreciative enough of their innate gifts, such as their sensitivity and empathy, their artistic and creative imaginations, and the ability they have to heal and soothe others. Money could be earned through a 'Neptunian profession': acting, modelling, painting, poetry, dance, fashion, photography, healing, the selling of alcohol or drugs, etc. Professions as varied as that of a chemist, clergyman or merchant marine could be connected to a 2nd house Neptune.

Finally, there is a tendency to imbue the material world with symbolic and emotional significance. An object or possession may be valued not so much for what it is, but for the feelings it inspires in them. Often, they can perceive the essence underlying the form itself.

Neptune in the 3rd

Neptune is where we are looking to be reconnected with a sense of wholeness and oneness in life. By contrast, the usual 3rd house type mind is one which analyses, compares, discriminates and observes the relationship of one thing to another. While Neptune in the 3rd can (just about) still do this, the mind must also be used for other 'higher' purposes — as the vehicle or eye through which the soul looks outward. On a deep level, those with Neptune in the 3rd know that, *divorced from love, the mind is like a pair of scissors which cuts life into shreds.*

On one level, Neptune in the 3rd can confuse and scatter the mind, giving rise to vagueness and woolly thinking. However, at other times, the Neptunian mind exhibits an uncanny insight into the undercurrents and subtleties in the environment. They sense the 'meta-message' or hidden nuances and meanings behind what is said or exchanged. What they lose in terms of precise analytical abilities, they gain by being able to view the bigger picture more clearly.

There are some dangers to bear in mind. Their desire to see what is beautiful and divine in their surroundings can produce a kind of selective perception in which only the good is seen and that which doesn't fit into this category goes unnoticed. They may be so open to the mind and opinions of others that they may think they are thinking their own thoughts when in actual fact they have picked up the point of view of somebody else in the environment. In some cases, they serve as spokespeople for others. Sometimes, they believe that knowledge is what will redeem them. As a result they may study avidly and yet never feel they know enough. Or they are gluttonous for other people to come along and say something which inspires them.

Neptune in the 3rd may not feel comfortable expressing itself through ordinary channels of communication. What they have to say or what they have experienced may be more aptly demonstrated through dance, poetry, song or a picture they paint or take with a camera. Often, there is a shyness in the early schooling situation. I have seen this placement in some cases of dyslexia. Or they may be confused in such a way that they turn up to appointments on the wrong day, take down numbers or addresses incorrectly, and invariably get lost or waylaid on short journeys. In extreme cases, it may indicate mental instability, hallucinations, and paranoia where they imagine all sorts of things happening 'out there' which are actually projections of their inner world.

Sacrifices may have to be made in Neptune's domain, and in the 3rd, this may entail a need to adjust and be extra-sensitive to a sibling who for some reason is a problem or has difficulties. In certain cases I have seen, the ghost of a dead sibling haunts one or both of the parents, and the remaining child has been confused with the one who has passed away. If a brother or sister has died, those with Neptune in the 3rd may carry a sense of guilt, imagining they are partially responsible for the death. (Neptune diffuses the boundary between the self and others, and in the 3rd, the person may feel that he or she is responsible for everything which happens in the immediate environment). A parent can help children with Neptune in the 3rd by respecting their imaginations and yet spelling things out as honestly and clearly as possible, bearing in mind what is age-appropriate.

I have also seen Neptune in the 3rd in the charts of children without siblings who long for companionship with the brother or sister they never had. Some may assuage loneliness and feel more complete by inventing imaginary playmates. In some cases of adopted children, Neptune is found in the 3rd, as if they are not sure where they truly fit in or belong. In a few examples of this placement, sacrifices had to be made in the area of education. They had to leave school to work for the family, or money was tight and an older brother or sister got there first.

A number of people I know with Neptune in the 3rd show exceptional ability as teachers — especially working with children who have learning difficulties. They can find ways to communicate with and understand the child that other teachers may not be able to grasp.

Neptune in the 4th (Pisces on the IC)

Someone with this placement once said to me that she felt as if she had swallowed a mirror. From deep down inside, those with Neptune in the 4th absorb and reflect the atmospheric influences around them. If possible, they should exercise caution in selecting the environments in which they live. Of course, discrimination and free choice are not always on the same menu as Neptune.

This is a very hard placement to pin down, and I have seen it operating in a number of ways. Some people with it, no matter what the aspects to Neptune are, have reported to me the joyful wonders of their idyllic early home life — children at play in the garden, the closeness of the family, mother's bread, daddy's knee, grandpa's stories, etc. And for many people, a positive 4th house Neptune indicates this kind of supportive and loving home background, which is such a good base for later development. However, some appear to spend much of their later years yearning to be back there, and comparing the problems and drudgery of adult life with the good old days. Some may have blended so thoroughly with the family, that they have never developed a more individualistic sense of who they are. The way they think and feel, and their tastes, opinions and proclivities, reflect those from the early home, full-stop. They may have come from what family therapists call 'enmeshed families': families who live tightly within closed systems, where there are unwritten rules that no one should behave differently from what is expected in case it upsets anyone else or causes undue disharmony. Neptune's price for remaining within the safe structure of such a family is that of one's own personal identity and freedom.

Others with this placement start by telling me of the joys of their early lives, and then look down, lower their voices and say, 'But then, it all changed when father lost his job, my brother became seriously ill, mother had an affair . . . etc.' Neptune is back to his old tricks again, asking for sacrifice and adjustment. In one case of a chart I did for a woman with Neptune in the 4th, I remember her describing the delights of her childhood: 'It was all so wonderful, I wish I could have those happy days back again — except of course those times I came home from school and found daddy lying drunk on the floor and mommy beat up . . .' In Neptune's house, a person's favourite coloured spectacles are rose.

Making sense of all this is not easy, but there are a few concrete things to be said about Neptune in the 4th. They will usually be called upon to make sacrifices on the home front. For instance, this placement shows up in the charts of people who, as children, had to be extra quiet and controlled in order not to disturb a chronically ill parent. In other cases I have seen, they were brought up in a collective environment — perhaps a boarding house or orphanage. Sometimes the home itself was also the institution where the parents worked, so that although the parents were there, they were not always available to the child. The child had to watch the parents constantly giving time and attention to other people, and this caused jealousy, insecurity and pain.

Difficult aspects to Neptune can indicate families which have been broken up or dissolved in some way. In certain cases, a 4th house Neptune may even mean the sacrifice or giving up of the homeland. Sigmund Freud, for instance, who left Austria to escape the Nazis, was born with Neptune in Pisces in the 4th. (Saturn in Gemini in the 8th squared his 4th house Neptune and we all know what he thought about the undercurrents in the early home environment.) Similarly, Neptune in the 4th could indicate the giving up of one's tradition and family patterns as in the case of the Duke of Windsor (Neptune in Gemini in the 4th ruling Pisces in the 1st). Others will seek their 'spiritual home and family' — not necessarily linked to blood ties. The house may be used as a meeting place for meditation groups, psychic sessions, or as a haunt for artists and musicians. Those with Neptune in the 4th might be very happy living by the sea.

If the 4th is taken to mean the father (the hidden parent), then he will carry something of the Neptunian projection. For some, it denotes a very sensitive, soft and feeling father, often poetic and romantic. The father may be over-idealized and then appear as a disappointment later in life when examined more realistically. It could indicate an absent or missing father, one of whom the child only has a vague recollection or an unclear image. I have seen cases where the father belonged more to the world than the child: he was a clergyman, or a busy doctor, or a famous opera singer, or a politician, or a well-known actor, or a diplomat. In these cases, the children are asked to sacrifice the personal father, and often have to find within themselves the kind of love and support they saw their fathers giving so freely to others.

Neptune in the 4th is sometimes an indication of skeletons in the family closet: an alcoholic, drug-ridden or mentally disturbed parent or close relative. In a few charts I have seen with this placement, there was uncertainty about who the real father was. Of these, two of them only found out in later years that the man they thought was the father actually wasn't.

This placement suggests deep spiritual longings which often surface in the second half of life. Hermann Hesse, the writer who immortalized the spiritual quest in his book *Siddhartha*, had Neptune in Taurus in the 4th ruling Pisces on the 3rd house of writing and communication.

According to many textbooks the later years for those with Neptune in the 4th could be marked by a peaceful seclusion during which they quietly disengage from life. There is the danger, however, that they could regress back to the position of a helpless child, especially if they felt their needs were really never looked after when they were small. The way we begin life is often the way we end it — unless we bring these unconscious patterns of childhood to the surface of awareness and do something to change them. With Neptune in the 4th, this is better done sooner rather than later.

Pisces on the cusp or contained within the 4th is similar to Neptune there. With Pisces on the IC the search for a broader, all-inclusive identity is probably the best foundation upon which to build the life.

Neptune in the 5th

In the 5th, Neptune wins some and loses some. On the one hand, this position bestows a rich and vivid imagination, creative flair and the natural ability to exteriorize the feelings in a grand and exuberant manner. On the other hand, circumstances they attract into their lives may require that they give and become what others want and need, rather than what they would like to be or do for themselves. But should these coincide — that is, when what they wish to give is what others want and need to receive — then probably nothing else in the chart will equal the joy and fulfilment promised by this placement.

Back to the sandbox. The first problem is whether or not little Neptune is even free to go out and play. 'Poor Mother works so hard at home — I should really stay in and help her.' 'No, don't think of me,' poor Mother says. 'It will be good for you to go out with your friends — I really don't mind (sigh).' Guiltily, but excitedly, Neptune floats on air to the playground, bubbling with all the fun he is going to have. But what's this, nobody is there — 'How strange, where could they all be? (pause) I wonder what I am missing?' 'Well I can still play on my own.' He climbs in the sandbox filled with the inspiration of the castles taking shape in his mind, when along comes Mercury. 'Sorry Neptune, your mother sent me — she needs you back home — mind if I borrow your shovel?'

Sometimes the more those with Neptune (or Pisces) in the 5th search for pleasure, the more it eludes them. It's not always this bleak — but they often are called upon to make sacrifices in the area of creativity. Some may give up a career in the arts for the sake of a more stable or routine existence. Some will give up a more stable and routine existence for the sake of a career in the arts. But whether or not a profession in this field is sought, they will benefit from any spare-time creative outlet which offers them a chance to express their feelings, emotions and splendid imagination.

Romantically, they are usually bursting at the seams. Imbuing the beloved with divine qualities, they embark on the romance of all times. The writer F. Scott Fitzgerald was born with Mars conjunct Neptune in the 5th — and his relationship with Zelda was the Great American Romance of the period. Besides exhibiting his feelings creatively, he also openly displayed (5th) his drinking (Neptune). (Along the same lines, the singer-comedian-actor Dean Martin has a 5th house Neptune as well.) Similar to Scotty and Zelda (in his case she proved a little too Neptunian to handle), Neptune in this house may bring complications in love. One version is falling in love with someone who is unattainable in some way. In this case, the loved one can be safely idealized and worshipped at a distance, or duly sacrificed with a flair surpassed only by Our Lady of the Camellias. Very often they identify love with a cause — 'This person needs me to save or fulfil him/her.' Or the reverse — 'The beloved will salvage and redeem me.' More positively though, people with Neptune in the 5th possess, through the expansiveness and numinosity of their love, a natural gift for uplifting and healing others.

Sacrifices may have to be made regarding children. If difficultly aspected, they may feel martyred by parenthood: 'If it weren't for the kids, I could have done . . .' They might idealize a child or turn the child into their source of salvation. 'If the child loves me against all odds, if the child is wonderful or successful, then my life is redeemed.' Obviously, there must be a willingness on the part of a parent with this placement to free the child to live his or her own life. The child may reflect Neptunian or Piscean qualities — in the sense of possessing unusual creative or artistic abilities, or the more challenging manifestations of this planet or sign — mental, physical or emotional disabilities. What is important is the 'spiritual growth' gained through the experience with children. In whatever sphere of life it is placed, Neptune may indicate a kind of suffering which has the effect of softening the individual. Invariably, the parent who loses or is compelled to give up a child will be profoundly affected and altered through what Neptune has to teach. Some people with Neptune in the 5th work well with disabled or troubled children and adolescents.

Obviously, if Neptune is adversely aspected they should be very cautious about gambling and speculation. By nature, Neptune offers no guarantees.

Neptune in the 6th

There are some basic conflicts between the principles of Neptune (Pisces) and those of the 6th house. Neptune yearns for wholeness, infinity and unboundedness, while the 6th house (the natural domain of Virgo) divides everything into its component parts, examines one thing at a time, and clarifies what something is by contrasting it to something else. While Neptune keeps falling apart in order to be put back together again in a new and better way, the 6th house likes everything labelled and neatly stored in its proper place. Obviously, we can't always have it both ways, and one or the other principle is going to have to bend. Sometimes the 6th house need for order and efficient functioning will suppress the Neptunian urges to relax, let go and just float freely. At other times, the dissolving effect of Neptune will undermine the structure and organization of everyday life and the body itself. Ultimately, the challenge for those with Neptune in the 6th is how to function within defined limits and boundaries and yet not lose sight of their connection to everything else around them.

Neptune in the 6th indicates a sensitive and delicate nervous system, what some writers call a weak etheric boundary or 'leaky aura'. As a result, those with this placement are prone to invasion from outside forces or are more susceptible to germs and illnesses in the atmosphere. They would be well advised to take up an exercise or technique which strengthens the nervous system, and they should be cautious to discover which foods do or don't agree with their system. They need to find that balance between indiscriminate indulgence (no boundaries) and over-preciousness in diet and life (too many boundaries). Usually they are sensitive to drugs and alcohol and may need much smaller quantities to feel the effects.

Illnesses are often emotional in origin and difficult to diagnose clearly. In some cases I have seen, they have been diagnosed incorrectly, given a wrong prescription, and treated for something they didn't have. Some will benefit by seeking treatment from the alternative or complementary medicines such as homoeopathy, naturopathy, acupuncture, etc. — which approach prevention and cure on a more subtle level than allopathic medicine in general.

Conversely, those with Neptune in the 6th may have healing abilities and sometimes choose work which gives expression to these gifts. Some will be deeply aware of the body as a vessel of the spirit. As with many other 6th house placements, illness can be understood as a message that something in life is not right and needs adjusting. The person's faith and attitudes will play a large part in the course of recovery. Sometimes, the psychological or spiritual awakening and understanding which comes as a result of illness will profoundly alter their whole slant on existence.

Though an illness such as cancer cannot be attributed to any one planetary placement, parallels exist between the dilemma of a 6th house Neptune and the problems caused by malignant tissue in the body. Due to X-rays, the intake of various toxins, or just because of an occasional slip-up in its functioning, the body produces cells which are not properly attuned to the needs of the whole organism. Normally, a person who is healthy and strong can fight the imperfection, but if the system is weak or overly stressed then the cell continues to malfunction. Multiplying without restraint, it produces more rogue cells — none of which are programmed to act in accordance with the maintenance of the system as a whole. The malignant growth can eventually undermine the entire body. The right relationship of the cell to the larger system of the body is analogous to the question raised by Neptune in the 6th — how to function as separate individuals and yet make adjustments and concessions to the needs of those around us.

Sacrifices may have to be made in the sphere of work, and they are often sensitive to the atmosphere in the office. In a few cases, they may be the scapegoats for what goes wrong or the victim of an employer's or co-worker's deceit. On the other hand, fellow workers might turn to them for salvation and support. If well-aspected, there is usually a close and uplifting rapport with associates. Some may look to a job to bring them all their happiness in life. In a few instances I have seen, they have had to work very hard while not initially receiving the recognition or renumeration they deserve for it. Employment could entail the use of Neptunian skills — careers in medicine and healing, chemistry, work which involves artistic imagination, and in some cases jobs in bars and pubs, or at sea.

Very often, they are not too interested in the mundane practicalities of everyday life. Any excuse will be found to avoid the drudgery of such unglamorous tasks as vacuuming, and such boring duties as paying bills on time. Conversely, a few may become obssessed with the daily chores, as if heaven on earth was achieved through good organization in life. (Whoever said 'cleanliness is next to godliness' might have had Neptune in this house.) Some will perform practical tasks as a form of service to others. Housework could also be used as an escape or way of avoiding other areas of the life that need dusting. Discrimination is advised in choosing servants, au pairs, or even the car mechanic — we are open to deception in the affairs of Neptune's house. Again, disillusionment or pain in the domain of Neptune helps us to recognize our limits and imperfections and open us to a greater and more comprehensive awareness of ourselves and life in general.

In its most positive sense, those with Neptune in the 6th can take a divinely inspired vision and bring it into concrete manifestation. They can also see divinity everywhere. There is a saying: 'In every particle of dust, there are present Buddhas without number.'

Neptune in the 7th

Those with Neptune in the 7th encounter complexities in the area of personal relationship which can serve to change and transform their consciousness and understanding of life. Through the joys of intimacy and closeness or through any pain, disillusionment or loss incurred in partnership, they can be reborn into a new level of awareness.

There are many different manifestations of this placement. Some people will be looking for a god or goddess to worship, to revere, and to save them. To assuage feelings of loneliness and isolation they often yearn to be absorbed into another person. Rather than taking responsibility to become a complete person in their own right, a partner may be sought to make them more whole. In this sense, they love others because they *need* them for something. Taken to an extreme, the other person becomes like an article of clothing they wear, or a piece of equipment they use, what Martin Buber calls an 'I-It' relationship. Neptune is not entirely happy with this situation — this planet's noble ideal of love is to love and not ask anything back in return. If those with Neptune in the 7th become too dependent on another person, they may find that, in one way or another, the partner lets them down or the relationship is disrupted.

Consequently, they are faced with having to develop for themselves what they sought in the other person, and learn a more selfless kind of love in the bargain. Wherever Neptune is placed in the chart, a lot is asked of us.

The other variety of Neptune in the 7th are those who are looking for someone to whom they can play saviour. Their idea of relating is to rescue and redeem the other person. Hence, the reputation of this placement for an attraction to victim types — alcoholics, drug addicts, criminals, unstable people with a shady or difficult past, etc. Some will be drawn to artists and inspirational types, such as the musical genius or the religious prophet, who need an inordinate amount of mothering and cleaning up after. Very often, the one who has done the looking after and rescuing ends up feeling martyred and unappreciated.

Unconsciously, some people with Neptune in the 7th believe that by giving something up they will be cleansed and purified. On the basis of this hidden agenda, they may fall in love with someone who isn't free or wholly attainable, such as a person already married. Obviously, this will involve adjustments on the part of the person with Neptune there, or perhaps relinquishing the relationship entirely. In some cases I have seen, those with Neptune here settle into platonic relationships, in which the desires of the flesh are 'transcended'.

Those with this placement are often genuinely called upon to give a great deal in relationships — to make sacrifices for the partner and be accepting of the limitations which the other person cannot easily resolve. Sometimes they exhibit a kind of unselfish love which is saintly and worthy of true respect. However, at other times they may allow themselves to be walked over as if they had no rights in the relationship. There is a fine line with Neptune between authentic selflessness and tolerance and just being a doormat.

Not surprisingly, with Neptune in the 7th there is often a very romantic and idealized notion of what a relationship should be, which doesn't account for the hard work involved. A yearning for perfection in the partner and in the partnership itself means that those with Neptune in the 7th might actually be very difficult people to live with. Unconsciously, they can be extremely critical and judging of flaws in the other person which don't match up to their concept of what their partner ought to be like or fail to match their notion of Love. Some present the facade of a perfect relationship to the public, when, in actual fact, it is very far from the ideal. More positively, there may be a spiritual meeting and union of two people, and an uncanny psychic rapport between them. However, no matter how divinely ordained the union might seem, there is still the need to adjust to the differences elicited by personal idiosyncrasies. Two soulmates can still argue about the manner in which the other squeezes the toothpaste tube.

After we strip away the fantasy, glamour, esctasy and romantic notions of love, what does Neptune leave us? Ultimately, this planet represents a non-attached kind of love, a love that does not cling, or swallow up any of the people involved. Not a union based on 'oughts' and 'shoulds' but one of reciprocity, *which respects the other person's need for acceptance, not approval.* As Marilyn Ferguson writes in *The Aquarian Conspiracy*, 'love is a context, not a behaviour.'[1] Somewhere in between demanding that the other person adjusts to us, or our always adjusting to the other person is the kind of love that Neptune envisions.

Besides just referring to marriage and close partnership, the 7th house is the way in which we meet society in general. Neptune in the 7th can encounter others from the stance of love, sensitivity and openness, or present a false front which suits any occasion. A number of artists and musicians whose charts I have done have this placement, as well as people who counsel and help others in some way. If Neptune is difficultly aspected, there can be the danger of scandal and problems with public lawsuits. The person may be 'scapegoated': that is, openly punished and admonished for what others secretly feel guilty about in themselves.

Neptune in the 8th

If Neptune can't be at home in the 12th, his next favourite house is that of his close brother Pluto, the 8th. Neptune's main thrust is the loss of boundaries and separateness: what better place to do this than in the house of sex, sharing and intimacy. And as a means of alleviating Neptune's perennial divine homesickness, the 8th house's association with death does the job quite well.

Freud made us aware that many seemingly innocent things can be symbolic of our sexual drive and interests. For instance, if you dream of smoking a cigar, is that really a cigar you are thinking of? However, it is also the case that sex itself may be symbolic. With Neptune (or Pisces) in the 8th, sex, rather than just simply being enjoyed for its own sake, is often the means to alleviate other very pressing psychological concerns.

For those with Neptune in this house, sex is a way of merging with other people, and hence transcending the limits of the isolated self.

Either through losing their own boundaries or engulfing those of another, they relieve much more than just a physiological tension. Reminiscent of the rites of Dionysus, in the throes of physical love, they satisfy the need to abandon and forget themselves. Sex is also a way of loosening the reins of personal control and responsibility for the self. They are captured and captivated by another; they are carried away by a force more powerful than themselves. It is a form of worship and reverence, a kind of divine seduction, which brings home to them that something exists which is bigger and greater than they are.

With Neptune in the 8th, physical intimacy is also a respite from loneliness, and much of the promiscuity and indiscretion associated with this placement may stem from this motive. Some may also feel that giving themselves sexually is a way of serving, pleasing or even healing others. It can also be a very convenient way of escaping from problems in other areas of the life.

I have seen many cases of people with this placement who are confused about their sexual identities. Neptune is so diffuse, so adaptable, so fluid and so shaped by its container, that they have difficulty knowing exactly what it is they do want. Conversely, problematical aspects to Neptune (from Saturn, for instance) also suggest a fear of letting go — a tension between holding on to boundaries and losing them. Some may even feel the need to transcend their libidinal desires altogether for the sake of channelling these energies in other directions. For others, sex may seem like a disappointment, and not quite as wonderful as it looks in the movies or what they read in books or hear from friends about it. And still others may feel that their way of purification and redemption is through sacrificing a sexual relationship with someone to whom they are strongly attracted. In some instances I have seen, they seemed to always desire and fantasize about people they were not involved with, rather than the person with whom they were engaged in a relationship. Neptune is never that content with what he already has. Besides, if we know a person too well, his or her alien magnetism eventually wears thin.

Many of the same processess apply to the exchange of values between people. Often they hope to gain many material benefits from a partner, but ultimately what is acquired is usually of a much less tangible nature. Strange complications and deceptive circumstances can affect the whole area of the partner's money and joint finances. At times they may be too influenced or even deceived by other people's values, or envious about what others own which they don't. In the end, their greatest satisfaction will come not from accruing other people's possessions but rather by helping another person to develop his or her own values and resources.

It is advisable that they are as straightforward as possible in business dealings and care should be taken in the selection of business partners. Neptune often brings confusion, and when signing contracts, the two parties should clarify exactly what the agreement is. Economic losses and gains will have an important psychological impact, and ultimately could impel them to find their security and salvation inwardly in values other than the material. In any case, they are well-advised to seek advice before making financial investments and in all issues concerning inheritance and taxation.

When Neptune is in any of the water houses, the person is extremely sensitive to and influenced by undercurrents and feelings in the atmosphere. Depending on the aspects to Neptune, the experience of intangible and non-material forces can operate constructively or destructively (Adolf Hitler had Pluto conjunct Neptune in the 8th). In positive cases, the person will receive guidance and inspiration as if out of nowhere or may be open to valuable instruction through dreams. It is as if they tap into an invisible realm where expanded vision and understanding becomes available just at the times when such broadened awareness is most necessary. For this reason, they can also serve as sources of comfort and inspiration for others who are experiencing crises. However, the psychic openness of this position can manifest in less desirable ways. In a few instances, they may feel 'possessed' — as if they have been taken over by something powerful outside of themselves. Sometimes they may receive deceptive or misleading guidance from some other dimension.

Since Neptune wants to go Home, and the 8th is the house of Death, those with this placement might entertain self-destructive fantasies when life gets too tough. These can be acted out through a misuse of drugs or alcohol. (Marilyn Monroe was born with Pisces on the cusp of the 8th — not only the cause of death but all the confusion and uncertainty around it reflect the influence of Pisces there.) Unless Neptune has hard aspects from Saturn, there is usually not a fear of death, since the desire to transcend boundaries is so very strong. In line with this, there will often be an interest in the metaphysical or occult.

Neptune in the 9th

Neptune in the 9th seeks redemption and salvation through a belief system. Those with this placement yearn to merge with something greater than the self through an often devotional adherence to a philosophy, religion, cult or guru figure. There is also an irresistible attraction to anyone or anything which promises the keys to heaven. Normally their philosophy or religion will require some form of sacrifice and relinquishment — of the ego, of their possessions, or of former attachments. Many with this placement will benefit enormously from the following of such doctrines. Others may join very strange, esoteric or 'cultish' groups, and lose themselves through these involvements. Some may believe that enlightenment will come if they can perfectly imitate their guru. They fall victim to what is known as 'the buddha disease' — dressing, eating and thinking exactly like the master, and forgetting the importance of just being themselves. They mistakenly believe that if they behave like an enlightened being they will become enlightened — forgetting that behaviour is a by-product of consciousness, and not the other way around. In other words, they 'mood-make' themselves into believing they are realized. Hard aspects to Neptune in the 9th (especially from the 12th) suggest the possibility of 'spiritual inflation' — someone who believes that he or she is God's messenger or that their own particular cult is the one with a monopoly on the truth.

With Neptune here, there is the possibility of disappointments with philosophical systems. If they are looking for that one thing which will be the answer to everything, then they are liable to disillusionment. In one particular meditation society for which I did a number of the disciples' charts, many of them had Neptune in the 9th: their guru turned out to be an alcoholic. In general with Neptune, pinning the hopes on anything external to save one, even if it is a very inspired philosophy or belief system, may prove a let-down until what is being sought externally is found within the self.

Neptune in the 9th describes a very open and impressionable mind, a vivid imagination, and an interest in what Maslow called 'the farther reaches of human nature'. They sense that they could be much more than they already are if they could only find a way to more fully expand and utilize their faculties and potentials.

They may be confused about what direction to take in higher education. In many cases I have observed, there was vagueness and vacillation about which subject to make the major area of focus. Some might believe that education is the answer to everything, or find a professor who is their special 'guru'. Others could become disillusioned with their university or course of study, or find themselves victimized by the system in some way. A few people I know with this placement incurred drug and alcohol problems while at university.

Keats wrote that he could 'never feel certain of any truth but from a clear perception of its beauty'. The idea that 'beauty is truth, truth beauty' is a very apt description of one sense of Neptune in the 9th. Similarly, for those with this placement, creative expression might be inspired by religious or transcendental images or subtle dimensions of experience, and they could serve as channels to awaken others to these. The philosophical writer Goethe was born with Neptune in the 9th. Bob Dylan, whose songs inspired a whole generation, was born with Neptune in this house ruling Pisces on the 3rd (communication). Neptune here could also indicate international fame as an actor, artist or musician, as in the case of Marlon Brando, Henri Matisse and Jimi Hendrix.

Neptune will express itself in relation to travel and long journeys. For some, travel will be a means of escape and a way of avoiding something in the immediate environment. Others may make pilgrimages to find enlightenment, or be drawn to certain lands which have a Mecca-like enchantment for them. They might envision a place, go there, and find it is very different from what they imagined. Some may feel a kind of spiritual tie with a country other than their own. Caution should be taken not to be deceived by others while in foreign countries.

If Neptune is difficultly aspected, there could be complications with in-laws, or one who is felt as a responsibility to the person in some way.

Neptune in the 10th (Pisces on the MC)

Neptune has many different faces in the 10th house of career and standing before the public. One manifestation of Neptune here is in those who find themselves idealized and worshipped by the public in general. In some way, they capture the collective imagination or come to represent a movement or force sweeping through society. There are many interesting examples: for instance, Karl Marx, whose very name evokes a whole philosophy of life and history, and who envisioned an ideal state under communism, was born with Neptune in Sagittarius in the 10th. John F. Kennedy, who as President embodied a new outlook and vision for America and was worshipped as a hero by many, was born with Neptune in Leo there. Assassinated while still in office, Kennedy also came to represent the sacrificial victim side of Neptune. In a sense, both Marx and Kennedy gave up their personal identities to represent and serve something greater than themselves — the collective's longing for redemption.

Tenth house Neptunes may embody various other principles,

anything from representing what is beautiful, stylish and glamorous to that of the outcast and public scandal. Clint Eastwood, who personifies the image of the perfect rugged hero, and Bruce Lee, the Kung-Fu master who embodied the graceful victor, were both born with Neptune in Virgo in the 10th. Besides politics and cinema, other Neptunian careers include social work, art, fashion, photography, music, dance, religious work and healing.

However, foggy Neptune in the 10th can indicate vagueness or confusion about which career to pursue. Some will be dissatisfied with the work if it is not felt as all-absorbing and inspirational. A few I have seen have worked very hard and devotedly in return for less recognition or remuneration than they deserved. One man with this placement worked for a large company which did many shady and corrupt deals, and yet he was the only one to be arrested and imprisoned for it. Some will feel that their salvation depends on finding the right work or serving the needs of others. In certain cases, they may be forced to give up their careers because of a greater influence over which they have no control. Again, Neptune nudges us along the path of spiritual growth and expansion in this way, as if we are redeemed and purified by having to let go and sacrifice what we are overly attached to.

If we take the 10th house to represent the mother, then she will probably carry the Neptunian projection. She might have been seen as a martyr or victim, someone who gave up her own identity for the sake of raising the family. In some cases I observed, the mother had artistic or creative potentials which were cut short for these reasons. The child may be guilty about feeling happy if the mother is so frustrated, unfulfilled and miserable, or they could blame themselves for the mother's condition. Or the mother may be so over-sensitive and delicate that the child ends up having to mother the mother. Although the desire to serve reflects a purpose in itself, those with Neptune in the 10th may find a connection between their choice of a service vocation later in life and experiences with the mother during childhood.

In other cases, the parent may be seen as the saviour or redeemer or someone so idealized that the child feels unworthy to live up to that image. Perhaps Neptune asked that the mother be let go of and sacrificed for any number of reasons. If the mother leaves, is ill, has to work many hours to make ends meet, or dies, then the child must 'give up' the mother, at least in her physical form. Later in life, the child may search for the lost ideal mother, or feel somehow inadequate because he or she was deprived of one. More positively, the mother may represent grace and gentleness, acting as a model of softness and compassion for the child.

Pisces on the MC or in the 10th house is similar to Neptune there.

Neptune in the 11th

The existential psychologist Viktor Frankl believes that the desire to serve and help others doesn't require a reductionist justification — such as that a person does worthy things because he or she is guilty about something from childhood. Rather he sees service as a genuine way of giving meaning to life.[2] In addition, caring for others can be the natural and immediate expression of a feeling of bonding and solidarity with those with whom we share this planet. Neptune in the 11th inspires this kind of altruism for its own sake.

Albert Einstein, born with Neptune here, beautifully summed up the challenge of this placement when he said that 'our task must be to free ourselves from this prison by widening our circle of compassion to embrace all living creatures.'[3] Many of those with Neptune in the 11th have a utopian vision and will join groups which promote humanitarian or social causes. They feel the need to participate with others in bringing their idea of truth, justice or beauty into the world. Galileo, born with Neptune in Gemini in the 11th, undermined the very foundation of the establishment in his search for truth. Alexander Fleming, who developed the life-saving drug penicillin, had Neptune in the 11th ruling healing and caring Pisces on the 10th house of career. Many of those with Neptune in the 11th will take up the cause of the underdog. If some segment of the population is suffering or mistreated, they feel this as deeply as if it is happening to them. Some will be more attracted to secret sects, artistic groups or spiritualistic and psychic circles. If Neptune has many hard aspects, the group may have fine ideals and intentions but somehow never fully bring these to manifestation.

The main thrust of Neptune in the 11th is to abandon the self to the group. Some may look to a particular group or cult as the means to redemption and salvation and make many sacrifices for its sake. In less politically minded people, group activities may simply be a way of escaping from the more mundane routines of life. They could lose themselves in a social whirl, seeking ever more glamorous friends and parties. Or the local pub may be the extent of their group involvement.

If Neptune is well-aspected, friends will be supportive and caring. Likewise, a person with Neptune in the 11th will usually be there to help and nurture associates in difficulty. However, if Neptune has difficult aspects, they could experience disillusionment or deception through friendships. They can easily feel that their ideals of comradeship are betrayed. Some may subtly manipulate a friend by making that person feel sorry for them. Discrimination should be exercised in the right choice of friends or groups — it is easy with Neptune here to abnegate personal responsibility if influenced by a 'bad' crowd. Friends may carry the Neptunian projection — ones who are artists, healers, romantic dreamers, or sometimes just off-beat.

Some with this placement may chase a goal which constantly eludes them or even set up a pattern of wanting things it would be impossible to have. Again, through confronting disillusionment in Neptune's house we are made aware of our limitations and reminded that something greater than us exists which is running the show. However, it is still advisable that they offset a tendency to be vague and vacillating about their direction in life by defining their goals as clearly and realistically as possible.

Neptune in the 12th

Neptune is strong in its own house, where the very best or the very worst qualities of this planet may manifest. Those with this placement will be highly sensitive to undercurrents, movements and unseen forces in the atmosphere. Sometimes they are more aware of these levels than what is actually happening on the surface level of life. Pierre Teilhard de Chardin (Neptune in the 12th in Taurus), the late Jesuit priest who has inspired many people with his mystical vision of all life culminating in an 'Omega' point of spiritual union, wrote that awareness can return to the point 'where the roots of matter disappear from view'.[4] At times, their uncanny vision can be confusing: they see or are told one thing and yet feel or sense something quite different occurring.

Some may be victimized by their own unconscious — that is, periodically swamped or overwhelmed by emotions and feelings which others have an easier time keeping at bay. Montgomery Clift was born with Neptune in the 12th. He had all the Neptunian acting talent and the glamour that goes with it, but he also suffered from severe guilt and depression he couldn't control, and consequently turned to drink and drugs as an escape route. A few people I know with this placement have reported experiences in which they felt their ego-boundaries dissolving and their ordinary 'lensing' of life go out of focus. For some, this was welcomed as a mystical or peak experience; but for others the experience was accompanied by disarming and frightening sensations of chaos and invasion.

If Neptune is not too adversely aspected, the unconscious mind can serve as a source of guidance and inspiration, allowing access to the 'inner, wise person'. There is an openness to the archaic memory of earlier forms of evolution and they can draw on this reserve of stored information with startling effect — as if they have wisdom and insight into experiences of which they have had no firsthand knowledge. There may be an interest in the philosophy of karma and reincarnation and possibly the belief that they are in touch with some of their previous lives. Understood properly, this could help them in more meaningfully meeting the present life. However, for some with this placement, dwelling on past lives could be a way of avoiding facing what is in front of them right now. Fantasizing about when they were Cleopatra or Joan of Arc might also add a bit of glamour to an otherwise dull existence, but it remains to be seen to what constructive use they put such beliefs.

Neptune in the 12th can denote very strong escapist tendencies: daydreams or fantasies can swallow them whole, and they might retreat from life by creating their own little worlds in which to live. For most people with this placement, times of seclusion and withdrawal will be necessary in order to re-centre and cleanse themselves of the 'psychic smog' which has been absorbed and accumulated from interaction with others.

One extreme of Neptune in the 12th may be those who feel that they have no control whatsoever over what happens to them (what some psychologists call an 'external locus of control'). While Neptune asks that we acknowledge a greater authority than ourselves, a total denial of personal power and responsibility is not a healthy situation, and is best kept in check wherever this planet is placed. Studies have linked depression and various other forms of psychopathology with people who feel that they have lost the influence to direct their lives. [5]

Similar to Venus in the 12th, those with Neptune here suffer because the world doesn't always live up to their expectations of what it could be. While they are hurt by the lack of beauty in the world, it is also possible that their sensitivity to beauty can be a means of their own self-healing. Beauty has a regenerative effect on the psyche. If they can make time in their lives to dwell on a sunset, linger by the sea on a night when the stars are visible, meditate in a chapel while the light shines through a stained glass window, or go to a gallery to view their favourite painting, they can often revitalize their own world-weary psyches. As Piero Ferrucci writes in *What We May Be,* in those moments a victory occurs 'over discouragement, a positive affirmation against resigning ourselves to the process of crystallization and death'.[6] In other words, those people with Neptune in the 12th do have a choice: *whether to see beauty or not.*

Beauty also has a self-transcending and revelatory power — opening Neptune in the 12th to new worlds and possibilities which others may not be able to glimpse. Taking responsibility to look for beauty in life will not miraculously erase all their problems, but it can lighten their load and balance out a tendency to err on the side of dissatisfaction. Teilhard de Chardin (Neptune in Taurus in the 12th) also wrote that the aim of evolution is 'ever more perfect eyes in a world in which there is always more to see.'[7]

Performing service is another way of freeing the self from pain and unhappiness, and giving meaning to life. Again, some common sense is required: some with this placement may throw themselves totally into other people's lives as a way of avoiding their own. Nonetheless, Neptune in the 12th could do very effective work within hospitals or institutions. Others may be found employed in museums, libraries and art galleries which protect and preserve the wisdom, beauty and riches of past and present.

Those with Neptune in the 12th might meditate on Jung's idea that certain problems in life can 'never be solved, but only outgrown'. Some new interest or vision arises and through this widening of view the insoluble problem loses its urgency. On one level we are caught in a storm, but viewing it from a different level shifts our perspective — like being on a mountaintop viewing the storm in the valley. The thunderstorm is still there and still has relevance, but we are now above it.[8] Those with Neptune in the 12th will have to learn to accept the good with the bad, the perfect with the imperfect, and the beautiful with the ugly. It helps if they can remember and reflect on what is known as Wittgenstein's dictum: 'The solution to the problem of life is seen in the vanishing of the problem.'[9]

27.
PLUTO AND SCORPIO THROUGH THE HOUSES

Like Uranus and Neptune, Pluto is another 'de-structuring' principle, inexorably pushing life on, and clearing away old forms to make way for the new. Similar to a snake shedding a skin, something pushes at us from deep within, impels us to move beyond old or outworn phases of life and leading the way to further growth and evolution. Eventually the new will become the old and that, too, will have to be relinquished for yet another phase to follow.

Pluto and Neptune in particular, both underworld gods, share certain similarities in that they each subversively undermine our old frameworks, forcing us to put our hands up and surrender. And yet, they differ dramatically in the way they do this. Like termites or woodworm eating away at the foundations of a house, Neptune slowly dissolves the rigidities of the old structure. With Pluto, however, the roof caves in on us, landing like a ton of bricks upon our heads. Tougher than Neptune, Pluto represents a growing pressure which gradually builds up to a climax, and then finishes us off. While Neptune coaxes us to change by giving us a sense that we can be cleansed and purified through sacrifice and suffering, Pluto *makes sure* that we let go by obliterating the old form entirely, until there is nothing left. Demanding that a cycle end and a new one begins, Pluto leaves us with little choice other than to change or die.

One of the oldest known recorded myths, 'The Descent of Inanna' (beautifully recounted in Sylvia Brinton Perera's book *The Descent to the Goddess*) describes the workings of Pluto in a house very clearly. Inanna is the goddess of the heavens, joyful, radiant and alive. Ereshkigal, whose name means 'the lady of the great place below' is her dark sister living in the underworld, and represents an earlier, matriarchal form of Pluto. Ereshkigal's husband has just died and Inanna decides to visit the underworld to attend his funeral. But instead of receiving Inanna gracefully, Ereshkigal greets her sister with a dark and poisonous stare and subjects Inanna to the same treatment that all souls must undergo when they enter Ereshkigal's realm. There are seven gates or portals leading to the underworld and at each one whoever passes must strip off a garment or jewel. The decorously regaled Inanna must pass through each of these seven portals, removing her robes and gems in the process so that by the time she faces her sister in the deepest underworld, she is completely naked and 'bowed low' before her. In other words, Pluto-Ereshkigal strips us of those things with which we have adorned ourselves, those things from which we have attained our sense of identity and 'aliveness'. Even though a highly unpleasant and demeaning experience, this is, the myth tells us, a destructive force that we must respect and bow to. After all, it is the work of a goddess, a divinity representing or serving some higher organizing centre or power. The house containing Pluto is where we may have to meet and pay homage in this way to Ereshkigal — a dark goddess, but a goddess nonetheless.

Ereshkigal then kills Inanna and hangs her on a meat-hook in the underworld: the beautiful and high-minded goddess of the heavens is left to rot. Similarly, the house Pluto inhabits is where we may have to face what is rotten in us. It is in this domain that we encounter the dark and undifferentiated sides of out nature — our overwhelming passions and obsessions, our lust for power, our raw sensuality, our jealousy, envy, greed, hate, rage and savagery, and our primal wounds and pains. We cannot be whole until these are brought to the surface, transmuted and properly reintegrated into the psyche.

This sounds unpleasant, and it often is, but we must remember that Pluto was also the god of buried treasure and hidden wealth. Through the upheaval he brings, disowned parts of ourselves banished to the unconscious and therefore out of reach, are reclaimed for conscious use and disposition. In this way, we reconnect to lost energy and also gain access to untapped resources and strengths into the bargain.

Inanna does not remain trapped in the underworld forever. Knowing she was going somewhere dangerous, she made previous arrangements for her release in case she found herself in trouble down there. Similarly, Pluto-Ereshkigal may stew us in our own juices, but we must also have the good sense not to remain stuck only in that which is loathesome or painful in life. Pluto breaks us down, but like Inanna, we must return again to the upper world and the everyday functioning of life — hopefully with a greater degree of self-knowledge, wisdom and wholeness.

Inanna escapes from the underworld through the help of two little androgynous men called 'the Mourners'. Small and unobtrusive, they slip into the underworld unnoticed and approach Ereshkigal, who herself is in great pain. Not only has her husband died, but she is also pregnant and having a difficult birth. In other words, something has died, but something is also being born. Instead of chastising Ereshkigal for the awful death of Inanna, the Mourners move very close to her and commiserate with her condition. Practising a kind of Rogerian therapy, they allow her the space to moan and bitch, mirroring back her woes and pains. The Mourners have been taught to affirm the life-force even when it expresses itself through misery, darkness and suffering. So grateful to be accepted in this way, Ereshkigal offers them any gift they wish. They ask that Inanna be returned to life, and Ereshkigal obligingly revives her. Inanna returns to the upper world, transformed and renewed, bringing with her fresh life for the crops and vegetation. Ereshkigal-Pluto destroys life, but also can create new life as well.

What can we learn from Pluto's house? Firstly, rather than understanding pain and crisis as a stigma or pathology, as something bad to be avoided at all costs, we can see these phases as part of a larger process leading to renewal and rebirth. Secondly, we learn that we cannot master or transform what we condemn, deny or repress — which is exactly how we normally deal with anything unpleasant. Instead, the Mourners hold the key: paying attention to and accepting Ereshkigal-Pluto as part of life allows the healing magic to work.

Something else is gained from being destroyed, from losing what has been precious, and from the disintegration of that which has once served as our source of identity and vitality. Through being stripped of everything, we are reminded of that part of us which is still there after all else has been taken away. We discover something deep within the self that sustains us even through the loss of former ego-attachments. This is the gift we retrieve in the house of Pluto: the knowledge of something in ourselves which is indestructible. Pluto releases the enduring from the merely transitory — and we are reborn with a sense of being alive which is unconditional and not contingent on the external or relative, phenomenal world providing us with certain 'props'.

Obviously, wherever Pluto sets up his altar in the chart, the affairs of that house are not to be taken at face value. Complexity and intrigue are the watchwords here. In Pluto's domain, we have to search for hidden causes and underlying, unconscious motivations. The isolated ego is not interested in supervising its own destruction. Pluto is the henchman of a deeper, core Self which employs this planet to break down the ego-boundaries and release more of who we really are. As Jung writes, 'there are higher things than the ego's will, and to these one must bow.'

Pluto deals in extremes, and we are capable of evincing the very worst or the very best of human nature in the area of life in which he is placed. When the omnipotence of the ego is called into question, we are terrified of being destroyed: accordingly we attempt to protect ourselves by ruthlessly or treacherously controlling what happens in Pluto's house. Not even knowing why, we may be driven to act compulsively and obsessively. And yet, in that same sphere, by acknowledging and serving a mysterious force more powerful than ourselves, we can potentially discover and exhibit our greatest strength, nobility, purpose and dedication. Not only are we significantly changed by what happens in that area, but it is also where we can act as a catalyst or trigger for the transformation of others. For some, the very force which moves history may overtake and work through them in Pluto's domain.

Scorpio on the cusp or contained within a house is similar in interpretation to Pluto there. The house with Pluto in it will influence any house where Scorpio is found. For instance, former President Nixon has Pluto in the 10th house and Scorpio on the cusp of the 3rd. A secretive, plotting and determined mind (Scorpio on the 3rd) would stop at nothing to achieve his obsessive need for power and standing in his career (Pluto in the 10th), and eventually brought about his own destruction and subsequent rebirth.

Pluto in the 1st

With Pluto in the 1st, an individual's personal style, destiny, and way of approaching life needs to include and recognize the nature of this planet. Above all, Pluto is both a creator and a destroyer, and those with Pluto in the 1st will express either one or both of these sides. It is better if they recognize their own destructive urges, otherwise they may unconsciously provoke events, other people, or their own bodies to act as agents of 'de-structuring' for them. In other words, one way or another the underworld realm of hidden thoughts, feelings and motivations must be reckoned with — they cannot escape untouched just trying to live on the surface level of life.

Those with Pluto here might employ their destructive urges for any number of reasons. For instance, if they feel that their progress or evolution is blocked or impeded by certain structures in their lives (such as a job or a relationship, etc.), then they will remove these to make room for new possibilities and further growth. If they don't acknowledge their frustration and do something positive about it, then they might act in such a way as to force the other person to break up the relationship or a boss to fire them from a job they don't like. As a general rule, it is dishonest and not to our advantage to displace responsibility for any 1st house planet onto other people or events.

In some cases, they may employ their destructive powers because there is something 'out there' making them feel vulnerable and endangering their sense of safety and security. Their philosophy in this instance is 'Get rid of it before it gets rid of me,' and they have the capacity to deal ruthlessly with life if necessary. There is a part of them which will promulgate almost anything for their own survival; or they may act like the scorpion who if cornered will sting itself to death first rather than giving something else the chance to defeat it. The primitive and instinctive drives of the nature will have to be 'owned' and accepted before being transformed or rechannelled. Some may swing to extremes and actually over-identify with the dark side of life, believing that they are 'badness incarnate'. In these cases, there is the need to discover that they are not just an Ereshkigal, but that they have a lighter and more worthy side (Inanna) to them as well.

Two examples illustrate the enormous variance in the use of Pluto's destructive energy. Adolf Eichmann, who engineered the elimination of millions of Jews, was born with Pluto in Gemini in the 1st ruling Scorpio in the 6th house of work. On the other hand, Copernicus, the father of modern astronomy used his 1st house Pluto differently: in establishing that the Earth actually revolved around the Sun rather than vice versa, he utterly destroyed a basic paradigm on which a whole era's view of life was based.

As can be expected, those with Pluto in the 1st will periodically orchestrate sweeping changes in their lifestyles. They might dramatically alter their physical appearances at some stage — such as shedding five stone or dressing in a radically different way. They might, usually when Pluto is triggered by transit or progression, drastically shift their outward or inner focus on life, as if they die and are reborn another person. For example Richard Alpert (Pluto in Cancer in the 1st) was a Harvard professor who after experimenting with hallucinogenic drugs went off to India and changed his name to Baba Ram Dass.

If Pluto is close to the Ascendent, the birth itself might have entailed a crucial life and death struggle. I have seen a few cases where the birth nearly brought about the death of the mother. Placed anywhere in the 1st, Pluto also suggests early years marked by difficulties and traumas, impressing on them that life is a struggle. Trusting the world will be a problem because their experience early in life has been that it is not necessarily on their side. Also, if they are so ruthless to survive, might not others be as well? Walking around anticipating disaster, they feel they must protect and barricade themselves against destruction and doom. For this reason, they are sometimes loners, who find it difficult to blend in or co-operate with others. For some, their need for power stems from this mistrust of life — if they are not in control, then terrible things might happen. Warding off evil can also be the root of obsessive-compulsive character patterns.

In Greek mythology, Pluto almost always stayed in the underworld; those few times he appeared on the surface, he wore a helmet which made him invisible. Likewise, those with Pluto in the 1st may protect themselves by being secretive and covert. If they show too much of what is happening inside, this may give others power over them. For this reason, they often appear mysterious and aloof. Bobby Fischer, born with Pluto in Leo in the 1st ruling Scorpio on the 5th (games and hobbies), effectively used the cunning and tactical side of this placement in gaining the title of World Chess Champion.

When those with Pluto in the 1st do come out and risk opening up, they do it with a serious intensity. Occasionally, suppressed feelings will erupt, inclining them to act in extreme ways. If Pluto is near to the Ascendant, their eyes may be keen and penetrating as if they are seeing deeply into what is happening around them. Some exude a powerful sexuality, such as Mick Jagger, with Pluto in Leo in the 1st ruling his 5th. Usually they have tremendous endurance, and can dedicate themselves one-pointedly to a cause or endeavour. Their will-power is enormous and they may battle between using this power constructively or destructively. Their lives may be a story of many ups-and-downs as if they need to experience both the best and worst of all possibilities.

Pluto in the 2nd

Like Uranus and Neptune in a house, Pluto implores the individual to probe more deeply into the meaning of that sphere and does not allow life to be lived in an ordinary or uncomplicated fashion in that area. Issues around the acquisition of money and possessions and the quest for security in general cannot be taken at face value if Pluto is placed in the 2nd.

With Pluto here, it is necessary to discover the underlying motivations which propel such strong and passionate feelings about money and security. For some, money is imbued with the power of a deity, which determines if they live or die. Money and power may be accrued as a way of controlling others, or as a safety gauge for those who feel that the world is out to destroy them. Material success may be sought as a way of enhancing their sexual attractiveness. Some may see amassing possessions as a way of extending their territory of influence and thereby regaining a sense of their lost infantile omnipotence. Or if they have been put down and belittled as children, then acquiring great wealth and status may be the way of proving their worth to the world.

Pluto sets up his altar of destruction in whatever house he occupies. Consequently, those with this placement may harbour a fear that something lurks in the shadows which threatens to wipe out their resources and possessions. They might hoard money in an attempt to counter-effect this danger. Pluto brings extremes, and they might experience both ends of the scale of poverty and wealth. If they have become too centred or identified with their bank accounts, cars or big homes, Pluto may destroy these external forms of self-definition, stripping away outer attachments or trappings so that they can discover who they are from inside themselves. They may even unconsciously provoke such a catastrophe so that an inner and more permanent sense of worth and security can be found.

The house position of Pluto shows where we might make a significant contribution to society. In the 2nd, the person may be in possession of certain skills and abilities which could influence and shape the world in some way. The innate resources and values to be developed are those of unusually deep perception, a powerful conviction, and an ability to be decisive in times of crises. Pluto can cut out and eliminate what is not essential, and thereby purify and streamline what it touches. Those with Pluto in the 2nd can take something which appears to be of little value and transform it into an object of worth.

Their incomes and sources of self-worth could be obtained through professions associated with Pluto: research work, the psychological, parapsychological and medical fields, mining and underground work, detective and undercover activities, antiques and refurbishing, etc.

Pluto in the 3rd

Like Uranus or Neptune in this house, Pluto in the 3rd aims to transcend the ordinary limits of the mind or intellect. Those with this placement often have a deep, penetrating and incisive mind able to 'laser through' to the heart of any matter. There could be an interest in extra-sensory perception or a desire to expose and freely talk about subjects which others find taboo (such as sex and death). Their minds are well-suited to any form of research or depth studies. Some might seek knowledge for the power and mastery it gives over others and the environment. Occasionally, they give birth to ideas which could have a transforming effect on society. The Protestant Reformationist Martin Luther is reputed to have been born with Pluto in Libra in the 3rd. Mary Baker Eddy, the founder of the Christian Science Church, also had Pluto in this house.

They may have a certain power with words. William Butler Yeats, the Irish Nobel Prize winning poet who had a deep mystical slant on life, was born with Pluto in the 3rd ruling Scorpio on the 9th house of philosophy. (The poet Robert Browning, the author of so many famous and immortal lines also has enduring Pluto in the 3rd.) However, Pluto's strength can be used treacherously as well; and those with this placement are often known for their cutting tongues and acute sensitivity to where another person's weakness lies. Negative moods could creep up and they can be overwhelmed by obsessive thoughts, as if their own minds betray them. Their thoughts can turn very destructive, and some will be afraid to speak because of a fear of what might come out. Others hide what is going on inside them in case exposing themselves would render them too vulnerable.

The 3rd house covers the early environment and the growing-up years. As children, we all have difficulty distinguishing between having wished for something and the belief that we have actually done the deed. For instance, if a little boy is angry at his sister for getting more attention than him, he may entertain a passing thought that he wishes she were dead. Let's say that the next day his sister falls out of a tree and breaks her leg. The boy in question might equate the negative wish he had with the accident and therefore believe that his bad thoughts caused it to happen. Taking whole or part blame for it, he will walk around guilty and afraid of being found out and punished for his evil doings. As we grow older we realize we are not so omnipotent, but those with Pluto in the 3rd may still harbour fears and guilts about the power of their thoughts and the bad things they made or make happen around them. The actor Peter Fonda was born with Pluto in Leo in the 3rd. Lois Rodden (*The American Book of Charts*) cites that when he was ten years old his mother committed suicide. Shortly after he shot himself in the stomach and consequently had psychiatric counselling at the age of eleven. All this is very Plutonian and it is possible that he was trying to punish himself for any guilt he might have harboured regarding his mother's death. Secret sins such as these can torment a child or adolescent with Pluto in the 3rd, and he or she may be terrified to tell anyone else about it. And where there is shame and guilt, anger and rage are not far away. Obviously, parents of children with Pluto in the 3rd should try to create an environment in which the child feels safe to talk about what is going on in his or her mind, rather than allowing thoughts and feelings to fester underneath too long.

The early environment may have been experienced by those with this placement as threatening or non-life-supporting and could leave the impression that they have to continually guard themselves against others. They will not easily forget a wrong-doing and may hold on to resentment for a very long time. The relationship with siblings is usually complex and ridden with undercurrents of sexuality, competition and intrigue. This placement often indicates difficulties with neighbours and problems with early schooling. For some, being sent away to boarding school is a major upheaval and felt as a kind of banishment or punishment for some imagined transgression.

Even short journeys can be harassing. They may arrive at a friend's for a quiet weekend in the country to discover they have stepped into the plot of an Agatha Christie thriller.

Those with Pluto in the 3rd are powerful on the mental plane and if they hold a certain attitude towards another person, they can 'box' the person in to such a degree that he or she inevitably acts out the projection. Therefore if they want someone's behaviour to change, they might try altering the context in which they are viewing that person. It is a basic fact of life that attention carries energy.

Pluto in the 4th (Scorpio on the IC)

Complexes, traumas and unresolved issues from early childhood often seethe below the level of conscious awareness if Pluto is in the 4th house. They may try to cut off their deeper feelings altogether, exerting rigid control over themselves as a way of defending themselves against these raw emotions. And yet there is always the sense of something dangerous lurking underneath which could overwhelm them in the end. For some, their whole life is built around suppressing what's down there, and in this respect they are dominated by those very things they are trying to keep at bay. Finding the self is like peeling an onion — layer upon layer has to be removed to reach the core. More than any other placement, this is the deep-sea diver who must plunge into the depths of the personal unconscious, bringing hidden complexes to light so that they can be examined, worked on and hopefully transmuted.

These complexes probably stem from their experiences in the early home environment (the family of origin) and may resurface later on in their private and domestic lives. Since the home sphere is where they feel most vulnerable, they may attempt to manipulate and control those around them so that nobody slips up and detonates their inner time-bomb. Obviously, this does not lend itself to the most relaxed of home atmospheres, in which there are probably many unwritten rules about what is or isn't allowed to be said or done. Wherever Pluto is in the chart is where we fear our own destruction. In the 4th, the bogeyman lurks under the bed, in the wardrobe, or stares at them from across the breakfast table. It is like living by the side of Mount Vesuvius.

Those with Pluto in the 4th might experience major reorientations in their lives through upheavals in the domestic sphere or the collapse of the family structure altogether. Although this is hardly likely to be easy, they have the capacity to rise out of the rubble reborn, hopefully wiser and with greater self-understanding. On the positive side, Pluto in the 4th is a good indication of strong regenerative powers and the ability to rebuild the self after any kind of breakdown. The survival instinct runs deep and resources they didn't know they had come to the fore at the time of crisis.

If we take the 4th house to represent the father, he could have been experienced as exceptionally powerful, dark or threatening. Children with this placement may be keenly aware of the father's passion, sexuality, frustrations and pent-up rage. Sometimes it is the death, disappearance or psychological distance of the father which affects them strongly. More positively, he could represent someone with great courage, fortitude and creative potency.

The 4th house describes how we end things, and with Pluto or Scorpio there, endings are often final and irrevocable. There may be the need to dramatically finish certain phases in the life, or cut themselves off from people or places to which they have previously been tied. The Duke of Windsor, who abdicated the crown and in that sense, his rightful inheritance, was born with Pluto conjunct Neptune in Gemini in the 4th.

Those with Pluto in the 4th may have a love and reverence of nature, an almost primeval tie with the earth and its mysteries. Attempting to fathom the secrets of nature, there may be an interest in oceanography and deep-sea diving, archaeology, psychology or metaphysics.

Some will be able to transmute their inner struggles and emotional churnings into creative expression. For instance, according to the time given by his father, Mozart was born with Pluto in the 4th. He composed some of his best works in periods of depression and illness. Through psychological exploration, deep inner reflection and meditation, and the nurturance of seeds of self-knowledge, those with this placement may mature into extremely wise and radiant sources of strength, inspiration and guidance for others. The Greek god Pluto was in charge of buried treasure, and those with this planet in the 4th just need to dig for it.

Scorpio on the IC or contained within the 4th house is similar in interpretation to Pluto there.

Pluto in the 5th

The key to working with Pluto in the 5th is the development of a healthy sense of one's own power and worth. Everyone has the need to feel important and special in some area of life, but with Pluto in Leo's natural domain, this could become an obsession. Excessive pride and an inflated self-opinion could bring many problems to those with this placement. However, too weak an ego, or too little a sense of their importance, value and effectiveness can also be the source of difficulties. In either case, they may resort to extreme gestures to prove their potency. Barbra Streisand, the singer-actress-writer-director whose drive, energy and apparent abrasiveness rub many people up the wrong way, was born with Pluto in Leo in the 5th.

As children, we feel that we are more likely to be protected by our parents if they find us enchanting and captivating. Therefore being somebody special is linked in our minds with warding off doom and disaster. For those with Pluto in the 5th, the need for love, approval and power may still be mixed up with the survival instinct. Barbra Streisand's father died when she was very young, and perhaps she felt that she was not special enough to keep him. Later, she felt neglected by her mother and new stepfather, which would have added more fuel to the fire already raging in her 5th house. Obviously, as in her case, this dynamic may spur some people on to high achievements. For others, it could mean bitter disappointment at the lack of their recognition and worth and angry resentment towards those who appear more successful. However, failing to win the status they seek may provide the impetus for further self-evaluation and self-knowledge.

For children with Pluto in the 5th, the sandbox could be the place where they scale new heights, or the scene for traumatic experiences.

It just can't be any old castle, but must somehow express from the depths of their feelings who they really are, complete with moat and secret chambers. Mars threw sand in the face of his friend who did a better castle; Pluto might go a step further — accidently on purpose kicking over the rival's castle, provoking a fight and breaking the friendship. It may be days or weeks later before Pluto returns to the sandbox at all. (It's reputed that when Ms. Streisand's film *Yentl* didn't receive the recognition she felt it deserved from the Academy of Motion Pictures, she boycotted the ceremonies that year altogether.)

Later in life, creative self-expression may still entail working through traumas, blocks and difficulties. However, the problems encountered serve to bring unconscious patterns and unfinished issues from early life to the surface where there is more chance of resolving them. Some with this placement will be able to give expression to creative works of great power which can awaken and transform others. Hermann Hesse, born with Pluto in the 5th ruling Scorpio on the cusp of the 11th, comes to mind. He is also reported to have struggled with bouts of depression and alcoholism. Nietzsche had Pluto in Aries in the 5th ruling Scorpio on the cusp of the 12th, and according to Rodden (*The American Book of Charts*) spent ten lonely years writing his major works. After completing these books, he died a year later, alone and insane.

For both men and women, this position of Pluto suggests that bringing children into the world could have a life-changing effect. Although this is generally the case for anyone who has children, the issues of parenting are somehow more far-reaching with Pluto in this house. For many men with this placement, becoming a father for the first time heralds a traumatic awakening to the fact that they are no longer the 'eternal youth' themselves. For a woman, it could indicate difficulty with child-bearing and she is wise to look after herself with extra care during the pregnancy. Issues around abortion and miscarriages are not uncommon with Pluto in the 5th. Even when an interrupted pregnancy cannot be helped, there is still the need to grieve and mourn for what is lost. As with Neptune in the 5th, the anguish incurred in such circumstances is more productively utilized if some meaning or purpose can be attached to the experience.

Parents with this placement may meet their own dark and subterranean sides through the behaviour of their children. The parent with Pluto in the 5th may over-control or try to dominate a child not purely out of a desire to love and protect, but because the parent is frightened that the child, if left to its own devices, might do something which is untoward or personally threatening. If this is the case, the children may have to break radically with the parent in order to establish more freely their own identities. In the long run, it is far better that the parent examine his or her own fears and complexes and what has given rise to them, rather than attempt to control life as a way of avoiding confronting these. Having said all this, I have seen many instances of Pluto in the 5th where the parent-child relationship is handled with strength and dignity.

With Pluto in the 5th, romantic pursuits may become entangled with the power drive and some degree of sexual compulsiveness. Those with this placement may fear the intensity of their sexual drive and try to inhibit it altogether or find ways to transmute libidinal expression into channels which they deem more acceptable. Others may derive a sense of potency through sexual conquest and attract love affairs which involve power conflicts, dramas and intrigues. Carried to extremes, they could use other people too much to prove their own worth — a form of psychological rape. True mutuality, sharing and respect for another person's integrity are the lessons to be learned if Pluto or Scorpio is in the 5th.

Pluto in the 6th

The 6th house is the meeting point of body and psyche, the point of connection between what we are inside and the forms with which we surround ourselves. Those with Pluto in the 6th can explore this connection in great depth.

When an underworld deity like Pluto sets up his altar in the 6th house of health, then physical illness cannot be taken at face value. In mythology, Pluto rarely came above ground, but in one instance it was to seek healing for a wound. In sickness accumulated poisons and toxins come to the surface which need to be eliminated in order for the body to function healthily again. The root causes of these problems, not just the outward symptoms, need to be treated if Pluto is in the 6th, or else the trouble may just reoccur at another time.

In short, those with Pluto in the 6th should explore the possibility that illness is an indication of problems elsewhere in the lives than just the body. It is a well-known fact that psychological issues play a part in aggravating a disease. Noxious agents are always present in the system, but whether we develop an illness depends on our ability to resist these. Negative thoughts and feelings, conscious or unconscious, take their toll on the body by weakening the system's natural defences, making us more susceptible to what we can normally combat. People with Pluto in the 6th may complain that their bodies have betrayed them when they fall ill, when in actual fact the body has only revealed that there is something awry in their mental and emotional states. The good news is — as the authors of *Getting Well Again* point out — that if people can make themselves psychosomatically ill, they can also become 'psychosomatically healthy'.[1] By examining their beliefs and feelings, those with Pluto in the 6th can move in the direction of altering not just their health, but their whole lives. The knowledge available to these people is the direct comprehension that the mind, body and emotions function as an integrated system.

Functioning as a unified whole means that every little thing in life has significance in relation to everything else. For those with Pluto in the 6th then, simple, everyday routines in life can take on great importance. Just choosing what clothes to wear in the morning or keeping the house clean can be fraught with great anxiety if Pluto is poorly aspected. They may contrive compulsive rituals in executing these tasks as if by doing them in this way they are warding off evil and destruction.

On the positive side, they have the capacity to work in a dedicated and undistracted fashion, with their total will behind a job. However, they can also take the need to be conscientious, responsible, practical and productive, and turn these into obsessions as if their very survival depended on these qualities. The desire to do a job right is felt with intensity, conviction and passion. Obviously, this zeal can make them difficult to work alongside with. They may be unduly irritable and critical of others who do not share their style and approach. Relationships with co-workers may be marred by uncomfortable undercurrents, sexual innuendoes, betrayals, treachery and intrigues. Power struggles could develop and they may resent and feel threatened by anyone in authority, unconsciously wishing to dethrone those in a higher position. If those with Pluto in the 6th are in the position of authority, the whole question of how they dispense power over subordinates comes sharply into focus.

Often there is the desire to improve on already existing methods of work. Compulsively searching for flaws, sweeping changes can be made in the name of increased efficiency. Their work must be deeply engaging and consuming, otherwise they will lose interest, and possibly 'set up' situations which force them to leave the job for another. Some may become ill to free themselves from work they abhor. Others may lose jobs because of conditions beyond their control — such as economic recession and redundancy. While the loss of employment can have a serious effect on their psychological well-being, examining the emotions and feelings which are brought to the surface by such contingencies could lead to greater self-knowledge and further growth.

Employment may be in a field which is 'Plutonian' by nature: undercover or detective work, mining, careers in psychology, medicine or psychiatry, or work involving nuclear energy. Taking one meaning of Pluto literally, some could work in junkyards, cemeteries or funeral parlours. Quite a few people I have seen with Pluto in the 6th are involved in various forms of neo-Reichian body-work.

In some cases, an accident or illness may produce irrevocable damage. The French artist, Henri Toulouse-Lautrec who was deformed as a result of a riding accident, was born with Pluto in Taurus in the 6th. But even if we are born with severe limiting restrictions, we are still responsible for the attitude we adopt to the handicap: we can live a life of bitter regret or find ways to give meaning to the life despite or maybe even because of it.

Pluto in the 7th

The Greek sovereign of the underworld was only seen to leave his kingdom for the upper world twice: once to heal a wound inflicted on him by Hercules, and once to abduct Persephone into his realm. Similarly, the workings of Pluto can be observed most clearly in illness and in the sphere of close relationships.

With Pluto in the 7th, it is in the area of partnerships that Pluto is encountered. Rather than viewing marriage or close union as merely a 'happily ever after' affair, it is wiser for those with this placement to understand relationships as catalysts or agents for personal transformation, growth and change.

Liz Greene says of Pluto in this house that 'the entry into the underworld comes through somebody else'. In other words, relationships will plunge them into deep emotional complexes which have lurked in the recesses of the psyche from as far back as early childhood (or even further, if one believes in karma and reincarnation). Through issues connected to partnership, parts of the nature which have been buried, repressed or kept under control by the ego will erupt messily into the everyday life. After the blast, there is the task of putting themselves back together again, hopefully with greater awareness and understanding of their own complexities.

If they are not wholly in touch with their own darker or undifferentiated sides, then they may project these qualities onto the partner. If they have not acknowledged their potential for ruthlessness, treachery, betrayal, jealousy, envy and possessiveness, they seem to attract or constellate such traits in other people. Again, the nature of life is towards wholeness: if we are not living that wholeness, then the outside brings it to us.

Wherever Pluto falls in the chart is where the god of death and destruction can be found. Some with this placement sense their own proclivities for destructiveness in the area of relationships and consequently live in fear that others might be capable of the same kind of behaviour. Or they may totally disown their own destructive energy by just attributing it to the other person. Because of a nagging apprehension that sooner or later the other person is going to disrupt the relationship, they have difficulty trusting the partner or feeling safe in a union. Attempting to avert such a catastrophe, they may try to dominate, possess and control the partner. Unfortunately, such behaviour often serves to drive the other person away, thereby bringing about the situation which they most dreaded. As in the case with Pluto in any house, the deity which brings the illness is also the one who brings the cure. To clean up the mess that our own unconscious complexes land us in, Pluto hands us a shovel and says 'Start digging.' In the process we may even unearth some very good reasons why it all had to happen that way.

I have seen many instances where those with Pluto in the 7th wanted to end a relationship but were afraid to do it for various reasons. Invariably, they somehow provoked the other person to do it for them.

Some may meet Pluto in the 7th through the death of a partner. If the partnership was a close, good one, then picking up the pieces after such a misfortune is a slow, gradual process with many phases. But wherever Pluto is, the capacity to rise again, like the Phoenix out of the ashes is also present; although Pluto may teach them to be more careful next time about deriving their identities wholly from something external to the self. Even if the relationship was fraught with fights and bitterness, the loss of a partner through death can still be devasting — especially if the person feels partially responsible for what has happened, or the partner died before pressing interpersonal issues could be resolved. It will be important for the remaining partner to do what he or she can to work through these feelings; otherwise any later relationship may be tainted by them. Pluto's house is easily haunted.

Pluto is a planet of extremes and in this sense it is oddly placed in the house which is concerned with balance, sharing and learning co-operation. The issue of who has the power in the relationship is brought sharply into focus. Some will give all their power over to the other person, as if they want to be swallowed up by the relationship. Others will not feel safe unless they are the ones in charge. In either case, the balance of power is unevenly shared and lessons of true mutuality are still to be learned. Sooner or later one or the other of the partners may feel the need to break free in order to grow beyond the constrictions of such an arrangement.

In many cases I have seen, those with Pluto in the 7th actually have difficulty eliminating or letting go of a relationship. For some, this evinces a kind of loyalty which is determined to keep working at it. For others, their identity may be so tied up in the partnership, that to lose it would be like death. In mythology, Pluto, compared to the other gods, was a relatively constant husband to Persephone, and was only unfaithful twice. In the first instance, he developed a mad passion for the nymph Minthe, but in his wild pursuit of her, he accidently crushed her underfoot. (It is possible that those with Pluto in the 7th can actually destroy a relationship because of their own intensity about it.) In the second case, he abducted one of the daughters of Oceanus into his kingdom, where she lived until she died a natural death.

Pluto may require the complete breakdown and elimination of an existing relationship to allow for the continuing individuation of each party. On the other hand, however, Pluto also suggests that a relationship can endure a number of mini-deaths and rebirths, coming up stronger each time, and lasting many, many years.

Those with Pluto in the 7th have the ability to help others through painful times of crises and transition. Some may have a profound influence on society in general. Two examples illustrate the social face of Pluto in the 7th. The fascist Italian dictator, Mussolini, had Pluto here ruling the 12th house of collective movements. By contrast, Betty Friedan, the indefatigable women's liberation leader, has Pluto in the 7th ruling Scorpio on both the 11th and 12th house cusps. This house placement of Pluto is also useful in the charts of lawyers, healers, counsellors and psychologists.

Pluto in the 8th

In a poem entitled 'In Tenebris', Thomas Hardy wrote 'If a way to the Better there be, it exacts a full look at the Worst.' He might have been thinking of Pluto in the 8th when he came up with these lines.

According to Freud, we are born with certain drives which push at us from within. But due to internal or external pressures, we become anxious about the expression of these impulses and set up defence mechanisms to restrict them. Two of these in particular —

drives of sex and aggression — give us a great deal of trouble. If they are denied altogether, they often erupt explosively in compulsive, uncontrollable behaviour. However, if we allow them free rein, there is the danger that they will control us rather than the other way around. The challenge for those with Pluto in the 8th is to explore and accept these drives and yet find ways to channel them purposefully and productively in the sphere of interpersonal relationships.

Sex and aggression are normally associated with the planet Mars. They appear to be endogenous, instinctive impulses which are a necessary part of our biological heritage. The value of sex is obvious in reproduction, and aggression or power is necessary for growth and mastery of life. Sexual arousal is, in many ways, akin to the physiology of anger. In fact, Kinsey reported fourteen physiological changes which are common to both sexual arousal and anger.[2] Even from our own experience we may know how often love turns to anger, or what starts out as an argument finishes up as an orgasm. But when we start talking about either repressing these drives or mastering them, we leave the field of Mars and enter the domain of Pluto.

Some people with Pluto in the 8th successfully master and skilfully guide their libidinal energy into impressive achievements. Winston Churchill, Leonardo da Vinci, Galileo and Bismarck — all men of exceptional power and drive — were born with Pluto in this house. This placement also denotes tremendous strength and resources in crises as well as the stamina to lead other people through difficult times. Besides reorienting their own use of power on the physical, mental, social, emotional or spiritual levels, they possess the ability to drastically alter the lives of those they come in contact with.

However, looking through *The American Book of Charts,* three other examples of Pluto in this house stand out. One is John Gacey, with Pluto in the 8th ruling Scorpio on the 12th and 1st. According to Rodden, he was considered an 'upstanding' and salient member of the community until he was indicted for the 'sadistic sexual assault and murder of thirty-two young men and boys' (buried, aptly for this placement, in his cellar). Albert Dyer was the friendly man patrolling the school crossing who one day abducted, raped and strangled three little girls — he had Pluto in Gemini in the 8th ruling a Scorpio Ascendant. Arthur Bremer, who gunned down Senator George Wallace, also had Pluto in this house. Rodden writes that 'his diary stresses his sexual frustration and preoccupation.'

When the natural energies of sex and aggression are obstructed in their development and expression, and left to fester in the underworld, they turn ugly and deadly. Unless examined and positively channelled, they accumulate power and burst into consciousness blasting through all ego-controls. Before the person knows it, all hell breaks loose.

Obviously, not all people with Pluto in the 8th are going to fall into the category of a Churchill or a child molester. And yet one thing is certain: a tremendous reserve of energy, what some would call 'coiled-up serpent power', lies in waiting.

The 8th house describes what passes between people, and with Pluto there, the token of exchange is intensity. Partnerships may involve power struggles, physical or emotional violence, or the breaking of taboos. Some have a propensity for tragic, tortured or transformative relationships in the tradition of Romeo and Juliet, or Tristan and Isolde. Behind the symbolism of the sexual act is a craving for self-transcendence or power. Fearing the excessiveness or the chaos of their powerful emotional drives, they may attempt to avoid close contacts altogether. Pluto in the 8th also sometimes describes conflict, treachery and intrigue around other people's money. Complications and long-drawn-out problems can arise over inheritances, taxes, business deals and divorce settlements, especially if Pluto is adversely aspected. Their value system in general may differ significantly from a partner's; or what the partner believes in may dramatically affect and change them. They may want to challenge and tear down what another person holds in esteem.

Besides having to deal with their sexual and aggressive drives, they will most likely need to grapple with issues around death. Freud felt that we all harbour a death-wish (Thanatos) and yearn to return to the tension-free state that we experienced before birth. This longing to break through limited boundaries, to tear the self down in order to dissolve into non-being may be strong for those with Pluto in the 8th. Some may flirt with death by putting themselves in dangerous or highly risky situations, or by unconsciously playing out self-destructive tendencies. Others may be fascinated by the whole topic and research extensively into life after death, reincarnation and related metaphysical concepts.

I have met a number of people with this placement who have had close brushes with death, and after a narrow escape came back to life and reassessed all their priorities. Others may have more than their fair share of experience with the deaths of those close to them. And yet, I have also encountered others with this placement who are absolutely terrified and anxious about their own deaths. They may need to be reminded that death is an inextricable part of life

— to deny death is also to deny life. If we fully acknowledge that we will one day die, then it can plunge us into living more authentically and appreciating each passing moment as fully as possible. St Augustine once wrote that 'it is only in the face of death that man's self is born.'[3] Death jolts us into life.

If they are not afraid of it, these people are closely attuned to energies at work on the deeper levels of life and will hear rumblings in the atmosphere far sooner than others. The sensory apparatus is something like those of animals who know beforehand when an earthquake is about to come. There is a desire to understand and even gain mastery over the secrets of nature and what some might term 'occult powers'. Sometimes without consciously being aware of it, these people work 'magic', influencing situations and other people through the manipulation of these subtle forces. Inexorably drawn to penetrate the realm of forbidden knowledge, they dare to explore levels of existence that others are unaware of or fear to approach.

Pluto in the 9th

I have observed that, in general, people approach the house in which Pluto is placed in two very broad but different ways. Some plunge into the affairs of the house, grappling with the deeper issues and implications of that realm, and inevitably are changed and transformed through what they experience there. Others, trying to preserve their already existing sense of self and fearing what this planet might do to them, close the door and try to shut Pluto out of the house altogether. They forget that he has an uncanny ability to break locks.

This same dynamic applies to Pluto in the 9th. On one level, the challenge for those with this placement is to join Pluto in a quest for a deeper awareness of the ultimate concerns of life. With Pluto here, religious and philosophical issues are often approached with a seriousness and reverence, as if their survival depended on coming to grips with the nature of God or existence. The spiritual drive can be obsessive and fanatical: they are often voracious to find answers and to discover the basic, irrefutable laws and patterns which govern life. In search of the truth, they reach for the bright heavens or plumb the dark undercurrents and depths of the psyche. And what they are really looking for is the ground under their own feet. How can life be faced unless there is something to stand on? Even if the ground is slippery and treacherous, it is still better than no ground at all.

Even if it should turn out that life has no givens, and there is no pre-ordained design or structure to existence, those with Pluto in the 9th still desperately need to find or create meaning. But Pluto is a destroyer as well, and sooner, or later their philosophies may be subjected to some sort of purgatory, or be torn down and constructed anew. In this sense, they are sometimes betrayed or let down by their cherished religion or beliefs. The collapse of a belief system may be an almost overwhelming experience, throwing them into deep despair and depression, until they are reborn again through another one.

Their dogmatism and self-righteousness could stem from the fear that if another person's philosophy contradicts their own, then what they believe in may have to be questioned. Rather than endangering the sanctity of what they worship and adore, they may try to control what everyone else believes in or convert all others to their side. The Spanish dictator Francisco Franco was born with Pluto in the 9th ruling Scorpio on the cusp of the 3rd.

The image of God is often coloured by what planet is in the 9th. For those with Pluto here, God may not be all justice, beauty and light. Probably omnipotent, He may have a dark side to His nature and occasionally decide He doesn't like them. He could delight in leading them to the edge of a precipice, dangling them there, or destroying them altogether no matter how 'good' they were. It is no wonder many of the people I have met with Pluto in the 9th have difficulty conceiving of a rosy future. As dire as this may sound, some real benefits arise out of their dilemmas. Firstly, they are forced to take a stand on suffering and find some meaning through it, even if it is a fate they can do nothing about. Secondly, they will try to derive as much as they can from every experience, engaging themselves in each and every moment far more completely than others who have a less harrowing concept of God.

I said earlier that some may not welcome Pluto in the house at all, although he invariably finds a way of sneaking in. Along these lines, I have met people with this placement who, afraid or thwarted by the search for truth, turn nihilistic. Diametrically opposite to those who use Pluto's constructive probing, these people are aimless and apathetic, and don't see the value in anything. Why bother if it all ends in death anyway? But this is exactly why they should bother. Death is probably the most important event in life, and we can't die well unless we have lived well. Cicero said 'To philosophize is to prepare for death.'[4] Unlike those with Pluto in the 8th, these people are not necessarily suffering from the repression or malfunctioning of sexual or aggressive instincts, but from the repression or frustration of an equally important and particularly human drive — the will to find meaning in life.

While the 8th house represents drives which push us from within, the 9th represents strivings or goals which pull us from without. For those with Pluto in this house, there is a strong pull to follow Pluto's lead, and yet much anxiety and trepidation about what they might encounter in the process. This dynamic applies to the pursuit of higher education and long journeys as well.

Experiences which evoke profound transformations can occur through higher education. Pluto is met within the halls of academia, either in the guise of an important professor who profoundly arouses them, or through conflicts and challenges which any particular course or educational system presents. In certain cases, they may drastically alter their major focus of study at some point during the education. A few people with Pluto in the 9th might make discoveries which require the rewriting of history, the revising of any discipline, and the elimination of that which is old and false in some system of thought. The zoologist Thomas Huxley, who lectured in natural history and profoundly affected the scientific thinking of his time, was born with Pluto in Aries here.

Long journeys represent another area in which a 9th house Pluto is activated. They can be transformed through travelling or through encountering and assimilating the knowledge and traditions of cultures other than their own. One famous example of this is the artist Paul Gauguin, with Pluto in Aries in the 9th ruling Scorpio on the 4th. He left his wife and children behind (Scorpio on the 4th) and emigrated to Tahiti, where he produced his most famous works and may have contracted syphilis; he later died of this disease in the Marquesas islands. There is a possibility that some people with Pluto in the 9th may project the unacceptable parts of their own psyches onto another race, religion or culture — persecuting and blaming something outside themselves for what is dark or evil in the world.

The relationship with in-laws might also be the sphere where Pluto is felt. For instance, if in difficult aspect to the Moon, the mother-in-law or sister-in-law might be seen as threatening or manipulative. The death of an in-law may have a profound effect on the life.

Pluto in the 10th (Scorpio on the MC)

If we take the 10th house to represent the mother, then those with Pluto here may see her as dark, threatening and possessing the ability to destroy them. She can be experienced as a witch, or someone who is primeval, ruthless and manipulative. They may sense a seething anger and pent-up frustration or sexuality emanating from her. They feel as if she is always there, somehow watching them, even if she is not physically present. In short, she is felt to be dangerous and untrustworthy. However, in reality, she may not be this sort of person at all, but the child with Pluto here, in certain cases, may experience her predominantly in this way. Or sometimes the early death or loss of the mother is the root of later problems in life.

As covered in the general discussion of the 10th house, our early experiences of the mother (our first container) will contribute to the way in which we relate to the larger container of society. If the image associated with a negative Plutonic mother is projected onto the world, then these people will fear that the world is a dangerous place intent on destroying them. Some with this placement may react to this by withdrawing from society altogether and having as little to do with the world as possible. Others may compensate for their dread of being devoured with an obsessional need for power and control over others. Attempting to regain a lost sense of infantile omnipotence, they strive to extend their territory of influence to include as much of the world as they can. If they are in control, if they are the ones in authority, then they feel safe. Their need for power can be so consuming that any means will justify achieving those ends, as in the case of President Nixon with Pluto in the 10th. Also, there is a distrust of anyone who has authority over them, a desire to dethrone or destroy those in charge before it's too late. For all these reasons, those with Pluto in the 10th need to re-evaluate and come to a deeper understanding of their underlying psychological motives for ambition, power or worldly success.

Of course, the above description is a one-sided explanation of Pluto projected in a negative light. It is possible that the mother may carry a positive Pluto association. She could be viewed as the great bestower of life, and experienced as an exceptionally capable source of comfort and support through all the contingencies of daily life. Some people I know with this placement have watched the mother struggle successfully with a personal crisis or a severe life trauma, and were most impressed with her ability to manage hard times and come out the other side renewed and regenerated. She then became a positive prototype for later challenging experiences with which they had to contend. In this way, as adults with Pluto in the 10th they model qualities of strength, will and endurance to other people.

Pluto's placement in the chart is where we periodically tear down, destroy or alter existing circumstances in order to create new ones. It is where we may be reduced to nothing in order to rise again. Not only did Nixon have it here, but his chief of staff H. R. Haldeman was born with Pluto in the 10th ruling the 3rd. He was convicted of conspiracy and spent a year and a half in gaol where he wrote a book called *The Ends of Power.* The actress Elizabeth Taylor, whose life and career has had many ups and downs, was born with Pluto in this house as well. In some cases, Pluto here may indicate the loss or leaving behind of an established career and the necessity to embark on a new vocation of an altogether different nature.

Those with Pluto in the 10th ultimately require a career which is deeply engaging, meaningful, and exciting. Either the work is of a 'Plutonian' nature or they approach the whole area of work with the kind of intensity and complexity associated with this planet. Some may be responsible for reforming existing institutions of society which are outworn or outdated. Other fields related to Pluto are those of medicine, psychology, and occult and psychic work (Uri Geller, the world-famous spoon-bender has Pluto here), investigative science and journalism, politics, mining, atomic research, etc. I have done charts for two people with Pluto in the 10th who were in jobs in which they were not allowed to reveal the exact nature of their work. (One of these had Scorpio on the cusp of the 3rd and spoke fluent Russian.) Some may engage in careers which reflect society's shadowy side — such as prostitution, crime or underworld involvement.

Occasionally, I come across people with Pluto in the 10th who tell me that they have no ambition. After talking with them for a while, it becomes clear that they still see themselves as 'small' compared to the big, powerful world (mother) out there. Usually, on some level, they are frustrated by the lack of influence they wield, or the unchallenging job they are already in. In certain cases, it strikes me that some people with Pluto in the 10th may not find their true vocation until they are more capable of using their power wisely and for the good of the larger whole, rather than for purely personal ends.

Scorpio on the Midheaven or contained within the 10th house is similar to Pluto there.

Pluto in the 11th

The philosopher and historian Will Durant wrote that 'the meaning of life lies in the chance it gives us to produce, or contribute to something greater than ourselves.' For many people, the family serves this purpose. But for others it could be a group that elicits a person's potential for nobility and gives him 'a cause to work for that shall not be shattered by his death'.[5] On one level, these ideas encapsulate the highest purpose of an 11th house Pluto: to be able to immerse themselves in something greater than they are which will live forever.

Groups are meant to break down boundaries and change those with Pluto in the 11th. For this reason, some people with this placement have great problems feeling comfortable within the group situation. The destructive energy of Pluto might be projected onto the group and they feel it is trying to destroy them. Deep emotional complexes are brought to the surface through group situations, and therefore it is the area of life through which important psychological transformations could occur. Even though it might be a frightening experience for these people, they could benefit from some sort of group therapy situation, where the undercurrents activated by the group can be openly discussed. Sometimes they end up playing the scapegoat or 'group shadow' figure, acting out what others in the group have repressed or denied.

Those with Pluto in the 11th could be drawn to groups interested in radical reform of society's existing structures and institutions. Some may be more interested in groups which focus on psychological growth, like *est.* Jerry Rubin, the American political activist of the sixties, was born with Pluto in Cancer in the 11th. Later, as is often the case with Pluto in the 11th house of goals and objectives, he changed his direction and joined groups of a more philosophical and psychological orientation. Jean Houston, a leading humanistic psychologist, runs groups on how to be a more fully realized and 'extended' human being — she has Pluto in the 11th as well. I have noticed that a number of musicians and conductors have this placement of Pluto — the band or the orchestra being the group which is essential to their work and expression. In certain cases, it is possible that someone with Pluto here might join a group as a 5th columnist, for the purpose of undermining or infiltrating it. Motives are not always that cut and dried where Pluto is concerned.

While zeal for a just cause is always a positive thing, a difficultly aspected Pluto in the 11th could give rise to what some psychologists call 'crusaderism'. These people are demonstrators in search of an issue, compulsively embracing one cause after another. The motives for such hard-core activism might be examined to see if it is not masking some deep fear about the purposelessness of their lives.

Pluto in the 11th also reveals itself through friendships. On a positive note, this could mean very deep and profound friendships which endure over many years and through periods of crisis and change. Invariably, however, there is a complexity about friendship with Pluto here. Betrayal may be an issue — they may be deceived or let down by someone they trusted or discover that they, themselves, have the ability to be ruthless and turn on another. The famous gangster John Dillinger, betrayed by the 'lady in red', was born with Pluto in this house ruling Scorpio on the 5th house of romance. The groups he belonged to were Plutonic, that is, of the 'underworld'.

Sexual rivalry or sexual undercurrents between friends can occur with Pluto in this house. A friendship may start as a sexual relationship and grow into something else, or vice versa. The loss or death of a friend might awaken a host of psychological and philosophical issues. Power conflicts between friends are also possible with this placement. They may fear that unless they control the relationship, the friend might do something to hurt them. With Pluto in the 11th, the reasons for forming friendships should be examined — are there secret or ulterior motives for wanting to be a particular person's friend? Conversely, they might suspect a friend of treachery in this respect.

The 11th house also describes a person's goals and objectives in life, and the ideals one wishes to realize in the future. With Pluto here, the whole manner in which they set about achieving goals and objectives may need to be periodically examined and revised. Some may exhibit unswerving concentration and one-pointedness while others lean towards an obsessiveness which justifies any degree of ruthlessness and deceit to ensure their aims. At some point in the life, there could be a significant reorientation of their sense of purpose, direction, or the part they are to play in the larger scheme of things.

If Pluto has many hard aspects to it, they may be confused about where they fit into the collective in general. Some may feel isolated or lonely, as if the flow of history is moving in a different direction from where they want to go. Liz Greene refers to this position as the 'doomsday prophet' who looks to the future and sees disaster. Rather than noticing what is going right, they notice first what is going wrong, or perceive the hidden seeds of destruction in what may seem like the best or brightest of plans. Like Cassandra in Greek mythology, they may find that others do not want to hear about this vision.

Pluto in the 12th

With Pluto in the 12th, there is a pressing need to bring what's weak, hidden or undeveloped in the psyche into clearer focus. As with Pluto in the 8th, some people might be so frightened of being overwhelmed by the nature or intensity of their deeper drives and complexes, that they exercise a tight control over these. However, very often it is not only 'neurotic' urges which are suppressed, but healthy, positive drives as well. The psychologist Abraham Maslow pointed out that many people not only evade what they deem is negative in themselves, but also block what is 'god-like' and laudable. He called this 'the Jonah Complex', the fear of our own greatness.[6] From my experience, certain individuals with Pluto in the 12th defend themselves not just against the so-called 'lower' or carnal drives, but also against such positive impulses as the desire to develop their 'higher' possibilities more fully, or to realize more of their innate potentials. To paraphrase Maslow, they are afraid to become that which they glimpse in their most perfect moments. Why?

The answer, in a nutshell, is *death-anxiety*. All change makes them highly anxious because it means the dissolution of what they already know themselves to be. Growth inevitably requires the breaking down of existing patterns or the letting go of what is familiar, and on some deep level they equate these kinds of changes with death itself. Part of them desperately yearns for growth and development, and yet another part mounts every campaign possible to ward off what they unconsciously feel is trying to kill them. Until they locate and make peace with their deep existential dread of non-being, they will keep displacing their fear onto whatever comes along which threatens to change them. Until they know they are afraid to die, they cannot fully live.

Roberto Assagioli, the founder of Psychosynthesis, a transpersonal approach to human development, was born with Pluto in Gemini in the 12th. Feeling that Freud concentrated too much on just the 'basement' of the human being, Assagioli devised his own psychological system to take every level of the building into account. A basic tenet of Psychosynthesis reflects the meaning of a 12th house Pluto: that *all* the elements of the psyche — both dark *and* light — can be consciously recognized, experienced, accepted and integrated into awareness. Through dream analysis, introspection, therapy and various exercises and techniques, those with Pluto in the 12th can release the energy trapped in unconscious complexes and redirect it towards strengthening and building the whole of the personality, including their 'higher' intuitive and emotional faculties. Provided they can track down and deal with their death-anxiety, people with Pluto in the 12th are well equipped to search out what is weak, blocked hidden or missing in the psyche. Indeed, what more appropriate place for them to exercise the innate investigative nature of Pluto than in the house of 'secret enemies' and 'behind-the-scenes activity'. And rather than waiting for angry and neglected parts of their own psyches to chase after them, they are well advised to go hunting for these first.

In the 12th, the destructive energy associated with Pluto can be used to remove that which is obsolete and detrimental to new growth. Or destructive energy can be improperly displaced and unleashed outwardly in a treacherous way or dangerously turned against the self. The difficulty for those with Pluto in the 12th, however, is that they are not simply dealing with the personal unconscious but with the collective unconscious as well.

A contemporary medical model theorizes that noxious bacteria and viruses are always present in the physical system, but the healthy or strong person is able to defend himself or herself from these taking over. Similarly, stress is everywhere in society, but some people have a better ability than others to prevent it from getting into their systems. Those with Pluto in the 12th are more sensitive to what is dark, destructive or overwhelming in the atmosphere than someone with, let's say, a well-aspected Venus in the 12th. While Venus there may feel that 'love is in the air', what might Pluto sniff? Some of them may unconsciously be 'taken over' by what other people have repressed — sexual drives, anger, hostility, etc. It is not unlikely for a child with this placement, for instance, to take on the role of family scapegoat or 'identified patient'. When tensions run too high at home, he is the one who gets sick or burns down the school. Starting a conflagration serves two purposes: it gives a concrete expression to the emotions he feels around him and it serves to divert the parental unit from their own interpersonal problems. Those with Pluto in the 12th can make better sense of their actions and behaviour if they view what they do and feel in relation to a larger scheme of things.

The 12th house represents the greater whole out of which we come and into which we are born. Pluto there has to contend with the less pleasant aspects of this inheritance — the collective shadow, that which society as a whole finds ugly or unacceptable. They may be required to acknowledge, integrate, and, if possible, transmute the anger, hate, destructiveness and rage accumulated over centuries. In this sense, they are in charge of society's waste disposal unit. They either act out the collective's shadow and thereby release this pent-up energy or they gather it inside themselves and find some way to creatively transform and redirect it. Two examples will clarify what I mean. Albert Speer, the Nazi who served as Hitler's minister for war and arms production, was born with Pluto in the 12th, ruling Scorpio on the 5th house of self-expression. He was somebody who supplied the weapons, in a quite literal sense, through which the collective's hate and aggression could be expended. Compare his role with that of Pope John Paul II, with Pluto in Cancer in the 12th also ruling his 5th, whose mission is to defuse the hostility of the world through invoking greater peace, goodwill and Christian love.

Some people with Pluto in the 12th may work to transform outmoded institutions or campaign to change laws which are no longer functioning as they should. Often, and sometimes in mysterious and obscure ways, they facilitate changes on the level of the collective. In a questionnaire composed by Marilyn Ferguson, author of *The Aquarian Conspiracy*, respondents were asked who had influenced them most in their lives. At the very top of the list was Pierre Teilhard de Chardin, with five planets including Pluto in his 12th. (Assagioli also was in the top seven mentioned.)[7]

Periodic withdrawals from life may be necessary in order to grapple with emotional complexes which have been awakened through social interactions. They might be significantly affected through brushes with institutions, such as confinements in hospitals or prisons. Assagioli (Pluto in Gemini in the 12th) was put into prison in the 1930s because his humanitarian and philosophical beliefs threatened the Fascist government of Italy at the time. When he was released, he told friends that it was one of the most beneficial and creative periods of his life. The American writer O. Henry spent three years in gaol writing some of America's best-loved short stories: he had Pluto in the 12th.

As these examples suggest, Pluto here gives the capacity to transform a crisis into something productive and useful, or make the most of even limited or restricted circumstances. Assagioli wrote that it was most often during times of crises that a person discovered *the will* (Pluto), awakening to the knowledge that he or she is a 'living subject, an actor, endowed with the power to choose'.[8] Even if those with Pluto in the 12th cannot change an unfortunate situation, they can still choose what attitude they are going to hold towards it. They have the ability to learn from failure and defeat and to understand the necessity of one cycle or phase of existence ending in order that another can begin. In this respect, a 12th house Pluto recalls one of Nietzsche's sayings: 'That which does not kill me, makes me stronger.' Even suffering and pain can have meaning if they make a person more whole.

Scorpio on the cusp or contained within the 12th is similar to Pluto there.

28.
THE MOON'S NODES THROUGH THE HOUSES

The Moon circles the Earth each month, crossing the plane of the ecliptic twice: once as it ascends from south to north, and then two weeks later as it descends from north to south, at the opposite side of the zodiac. The ascending point is the north node, also known as Rahu, *Caput Draconis* or the Dragon's Head. The descending point is the south node, also referred to as Ketu, *Cauda Draconis,* or the Dragon's Tail. The north node and south node will always fall in opposing signs and houses.

Since the nodes of the Moon occur where the Moon crosses the apparent path of the Sun around the Earth, they symbolically link the Sun, Moon and Earth together. Understood in this way, the houses highlighted by the nodal axis indicate the spheres of life where we might successfully fuse or integrate the complementary solar and lunar principles within the personality. A brief recapitulation of the inherent conflict between the Sun and Moon principles will make the function of the nodes clearer.

Ishtar, a typical Moon goddess, was worshipped as 'the all-accepting one'. Sometimes symbolized as a prostitute who 'gave herself' to anyone who came along, icons of her were placed on the window sills of ancient Babylonian homes. In a non-discriminating and non-choosing way, Ishtar went with whatever happened. If she was feeling joy, she gave herself to joy. If she was feeling pain, she gave herself to pain. In this sense, the Moon is identified with the emotions and feelings, and with the instinctual urges of the body.

Acting out of habit and stored memory-impressions, the Moon represents the regressive pull back into the past. Past experiences condition our expectations and behaviour later in life. If, as children we only had Mother's full attention if we were sick, then a lasting impression would be recorded into consciousness that the way to be noticed was to be ill. Later in life, we might instinctively fall sick if we felt in need of attention. In this sense, the Moon is repetitive and 'lazy'. But, many of the Moon's stored memory-impressions from the past are useful later in life: the Moon principle allows us to draw on a reservoir of instinctual wisdom — acquired not only in early childhood but inherited from our ancestral and animal past and coded in every cell of our bodies. *The house occupied by the south node of the Moon is a sphere in which, for better or for worse, we act instinctively and from habit.*

Complementing the principle of the Moon, the Sun represents the Hero. The hero does not necessarily let himself be seduced by the Moon goddess. The Sun or heroic principle is the proponent of the will — the 'organ of the future', while the Moon aligns herself with the memory — 'the organ of the past'.[1] The will is suggestive of resolution and determination, and of self-generating rather than reactive behaviour. Resisting the pull from the past, the Sun has the power to provoke change, implement choice, and spontaneously inaugurate a series of successive actions. While the Moon is swayed by feelings and instincts, the Sun chooses to create the situation as it sees fit, guided by the direction it wants to take. *The house in which the north node of the Moon is placed requires the exercising of the solar, heroic principle.* This area of life is a fresh field of experience hallmarked for us to explore and conquer. Developing ourselves in that area brings forth previously untapped potentialities and adds to our repertoire of skills. Through attending to this domain we create new experiences for ourselves and generate new possibilities. The struggle to master and expand ourselves in that spectrum of life inspires a deep sense of purpose and direction.

An analogy can be drawn between the north and south nodes and the human brain. One part of the brain stores what is inbred and instinctual and serves to maintain the organism. However, another area of the brain — *the cerebral cortex* — is a more recent evolutionary development. The cortex is not required to maintain life: it can be removed and yet life-processes like the functioning of the heart, digestion, lungs and metabolism will continue. The cortex serves a different and yet very important purpose — it governs all the higher psychological capacities of humans, such as thought, imagination and the organization of experience. With the development of the cerebral cortex, we are no longer bound to meet life in an instinctive and stereotyped way, but we have gained the capacity to be self-reflective. The cortex enables us to be conscious of being conscious. We can now imagine different possibilities and make choices to bring the desired ones about.[2] It would appear that the south node corresponds to the instinctual seat of the brain, while the north node relates to the cerebral cortex.

To open the door to the north node's house, we first have to overcome a tendency to stay too long in the area of life or way of being suggested by the opposite placement, the house of the south node. The south node is the domain of capacities already developed. Like the Moon goddess, we are drawn to that sphere instinctually and from habit. It serves as a kind of resting place, an area of life where we can digest experience and recharge our batteries before embarking on new and unknown territory. I must emphasize that many of the pre-coded patterns and capacities of the sign and house placement of the south node are undoubtedly precious and are not to be unduly discarded and neglected. But some of these tendencies might have played out their usefulness and are followed because that is simply what is easiest to do. The door to the south node's house is easily opened and we may unconsciously escape into this domain to avoid the struggle of growth in other directions. Entering the house of the north node takes more doing: the key is turned through the exercise of the will and the effort of choosing. Lazy people don't pass through the threshold.

The houses brought into contention by the nodal axis provide the fields of experience which awaken us to the archetypal conflict between unconscious, habitual behaviour (the Moon) and conscious choice (the Sun). The south node represents what has already been packed in the suitcase when the journey began. We have it at our disposal. The north node points to new acquisitions and wealth we can purchase along the way, providing we are willing to pay the price and make the effort to shop around. It doesn't have to be an either/or situation between the south and north node spheres. And/and is possible and preferable. But if the field of experience associated with the south node is overdone at the expense of the north node, then growth is slowed down. We don't pick up anything new along the way.

North Node in the 1st, South Node in the 7th

These people should learn to stand on their own feet, making decisions and choices based on what they need or want for themselves. They must honour who they are. The line of least resistance is to allow others to dominate them and to over-adjust by trying to be too much what others need or want them to be.

South Node in the 1st, North Node in the 7th

These people tend to live too much for themselves, only looking out for Number One. They need to learn more about co-operation and compromise, through adapting themselves more readily to what others need and require, especially in the area of close partnershisp and marriage.

North Node in the 2nd, South Node in the 8th

They should develop their own resources and values rather than relying on the resources and values of other people. There is the need to earn money in their own right, even if they could live comfortably off others. In this way, they gain a truer sense of their self-worth. There is a need to come to terms with and accept the world of form and matter.

South Node in the 2nd, North Node in the 8th

They may have rigid value systems which need to be altered by taking other people's viewpoints and beliefs into consideration. Some may feel that allowing others to help or support them is a sign of weakness, and that self-sufficiency in all matters is the priority. They should endeavour to help other people develop a greater sense of self-worth. They may need to learn that pain and crises, rather than just being things to be avoided at all costs, often bring opportunities for growth and positive change.

North Node in the 3rd, South Node in the 9th

There is the need to develop the capacity to think rationally and logically rather than being overly swayed by blind faith. Their intuitive vision may be good, but the issue is integrating this into the everyday life. It is worth exploring all the possibilities at hand and what the immediate environment has to offer, before rushing far afield to seek what they are after.

South Node in the 3rd, North Node in the 9th

There may be too great an emphasis on the rational and logical mind and they need to develop the more intuitive, feeling and creative side of the brain. There is a danger of being too provincial, and they should expand their awareness by exploring other cultures and belief systems rather than just the ones they have known during childhood.

North Node in the 4th, South Node in the 10th

Growth comes through 'inner work' on the self. Rather than basking in outward achievement and being in the limelight, these people should take time to develop the private and personal sphere of life, especially the home base. In other words, the home and soul should not be neglected for the sake of worldly success. Activities which are nourishing to the feeling life of the person and which enhance psychological self-knowledge are encouraged.

South Node in the 4th, North Node in the 10th

There is the need to venture from the home base and balance any tendencies towards morbid introspection or hiding the self away through finding a job or career which serves the collective in some way. In a woman's chart, this indicates that just being a housewife is not enough. Reclusive or introverted tendencies may vie with the need to develop some sense of their own authority, power and usefulness through a career.

North Node in the 5th, South Node in the 11th

There is the need to further develop their personal creativity, giving more spontaneous expression to the self and feelings. Anything which augments their sense of specialness and uniqueness should be encouraged, rather than just blending in with the crowd. Taking on communal goals and objectives rather than defining their own needs and wishes can be detrimental to individuation. In other words, it is too easy to be swayed by others rather than standing up for the self.

South Node in the 5th, North Node in the 11th

These people should be encouraged to become involved with group endeavours. There is a need to develop social and/or political awareness, to promote a common cause rather than just being concerned with their own personal affairs or interests.

North Node in the 6th, South Node in the 12th

More attention needs to be paid to the efficient and practical management of everyday life. Not accepting the responsibilities of mundane existence, there can be too much day-dreaming, or a secret desire to be rescued, saved and looked after by others. Developing and refining their skills, talents, resources and practical capabilities will give more satisfaction. The body needs to be cared for and respected.

South Node in the 6th, North Node in the 12th

Greater sympathy and understanding of others is needed to balance an overly critical or judgemental nature. They could be too controlled and rational, believing only in that which can be seen, proved, measured or tested. The 'heart centre' needs to be opened so that they feel connected to something greater than themselves. In this way, life becomes richer and more meaningful.

29.
THE POSSIBLE EFFECTS OF CHIRON THROUGH THE HOUSES

In 1977 a tiny planetoid named Chiron was discovered between the orbits of Saturn and Uranus. The sighting of a new celestial body heralds a change of consciousness in society and reflects crucial historical developments. For instance, Uranus' discovery in 1781 can be linked to a period of revolution and rebellion: America was rebelling against England, class war raged in France, and Napoleon was soon to march through Europe. Neptune was located in 1846, coinciding with the Romantic Age and the yearning for something more ideal as expressed through the rise of welfare movements for the poor, young, sick and needy. And in 1848 a wave of revolutions swept across Europe. Pluto's discovery was synchronous with the rise of fascism and totalitarianism on the one hand, and the emergence of the new science of psychology, in which uncharted depths of the mind were probed, on the other. If Chiron is to follow suit, we can turn to mythology to glimpse its connection to critical developments in the evolution of the collective. Moreover, grasping Chiron's archetypal significance will enable us to deduce its possible effects in a house.[1]

Chiron's father was Saturn, and his mother Philyra, one of the daughters of Oceanus. According to the legend, Saturn's wife, Rhea, caught her husband and Philyra in the act of coupling. To escape, Saturn changed himself into a stallion and ran away. The product of the union was Chiron, the first Centaur, born with a body half human, half animal. Distraught at giving birth to what she felt was a monster, Philyra prayed to the gods to relieve her of the burden of her newborn child at any cost. In reply, they took Chiron away and turned Philyra into a lemon tree.

Chiron's first wound is the rejection by his mother, and wherever Chiron is housed in the chart is an area of life in which we might be sensitive to rejection. On a symbolic level, this may reflect the 'fall from grace' we all experience when the contracting womb thrusts us out into the harsh world. Trapped within a separate and distinct physical body, we lose that sense of oneness with all life. Chiron's house placement may show where being in the body creates a problem — where our earthly physical drives and urges could be in conflict with pulls towards something transcendent, pure and divine. Chiron, the son of Saturn, was part divine and yet part animal. We, too, are neither wholly one or the other and the house position of Chiron could indicate where this conflict is most keenly felt.

Raised by the gods, Chiron grew to be very wise. His animal side invested him with an earthy wisdom and a closeness to nature. He was what the American Indians called a *shaman,* a wise medicine-man. Well-versed in the medicinal properties of various herbs, he practised healing and naturopathy. But his knowledge was not limited to the sphere of healing — he studied music, ethics, hunting, war and astrology. Stories of his great wisdom spread far and wide, and inevitably various gods and high-ranking mortals brought their children to Chiron to be educated. Becoming a kind of foster parent to divine children, he taught Jason, Hercules, Asclepius and Achilles, among others. In an excellent lecture on Chiron, Eve Jackson points out that the principal subjects he taught were warfare and healing.[2] In this sense, he was conversant with the art of creating wounds and then healing them. The house position of Chiron may show where we have been wounded or damaged in some way and yet through that experience gain a kind of sensitivity and self-knowledge which enables us to better help and understand other people. Ms. Jackson associates Chiron's discovery with the rise of popular interest in psychotherapy, a profession in which painful psychological wounds are brought to the surface in the process of healing. Indeed, Chiron appears to be strongly placed in the charts of many healers and therapists.

Chiron prepared people to be heroes. Teaching not only survival skills, he also instilled cultural and ethical values. His pupils were adept at surviving in the world, but they were also capable of performing noble feats and deeds in the service of their country or greater whole of which they were a part. The house position of Chiron may indicate not only where we can teach others, but also where our own heroic potential could come to the fore — an area of life in which we go beyond just being ordinary and yet don't lose touch with 'real life'. Chiron's orbit swings erratically between Saturn and Uranus, and therefore provides a link between these two principles. In Chiron's house, it is possible that Uranus' bold new insights and revelations can be applied practically and within the confines of what is acceptable to the establishment. Chiron marries instinct with intelligence: in his house we can be inventive, intuitive, and yet down-to-earth as well.

While involved in a drinking bout with some of the more raucous centaurs, Hercules accidently wounded Chiron in the knee with a venomous arrow. The poison was from the deadly Hydra and produced a wound which was incurable even with Chiron's own medicine. So we have a curious phenomenon: the great healer himself suffered from a wound which could not be healed. I have noticed that Chiron is often prominent in the charts of disabled people, many of whom fashion a meaningful life for themselves through being of service to other people. Also, it appears that the best therapists are the ones who are most aware of their own psychological imperfections and neuroses. In his book, *Power and the Helping Professions,* Adolf Guggenbühl Craig points out 'that the patient has a physician within himself but also that there is a patient in the doctor.'[3] The healer who is in touch with his or her own pain and weakness is better able to help patients constellate the inner healer in themselves.

As a reward for all the services he had performed, Chiron was given the gift of immortality by the gods. Therefore, he was in a strange position: he could neither recover from his wound, nor die. Finally a solution to his predicament was found. Prometheus had been banished to the underworld as a punishment for stealing fire from the gods. His release was contingent on someone else taking his place in Tartarus. Chiron, no longer wishing to be immortal, agreed to exchange places with Prometheus. In this sense, Chiron and Prometheus needed one another. They represent the blending of two different kinds of wisdom: Chiron took earthly wisdom and used it for higher purposes, while Prometheus took fire from the gods, symbolic of creative vision, and brought it down to earth. Chiron's house is where we need to integrate fiery vision with practical common sense.

Chiron chooses death. He accepts its necessity, neatly making arrangements for it, so that he faces its reality with peace and nobility. Partially inspired by the work of Elisabeth Kübler-Ross, this concept of accepting and preparing for death has recently come to many more people's attention. Chiron's attitude towards dying, and his holistic understanding of health, healing and education, are all signs of our times.

It is too soon to be certain of the sign rulership of Chiron. Given the centaur connection, some astrologers believe that Chiron should be associated with Sagittarius. Others feel Virgo is appropriate because of his association with healing and practical wisdom. Present-day advances in computer technology and methods of statistical research are being applied in assessing the significance of Chiron; in the meantime, it is hoped that the following brief examples of Chiron's possible effects in the different houses will shed some light on its influence in the chart.

Chiron in the 1st

With Chiron in the 1st, the wounding can occur early in life. For instance, one woman I know with this placement was born with a condition commonly called 'brittle bones'. Because of her delicate state, the doctors advised her mother that the child should not be picked up or held, and in this way, as an infant, she was deprived of a necessary physical solace and closeness. Other placements in her chart indicate a very powerful will, and she bravely worked within the limitations of her handicap to become strong and self-sufficient. At the time of our reading, transiting Uranus was conjunct her 1st house Chiron and she was hoping to begin a training as a physiotherapist.

Another example is an artist born with Chiron in Sagittarius in the 1st house conjunct the Ascendant. Severely stricken with an atrophying disease of the nervous system, he nonetheless used what strength he had to teach painting to young people. Although Chiron chose to die, he was rewarded by the gods for his good work by being made part of a constellation in the heavens for all to see for all eternity. Similarly, although this man died while still in his early thirties, like the immortal Chiron his memory and influence live on through his paintings and the future artwork of those he taught.

Both these people personify the wounded-healer/teacher nature of Chiron and serve as a source of inspiration not only for disabled individuals but also for many of the able-bodied people who have known them.

In her study of the charts of sixty-nine healers/therapists Eve Jackson found that eleven of these had Chiron in the 1st.

Chiron in the 2nd

The ability Chiron had to apply spiritual, philosophical and ethical insights to everyday life and practical matters is highlighted with Chiron in the 2nd. Elisabeth Kübler-Ross, whose pioneering work in the field of death and dying has been of practical use to both dying people and their families, was born with Chiron in Taurus in the 2nd. Her work came to the fore just as Chiron was returning to its own place in her chart (Chiron's cycle is roughly 50 years).

I have also seen Chiron in the 2nd in the chart of two people who suffered great pain through bankruptcy and financial collapse, and yet used the experience to broaden their philosophical and psychological understanding of life and themselves.

Chiron in the 3rd

A woman who cured herself of cancer using special diets and visualization techniques is now writing and distributing information about combating the illness in these ways: she has Chiron in Sagittarius in the 3rd house of communication. I have observed this placement in the charts of other people who write on the subject of medicine and healing.

Their wounding may come during adolescence and the growing-up years. Some with this placement may have difficulty fitting into the early schooling situation or have learning or speech difficulties. In a few cases, those with Chiron here had brothers or sisters who were ill or afflicted in some way, and their formative years were marked by the need to be sensitive to their sibling's condition.

Chiron in the 4th

If the 4th house is taken to be the father, then he may carry the Chiron projection. The child with this placement may be exceptionally sensitive to his wounds, or view the father as a kind of teacher or mentor. One woman I know with Sun conjunct Chiron in the 4th was, as a young girl, abandoned by her father shortly after her mother died of cancer. This early rejection contributed to her receptivity to the pain, needs and feelings of other people.

It is possible that in the later years of life, those with this placement may develop a latent interest in various forms of healing.

Chiron in the 5th

The 5th house is associated with children and young people, and those with this placement could serve as teachers to the young. One woman with Chiron here overcame heroin addiction and now works helping adolescents with drug problems.

It has already been mentioned that Chiron's house placement may show where our earthly physical drives and desires could conflict with pulls towards something transcendent, pure and divine. I did a chart for a very religious man with Chiron in the 5th who was tortured by sexual desires for pubescent girls and boys. Through psychotherapy and prayer, he has successfully transmuted these urges into constructive channels and expresses his love of children by working as a tutor and counsellor for 'problem' adolescents.

Prince Charles is born with Chiron conjunct his Sun in the 5th house of creative self-expression. Eve Jackson quotes from an interview he gave: 'Ever since I was a child, I've been interested in medical matters and in the business of healing — I've always wished I could heal.' In recent years he has expressed his wholehearted support and enthusiasm (5th house) for holistic medicine.

Chiron in the 6th

To some degree, Chiron suffered by being trapped in a body he didn't like. I have seen this placement in the charts of a few people who felt uncomfortable or limited within the physical body. One was an unusually tall woman and another a rather short man. However, the kind of psychological adjustments that they had to make contributed to their sensitivity and understanding of the pain of other people. The man in question has worked extensively and productively with handicapped people of all ages.

Recalling Chiron's holistic approach to medicine, this placement shows up frequently in the charts I have seen of therapists who work with the body — those who use neo-Reichian techniques, massage, and herbal remedies, etc.

Since Chiron was so adept in the art of survival skills, it is likely that those with Chiron in the 6th have the potential to master practical crafts such as cooking, sewing or other kinds of useful handiwork.

Chiron in the 7th

With this placement, it is possible that the nature of Chiron could be projected onto the partner, who might be seen as obviously wounded, either physically or psychologically. Or it may be that the partner is viewed as a kind of teacher or wise mentor. Conversely, those with Chiron here could act as a teacher to another person.

Chiron's feeling of rejection can come through a relationship if this planet is placed in the 7th. The hurt of a painful separation from a loved one may bring up deep wounds which soften, sensitize and transform even the most hard-hearted people. Or they could experience frustration at the discrepancy between an idealized notion of love and the reality before them.

Chiron in the 8th

Those with Chiron in the 8th may be sensitive to sexual rejection, or feel inadequate or confused about their sexual identity. Strong libidinal drives could conflict with their more spiritual or religious inclinations.

It is likely that they are extremely receptive to any painful undercurrents in the atmosphere, and possess latent healing abilities which they should be encouraged to develop. Some may be able to teach others about the deeper mysteries or subtle dimensions of life. The 8th house is associated with death, and those with this placement may want to study the example of the famous centaur who chose death with peace and equanimity.

Chiron in the 9th

The 9th house will highlight Chiron's ability to take intuitive and innovative insights and apply these in a practical manner. They are likely to make very capable teachers. The highly respected and deep-thinking astrologer John Addey was born with Chiron in Aries in the 9th house conjunct the Midheaven. Crippled with an incurable form of rheumatism, he worked as a teacher for disabled people. Furthermore, he once remarked that he would have probably been all too happy to spend his days between golf and horses had it not been for his illness which forced him to stay still for a moment and reflect on life. His wound impelled him to turn his attention to the 9th house matters of philosophy and astrology. With the clarity and finesse of the mythological Chiron, Addey related the abstract and theoretical concept of harmonics in a practical way to chart analysis.

Chiron in the 10th

Any planet in the 10th will be linked to career and profession. Of the sixty-nine charts of healers/therapists Eve Jackson studied, fifteen of these had Chiron in the 10th. In short, the person's function in the world could well reflect the healing qualities of the Greek Chiron. Nevertheless, Chiron was unsure where he fitted in — he was half divine and half animal, and those with Chiron here may be uncertain of how they are to fit into society, of the role they are meant to play in the collective scheme of things.

A 10th house Chiron may also describe a feeling of rejection by the mother, and the consequent psychological pain and growth that stems from such an experience. It is also possible that the mother might have carried the Chiron projection — she was seen as wounded or afflicted in some way or conversely mirrored Chiron's healing and philosophical nature.

Chiron in the 11th

Those with Chiron in the 11th could be involved in the running of various kinds of therapy or healing centres. They might be sensitive to the pain in society and perhaps concerned with helping or teaching those who are oppressed or downtrodden. There may be a nagging fear of rejection or slight within the context of groups and friendships or some hurt incurred through such involvements. Ultimately this pain could act as a catalyst for further self-knowledge and self-understanding.

Friends may carry any of the connotations of Chiron — either people involved in the healing/teaching profession or those who are obviously psychologically or physically vulnerable. Those with Chiron here may serve as mentors to their friends, or look to their associates for guidance, direction and support.

Chiron in the 12th

In Eve Jackson's study, the third most frequent position of Chiron in the charts of healers/therapists is the 12th house. Of these, two distinct groups were noted: those who practised 'spiritual healing', such as the laying on of hands or even absent healing and those who worked primarily with dreams or guided imaging. I did a chart for a woman disabled from birth who has the Sun conjunct Chiron in the 12th; she now works as a psychological counsellor in a hospital (12th house of institutions).

For those with Chiron in the 12th, unhealed wounds may be buried deep in the unconscious or stem from a difficult pre-natal experience. The psychologist Arthur Janov, author of *The Primal Scream,* was born with Chiron in the 12th in Aries: he feels that the way to reconnect to one's true power and vitality (Aries) is through releasing these deeply entrenched early traumas.

Reincarnationists might propose that those with 12th house Chirons have had connections with healing or teaching in previous lives. In any case, those with this placement have the potential to tap a rich source of practical wisdom stored in the recesses of their own psyches.

30.
A CASE STUDY

Any placement in the horoscope can only be understood in the context of the entire chart. No matter how well the meaning of a planet in a house is comprehended, we still have to consider many other factors in order to fully interpret the significance of any house. These include:

1. The aspects to the planet(s) in the house.
2. The sign on the cusp and other signs in the house.
3. The ruling planet of the sign on the cusp, and its placement by house, sign and aspect.
4. The ruling planet(s) of any other sign(s) in the house and their placement by house, sign and aspect.

The following case discussion is included to help clarify the art of synthesizing these different chart factors in reference to the houses.

Kate: A Woman in Search of Her Own Power
Kate is an attractive woman in her early forties. While keeping a secretarial job as a means of earning a regular income, she uses her free time to study psychology and healing. Recently, she has begun to counsel people on a part-time basis, and has led a number of groups on various aspects of 'spiritual healing' and self-healing. At present Kate is single, but she has been married twice — her first husband died suspiciously from a mixture of drugs and alcohol, and she was divorced from her second husband in 1972. She has a sixteen-year-old daughter (Sally) whom she has raised almost entirely on her own.

Kate and I have met twice over a period of two years to interpret her chart. A clear correlation between her house placements (see Figure 16) and what she has reported to me about her life can be

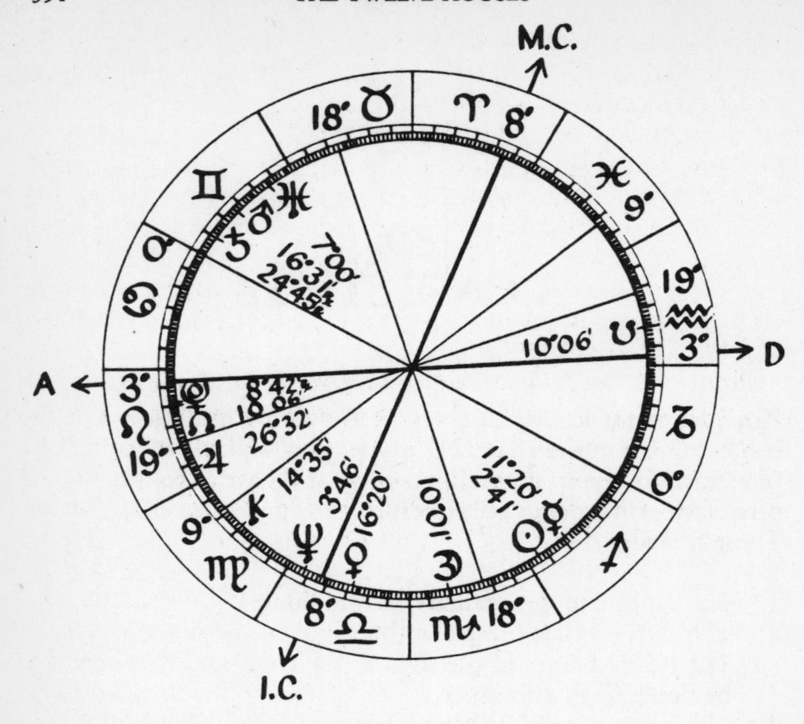

Fig.16 KATE

9.20 p.m., November 25th, 1943.
Bloxwich, England.

seen in these details of her case history, clarifying how the energies in a house actually manifest in the unfoldment of the life-plan.

Ascendant and 1st House
Those with Leo on the Ascendant create a world in which the need to develop their power, authority and creative expression (Leo) is the means of defining their individual selfhood (1st). Because the Ascendant ruler — the Sun — is placed in the 5th, self-discovery is also linked to the 5th house: Kate told me that raising a child on her own (5th house — children) has contributed more than

anything else to her sense of power and capability. It is also through the spare-time activities (5th) of studying psychology and healing that Kate's real inner self has been touched.

At first glance, it might seem that the Sun in Sagittarius in the fiery 5th should have no problems freeing the creativity and self-expression. But in Kate's case, the Sun (the chart ruler) is aspected by all three outer planets, suggesting the battles, challenges and breakthroughs she has faced in finding her own identity and confidence. Kate told me that she was afraid of her own power for a long time — particularly in the 'psychic' area, 'which terrified me and I tried to fight off'.

Pluto in the 1st denotes that life is viewed as a struggle with many traumatic ups and downs and occasional sweeping changes. Her two marriages involved either emotional or physical violence, and both ended rather drastically. (More on this will be covered in the 7th house.) Pluto is close enough to the Ascendant to suggest something difficult about her birth. Kate was born six weeks late during World War II and the delay put her mother under terrific strain. Throughout Kate's life, transitions into new phases of being are accompanied by mounting tension and a slow, gradual build-up to change.

Pluto marked her early years, and at the age of 5½ (as the progressed Ascendant conjuncted Pluto) she nearly died of bronchial pneumonia. At the same time, she was cut off from her grandmother — the one family member to whom she felt close and who had been a surrogate mother since Kate's birth. She compared this period with later ones in her life; 'It was like going through a tunnel alone, with no support.' True to her 1st house Pluto, she also kept her deepest feelings and fears bottled up inside her, but the 'occasional small event would trigger huge eruptions in me'. Kate once said, 'Perhaps when I learn to live harmoniously with my own darkness, I will be ready to fully accept and express all that I am.' With Pluto in the house of self, the journey to find who she really is must include a descent into the underworld.

Kate commented: 'Finding myself has been a major task — projecting myself out to the world looks like taking the rest of my life!' This statement reflects the north node in Leo in the 1st — again highlighting the need to find her identity, power and creativity in her own right and often against difficult odds.

2nd House

Benevolent Jupiter is in Kate's 2nd house. In keeping with the nature of this planet, Kate remarked, 'I always seem to have the ability to scrape up what's most needed from somewhere just when things are really bad.' She commented that the way money comes to her when she is desperate has contributed to her feeling that she is 'connected to something greater — it all does have a purpose and ultimately that is good and positive.'

The 2nd house is what we value, and Kate definitely values her freedom (Jupiter). 'I don't value material things — in fact, I can't wait until Sally is old enough to leave home — then I shall be free to travel and go where I please.' The 2nd house Jupiter squares the 5th house Sun. The kind of growth gained from being a parent (Sun in 5th) is important to her and yet conflicts with (squares) the freedom (Jupiter in the 2nd) which she so dearly treasures. Jupiter in the 2nd rules Sagittarius in the 5th; proving she could support Sally has given Kate greater confidence, optimism and courage.

Kate herself said that her real values are 'spiritual ones — a yearning for meaning and transcendence' (Jupiter). She believes in the magical and uplifting qualities of certain objects, and has certain minerals and rocks around the house which she will hold in her hand to draw strength and healing when needed. In this sense, the material world is imbued with the protective, inspirational attributes of Jupiter.

3rd House

The 3rd house describes one's mental style, early education, way of communicating, and relationship with siblings. Neptune in the 3rd often exhibits an uncanny insight into the undercurrents at work in the environment. From Kate's description of her early life, it appears that there was an unwritten family rule that 'nothing was ever talked about overtly.' Kate sensed many things were wrong with her parents' marriage, but it wasn't until her early teens that her suspicions were openly confirmed.

Neptune often has to make sacrifices in the house in which it is placed. In the 3rd, Kate had to make many adjustments to the needs of her younger brother, who was epileptic, although his condition was never properly explained to her. All this highlights the atmosphere of loneliness and alienation Kate felt in the early home. With Neptune in the 3rd ruling Pisces on the 8th, and a Pisces mother and father, Kate learned to keep everything she was feeling hidden away — quite a difficult assignment for someone with Sun in Sagittarius in the 5th and Leo rising.

Neptune is associated with faith and religion and the 3rd with education. At age seven, Kate was sent to a Church of England school. Restless Mercury rules the cusp of her 3rd house, and the family moved home six times during Kate's growing-up years. When she was eleven, they moved from a large town to a tiny village where she experienced enormous problems adjusting. In true Neptunian fashion, Kate wanted to fit in and be part of something, and yet this constantly eluded her. She reminisced:

> I wouldn't even open my mouth in school because my accent was different from everyone else in the class. When I did speak, nobody could understand me. Nobody knew I was intelligent even though I always did well on exams.

With Neptune, the planet of mystery, in the house of education, Kate was a mystery to the other girls at school.

Later in life, Kate's 3rd house Neptune manifested in psychic powers: she has the ability to 'pick up on' other people's thoughts and admits to 'seeing things around me that others just don't see'. She has experienced telepathic contact and communication with people at a distance (Neptune rules Pisces on the 9th house cusp). She also freely confesses to day-dreaming (Neptune in the 3rd) about all the places she would love to visit (Pisces on the cusp of the 9th).

Her second husband brought out the link between Neptune in the 3rd and Pisces in the 8th (what is shared between people). He constantly lied to her about important things. She said:

> His lying and deceit took me to the depths of despair. I thought I was going insane. But it was that experience which indirectly led me to the acceptance of my psychic gifts — I could always tell when he was not being truthful. I knew when he had a car accident 250 miles away and I 'saw' his supposedly dead daughter who turned out to be very much alive and exactly as I had 'seen' her.

Kate feels that all the pain in her growing-up years and problems at school have contributed to her desire to want to help others who are suffering. This attitude reflects the placement of Chiron, the wounded healer, in the 3rd.

Virgo on the 3rd and Mercury in the 5th suggests that her work (Virgo) could involve some sort of writing. Besides secretarial jobs in law and advertising, she has done volunteer work on an audio magazine for blind people. She has written articles for various journals on metaphysical philosophy and alternative medicine (literally 3rd house writing about esoteric — Neptunian — things). She also undertook a volunteer training as a nurse and has studied healing with various teachers. In this sense, she has studied (3rd house) how to help and rescue (Neptune) others around her.

IC and 4th House

Appropriately with Venus and Libra at the IC (and Neptune conjunct it from the 3rd), Kate found her father easy to get along with and very easy 'to get around'. She saw him as weaker than the mother (Aries on the MC), who covertly dominated him. Kate also mentioned that she learned a great deal about music and art from her father.

There is a link between the 4th house Venus and Taurus on the cusp of the 11th, the house of friends. When Kate was fourteen, she had a girlfriend who was three years older. It turned out that this girl was having an affair with Kate's father (ruler of the 11th, Venus, in the 4th trine Uranus in the 11th). Her father would come to Kate's room at night and sit crying on her bed, because his girlfriend was at the pub with boys her own age.

Kate's Moon in Scorpio squared to Pluto describes the uncomfortable undercurrents in the home stemming from her hen-pecked father's infidelity. He actually told Kate that he was waiting to divorce her mother until Kate had finished school. Apparently inheriting (4th house) some of her father's sense of being caged by women, Kate is not comfortable in her own female body and feels tied down by the mothering role herself. In many ways, she is still fighting her father's battle to break free of the 'restricting feminine' shown by the Moon squared to Pluto, widely inconjunct Uranus, and ruling Cancer on the 12th house cusp of unresolved issues from the past.

The 4th house is how we end things, and the Moon in Scorpio squared to Pluto suggests some traumatic endings. Kate's first husband died of alcohol and drug poisoning after they split up. Shortly after she left her second husband he had a mental breakdown, broke into where she was living, and tried to strangle her.

Yearning for a more ideal home situation (Venus in Libra in the 4th) she dreams of a 'congenial home — a cottage in Cornwall where I feel that I belong' and is hopeful that some good relationships are yet to come. Recently she has undergone primal therapy to reconnect with the buried emotions from the past (transiting Pluto and Saturn are in the 4th).

5th House

Kate admits that she never really wanted a child and even before she knew she was pregnant, she was severely depressed and ill (Scorpio on the cusp of the 5th and its ruling planet, Pluto, squared to the Moon in Scorpio). The baby was conceived in Africa where she and her first husband, Jim, were living. He was a Catholic and told her that if difficulties arose during the birth, he would advocate saving the child and sacrificing the mother. Kate had a strong intuition that both she and the child would die if she had the baby in Africa. Unconsciously trying to provoke a split, she argued and fought with her husband during the pregnancy and flew back to England to have the baby (Sagittarius in the 5th — long journeys associated with childbirth). The English hospital was well-equipped for emergencies, and in the end she needed a vacuum extraction. The Sun trine to Pluto and the Sagittarian influence in the 5th suggests her capacity to escape from danger.

The Scorpio/Sagittarius combination in the 5th reflects a split in Kate: one part of her is depressive, cynical, and sometimes suicidal (Scorpio in the 5th ruled by Pluto in the 1st), while another part is optimistic, philosophical, and full of abiding hope (Sun in Sagittarius in the 5th). But the Sun in Sagittarius does not come into its own without a struggle against the darker forces which beckon her to 'end it all.' In a serious tone, she told me: 'I feel that the near-death in childbirth was a rebirth into a higher level of awareness, although it took many years for this to come through.'

Sally was born with Jupiter in the 12th house (she was conceived abroad) and Pluto in the 1st (reflecting Kate's 1st house Pluto and Scorpionic 5th). Kate feels that she is, at present, in a tight bind with Sally: she has brought her up to be independent and free-thinking and yet cannot accept many of the things her daughter wants to do. This conflict mirrors the tension between fearful and controlling Scorpio in the 5th and liberal, easy-going Sagittarius there.

Kate's early environment was not conducive to play. The Scorpionic 5th house and the Moon squared to Pluto suggests an atmosphere where so much was kept hidden and under the surface that it felt dangerous and risky to let go and be spontaneous. Consequently, much of Kate's innate creativity (shown by the Sun and Mercury in Sagittarius in the 5th) was suppressed and undeveloped. It was only after she left her second husband that she began experimenting with making collages and then writing — what Kate felt was an 'important breakthrough'. Eventually, her spare-time pursuits (5th) became much more meaningful than the secretarial work she did to earn a living. At the age of thirty-two, she enrolled in college to broaden and expand her mental capacities. Only then did she realize she was intelligent.

The 5th is associated with romance, and with the Sun there, her romantic involvements could contribute to her sense of identity and worth as a person. Kate told me: 'It was also through love affairs that I discovered I was capable — the men I met seemed to have so much confidence and faith in me — they believed in me.' The Sun in the 5th trines Pluto in the 1st and her identity was transformed through some of these relationships. Uranus is transiting her 5th house at present and she is utilizing and expanding more of her talents and skills. Recently she said 'I am fed up with being surrounded by people who don't know there is a real me in there, who also has needs.'

With the Sun in the 5th ruling her Ascendant, her way to the 'real me' is through freeing her positivity, joy and self-expression. In order to do this, she first has to release and transmute the deep pain, doubts and fears suggested by Scorpio on the cusp of the 5th and Pluto in the 1st squared to the Moon in Scorpio in the 4th. She remarked:

> Every time an avenue is blocked, or appears to be, it continually throws me back into uncertainty and pain. I try to rearrange the pieces yet again and come up with an answer which will show me a way out for the future.

6th House

With Capricorn on the 6th, Kate admits that she has lessons to learn in handling the routine requirements of everyday life: 'I'm not good at running everyday affairs — I always pay the red electricity bill and keep losing important papers.' Although she generally relates well with co-workers, she has recently had difficulties with a friend with whom she leads healing groups. (Saturn rules the 6th and is in the 11th, the house of friends, conjunct fiery Mars.)

Since Saturn is in the dual sign of Gemini, there is a suggestion of two jobs. As already mentioned, her part-time work involves healing and counselling but her daily bread is earned through secretarial work. She feels that it will be in the second half of life that she 'comes into her real work' (slow Capricorn on the cusp of the 6th).

The 6th house of health is linked to the house of groups (ruler of the 6th in the 11th) indicative of her participation in healing groups and circles. She has devised various visualization exercises that people can use to facilitate the self-healing process. In terms of her own health, she notices that her back and shoulders go rigid when she is feeling strained and uptight (Saturn rules the muscular framework of the body and Gemini is associated with the arms and shoulders). Skin problems (Saturn) continue to plague her, which may be a sign that something she is holding in wants to be released. Capricorn rules the knees, and at the age of six she fell down some steps and badly scraped her knee. An infection set in, and she still bears a scar there.

Descendant and 7th House

With free-thinking Aquarius on the cusp of the 7th and its rulers, Saturn and Uranus, in the forward-looking 11th house, her attitude towards relationship needs to extend beyond a wholly conventional framework. It would be difficult for her to remain in a partnership merely for reasons of security or out of a sense of duty: 'I'd rather be alone than with someone I don't fit with. It has to be someone I enjoy being with — a mental thing.' (Both the rulers of the 7th are in the mental, communicative sign of Gemini in the 11th house of friends.)

While all but one of the other girls in the village school she attended managed to become pregnant and engaged in their last year there, Kate resisted going along with the crowd 'Getting pregnant and rushing into marriage was the last thing I wanted.' Eventually she befriended Jim who worked as a merchant marine. The relationship was unusual (Aquarius on the Descendant) — he was so long away at sea, they hardly saw each other. In time they were married. They both liked to travel, and when Jim was offered a job in Africa, they went there to live. In true Uranian fashion (ruler of the 7th) marriage took Kate from the Midlands to exotic Africa. The day she landed at the airport to join her husband who was already there, a revolution broke out in the country. The honeymoon was over. She told me: 'By the time we were in Africa in the middle of a civil war, it was a bit late to realize I was living with a stranger.' Aquarius and its ruler Uranus in the 11th are both associated with collective upheavals of a political nature and this was the backdrop to her marriage situation. Their troubles multiplied when he started drinking and she became pregnant with Sally. She felt trapped by him (Sun opposition Uranus, the ruler of the 7th). She came back to England to have the baby, and six months later Jim died.

Two years later she met Bob, her second husband. Although Bob legally adopted Sally, he became jealous of the attention Kate gave to the baby, and he resented her doing anything without him. Transiting Neptune was conjuncting her Sun in the 5th at the time and opposing her natal Uranus, the co-ruler of the 7th. Bob was a shift-worker and he expected her to adjust totally to his needs. 'If he was at work, I was expected to stay at home. And when he was at home sleeping during the day, he wanted me at home as well. He even bought the food so I didn't have any reason to leave the house.' One day, she caught him beating Sally. When Kate announced that she could take no more, he beat her up and kept her and the baby prisoner in the house for a week. (Both rulers of the 7th, Saturn and Uranus, are conjunct Mars — suggestive of the violence Kate attracted.) Finally, Bob went to work to collect his pay, and Kate escaped with the baby and some belongings.

Looking back on the break-up of her second marriage, she commented. 'Certainly my spiritual awakening began when I was totally in despair from that experience.' (Transiting Neptune conjunct the Sun opposing the 7th house ruler, Uranus, which is natally trine to Neptune and sextile Pluto.) She realized that until she more fully defended her own needs and wants she would trap herself into relationships which were doomed to violence and failure. 'I had to learn to stand alone after that.' She swung to the other extreme and didn't want anyone close to her.

As the south node in the 7th suggests, trying to derive her identity solely by being somebody's wife was not going to work for her. She took a deep breath and willingly stepped into her north node in Leo in the 1st.

8th House

The 8th house is a continuation of the 7th, denoting what is shared between partners, and the issues that intimacy evokes. Because both rulers of Kate's 8th house cusp, Saturn and Uranus, are conjunct Mars, we can expect that sparks will fly. Until she could honour and respect her own power, she projected it onto her husbands and then had to fight with them to wrench it back.

Saturn, a co-ruler of the 8th house of the partner's money is sextile to Jupiter in the 2nd. When her first husband died, she used the money from his life insurance policy to buy a house. Her second husband spent all the marriage trying to get his hands on that money. But Kate kept the house in her own name, remarking it was 'one of my few sensible actions during that time'.

The finality of the endings of the relationships is shown by Uranus, another co-ruler of the 8th, sextile to her 1st house Pluto. The 8th house is also associated with what is subtle, mysterious and hidden in life. Saturn and Uranus, the co-rulers of Aquarius on her 8th house cusp, are both placed in the 11th house of groups. This suggests her link with a spiritualist church and her association with various psychic and healing circles, where 'I found myself accepted for what I was and valued for my "strange powers", which could then be shared with others.'

Some of Pisces is also in the 8th and its ruler Neptune is in Libra in the 3rd, but very near the IC. Again, this reveals her abilities as a medium — she registers and 'takes in' the hidden feelings of other people. Neptune's placement near the 3rd/4th cusp and its link to Pisces in the 8th house of intimacy also suggests that unresolved dilemmas from her growing-up years will infiltrate later close involvements. As already mentioned, she was still fighting her father's battle to free himself from the restrictions of a wife and children. In her relationships, all the charged undercurrents which polluted the atmosphere of the early home clamoured to be brought to the surface and examined. The issue of freedom versus restriction in relationship plagued both her marriages until she succeeded in acknowledging her own rights as a person. She kept recreating the past in order to free herself from it.

9th House

With the ruler of the 9th, Neptune, in the 3rd house of the mind, her thoughts will naturally turn to religion and philosophy. When Kate went back to college (9th house), she took a Religious Studies course, and wrote a thesis on spiritualism. In true Piscean fashion, she dreams of the time her life assurance policy comes to fruition and she can use the money to travel around the world, visiting the sacred sites of Egypt and other faraway lands.

Some of Aries is in the 9th house, and its ruler Mars is conjunct Uranus. She has brushes with Mars and Uranus on long journeys. As the plane she was on landed in Africa, it flew over jeeps and tanks coming to close the airport. Just as a plane she was on had left Athens airport, another plane blew up on the runway.

Aries in the 9th is also shown in the way Kate learned to stand up for herself at college (something she had never done earlier in school). When her tutor, an ordained minister, commented that he thought 'spiritual healing' was rubbish because he didn't know anyone who had been healed in that way, Kate sharply retorted with 'How long has your ignorance been the criteria for judgement?' The ruler of Aries is conjunct Uranus and Saturn and opposition Mercury.

MC and 10th House

Kate's mother was bursting with tension and anger (Mars, ruler of MC conjunct Uranus) and yet kept denying anything was wrong (Mars conjunct Saturn). Mother's rule was that nothing threatening should be talked about or discussed (Mars, ruler of the MC is in Gemini conjunct Saturn). She tried to control and dominate Kate and the rest of the family so that they wouldn't do anything to upset her. In the end, Kate left home (and the country) as soon as she could, and her father finally left home to live with another woman. After seventeen years' separation, Kate's mother still tells people that her husband is coming back to her, and refuses to grant a divorce. This attitude reflects the tenacity of the MC ruler, Mars, sandwiched between Saturn and Uranus, and the refusal to accept change.

The ruler of the MC is conjunct the co-rulers of the 7th linking the house of the mother with the house of marriage. Kate kept attracting men who tried to dominate her in the same way that her mother had done. Perhaps she was hoping to repeat the past in order to change and resolve the old tension with the mother: to turn a controlling person into someone more flexible and giving. Twice failing to do this, each time she had to again break free of the restrictive mother/husband figure. Having become conscious of this pattern through self-analysis and some therapy, she is no longer unconsciously bound to its repetition. At last accepting herself, she is no longer compelled to find a monster whom she must convert and cajole into someone who accepts her as she is.

As Kate grows more confident, her Aries Midheaven becomes increasingly obvious. She told me that following college she was able to talk herself into a job for which she didn't have the proper qualifications. It was in advertising and public relations, and she turned out to excel at the work in spite of her lack of experience. However, she had conflict with the Aries boss who demanded that she go to bed with him (Aries on the cusp of the 10th, the house of authority figures). According to Kate, he believed that if a woman worked for him, he owned her. She mimicked his words: 'No woman has ever said no to me, you are not going to be the first.' Having discovered her own rights and authority and her own Aries Midheaven, she *was* the first.

The ruler of the Midheaven is in Gemini and her work has always involved secretarial duties and writing. In the past few years, she has started leading some weekend seminars with a friend in various techniques of healing (ruler of the MC in the 11th). At first, she was shy and thought her friend was the one who knew more. Now Kate admits that she, herself, has something important to teach and communicate. Although other people had often seen her as strong and capable, she has finally fully 'owned' this side to her personality. Synchronously, more and more people are approaching her for help and guidance. She looks all set to eventually establish herself full time in the counselling and healing profession, in which she can be her own boss (Aries on the 10th, and Mars conjunct Uranus).

11th House

Saturn and Uranus in the 11th reflect the duality which Kate meets in the sphere of friendship: 'I have two entirely different groups of friends who would probably never get along with each other. At parties we actually have two shifts to accommodate them both.' One group mirrors Saturn — they are conventional and straight-laced; the other group comprise her Uranian friends — those who are involved in some form of alternative healing, psychology or spiritualism. Sometimes it is her friends who push her into new things, but at other times, Kate acts as the catalyst for changes in them (Mars and Uranus in the 11th). Mercury in the 5th opposes the Mars and Uranus in the 11th and occasionally she has 'rip-roaring' philosophical battles with her friends, some of which result in the termination of the relationship. Taking a Uranian stand, Kate told me: 'It's usually that they cannot accept my right to my own viewpoint and try to force theirs on me. I don't really care what anyone believes so long as they also respect my rights to my beliefs.' She admits the need to 'occasionally administer a kick up the backside to my friends, which blasts them into a new orbit'.

Many of her friends are people she has met through work (Saturn in the 11th rules the 6th house of work, and Mars in the 11th rules the 10th house of career). Recalling the connection between the 11th house of social reform and the 6th and 10th houses of work, she is often the spokesperson standing up for injustices in the office. However, she adds that 'even when I try to assert myself and apparently succeed, disaster follows on.' (Mars is caught between Saturn and Uranus.) She once convinced a boss that the work he was giving her was not what she had been contracted to do. Feeling it was indescribably boring and a waste of her abilities, she confronted him with her objections. He totally agreed with her, and then a few weeks later sacked her from the job.

With Saturn in the 11th and 'lazy' Venus in Libra ruling Taurus on the cusp, she confesses to having difficulty setting goals — 'I often just fall into whatever comes along.' Clearer about her long-term objectives than her immediate aims, she knows she wants a healing centre cum home in Cornwall but that 'it will take a long time to realize that dream.' (Venus in the 4th house of the home rules the 11th house of goals and groups.) Right now, her greatest interest and enthusiasm comes through the groups she is running, although 'each one is an enormous challenge which stretches me considerably.' The 11th house is the desire to become greater than we already are: Saturn there is frightened of expanding her boundaries, but Mars and Uranus must take up the challenge. Via Mars and Uranus in the 11th house of groups and friends, Kate has tapped a vast resource of energy, authority and power. She has come a long way from the quiet girl who was afraid to open her mouth at school.

12th House

When Kate explored some regression and rebirthing exercises with a therapist, she experienced the womb as a hateful place in which she felt trapped and imprisoned. This recollection reflects the Moon in Scorpio ruling Cancer on the cusp of the 12th squared by Pluto and inconjunct Uranus. As already mentioned, she was six weeks late being born and the space available in the womb must have become tighter and smaller — what she described in her rebirthing session as 'a hostile environment'. The 12th house indicates feelings that are in the back of our mind before we are born. Right from life in the womb (as the difficultly aspected Moon ruling the 12th suggests) Kate was not comfortable with the situation in which she was placed, and yet didn't assert herself to get out. Later on, her own tendency to hold herself back finds a good 'hook' in the repressive domination of her frightened mother. Symbolized by the regressive 4th house Moon in Scorpio inconjuncted by freedom-loving Uranus in Gemini in the 11th, it is not so much the actual mother Kate had to release herself from, but rather that part of her own self which wouldn't let her be free. Her conflict between holding back and pushing forward is also mirrored by the father's dilemma between staying with the wife and family or establishing a new life with his mistress (the ruler of the 12th is in the 4th — the house of the father).

Cancer on the cusp of the 12th is another indication of Kate's psychic abilities. Although neither her mother nor father professed to having such proclivities, both her grandmothers dabbled in spiritualism. As shown by the ruler of the 12th in the 4th, Kate inherited her psychic and healing faculties. The 12th house ruler, the Moon, in square to Pluto depicts the struggle Kate had in accepting these gifts — though, in doing so, her life has been transformed. Having freed something intrinsic to her nature, it is not surprising that the 5th house Sun in Sagittarius ruling Leo on her Ascendant compels her to enlighten and help others in this way.

Kate was recently in a car accident in which she was pinned to the wreckage by her seat belt and couldn't release herself. She wrote in a letter about the incident:

> The experience with the car seems to exactly fit my life. I feel trapped, blocked, helpless, powerless to move, and oh so anxious to get out . . . a knight in almost shining armour rescued me that time, now I feel I need to do it myself.

After such a 12th house experience, we arrive, full circle, back to heroic Leo on the Ascendant.

CONCLUDING THOUGHTS

> Astrology cannot make a man's choice for him any more than a road map, of its own volition, can choose whether or not one will undertake a journey.
>
> Liz Greene

An apple tree 'knows' that it is meant to bear apples. It does this without striving or making great effort, but simply as an expression of its inner nature. Like the apple tree, each human being, on some deep level, knows what he or she is 'supposed to become'. But unlike apple trees, we have lost touch with this knowledge. Consequently, we are disconnected from our own natures and from the totality of life.

Properly understood, astrology provides us with the symbolic framework through which to rediscover the basic principles and patterns that govern and describe our own unique development. If we listen, the chart can 'tell' us what 'we should know about ourselves but have become too civilized to discern'.[1]

You have probably read through your different house placements and are considering and digesting what has been written in this book. Or you are concerned how to apply what you have read to those close to you or to clients. Whatever the case, the more you discover in yourself, the more you can see in others.

The birthchart helps us to become aware of what we could be. But the choice to act is ours alone. The chart can't do this for us. And, in the words of a Japanese proverb, 'To know and not to act, is not to know at all.'

It might be helpful to reflect on this old Jewish story:

> The Hasidic rabbi, Susya, shortly before his death said 'When I get to heaven, they will not ask me, "Why were you not Moses?" Instead, they will ask "Why were you not Susya?" Why did you not become what only you could become?" '

Why don't you become what only you can become?

APPENDIX 1. THE TWELVE HOUSES: A SUMMARY OF KEY CONCEPTS

Ascendant and 1st House (naturally associated with Mars and Aries)
That facet of universal being which seeks to express itself through each of us. The lens through which we perceive the world. The focus we bring into life. The kinds of functions most valuable in discovering our unique identity. Our relationship to the archetype of initiation — how we get things started. The experience of our birth and the way we enter new phases of life. How we meet life in general. The atmosphere of the early environment. The effect we have on others. The quest on which the hero embarks. Some indication of physical vitality and physical appearance.

2nd House (naturally associated with Venus and Taurus)
The differentiation of the body out of the universal matrix of life. The awareness that mother's body is not our own. The attachment of our identity to the body (the body-ego). The forging of a more solid sense of 'I' or personal ego. Giving the self more definition, boundary, and shape. Our innate wealth. Inherent faculties or capabilities which we can develop further. Resources or attributes which give us a sense of value or worth. What constitutes security for a person. Things to which we attach ourselves. What we possess or hope to possess. Money and the material world — our relationship and attitude to these things. What we value. The desire-nature.

3rd House (naturally associated with Mercury and Gemini)
The differentiation of the mind from the body (the mental ego). The development of language and the ability to distinguish subject from object, actor from the action performed. The concrete mind, or left-brain processes. How we use our mind — our mental style. Exploring the immediate environment. Naming and classifying things. The discovery of relativity: how do we compare to what is

around us? How do these things compare and relate to one another? The general context through which we view the immediate environment. Siblings — our bond with them. What siblings are like. What we project onto them. Other relatives — uncles, aunts, cousins. Neighbours. The early school experience. All forms of communication — writing, speaking, information exchange. Short journeys. The growing-up years in general (roughly ages 7 to 14).

The Imum Coeli and 4th House (naturally associated with the Moon and Cancer)
Self-reflective consciousness and the assimilation of experiences from the first three houses. The integration of mind, body and feelings around a central 'I'. A sense of the 'me-in-here' who is experiencing and doing. The maintenance of the individual characteristics of the self in a stable form. What we find when we retreat back into ourselves. Our inner base of operation. The home. What we are like in private. The roots of the being. The soul as intermediary between ourselves and events. The influence on us of our family of origin. The atmosphere in the early home and early conditioning. Qualities we carry which stem from our racial or ethnic origins. The influence of the 'hidden parent' — usually the father. The inborn image of the parent in question. How we end things. Conditions surrounding the end of life.

5th House (naturally associated with the Sun and Leo)
The urge to distinguish ourselves as unique and special. The urge to expand and extend our territory of influence. The desire to be central, to have something revolve around us. Generativity, the ability to produce. The outpouring of the self and the urge for creative self-expression. Artistic expression. Those pursuits which make us glad to be alive, which engage our heart and whole being. Recreation, hobbies, spare-time amusements, pleasures, sporting events, gambling and speculation. Romance — what kind of person ignites us and what happens during love-affairs. Sex — the ability to attract other people to us and please them. The joy we feel being loved. Children, the physical extension of the self. What our children are like, or what we project onto them. The inner child in us. Play. Personal flair.

6th House (naturally associated with Mercury and Virgo)
Further refinement and differentiation of the self. Characterizing the self by how we differ from other people. Reducing things to parts (left brain). Discrimination and selectivity. Assessing the use we make

of our power, energy and capabilities. The relationship between what we are inside and what surrounds us on the outside; the correlation between the inner world of mind and feelings and the outer world of form and the body. The bodymind connection. The adjustment to necessity and living life within boundaries. Mundane everyday reality, daily rituals. Our relationship to servants, hired help, employees. Our own qualities as a server. How we approach work and our relationship to co-workers. Craftsmanship, attention to detail, perfection and technical proficiency. Relationships of inequality. Health issues: the nature of physical problems and underlying psychological significance of certain illnesses.

Descendant and 7th House (naturally associated with Venus and Libra)

Reconnecting the 'I' to the 'not-I'. The kinds of activities which provide us with the realization of the significance of others. Relationships based on mutual commitment, legal or otherwise. The marriage partner or 'significant other'. The kind of partner to whom we are attracted. What we wish to import from others. What in ourselves we project onto a partner. What we bring into relationship. Open enemies: what we see in other people that we don't like in ourselves. The general atmosphere in close relationships. How we meet society. The process of collectivization and socialization. The lower courts. How much do I blend and co-operate versus how much do I assert my individuality?

8th House (naturally associated with Pluto and Scorpio).

That which is shared between people. Other people's money. How we fare financially in marriage or business partnerships. Inheritance, legacy, taxation, banking, accountancy, investments, etc. How the partner's value system interacts with our own. What happens when two people are intimately connected and attempt to merge with one another. Relationships as catalysts for change. Destroying old ego-boundaries and opening new ones. Periods of cleansing and renewal. The drawing to the surface of unresolved issues from early bonding relationships through present relationships. The raising of what is 'dark', instinctual, and passionate in us. The raging infant in us. Containing and transforming raw, primordial energy. Sex as a means of transcending the separate-self sense. Divorce proceedings. Death: physical death or the death of an ego-identity. How we die and meet transitions. The discovery of that which is indestructible in us. Self-regeneration. Our sensitivity to the eco-system and the sharing of the resources of the planet. The astral plane — our sensitivity to invisible or intangible planes of existence.

9th House (naturally associated with Jupiter and Sagittarius)
The search for meaning, purpose, direction and guidelines in life. Seeking the truth and fathoming the underlying patterns and laws which govern existence. The higher mind, intuitive thought processes, and the workings of the right brain. The ability to imbue an event with significance and the symbol-making capacity of the psyche. The style in which we pursue religious and philosophical issues. The god-image. What pulls us forward. Viewing life at a distance. Travel and long journeys. Our view of life's journey. Journeys of the mind and higher education. Codified systems of collective thought. The dissemination of ideas — teaching, publishing, preaching and promotional work. The higher courts. The ability to sense the direction in which something is heading. Relationship to in-laws. A possible indication of career.

The MC and 10th House (naturally associated with Saturn and Capricorn)
The integration of the self into society. Fulfilment of the individual personality through serving and influencing society. Profession, vocation, and career — our office and status in life. How we approach work. The atmospheric conditions we encounter in the sphere of career. How we wish to be seen to be working. What we wish to be remembered for contributing to the world. Our style before the public and the image we wish to promote. Needs for achievement, recognition and praise. Ambition. The image of the 'shaping parent' (usually the mother). The connection between our relationship to mother and the way we relate to the world later in life. What we feel the world/mother requires of us. Our attitude to authority figures and the government.

11th House (naturally associated with Saturn, Uranus and Aquarius)
The urge to become something greater than what we already are, to move beyond existing images of the self. The identification with something larger than the self. Circles of friends, types of friends, how we behave with friends, and what we project onto them. Groups, systems, organizations. The nature of groups we join, our role in groups, how we feel in the group, what we project onto groups. Our sensitivity to new trends and currents in the atmosphere. Social reform and causes. Goals, objectives, hopes and wishes. What we encounter

when pursuing our aims. Group consciousness and the interconnectedness of all life. The global super-organism, global brain and group mind.

12th House (naturally associated with Neptune and Pisces)
The yearning to return to the original state of unity. Sacrificing the separate-self sense to merge with something greater and yet fearing the dissolution of boundaries. Nebulousness, confusion, empathy and compassion. Escapist tendencies. Meditation and prayer. Immersion in alcohol and drugs and other substitute gratifications for wholeness. Service — to others, causes, beliefs or to God. Behind-the-scenes activity, unconscious patterns and complexes. Being swept away by unconscious compulsions. Hidden enemies, external or internal saboteurs. Influences from causes or sources we don't always remember. The umbilical effect and life in the womb. *Karma,* what we bring over from past lives. Energies which sustain or undo us. Access to the collective unconscious, mythic images and the imaginal realm. The unconscious as a storehouse of the past but also as the reservoir of future possibilities. How we fare or what we meet in hospitals, prisons, museums, libraries and other institutions. Some indication of career. What we feel will redeem us — what we hope will give us immortality.

APPENDIX 2. THE QUESTION OF HOUSE-DIVISION

The only true absolute is that there are no absolutes.

Irvin Yalom

Astrologers disagree with one another over many issues, but most frequently about the houses. They squabble over the exact number of houses there should be and whether these ought to be counted clockwise or anti-clockwise. Some argue that cusps belong in the middle of a house, not at the beginning. Others insist that there is no justification for houses at all. But the fiercest battle raging over the houses is the question of which system should be used to divide them.

A properly controlled statistical study of the various systems is necessary but conducting such research is not easy. Reliable birth-times and accurate calculations would have to be ensured. Although planets sometimes change houses in different systems, it is still very tricky to validate that one placement 'fits better' than another. The most reliable research would test the correlation of events in a person's life with transits, directions, and progressions to the house cusps. But there are so many different techniques of progression that this approach also runs into numerous complications.

Unfortunately, the various astronomical and philosophical issues upon which dividing the houses is based are so complex and abstruse that even a practised astrologer holding an honours degree in trigonometry will still have difficulty in choosing which system is the 'right' one. Each has its own merits and disadvantages. It may be that one method is more appropriate for predicting events, another for a psychological reading, etc. Teachers can offer some guidance, but ultimately students of astrology will have to decide for themselves which system of house-division they prefer. There are certainly enough to choose from. All I can do is present some of the existing alternatives and briefly introduce the assumptions on which they are based. The reader is then referred to those books which describe house systems in much greater detail, listed at the end of the Appendix.

In *Natal Charting,* John Filbey classifies the most important of the twenty-five or so existing systems under three headings: the ecliptic systems, the space systems and the time systems. I will follow suit, giving a few examples of each.

The Ecliptic Systems

In these methods of house-division, the house cusps are determined by divisions of the ecliptic, the apparent path of the Sun around the earth. The four best known of these are the Equal House System, the Porphyry House System, the Natural Graduation House System and the M-House Method. Let's look more closely at two of these.

The Equal House System

Equal House is the most popular and oldest (stemming from 3000 BC) of the Ecliptic Systems, recently promoted by Margaret Hone, Robert Pelletier and others. Mathematically, it is very simple. Starting from the Ascending degree, the ecliptic is divided into twelve equal houses of thirty degrees each. Because the meridian is hardly ever exactly perpendicular to the horizon, the MC-IC axis does not usually coincide with the cusps of the 10th and 4th houses, as in most other systems. However, Equal House advocates still recognize the MC and IC by noting these points in the chart.

The beauty of this method is its simplicity. Proponents praise the way it clearly reflects the twelvefold division of the signs of the zodiac. Hone and Holden both stress that 'the houses grew out of the signs' and therefore it is fitting that the ecliptic should be similarly divided to form the houses.[1] Hone, pleased that the Equal House System avoids the problem of intercepted houses, commends its 'great convenience' in making aspects easier to find.[2] Pelletier, arguing in favour of this system, writes 'it seems superfluous to demand mathematical or astronomical precision of a frame of reference for houses that is purely symbolic'.[3]

Rudhyar is infuriated by the Equal House Method, feeling it over-emphasizes the horizon at the expense of the equally important vertical meridian axis, as if it considers 'lying down the only significant position for man'.[4] Freeman also feels Equal House threatens the significance of the MC by allowing 'it to fall where it will'.[5] Similarly, Liz Greene objects to the neglect of the MC-IC axis, to which she attributes the physical and psychological inheritance passed on by the parents. By not assigning this axis its proper place, the Equal House System, in her view, neglects the person's 'fate'.

For instance, assume that the ***nonagesmal,*** or cusp of the 10th house in the Equal House Method, is in Libra, but the actual MC is in Scorpio. The person may dream of being a great artist or beauty queen (Libra) but due to family background, physical restrictions or practical considerations (MC) is actually better suited to a Scorpio-type career such as a psychologist or surgeon. In other words, an Equal House chart shows an internal, idealized image of what we would like to be; but the chart erected using a Quadrant system (one in which the MC and 10th house cusp coincide) shows what is actually permitted to us. For this reason, I prefer to use a chart set up by one of the Quadrant systems.

In his essay, 'Thoughts on the Use of House Systems', Michael Munkasey believes that because the Equal House System emphasizes the ecliptic or Sun's path, it highlights the importance of the solar principle — which he defines as the 'ego or creative self'. He writes that 'if you want to emphasize or measure a Sun function, you should use the equal house or another ecliptic system.'[6] Because the 'houses divided by this system refer their meaning directly to the Ascendant,' Michael Meyer suggests that the Equal House chart enhances an understanding of the significance of the Ascendant in the person's life.[7]

The Porphyry System

Devised in the third century AD, the Porphyry System also uses the ecliptic as its circle of reference. Like the Equal House Method, the Ascendant is taken to be the cusp of the 1st house, but unlike Equal House, the MC always coincides with the cusp of the 10th. The other house cusps are determined by trisecting the space between the quadrants into three equal sections along the ecliptic. The value of this system was that Porphyry incorporated the four angles into the house cusps. The system is criticized, however, because there is really no logical reason why the unequal space of the quadrants should be divided equally. It is not in much use today.

The Space Systems

In the Equal House System and the Porphyry System, the ecliptic was divided to determine the house cusps. But there is no particular reason why the ecliptic should be chosen over other possible circles of the celestial sphere. The basis of the Space Systems is to take another great circle — such as the celestial equator, the horizon or the prime vertical — divide it into twelve equal parts and project these divisions onto the ecliptic. Some of the Space Systems are the Campanus House System, the Regiomontanus House System, the Morinus House System and the East Point House System. Let's look at the two most popular of these.

The Campanus House System

The inventor of this system, Johannes Campanus, was a well-known mathematician of the thirteenth century. While he accepted Porphyry's idea that the four angles of the chart should coincide with the 1st, 4th, 7th and 10th house cusps, he looked around for something other than the ecliptic as the main frame of reference. He chose the *prime vertical,* a great circle which passes through the east and west points of the horizon as well as the zenith (the point in the heavens immediately overhead at any place) and the nadir (the point opposite to the zenith). Campanus divided the prime vertical into equal segments of thirty degrees each. The great circles which passed through these points and the north and south points of the horizon formed the house boundaries.

By selecting the prime vertical rather than the ecliptic as his primary focus, Campanus broke with the tradition of always using the apparent orbit of the Sun and the planets (the ecliptic) as the main astrological frame of reference. A precedent was set: the position of a planet in respect to the horizon and meridian of the place of birth assumed more significance than the position of the planet along the ecliptic. In other words, the space around the locality of birth became as important a consideration as the zodiac itself. Instead of the houses being projected onto the zodiac, the signs and the planets were now viewed in relation to the houses.

However, the Campanus System (as well as the other space systems) present a problem in the higher latitudes where, in this case, the angle of the ecliptic to the prime vertical becomes more acute. The result is that the longitudinal position of the house cusps in respect to the ecliptic become more unequal, and the houses greatly distorted. This difficulty does not arise with the ecliptic systems of house-division. Margaret Hone is dubious about accepting any system which fails in some part of the world. Dane Rudhyar is more practical about it and suggests that 'each hemisphere of the Earth and the polar regions must have its own kind of astrology.'[8]

Like Campanus, Rudhyar believes that while the Sun and planets are basic to astrology, they needn't be the only essential frame of reference. In his 'person-centred' approach to chart interpretation, he uses the Campanus System because it so fully acknowledges, 'the space at the center of which the individual stands.'[9] He proposes that the Campanus System might even be the basis for the future development of a 'birth-sphere' or three-dimensional birthchart.

The Regiomontanus House System
In the fifteenth century, Johannes Muller, also known as Regiomontanus, modified the Campanus System. Rather than choosing the prime vertical as his primary frame of reference, he divided the celestial equator into equal arcs of thirty degrees and projected these onto the ecliptic. The practical advantage of this system is that it produces less house distortion in the higher latitudes than the Campanus method. Again, by going beyond the ecliptic to the great circle of the celestial equator, he put a greater emphasis on the Earth's own daily rotation than on the movement of the Earth around the Sun. This system was very popular until 1800, and is still used by many European astrologers.

Munkasey proposes that all the space systems, in utilizing other circles beside the ecliptic, give the chart a lunar influence. By this he means they include 'some subconscious aspects of personality development', personality traits which are not consciously recognizable.[10]

The Time Systems
In these systems, the house cusps are found by equally dividing the time it takes for a chosen point (such as the Ascendant or Midheaven) to travel an arc of the celestial sphere. The best-known time systems are the Alcabitus House System, the Placidus House System, the Koch or Birthplace House System and the Topocentric House System. We will look more closely at three of these.

The Placidus House System
This method was devised by a Spanish monk, Placidus de Titus, in the early seventeenth century. Mathematically, it is one of the most difficult house systems to calculate. Put very simply, the 11th and 12th house cusps are found by trisecting the time it takes any degree of the ecliptic to travel from the Ascendant to the Midheaven (semi-diurnal arc). Likewise, the time it takes any degree to travel from the IC to the Ascendant (semi-nocturnal arc) is trisected to give the 2nd and 3rd house cusps.

At first, the system was opposed by astrologers because of its time-based factor. However, Geoffrey Dean points out that it is no more based on time than any other system, 'because all systems can be described in terms of the division of time'.[11] The system eventually achieved great popularity, helped by the fact that the nineteenth-century astrologer Raphael published an almanac including a Placidean table of houses.

The main problem with this system arises from the fact that in latitudes greater than 66½ degrees, many degrees never touch the horizon at all. In other words, in these high latitudes certain degrees of the ecliptic can never become the Ascendant. The whole system is based on the time it takes for a degree to move from the Ascendant to the Midheaven. If a certain degree never rises, no time-interval can be determined, and therefore this degree cannot form the cusp of any house.

Munkasey writes that the Placidus System is 'good for emphasizing overall life goals'. He also notes that this system provides 'meaningful timing answers in horary and electional astrology'.[12] Martin Freeman prefers the time-based systems 'because astrology is so intimately involved with time'.[13] Zipporah Dobyns, Liz Greene, Christina Rose and Darby Costello, leading 'psychological astrologers', use this system and are satisfied with its results. Whatever its strengths and failings, more astrologers use the Placidus Method than any other form of house-division.

The Koch System (Birthplace House System)

The first tables for this method were published in 1971. Its author, Dr Walter Koch proclaimed that at long last a solution had been found to the problem of house-division. The system is based on a 'time dynamic', evaluating the position of all points on the ecliptic in respect to the Ascendant and the birthplace. The trigonometry involved is complex, using the arc of *oblique ascension* (small circle which marks the path of a planet during its twenty-four hours of motion) of the place of birth.

Although Koch claims that his system is the only method which calculates the chart for the exact birthplace, Dona Marie Lorenz contends that Koch's methods are 'no more birthplace centred than any method that utilises the longitude, latitude, and time of the event for calculating the houses'.[14] Like the Placidean method, it fails at the polar regions.

The German astrologer Edith Wangemann is a keen advocate of the Koch System. She tested it against other methods of house-division and found that it was the most consistently accurate in correlating facial features with the cusps of the chart.[15] Munkasey believes that the system is exceptionally good for determining 'where you are and where you are going, your current choices'.[16]

The Topocentric House System

This system is a further refinement of the Placidus Method. (Below 50 degrees of latitude, the house cusps are within one degree of the Placidean cusps.) Again, the trigonometry is complicated, and the reader should refer to the books mentioned at the end of the Appendix. What makes this system so interesting, however, is that it is the only one which has not been derived theoretically. Rather, it was devised through an empirical study of the nature and timing of events. Based in Argentina, Wendel Polich and A. P. Nelson Page studied the events in the life of a person whose birth-time was known precisely. House cusps were determined by plotting the primary directions which related to these events. The founders discovered that the cusps of these houses lay on a plane passing through the location of birth, and not on a great circle.

The Topocentric System has been verified by Geoffrey Cornelius and Chester Kemp in England. Dean reports that a fifteen-year test of this system carried out by Marr shows that primary directions to Topocentric house cusps successfully correlate with the events associated with the house.[17] This suggests that it is a good system to use for the timing of events. Another advantage is that no problems occur in the polar region.

A more full and detailed discussion of this system is found in *Recent Advances in Natal Astrology* compiled by Geoffrey Dean, published under the aegis of the Astrological Association of Great Britain in 1977. Excellent explanations of all the systems mentioned in this appendix as well as some others can be found in Ralph William Holden's book, *The Elements of House Division,* published by Fowler (1977). *Tools of Astrology: Houses* by Dona Marie Lorenz, published by Eomega Grove Press (1973) discusses the various house systems and includes tables of houses for nine of them. It's probably best for the beginning student to select one method to start with and then later experiment with others in deciding which one he or she prefers. There is no right or wrong system. A photograph of a tree is still a tree no matter what stance you take it from. The angle you choose, like the house system you select, depends on the purpose and perspective you have in mind. Life is full of alternatives.

NOTES

Introduction

1. St Augustine cited in Irvin Yalom, *Existential Psychotherapy,* Basic Books, New York, 1980, p. 280.
2. Carl Rogers quoting Kierkegaard cited in Rowan, *The Reality Game,* Routledge and Kegan Paul, London, 1983, p. 62.
3. Rowan, p. 62.
4. Rollo May cited in Yalom, p. 279.
5. Abraham Maslow, *Toward A Psychology of Being,* Van Nostrand, New York, 1968, p. 5.

Chapter 1

1. Dane Rudhyar, *The Astrology of Personality,* Servire/Wassenaar, Netherlands, 1963, p. 223.
2. Dane Rudhyar, *The Astrological Houses,* Doubleday, New York, 1972, p. 38.
3. Sue Walrond-Skinner, *Family Therapy,* Routledge and Kegan Paul, London, 1976, pp. 23-4.

Chapter 2

1. Martin Freeman, *How to Interpret a Birth Chart,* Aquarian Press, Wellingborough, Northamptonshire, England, 1981, p. 13.
2. Dane Rudhyar, *The Astrology of Personality,* p. 219.
3. Freeman, p. 59.
4. Dane Rudhyar, *The Astrological Houses,* title page.
5. Zipporah Dobyns and Nancy Roof, *The Astrologer's Casebook,* TIA Publications, Los Angeles, California, 1973, p. 6.
6. Dane Rudhyar, *The Astrological Houses,* p. 38.
7. Jean Houston, *'Creating A Sacred Psychology',* Wrekin Trust Cassette No. 81, Hereford, England.

Chapter 3

1. Arthur Koestler cited in Ken Wilber, *The Atman Project,* Theosophical Publishing House, Illinois, USA, 1980, p. 8.
2. Geoffrey Dean, *Recent Advances in Natal Astrology,* The Astrological Association, London, 1977, pp. 399-411.
3. Marion March and Joan McEvers, *The Only Way to Learn Astrology,* Vol. 3, Astro Computing Services, California, 1982, pp. 211-30.

Chapter 4

1. C. G. Jung, *Psychology and Alchemy,* Vol. 12, para. 32, Collected Works of Jung, Princeton, New Jersey, Princeton University Press.

Chapter 5

1. Peter Russell, *The Awakening Earth,* Routledge and Kegan Paul, London, 1983, p. 103.
2. Wilber, p. 29.
3. Marilyn Ferguson, *The Aquarian Conspiracy,* Granada, London, 1981, p. 81.

Chapter 6

1. James Hillman, *Re-Visioning Psychology,* Harper Colophon Books, Harper & Row, 1975, p. IX.
2. Liz Greene, *Relating,* Coventure Ltd., London, 1977, pp. 201-2.

Chapter 8.

1. Fritjof Capra, *The Tao of Physics,* Fontana/ Collins, England, 1981, p. 127.
2. Søren Kierkegaard cited in Rowan, p. 62.
3. Pierre Teilhard de Chardin cited in Ferguson, p. 201.

Chapter 9

1. Michael Meyer, *A Handbook for the Humanistic Astrologer,* Anchor Books, New York, 1974, p. 29.
2. Greene, pp. 137-8.
3. Carl Jung, *Aion,* Routledge and Kegan Paul, London, 1959, p. 71.
4. Rabbi Hillel cited in Yalom, p. 367.

Chapter 11

1. Ferguson, p. 82.
2. St Catherine cited in Ferguson, p. 108.

Chapter 13

1. Russell, p. 13.
2. Russell, pp. 106-7.
3. Russell, p. 127.
4. Capra, p. 17.
5. Russell, pp. 174-5.
6. Pierre Teilhard de Chardin cited in Ferguson, p. 52.
7. Russell, p. 82.

Chapter 14

1. Ken Wilber, *Up From Eden,* Routledge and Kegan Paul, London, 1983, pp. 25-6. See also Dianne Binnington, *The House of Dilemma,* Snowhite Imprints, Bristol, England, 1981.
2. Wilber, *Up From Eden,* pp. 13-15.
3. Jung cited in Ferrucci, *What We May Be,* Turnstone Press, Wellingborough, Northamptonshire, England, 1982, p. 44.
4. Colin Wilson, *The Philosopher's Stone,* Warner Paperback Library, New York, 1974, p. 7.
5. Rollo May cited in Yalom, p. 278.
6. Michel Gauquelin, *The Truth About Astrology,* Hutchinson, London, 1984, p. 30.

Chapter 15

1. Gauquelin, p. 30.

Chapter 18

1. Thomas Mann cited in Jaffee, *The Myth of Meaning,* Penguin Books, New York, 1975, p. 30.

Chapter 19

1. William Blake cited by Martin Butlin in *William Blake,* Tate Gallery Publications, London, 1978, p. 17.

Chapter 20

1. Sallie Nichols, *Jung and the Tarot,* Samuel Weiser, Maine, USA, 1980, p. 52.
2. Russell, p. 125.
3. Epictetus cited in Ferrucci, p. 105.
4. Schweitzer cited in Ferrucci, p. 105.
5. Rudhyar, *The Astrological Houses,* p. 164.

Chapter 21
1. Assagioli cited in Ferrucci, pp. 191-2.

Chapter 24
1. Jean Houston, *The Possible Human*, J. P. Tarcher, Los Angeles, California, 1982, p. 101.

Chapter 25
1. Jane Malcomson, 'Uranus and Saturn: Castration and Incest, Part I', *The Astrological Journal*, the Astrological Association, London, Summer, 1982.
2. Rudhyar, *The Astrological Houses*, p. 198.
3. Naumann, *The American Book of Nutrition and Medical Astrology*, Astro Computing Services, California, 1982, p. 9.
4. Laing cited in Shaffer, *Humanistic Psychology*, Prentice-Hall, New Jersey, USA, 1978, p. 50.
5. Laing cited in Shaffer, p. 56.
6. Liz Greene, *The Outer Planets and Their Cycles*, CRCS Publications, Reno, Nevada, 1983, p. 57.
7. Liz Greene, *The Outer Planets and Their Cycles*, p. 57.

Chapter 26
1. Ferguson, p. 435.
2. Yalom, p. 444.
3. Einstein cited in Russell, p. 129.
4. Teilhard de Chardin cited in Ferguson, p. 201.
5. Yalom, p. 262.
6. Ferrucci, p. 188.
7. Teilhard de Chardin cited in Ferguson, p. 71.
8. Jung cited by Jacobi in *The Psychology of C.G. Jung*, Routledge and Kegan Paul, London, 1968, pp. 134-5.
9. Wittgenstein cited by Yalom, p. 482.

Chapter 27
1. O. Carl Simonton, Stephanie Simonton, James Creighton, *Getting Well Again*, Bantam Books, Toronto, 1981, p. 24.
2. Anthony Storr, *Human Aggression*, Penguin, London, 1982, p. 34.
3. St Augustine cited in M. Montaigne, *The Complete Essays of Montaigne*, trans. Donald Frame, Stanford University Press, California, 1965, p. 63.
4. Cicero cited in Montaigne, *Complete Essays*, p. 56.

5. W. Durant, *On the Meaning of Life,* Ray Long and Richard Smith, New York, 1932, pp. 128-9.
6. Maslow cited by Haronian in 'The Repression of the Sublime', Psychosynthesis Research Foundation, New York, 1967.
7. Ferguson, pp. 462-3.
8. Assagioli cited by Keen, 'The Golden Mean of Assagioli', in *Psychology Today,* December 1974.

Chapter 28

1. Hannah Arendt cited by Yalom, p. 291.
2. Russell, pp. 19-20.

Chapter 29

1. Tony Joseph, 'Chiron: Archetypal Image of Teacher and Healer', in *Ephemeris of Chiron,* Phenomena Publications, Toronto, 1982, p. 9.
2. Eve Jackson, 'The Wounded Healer', lecture presented to Astrological Association Conference of Great Britain, Sept. 1984.
3. Adolf Guggenbühl Craig, *Power in the Helping Professions,* Spring Publications, Zurich, 1978, p. 91.

Concluding Thoughts

1. Liz Greene, 'Cycles of Psychic Growth', Wrekin Trust Lecture 64, 1977, p. 6.

Appendix 2

1. Holden, *Elements of House Division,* Fowler, London, 1977, p. 39.
2. Hone, *The Modern Textbook of Astrology,* Fowler, London, 1951, p. 284.
3. Pelletier, *Planets in Houses,* Para Research, Maine, 1978, pp. 13-14.
4. Rudhyar, *The Astrological Houses,* p. 34.
5. Freeman p. 60.
6. Michael Munkasey, 'Thoughts on the Use of House Systems', in Pelletier, *Planets in Houses,* p. 364.
7. Meyer, p. 121.
8. Rudhyar, *The Astrological Houses,* p. 34.
9. Op. cit., p. 26.
10. Munkasey, p. 365.
11. Dean, p. 167.
12. Munkasey, pp. 365-6.

13. Freeman, p. 60.
14. Dona Marie Lorenz, *Tools of Astrology: Houses*, Eomega Grove Press, Topanga, California, 1973, p. 26.
15. Wangemann cited by Dean, p. 407.
16. Munkasey, p. 366.
17. Dean, p. 174.

SUGGESTED READING

Alexander, Roy, *Chart Synthesis,* Aquarian Press, Wellingborough Northamptonshire, England, 1984.
Arroyo, Stephen, *Astrology, Karma, and Transformation,* CRCS Publications, California, 1978.
Arroyo, Stephen, *Astrology, Psychology, and the Four Elements* CRCS Publications, California, 1978.
Begg, Ean, *Myth and Today's Consciousness,* Coventure Ltd, London, 1984.
Binnington, Dianne, *The House of Dilemma: A Prospect of the Twelfth House,* Snowhite Imprints, Bristol, England, 1981.
Capra, Fritjof, *The Tao of Physics,* Fontana/Collins, Suffolk, England, 1981.
Capra, Fritjof, *The Turning Point: Science, Society, and the Rising Culture,* Fontana, London, 1982.
Dean, Geoffrey, *Recent Advances in Natal Astrology,* Astrological Association, London, 1977.
Dickson, Anne, *A Woman in Your Own Right,* Quartet Books, London, 1982.
Ferguson, Marilyn, *The Aquarian Conspiracy,* Granada, London, 1981.
Ferrucci, Piero, *What We May Be,* Turnstone Press, Wellingborough, Northamptonshire, England, 1982.
Freeman, Martin, *Forecasting by Astrology,* Aquarian Press, Wellingborough, Northamptonshire, England, 1982.
Gauquelin, Michel, *The Truth About Astrology,* Hutchinson, London, 1984.
Greene, Liz, *Saturn,* Samuel Weiser, New York, 1976.
Greene, Liz, *Relating,* Coventure Ltd, London, 1977.
Greene, Liz, *The Outer Planets and Their Cycles,* CRCS Publications, Reno, Nevada, 1983.

Greene Liz, *The Astrology of Fate,* George Allen and Unwin, London, 1984.

Houston, Jean, *The Possible Human,* J. P. Tarcher, Los Angeles, California, 1982.

Huber, Bruno and Louise, *Life Clock: Age Progression in the Horoscope V.I.* Samuel Weiser, York Beach, Maine, 1980.

Kübler-Ross, Elisabeth, *On Death and Dying,* MacMillan, New York, 1969.

McEvers, Joan and March, Marion, *The Only Way to Learn Astrology,* Vol. 3, Astro Computing Services, San Diego, California, 1982.

Malcomson, Jane, 'Uranus and Saturn: Castration and Incest, Part I', *The Astrological Journal,* Astrological Association, London Summer 1982.

Mann, A. T., *Life Time Astrology,* George Allen and Unwin, London, 1984.

Maslow, Abraham, *Toward A Psychology of Being,* Van Nostrand, London, 1968.

Moore, Marcia, and Douglas, Mark, *Astrology: The Divine Science,* Arcane Publications, Maine.

Naumann, Eileen, *The American Book of Nutrition and Medical Astrology,* Astro Computing Services, California, 1982.

Perera, Sylvia Brinton, *The Descent to the Goddess,* Inner City Books, Toronto, Canada, 1981.

Rose, Christina, *Astrological Counselling,* Aquarian Press, Wellingborough, Northamptonshire, England, 1982.

Rowan, John, *The Reality Game: A Guide to Humanistic Counselling and Therapy,* Routledge and Kegan Paul, London, 1983.

Rudhyar, Dane, *The Astrological Houses,* Doubleday, New York, 1972.

Russell, Peter, *The Awakening Earth,* Routledge and Kegan Paul, London, 1982.

Simonton, Carl; Simonton, Stephanie; Creighton, James, *Getting Well Again,* Bantam Books, Toronto, Canada, 1981.

Storr, Anthony, *Human Aggression,* Penguin Books, London, 1982.

Thornton, Penny, *Synastry,* Aquarian Press, Wellingborough, Northamptonshire, England, 1982.

Wilber, Ken, *The Atman Project: A Transpersonal View of Human Development,* Theosophical Publishing House, Wheaton, Illinois, 1980.

Wilber, Ken, *Up From Eden: A Transpersonal View of Human Evolution,* Routledge and Kegan Paul, London, 1983.

Yalom, Irvin, *Existential Psychotherapy,* Basic Books, New York, 1981.

SOURCES FOR CHART REFERENCES

The data for charts mentioned in this book is taken from the 'Accurate Data' section of Lois Rodden's *The American Book of Charts*, (Astro Computing Services, San Diego, California, 1980) with the following exceptions.

The Gauquelin Book of American Charts (Michel and Francoise Gauquelin, Astro Computing Services, San Diego, California, 1982):
Candice Bergen, John DeLorean, Ava Gardner, Hugh Hefner, Arthur Janov.

The Only Way to Learn Astrology, Vol. 3 (March and McEvers, Astro Computing Services, San Diego, California, 1982):
Ed Asner, Tracy Austin, Robert Browning, Mary Baker Eddy, Betty Friedan, Elisabeth Kübler-Ross, Marilyn Monroe, Roman Polanski, Pope John Paul II, Princess Diana, Barbra Streisand, Elizabeth Taylor.

The Outer Planets and Their Cycles (Liz Greene, CRCS Publications, Reno, Nevada, 1983):
Carl Jung, John F. Kennedy, Nikolai Lenin, Karl Marx.

Astrological Aspects (Rudhyar and Rael, ASI Publishers, New York City, 1980):
Mohandas Gandhi, Krishnamurti, Albert Schweitzer.

A Handbook for the Humanistic Astrologer (Michael Meyer, Anchor Books, New York, 1974):
Richard Nixon.

The Astrological Association of Great Britain:
John Addey, Margaret Thatcher.

GENERAL INDEX

INDEX OF PEOPLE